The Sounds of Spanish

This accessible textbook provides a clear introduction to the sounds of Spanish, designed particularly for English-speaking students of the language. Assuming no prior knowledge of linguistics, it explains from scratch the fundamentals of phonetics (the study of sounds) and phonology (the study of sound systems) and describes in detail the phonetic and phonological characteristics of Spanish as it is spoken in both Spain and Latin America. Topics covered include consonants, vowels, acoustics, stress, syllables, intonation and aspects of variation within Spanish. Clear comparisons are made between the sounds of Spanish and those of English, and students are encouraged to put theory into practice with over fifty graded exercises. Setting a solid foundation in the description and analysis of Spanish sounds, *The Sounds of Spanish* will help students improve their pronunciation of the language, and will also be useful to those studying the linguistic structure of Spanish for the first time. All the sounds discussed in this book are demonstrated on *The Sounds of Spanish* audio CD, included with this book.

JOSÉ I. HUALDE is Professor in the Department of Spanish, Italian and Portuguese and the Department of Linguistics at the University of Illinois, Urbana-Champaign. He is co-author of *Introducción a la lingüística hispánica* (Cambridge University Press, 2001), author of *Basque Phonology* (1991) and editor of *Generative Studies in Basque Linguistics* (1993), *Towards a History of the Basque Language* (1995), and *A Grammar of Basque* (2003). He has also published a large number of articles and book chapters, mostly on topics in Spanish, Romance and Basque phonology.

The Sounds of Spanish

José Ignacio Hualde

CAMBRIDGE UNIVERSITY PRESS
Cambridge, New York, Melbourne, Madrid, Cape Town, Singapore, São Paulo, Delhi

Cambridge University Press
The Edinburgh Building, Cambridge CB2 8RU, UK

Published in the United States of America by Cambridge University Press, New York

www.cambridge.org
Information on this title: www.cambridge.org/9780521545389

© José Ignacio Hualde 2005

This publication is in copyright. Subject to statutory exception
and to the provisions of relevant collective licensing agreements,
no reproduction of any part may take place without
the written permission of Cambridge University Press.

First published 2005
Reprinted 2009

Printed in the United Kingdom at the University Press, Cambridge

A catalogue record for this publication is available from the British Library

Library of Congress Cataloguing in Publication data
Hualde, José Ignacio, 1958–
The sounds of Spanish / José Ignacio Hualde.
   p.   cm.
Includes bibliographical references.
ISBN 0 521 54538 2 (paperback)
1. Spanish language – Phonetics.   2. Spanish language – phonology   I. Title.
PC4135.H83   2005
461'.5 – dc22   2004061593

ISBN 978-0-521-54538-9 paperback

Cambridge University Press has no responsibility for the persistence or accuracy of URLs
for external or third-party internet websites referred to in this publication, and does not
guarantee that any content on such websites is, or will remain, accurate or appropriate.
Information regarding prices, travel timetables and other factual infromation given in
this work are correct at the time of first printing but Cambridge University Press does
not guarantee the accuracy of such information thereafter.

Contents

List of figures xii
Preface xv
List of abbreviations xvii
Chart of the international phonetic alphabet xix

1 Introduction *1*
1.1 The phonemic principle *1*
1.2 Sounds and symbols: orthographic and phonemic representation *2*
1.3 More on Spanish orthography *3*
    1.3.1 Letters with more than one phonemic value *3*
    1.3.2 Phonemes spelt differently in different contexts *4*
    1.3.3 Phonemes spelt in more than one way in the same context *4*
1.4 Phonemes and allophones *6*
1.5 Phonology and phonetics *12*
1.6 The International Phonetic Alphabet: advantages and shortcomings *15*
    Exercises *17*

2 Variation in Spanish pronunciation *18*
2.1 Variation in pronunciation: dialects, sociolects, styles *18*
2.2 Main geographical varieties of the Spanish language in Spain *19*
    2.2.1 Northern-Central Peninsular Spanish *20*
    2.2.2 Southern Peninsular Spanish *21*
    2.2.3 Canary Island Spanish *22*
2.3 Main geographical varieties of the Spanish language in Latin America *23*
    2.3.1 Mexico (and the USA) *25*
    2.3.2 Central America *27*
    2.3.3 Caribbean *28*
    2.3.4 Andean Region *29*

       2.3.5 Paraguay *30*
       2.3.6 Chile *30*
       2.3.7 River Plate *31*
2.4 More on the limitations of dialectal classification *31*
2.5 Other varieties of Spanish *33*
2.6 The Ibero-Romance languages *35*
2.7 The notion of standard language. Is there a standard Spanish pronunciation? *35*
2.8 What's in a name: Castilian or Spanish? ¿*Castellano o español*? *37*
      Exercises *39*

3 Consonants and vowels *41*

3.1 Consonants and vowels *41*
3.2 Description and classification of consonantal sounds *41*
       3.2.1 Manner of articulation *41*
       3.2.2 Place of articulation *46*
       3.2.3 Activity of the vocal folds: voiced and voiceless consonants *50*
3.3 The Spanish consonant inventory *52*
3.4 Description and classification of vowels: the Spanish vowel system *52*
3.5 Glides *54*
3.6 Dialectal differences in phoneme inventory *55*
      Exercises *56*

4 Acoustic characterization of the main classes of Spanish speech sounds *58*

4.1 Introduction *58*
4.2 Vowels and voiceless plosives *59*
4.3 Fricatives and affricates *63*
4.4 Voiced plosives and approximant allophones of /b d g/ *64*
4.5 Sonorant consonants *68*
      Exercises *69*

5 The syllable *70*

5.1 Introduction *70*
5.2 Syllable structure *70*
5.3 Syllabification rules: consonants *73*
       5.3.1 The CV rule *73*
       5.3.2 Consonant clusters *73*
       5.3.3 Codas *74*
       5.3.4 Adaptation of word-initial consonant sequences in borrowings *77*

Contents

5.4 Syllabification rules: vocoids (vowels and glides) *77*
    5.4.1 Lexical distribution of exceptional hiatus *81*
    5.4.2 Historical origin of diphthong/hiatus contrast *86*
5.5 Resyllabification and contraction processes *87*
    5.5.1 (Re-)syllabification of consonants across word and prefix boundaries *87*
    5.5.2 Syllable contraction across word boundaries *89*
    5.5.3 Reduction of word-internal vowel sequences in colloquial speech *91*
    5.5.4 Sequences of three or more vocoids *93*
5.6 Contrasts in syllabification *94*
5.7 Syllable contact *95*
5.8 Sequences of identical consonants across word boundaries *97*
Exercises *98*

6 Main phonological processes *102*

6.1 Introduction *102*
6.2 Neutralization of phonemic contrasts *102*
    6.2.1 Neutralization and phonological schools *104*
6.3 Assimilation *107*
    6.3.1 Consonant-to-consonant assimilation *107*
    6.3.2 Consonant-to-vowel assimilation *108*
    6.3.3 Vowel-to-vowel assimilation *109*
    6.3.4 Vowel-to-consonant assimilation *110*
6.4 Dissimilation *110*
6.5 Weakening and deletion *111*
6.6 Strengthening *112*
6.7 Epenthesis *113*
6.8 Metathesis *114*
6.9 Consequences of the overlap of articulatory gestures *114*
Exercises *117*

7 Vowels *120*

7.1 The Spanish vowel system from a typological perspective *120*
7.2 Spanish and English vowels contrasted *124*
7.3 Acoustic characterization of Spanish vowels *127*
7.4 Dialectal phenomena involving vowels *128*
    7.4.1 Eastern Andalusian vowels *130*
    7.4.2 Metaphony and pretonic vowel raising in Asturian and Cantabrian dialects *131*
Exercises *135*

8 Plosives *138*

8.1 Voiceless and voiced plosives: main allophones *138*
8.2 The voiced/voiceless contrast by phonological context *138*
    8.2.1 Utterance-initial plosives *138*
    8.2.2 Intervocalic plosives *141*
    8.2.3 Postconsonantal plosives *144*
    8.2.4 Syllable-final plosives *146*
8.3 Spanish and English plosives in contrast *149*
    Exercises *151*

9 Fricatives and affricates *152*

9.1 Affricates *152*
9.2 Fricatives *153*
    9.2.1 /s/ and /θ/ *153*
    9.2.2 Variation in the articulation of /x/ *154*
    9.2.3 Summary of dialectal variation in the place of articulation of the fricatives *155*
    9.2.4 /s/ and /θ/ and Spanish 'jota' in historical perspective *155*
    9.2.5 Syllable-final and word-final fricatives *159*
        9.2.5.1 Voice assimilation of coda fricatives *159*
        9.2.5.2 Aspiration and deletion of /s/ *161*
9.3 On the phonemic status of /j̞/ *165*
    Exercises *172*

10 Nasals *173*

10.1 Nasal phonemes *173*
10.2 Nasals in coda position *174*
    10.2.1 Word-internal coda nasals *174*
    10.2.2 Word-final nasals *176*
    Exercises *177*

11 Liquids (laterals and rhotics) *178*

11.1 Liquid consonants: laterals and rhotics *178*
11.2 Laterals *178*
    11.2.1 Phonemes and allophonic distribution *178*
    11.2.2 The fate of the lateral palatal /ʎ/: *yeísmo* and related phenomena *179*
11.3 The rhotics *181*
    11.3.1 Phonemes and allophonic distribution *181*
    11.3.2 Historical origin of the tap/trill contrast *185*
    11.3.3 Dialectal phenomena involving the rhotics *186*

Contents

11.4 Neutralization and deletion of liquids in the coda of the syllable in Spanish dialects *188*
Exercises *189*

12 Main morphophonological alternations *190*

12.1 Morphophonological rules *190*
12.2 Historical origin of morphophonological alternations *192*
12.3 Alternations between diphthongs and mid vowels: *e/ie, o/ue* *193*
    12.3.1 Verbs with *e/ie, o/ue* alternations *193*
    12.3.2 The mid vowel/diphthong alternation in derivational morphology *196*
    12.3.3 Historical origin of the alternation between diphthongs and mid vowels *198*
12.4 Alternation between high and mid vowels in verbs: *i/e, u/o* *200*
12.5 Verbs with velar increment *202*
    12.5.1 Historical origin of the velar increment *202*
12.6 Other alternations in verbs *204*
12.7 Plural formation *205*
    12.7.1 Historical origin of the *-s/-es* allomorphy of the plural suffix *207*
12.8 Feminine *el* *210*
    12.8.1 Historical origin of feminine *el* *211*
12.9 Diminutives *212*
    12.9.1 Historical origin of the alternation *216*
12.10 Morphophonology and phonological schools *217*
Exercises *218*

13 Stress *220*

13.1 What is stress? *220*
13.2 Generalizations regarding stress in Spanish *221*
13.3 Stress properties of nouns and adjectives *222*
    13.3.1 Unmarked, marked and exceptional stress patterns *222*
    13.3.2 Proparoxytones *224*
    13.3.3 Consonant-final paroxytones *224*
    13.3.4 Unifying the statement of stress patterns for consonant- and vowel-final nouns and adjectives *225*
    13.3.5 Stress in compounds *226*
    13.3.6 Stress in truncated forms *227*
13.4 Adverbs *228*
13.5 Verbs *228*
    13.5.1 Present tense (indicative and subjunctive) and imperative *229*
    13.5.2 Past tenses *231*
    13.5.3 Future and conditional *232*
    13.5.4 Compound tenses *233*

13.6 Grammatical words *233*
- 13.6.1 Pronouns *233*
- 13.6.2 Determiners *234*
- 13.6.3 Prepositions *234*
- 13.6.4 Question words (interrogative pronouns) *235*
- 13.6.5 Conjunctions *235*

13.7 The Latin stress system and its continuation in Spanish *236*

13.8 Phonetic correlates of stress *239*

13.9 Secondary stress *246*

13.10 Lexical stress and orthography *246*
- 13.10.1 Basic orthographic accent rules *246*
- 13.10.2 Diacritic use of accent marks to indicate hiatus *248*
- 13.10.3 Monosyllables and pseudo-monosyllables *248*
- 13.10.4 Diacritically distinguished pairs *249*
  - 13.10.4.1 Monosyllabic segmental homophones *249*
  - 13.10.4.2 Question words *250*
  - 13.10.4.3 Demonstratives *251*
  - 13.10.4.4 Other cases of diacritic accent *251*

Exercises *252*

14 Intonation *253*

14.1 Tone and intonation *253*

14.2 The atoms of intonation *254*

14.3 Simple declarative sentences: nuclear and prenuclear accents *255*

14.4 Differences from English in the placement of nuclear accents *257*
- 14.4.1 Repeated information *258*
- 14.4.2 Object pronouns and indefinites *258*
- 14.4.3 Final predicates and adverbials *259*
- 14.4.4 Narrow focus *260*

14.5 Non-neutral declarative sentences *260*
- 14.5.1 Old and new information *260*
- 14.5.2 Contrastive narrow focus on nonfinal words *264*
- 14.5.3 'Circumflex' declarative contours *266*

14.6 Questions *267*

14.7 Intonation and phrasing *271*

14.8 A note on rhythm *272*

14.9 A note on dialectal differences in prosody *273*

Exercises *274*

Appendices *276*

Appendix A Summary of main aspects of Spanish pronunciation in contrast with English *276*
    A.1 Aspects of variation *276*
Appendix B Why isn't Spanish orthography completely phonemic? *277*
Appendix C Spanish among the Ibero-Romance languages *281*
    C.1 A brief historical overview *281*
    C.2 The other languages of Spain today and their influence on the pronunciation of the regional form of Spanish in bilingual areas *286*
        C.2.1 Galician and related varieties *287*
        C.2.2 Modern descendants of Old Leonese *288*
        C.2.3 Aragonese varieties *289*
        C.2.4 The extinct Navarrese Romance *289*
        C.2.5 Catalan *289*
        C.2.6 Aranese Gascon *290*
        C.2.7 Basque *290*
        C.2.8 English and Spanish in Gibraltar *293*
        C.2.9 Ceuta and Melilla *293*
Appendix D Bilingualism in Latin America *293*

Glossary of technical terms *295*
References *303*
Index *313*

Figures

2.1	Main dialectal areas of Latin American Spanish.	page 26
2.2	Areas without weakening of preconsonantal and final /s/ and area where the palatal lateral phoneme /ʎ/ has been preserved.	32
3.1	Articulators.	42
3.2a	Apical /s/.	48
3.2b	Predorsal (laminal) /s/.	49
4.1	Waveform of a production of *apetito*.	59
4.2	Quasi-periodic waveform of /i/ from /apetíto/.	60
4.3	Waveform of the vowel /a/ produced with a fundamental frequency of about 100 Hz.	61
4.4	Spectrogram of *apetito*.	62
4.5	Waveform of /osítos/.	62
4.6	Waveform of /-os/ from Fig. 4.5.	63
4.7	Spectrogram of /osítos/.	64
4.8	Spectrogram of *hacha* /át͡ʃa/.	65
4.9	Spectrogram of *sabe todo* /sábe tódo/ 's/he knows everything'.	65
4.10a	Spectrogram of *ave* /ábe/ [áβe] 'bird'.	66
4.10b	Spectrogram of Eng. *abbey* [æbi].	66
4.11	Spectrogram of *paso* /páso/ 'step' and *vaso* /báso/ 'glass'.	67
4.12	Spectrogram of *caro* /káro/ and *carro* /kář̥o/.	67
4.13	Spectrogram of *la lana* 'the wool'.	68
5.1	Spectrogram of the examples *la liana*, with exceptional hiatus, and *italiana*, with a diphthong.	96
5.2	Waveforms and spectrograms of the contrasting triplet *pie* 'foot', *pié* 'I chirped' and *píe* '(that) I / s/he chirp'.	100
6.1	Partial voice assimilation of /s/ as anticipation of the laryngeal gesture.	115
6.2	Nasal assimilation.	116
6.3	Intrusive plosive.	116
7.1	Spectrogram of /pipepapopu/.	127
7.2	Formant chart of Spanish vowels.	129

7.3	Raising of stressed vowels in metaphony contexts in Lena Asturian.	133
8.1	Spectrogram of *paso* /páso/ and *vaso* /báso/.	140
8.2	Waveforms of /pa/ and /ba/.	141
8.3	Waveform and spectrogram of *pidió todo* /pidió tódo/.	142
8.4	Spectrogram of *la bodega, la petaca* /labodégalapetáka/.	143
8.5	Waveform and spectrogram of *tienta* /tiéɴta/ and *tienda* /tiéɴda/.	144
8.6	Spectrogram of *rasco* /r̄ásko/ and *rasgo* /r̄ásgo/.	145
13.1a	Spectrogram of *hipopótamo*.	240
13.1b	Spectrogram of *hippopotamus*.	240
13.2	Waveform, intensity and F0: *mi número, me numero, me numeró*.	241
13.3a	Waveform and F0: *mi número de velas*.	242
13.3b	Waveform and F0: *me numero de veras*.	242
13.3c	Waveform and F0: *me numeró de veras*.	243
13.4	Waveform, intensity and F0: *¿Pero número? ¿Pero numero? ¿Pero numeró?*	244
14.1	Waveform and F0: *Miraban a Mariano*.	255
14.2	Waveform and F0: *Miraban a Mariano* (falling nuclear accent).	257
14.3	Waveform and F0: *Mariana miraba la luna* (new information).	261
14.4	Waveform and F0: *Mariana miraba* ₕ₋ *la luna*.	262
14.5	Waveform and F0: *Emilio viene* ₕ₋ *mañana*.	262
14.6	Waveform and F0: *Emilio* ₕ₋ *viene mañana*.	263
14.7	Waveform and F0: *Eᴍɪlio viene mañana* (narrow focus).	264
14.8	Waveform and F0: *Maʀɪana miraba la luna* (narrow focus).	265
14.9	Waveform and F0: *Mariana miʀaba la luna* (narrow focus).	266
14.10	Waveform and F0: *Miraba la luna* (circumflex declarative contour).	267
14.11	Waveform and F0: *¿Cuándo llega Mariano?* (neutral pronominal question).	268
14.12	Waveform and F0: *¿Cuándo llega Mariano?* (pragmatically marked pronominal question).	269
14.13	Waveform and F0: *¿Miraban a Mariano?* (neutral yes/no question).	269
14.14	Waveform and F0: *¿Miraban a Mariano?* (circumflex interrogative pattern).	270
14.15	Waveform and F0: *Cuando llegó Manolo, me dio la vela*.	271
14.16	Waveform and F0: *Cuando llegó, Manolo me dio la vela*.	272
C.1	Ancient languages in the Iberian Peninsula.	283
C.2	Linguistic situation in the Iberian Peninsula in the tenth century.	284
C.3	The languages of the Iberian Peninsula in the fifteenth century.	285
C.4	The languages of the Iberian Peninsula today.	287

Preface

The idea for this book was suggested to me by Dr Katharina Brett, of Cambridge University Press. The proposal was to write a book that could be used as a text for an introductory course in Spanish phonetics and phonology, but could also serve for independent study and as a reference book for anyone interested in obtaining information about Spanish pronunciation, following the model of Bernard Tranel's *The Sounds of French*. That is what I have tried to accomplish in these pages.

The first six chapters are of a general nature. In Chapter 1, the basic concepts of phonological analysis are introduced. Chapter 2 offers an overview of geographical and social variation in Spanish pronunciation. Chapter 3 provides an introduction to the articulatory analysis of Spanish vowels and consonants, and Chapter 4 does the same thing from an acoustic perspective. The structure of the syllable in Spanish is the subject of Chapter 5, and Chapter 6 illustrates the main types of phonological process. In Chapters 7–11, the different classes of Spanish phonemes are discussed in some detail.

Alternations in sounds between related words, like the one observable in the first syllable when we compare *puedo* 'I can' and *podemos* 'we can', for instance, are usually not discussed at all in books on Spanish phonology written from a structuralist perspective (e.g., Quilis 1993). On the other hand, these facts take a central role in books on Spanish phonology with a generative orientation (e.g., J. Harris 1969, or Núñez-Cedeño and Morales-Front 1999) and knowledge of these phenomena is usually an important component of the Spanish phonology curriculum at North American institutions. In the present book, morphophonological alternations are treated in a separate chapter, Chapter 12. The two last chapters are devoted to Spanish stress (Chapter 13) and intonation (Chapter 14). The volume is complemented with four appendices on topics such as Spanish orthography and bilingualism in Spain and Latin America. There is also a glossary of important terms. These terms appear in small capitals in the text on their first occurrence, and again when reference to a definition seems appropriate. Incidentally, Latin roots of Spanish words, for which the usual convention is to use small capitals, are, in addition, italicized in this book, in order to visually distinguish them from glossed terms.

I have tried to be even in my coverage of both Latin American and Peninsular Spanish. It is, however, unavoidable that those varieties with which I have more familiarity are better represented.

To finish this preface, I want to thank Kate Brett, Helen Barton, Mary Leighton and Karl Howe of Cambridge University Press; my copy-editor, Leigh Mueller; and an anonymous reader. For comments and help of various kinds, I am grateful to Jennifer Cole, Erin O'Rourke, Marta Ortega, Pilar Prieto and Erik Willis. *Este libro se lo dedico a mis padres.*

Abbreviations

A	Adjective
And.	Andean
Andal.	Andalusian
Arg.	Argentinian
Ast.	Asturian
augm.	augmentative
Bol.	Bolivian
Bq.	Basque
CA	Central American
Can.	Canary Islands
Car.	Caribbean
Cast.	Castilian
Cat.	Catalan
Chil.	Chilean
Col.	Colombian
CR	Costa Rican
Cu.	Cuban
dim.	diminutive
Dom.	Dominican
Ec.	Ecuadorian
Eng.	English
Fr.	French
IPA	International Phonetic Alphabet
It.	Italian
Gal.	Galician
Lat.	Latin
LatAm.	Latin American
Mex.	Mexican
ModSp.	Modern Spanish
N	Noun

List of abbreviations

NMex.	New Mexico
OSp.	Old Spanish
Par.	Paraguayan
Port.	Portuguese
PR	Puerto Rican
RAE	Real Academia Española
RP	Received Pronunciation
SA	South American
Sp.	Spanish
subjunct.	subjunctive
V	Verb

Chart of the International Phonetic Alphabet (revised 1993, updated 1996)

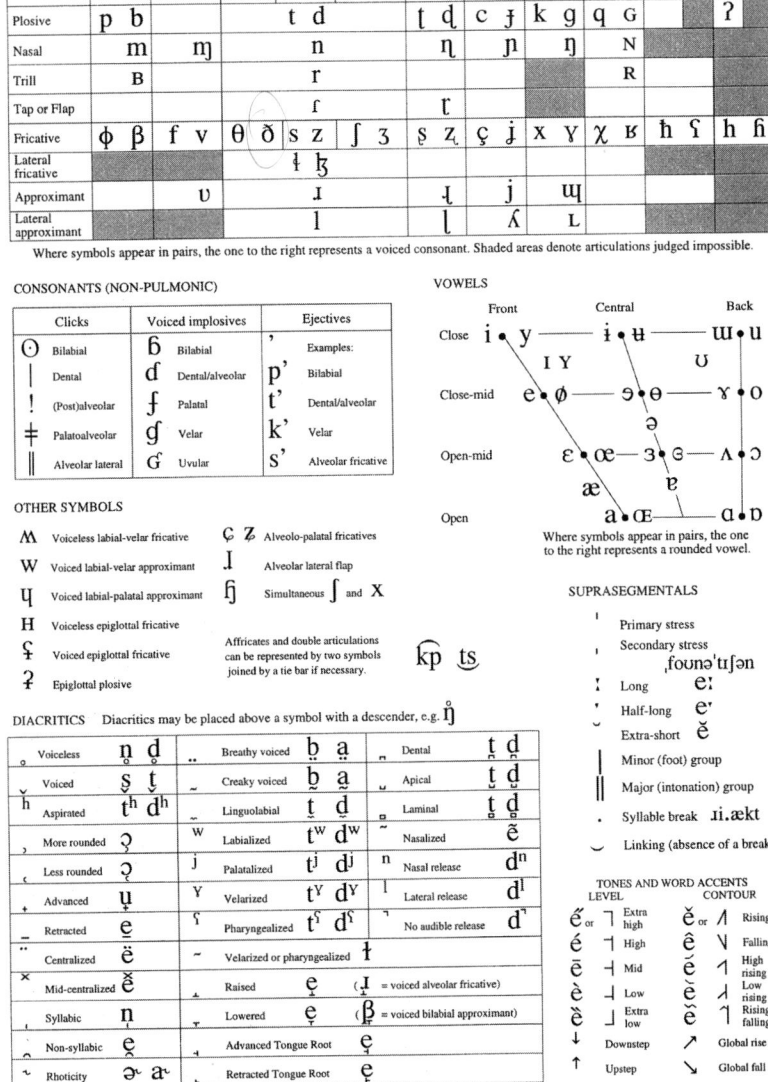

1 Introduction

1.1 The phonemic principle

An important feature of all human languages is that the meaningful utterances that we use to communicate with each other verbally are made up of a small number of building blocks, a handful of sounds, consonants and vowels, that, by themselves, are meaningless. Thus, for instance, in the Spanish word *sopa* 'soup' we recognize four distinct sounds or PHONEMES, *s-o-p-a*. These are the same sounds that, in different orders, are used to produce the words *paso* 'step; I pass' and *sapo* 'toad'. It is important to realize that these sounds do not possess any meaning in themselves. The Spanish word *sopa* means 'soup', but the sound /s/ does not mean anything. Although *sopa, paso* and *sapo* all use the same four sounds of the Spanish language they do not share any feature of meaning. The crucial thing about phonemes is that they are contrastive. If we replace a phoneme in a word with a different phoneme – or change the order of phonemes in the word – we don't have the same word anymore.

Individual languages, of course, vary in the specific sounds that they use, but the number of contrastive sounds in a language is always small, if we consider the number of words, the size of the vocabulary that is constructed by putting together these consonants and vowels in different combinations. In Spanish there only five vowel phonemes and fewer than twenty consonant phonemes – the exact number depends on the dialect. English has a slightly larger consonantal inventory (twenty-four or so) and more than twice as many vowel phonemes as Spanish.[1]

---

[1] The number of phonemes in Spanish comes close to the cross-linguistic average of 25 (Maddieson 1984). Extreme cases are the Amazonian language Pirahã (Brazil), with only 10 phonemes, including 7 consonants and 3 vowels, and, at the other end of the spectrum, the Khoisan language !Xū (Southern Africa), with 119 phonemes (Trask 1996, under 'Phoneme system').

In addition to segmental phonemes, consonants and vowels, languages may also have contrasts of meanings among words that depend on SUPRASEGMENTAL or prosodic features, such as WORD-STRESS and TONE. In Spanish, word-stress is contrastive or phonemic, as we can see from the fact that *paso* 'step; I pass', with STRESS on the first syllable, and *pasó* 's/he passed', with stress on the second, are different words: changing the position of the stress produces a concomitant change in meaning.

Unlike, for instance, Chinese or Yoruba, on the other hand, tone is not lexically contrastive in Spanish. Whether we say *pan* with a falling tonal contour or with a rising contour, we still have the same word meaning 'bread'. In both Spanish and English we may use a rising contour to ask a question (*¿Quieres pan?* 'Do you want bread?') and a falling contour in a statement (*Quieres pan.* 'You want bread'), but this is purely a matter of INTONATION and, unlike the position of the stress, does not affect the identity of words.

1.2 Sounds and symbols: orthographic and phonemic representation

Alphabetic writing is based on the possibility of identifying the contrastive sounds or phonemes of the language. In an ideal phonemic orthography there would be a one-to-one relationship between letters and phonemes: each letter would represent a different phoneme and each phoneme would be written with a different letter. Of course, actual alphabetic orthographies, used in real languages, depart from this ideal to a greater or lesser extent for all sorts of reasons, which we briefly address in Appendix B for Spanish.

In the conventional orthography of Spanish, there is an almost perfect correspondence in one direction, from written form to pronunciation: generally, there is only one possible way to read a given sequence of letters. Exceptions are very few indeed (see next section). Anyone who has learned the sound values of Spanish letters and letter combinations can accurately 'sound out' any word or text written in Spanish, even without knowing the meaning of the words. Unlike English speakers, Spanish speakers never have to consult the dictionary to verify the pronunciation of a written word that they have not seen before (unless it is perhaps a foreign proper name or a word from another language).

In the other direction, from sound to letter, there are more difficulties. It is not the case that native Spanish speakers always know how to spell all words. The same sound or sound combination can be spelled in two or more different ways in several instances.

Since in this book we will be concerned with pronunciation, we need a more accurate way of representing sounds than that provided by standard orthography. There are also other reasons for using a different transcription system from ordinary orthography – a phonetic alphabet. Regional varieties of Spanish differ in aspects of pronunciation, but these differences are often hidden under a common spelling system. In addition, we will be comparing the sounds of Spanish with the sounds of English, and occasionally with those of other languages, for which purpose we need a common way to represent sounds which is independent from the spelling conventions of each of these languages. For these reasons we need to use a phonetic alphabet.

When we talk about phonemes, we will put them between slanted lines in order to indicate clearly that we are making reference to phonemes, not to conventional orthography. Thus, for instance, we may say that a phonemic transcription of Spanish *halo* 'halo' is /álo/, since the *h* is not pronounced; it does not represent any phoneme at all. We will also, for instance, transcribe *casa* 'house' and *queso* 'cheese' as /kása/ and /késo/, respectively, in order to make clear that these two words start with the same phoneme, in spite of the fact that different letters are used to represent this sound in the conventional spelling. Notice also that in our phonemic transcriptions we will mark word-stress even when this is not indicated in conventional spelling, according to the orthographic rules, since, as we already know, word-stress is phonemic in Spanish.

With minor adaptations, the symbols that we will use in our phonemic transcriptions are those of the International Phonetic Alphabet or IPA (see table on p. xix). Some of the symbols of this alphabet are ordinary letters of the familiar Roman alphabet. We are following the IPA, for instance, in using /k/ to represent the initial consonant of *casa* /kása/, *queso* /késo/ and *kilo* /kílo/. As we will see, the IPA also uses some special symbols to represent certain sounds. Because Spanish orthography follows the phonemic principle to a great extent, as we said, our phonemic representations in general will not differ greatly from the way words are normally spelled.

1.3 More on Spanish orthography

1.3.1 Letters with more than one phonemic value

Although reasonably effective, Spanish orthography has some non-phonemic aspects. There are only a couple of cases where the way a word is pronounced is not completely predictable from the spelling. One is the pronunciation of the letter *x* in a few proper names, such as *México* (where it has a very different value from, for instance, that in *taxi*). The other case is presented by some sequences of vowels where, as we shall see in detail in Chapter 5, some speakers make a contrast not reflected in the orthography, so that, for instance, *duelo* has two syllables, *due-lo*, but *dueto* has three, *du-e-to*. Leaving these minor details aside, there are no ambiguities in letter-to-phoneme correspondences.

1.3.2 Phonemes spelt differently in different contexts

There are more complications in the other direction; that is, in the phoneme-to-letter mapping. Some phonemes are written with different letters depending on the context. Thus the phoneme /k/ is written as *qu* before *e* and *i* as in *queso* /késo/ 'cheese', *quiso* /kíso/ 's/he wanted', and with the letter *c* in other contexts, as in *casa* /kása/ 'house', *cosa* /kósa/ 'thing', *Cuba* /kúba/ (the letter *k* is also used in a few technical and foreign words, such as *kilo*). Similarly /g/ is written as *gu* (with silent *u*) before *e* and *i*, as in *guerra* /gér̄a/ 'war', *guisa* /gísa/ 's/he cooks'. To indicate that the *u* is pronounced after *g* a dieresis is used in standard Spanish orthography, as in *agüita* /aguíta/ 'water, dim.', *cigüeña* 'stork'.

There are some other minor complications. The letter *y* is used to represent the vowel /i/ in the conjunction *y* 'and' and is also used after a vowel in word-final diphthongs, but not in diphthongs in the middle of the word, so that the same sequence of sounds is written in one way in *rey* 'king' and in a different way in *reina* 'queen'. This is a minor rule of spelling that can be easily remembered.

Spanish has two 'r sounds' (or RHOTICS): a strongly trilled /r̄/, as in *guerra* /gér̄a/ 'war', *roca* /r̄óka/ 'rock', *honra* /ónr̄a/ 'honor', and a tapped /ɾ/ as in *pero* /péɾo/ 'but'. These two sounds only contrast in word-internal intervocalic position (that is, between two vowels inside a word), where the trill /r̄/ is written as *rr* and the tap /ɾ/ as *r*. Notice, however, that a single *r* is also used to represent the trill in positions where there is no contrast, because the tap is not found there in any words; that is, word initially (*roca*, *rey*) and after the consonants /n/, /l/ and /s/ (*enredo* 'tangle', *alrededor* 'around', *israelita* 'Israeli').

1.3.3 Phonemes spelt in more than one way in the same context

The real thorny details of Spanish spelling however – those that create problems for school children and other writers – have to do with the fact that in a few cases the same phoneme is spelt in different ways in exactly the same context.

a) To begin with, the same sound is written in three different ways in *dije* 'I said', *gente* 'people' and *México*. Following the conventions of the IPA we will represent this sound – 'a hard aitch' as in Scottish *loch* and in German *Bach* (or, in more technical terms, which we will learn later, a VOICELESS VELAR FRICATIVE) – as /x/ everywhere in PHONEMIC TRANSCRIPTION: /díxe/, /xénte/, /méxiko/. In the standard Spanish orthography the letter *x* represents

1.3 More on Spanish orthography

a voiceless velar fricative only in a few names such as *México* and *Oaxaca*. Aside from such names, the letter *j* is always used in /xa/, /xo/, /xu/ (*jarra* 'jar', *jota* 'a dance; letter j', *juzgar* 'to judge'). The phonemic sequences /xe/, /xi/, on the other hand, are written with *j* in some words (as in *jefe* 'boss', *jinete* 'rider', *jirafa* 'giraffe', *paje* 'page, servant') and with *g* in some other words (as in *gesto* 'gesture', *genial* 'genial', *girar* 'to turn around', *página* 'page of a book'), without any immediately obvious reason for the choice. This, in fact, represents one of the main challenges for Spanish-speaking children learning to write in their language. The Spanish poet Juan Ramón Jiménez (1881–1958) proposed to do away with what for him was an absurd complication of the orthography and wrote /xe/, /xi/ always with *j*, as in his *Antolojía poética* (more conventionally spelt *antología*). This orthographic reformation was also adopted in Chile for some time, but since nobody else followed suit, the Chileans finally gave it up. One just has to memorize which words are spelled with *ge*, *gi* and which with *je*, *ji*.

b) Spanish orthography distinguishes between the two letters *b* and *v*. For (most) Spanish speakers, however, this orthographic distinction does not have any reality in their pronunciation: *beso* and *vaso* are pronounced /béso/ and /báso/, respectively, with the same sound. Similarly, the different spelling of the underlined sequences in *com<u>b</u>ate* 's/he fights' and *con<u>v</u>ersa* 's/he converses' is purely a matter of orthographic convention, since they are pronounced in exactly the same way.[2]

c) Nowadays, the great majority of Spanish speakers pronounce orthographic *y*, as in *yeso* 'plaster' and *ll*, as in *llama* 'flame; s/he calls; llama', in exactly the same manner, /jéso/, /jáma/. This is yet another case where the same phoneme is spelt in two different ways in different words. There was a time, however, when this orthographic distinction was a phonemically real one, and, in fact, there are still speakers both in Spain and in the Andean region of South America who pronounce the sound spelt *y* differently from the sound spelt with a double *ll*. For these speakers, *ll* represents a phoneme which sounds approximately like the English sequence *li* in *million* or, more accurately, like Italian *gli* (it is a PALATAL LATERAL, represented with the symbol /ʎ/ in IPA). Nevertheless, this distinction in pronunciation is rapidly disappearing even in the areas where it had been preserved until recently and it is normally not found any more in the speech of the youngest generations.

---

[2] Bilingual speakers whose other native language has a sound /v/, such as some English–Spanish speakers in the USA and some Catalan–Spanish bilingual speakers in Majorca and other areas, may have this phoneme in their Spanish, though. Some school teachers, especially in Latin America, also insist on artificially introducing a distinction in pronunciation between orthographic *v* and *b* as a way to aid in the memorization of the standard spelling of words.

Knowing which words are spelled with *y* and which with *ll* is thus another source of orthographic problems for most Spanish speakers.

d) Most speakers of Peninsular Spanish have a phonemic contrast between /s/ and /θ/, a sound similar to that in English *think, thorn* (a VOICELESS INTERDENTAL FRICATIVE). Standard Spanish orthography offers a straightforward representation of this phonemic contrast: /s/ is written as *s*, as in *sopa* 'soup', *casa* 'house', and /θ/ is written as *c* in the sequences *ce, ci*, as in *centro* /θéntɾo/ 'centre', *circo* /θíɾko/ 'circus', *Cecilia* /θeθília/, and as *z*, elsewhere, as in *caza* /káθa/ 'hunt', *zapato* /θapáto/ 'shoe', *zona* /θóna/ 'zone', *zurdo* /θúɾdo/ 'lefthanded', *pez* /péθ/ 'fish', *piscina* /pisθína/ 'pool'. (The only anomaly is presented by some technical terms and proper names where the sequences *ze, zi* are used instead of *ce, ci*, as in *zinc* /θínk/, *zigzag*, *enzima* /enθíma/ 'enzyme' – compare with the homonymous *encima* /enθíma/ 'above' – *Zenón, zepelín* 'zeppelin'.) In standard Peninsular Spanish there are a number of /s/ - /θ/ MINIMAL PAIRS, that is, pairs of words that differ only in that one member of the pair has one phoneme and the other has the other: *ves* /bés/ 'you see', *vez* /béθ/ 'time'; *sien* /sién/ 'temple, side of the head', *cien* /θién/ 'a hundred'; *sima* /síma/ 'abyss', *cima* /θíma/ 'summit'; *sebo* /sébo/ 'lard', *cebo* /θébo/ 'bait', *abrasa* /abɾása/ 'it burns', *abraza* /abɾáθa/ 's/he hugs', etc.

Speakers from all of Latin America, as well as the Canary Islands and parts of Andalusia, however, lack this phonemic contrast. For them, these words all contain the same phoneme, /s/: /sópa/, /kása/ (both *casa* and *caza*), /séntɾo/, /síɾko/, /sesília/, /sapáto/, /sóna/, /súɾdo/, /pés/, /pisína/, etc. For speakers lacking the phoneme /θ/ – that is, for the vast majority of native speakers of Spanish – the different ways to represent the phoneme /s/ in spelling is another major respect in which conventional orthography differs from pronunciation.

e) Finally, as already mentioned, the letter *h* is always silent in Spanish and does not represent any phoneme. The sequences *haber* 'to have' and *a ver* 'to see', for instance, are completely identical in pronunciation, /abéɾ/.

Other than these relatively few complications, conventional Spanish orthography is phonemic.

The phonemes of the Spanish language are listed in Table 1.1, along with their representation in conventional orthography. The terms used to group these phonemes in classes will be explained in later chapters.

1.4 Phonemes and allophones

We noted above that Spanish, like all human languages, uses a rather small number of contrastive building blocks of sound or phonemes. A given phoneme is not always realized in the same manner, however. The pronunciation of all

1.4 Phonemes and allophones

Table 1.1 (Part I) Spanish phonemes and orthographic correspondences (General Latin American Spanish).

Phoneme	letter	examples
Vowels		
/a/	a	*casa* /kása/ 'house'
/e/	e	*mesa* /mésa/ 'table'
/i/	i, y	*pino* /píno/ 'pine', *y* /i/ 'and'
/o/	o	*copa* /kópa/ 'cup'
/u/	u	*cuna* /kúna/ 'cradle'
Plosive consonants		
/p/	p	*pelo* /pélo/ 'hair'
/b/	b, v	*boca* /bóka/ 'mouth', *vaca* /báka/ 'cow'
/t/	t	*toro* /tóɾo/ 'bull'
/d/	d	*dama* /dáma/ 'lady'
/k/	c, qu, k	*capa* /kápa/ 'cape', *queso* /késo/ 'cheese', *kilo* /kílo/
/g/	g, gu	*garra* /gár̄a/ 'claw', *guerra* /gér̄a/ 'war'
Affricate consonants		
/tʃ/	ch	*chico* /tʃíko/ 'boy; small'
Fricative consonants		
/f/	f	*foca* /fóka/ 'seal'
/s/	s, c(e,i), z*	*saco* /sáko/ 'bag', *cena* /séna/ 'supper', *escena* /eséna/ 'scene', *azul* /asúl/ 'blue'
/x/	j, g(e,i), x[a]	*jota* /xóta/ 'a dance', *gente* /xénte/ 'people', *mexicano* /mexikáno/ 'Mexican'
/j/	y, ll*	*yeso* /jéso/ 'plaster', *llano* /jáno/ 'flat'
Nasal consonants		
/m/	m	*mes* /més/ 'month'
/n/	n	*nada* /náda/ 'nothing'
/ɲ/	ñ	*año* /áɲo/ 'year'
Lateral consonants		
/l/	l	*loco* /lóko/ 'crazy'
Rhotic consonants		
tap /ɾ/	r	*coro* /kóɾo/ 'choir'
trill /r̄/	rr, r	*corro* /kór̄o/ 'circle', *rosa* /r̄ósa/ 'rose', *honra*[b] /ónr̄a/ 'honour'

Additional notes

[a] The letter *x* normally (but not always) represents the group /ks/: *taxi* /táksi/.

[b] Orthographic *h* does not represent any phoneme (it is silent): *harina* /aɾína/ 'flour'.

*Table 1.1 (Part II) Phonemic contrasts found only in some dialects.

1. /s/ vs /θ/ Only in Northern-Central Peninsular Spanish (northern and central Spain)

/θ/	z, c(e,i)	*cena* /θéna/, *escena* /esθéna/, *azul* /aθúl/
/s/	s	*saco* /sáko/ 'bag'

2. /ʝ/ vs. /ʎ/ Only in parts of Spain, the Andean region and Paraguay

/ʝ/	y	*vaya* /báʝa/ 'that s/he/I go'
/ʎ/	ll	*valla* /báʎa/ 'fence'

sounds may depend on factors such as which other sounds it is in contact with, whether we are speaking fast or slowly, and the degree of formality in the speech situation. In fact, it is much closer to the truth to state that the same sequence of phonemes is never pronounced in exactly the same manner, not even in two repetitions of the same word by one speaker. For our purposes, we can safely ignore much of this variation (which is, on the other hand, very important for speech recognition engineers). Nevertheless, some aspects of variation are both systematic within a language and not necessarily found in other languages. It is with these linguistically significant aspects of variation in the realization of phonemes that we need to be primarily concerned.

Consider for instance the Spanish word *candado* 'lock'. In terms of phonemes we could write this as /kandádo/. Native Spanish speakers, however, pronounce the two instances of the phoneme /d/ in this word in quite different manners. For the first /d/, the tip of the tongue makes firm contact with the root of the upper teeth. This is what we will call a PLOSIVE or oral STOP consonant; a DENTAL plosive, since the contact is with the teeth. For the second /d/, on the other hand, there is no such firm contact. The tip of the tongue only approaches the teeth without adhering to them. Its articulation is that of an APPROXIMANT consonant (see 8.2.2).[3] In fact, between two vowels (and in some other contexts that we shall specify), Spanish /d/ is much more similar – although not completely identical – to the English *th* sound in words such as *though, gather, brother* (not the one in *think*!). We will use the symbol [ð] to represent this sound. We say that plosive [d] and approximant [ð] are two variants or ALLOPHONES of the phoneme /d/ in Spanish. Notice that we use brackets [ ] to represent allophones. We also use brackets in the transcription of whole words and sequences, when we go beyond phonemic distinctions to include

---

[3] In many books on Spanish phonology, this sound is classified as a 'fricative'. As explained in 8.2.2, the term 'approximant' is more accurate for the CONTINUANT allophones of /b d g/ in Spanish, whereas the English sound in *though, gather*, etc., is a fricative.

1.4 Phonemes and allophones

non-contrastive, allophonic details. We may say that the word /kandádo/ is normally pronounced [kandáðo], with two different allophones of /d/.

We have just said that all sounds are influenced by their environment, giving rise to allophonic variants. The amount of allophonic detail that we include in a phonetic transcription of an utterance will depend on which aspects of pronunciation we want to emphasize. A phonetic transcription that includes a lot of non-contrastive detail is called a NARROW PHONETIC TRANSCRIPTION, whereas a BROAD PHONETIC TRANSCRIPTION only includes a few details of particular interest.

In our example, /kandádo/, the first vowel would often present some nasalization under the influence of the following /n/. We could note this by including a nasalization diacritic over this vowel, [ã]. The phoneme /n/ would also normally modify its articulation becoming dental before dental /d/. This could also be indicated with a dental diacritic, a little tooth, under the segment, [n̪]. Finally, in the ending /-ado/ the approximant allophone of the phoneme /d/ is often given a very short duration, which we can indicate by means of a smaller superscript [ᵟ]. A narrower transcription of a typical rendition of /kandado/, including these details, would thus be [kãn̪dáᵟo] (we do not include the dental diacritic under [d] because this sound is always dental in Spanish). In general, our phonetic transcriptions will be fairly broad, among other things because, in this book, we are mostly interested in describing those features of Spanish pronunciation that will be common across speakers and contexts, rather than being interested in the minute details in which two renditions of the same sentence are different, for instance.

Going back to our example, Spanish speakers are not generally aware that they pronounce /d/ in two different ways, plosive [d] and approximant [ð], depending on the context. These are two systematically different, but non-contrastive, pronunciations of the same phoneme /d/. One reason why Spanish speakers may not be aware that they do not always pronounce /d/ in the same manner is that a word-initial /d/ will be pronounced as a plosive [d] in some contexts, including after a pause and after /n/, as in *con días* /kon días/ 'with days', pronounced [kon̪días], and as an approximant consonant [ð] in other contexts, including after a vowel, as in *para días* /paɾa días/ 'for days', pronounced [paɾaðías]. The difference between [d] and [ð] is not contrastive in Spanish, but it is nevertheless systematic. A pronunciation such as [ládo], with a plosive [d], cannot be something different from [láðo], but it would be a funny way to say *lado* /ládo/ 'side'. Chances are that one would not be misunderstood by producing the wrong allophone, but only someone who is not a native speaker of the language would pronounce [ládo] instead of [láðo] in non-emphatic speech.

Table 1.2 Example of phoneme with two allophones in complementary distribution.

Phoneme	Allophones	Context
/d/	[d]	after pause, /l/ and /n/
	[ð]	elsewhere

The sounds [d] and [ð] are two allophones of the phoneme /d/ in Spanish which are found in COMPLEMENTARY DISTRIBUTION: one allophone, [d], occurs in certain environments (after pause, /n/ and /l/) and the other in all other phonological contexts (in the most widespread standard pronunciation).

To repeat, two allophones of a phoneme are said to be in complementary distribution when they occur in different contexts: one allophone occurs in a given environment or set of environments and the other is found elsewhere.

The Spanish phonemes /b/ and /g/ also have plosive [b], [g] and approximant [β], [ɣ] allophones in complementary distribution, as we can see in examples such as *ambos* [ámbos] 'both', *envía* [embía] 's/he sends' vs *sabe* [sáβe] 's/he knows', *lava* [láβa] 's/he washes', for phonemic /b/, and *tengo* [téngo] 'I have' and *lago* [láɣo] 'lake', for /g/. We will study this phenomenon in detail in Chapter 8.

English has two rather similar (although not identical) sounds to the two allophones of Spanish /d/, as in *dough* and *though*, respectively, but in English these are distinct phonemes. As we see, two sounds that are allophonic realizations or variants of the same phoneme in one language can be separate phonemes in another language.

To give another example comparing Spanish and English, in English there is a contrast between a phoneme /s/ that occurs in *Sue*, *rice*, and another phoneme /z/ in words such as *zoo*, *rise*. The existence of these MINIMAL PAIRS shows that /s/ and /z/ are indeed distinct phonemes in English. Both sounds also occur in Spanish, but with a very different status: the sound [z] is simply a possible realization of /s/ before certain consonants (before VOICED consonants) as in *desde* /désde/ [dézðe] or [désðe] 'from', *mismo* /mísmo/ [mízmo] or [mísmo] 'same'. It does not occur anywhere else in the language. We conclude that in Spanish the sound [z] is not a distinct phoneme, but only an allophonic variant of the phoneme /s/ in a specific environment.

Let us consider one more example of two sounds that are simple allophones of the same phoneme in Spanish but different phonemes in English. Many Spanish speakers (for instance in Andalusia, the Caribbean and Peru) pronounce final *-n* as in *pan* 'bread', *atún* 'tuna fish', with the final sound found in English

1.4 Phonemes and allophones

Table 1.3 Phonemic status of the sounds [s] and [z] in English and Spanish: two separate phonemes in English but two allophones (variants) of the same phoneme in Spanish.

English: two distinct phonemes, /s/ and /z/		
Phonemes		
/s/	*Sue, price, rice*	
/z/	*zoo, prize, rise*	
Spanish: [z] is an allophone of /s/		
Phonemes	Allophones	Contexts
/s/	[z]	before a voiced consonant: *desde, mismo, rasgo*
	[s]	elsewhere: *saco, ese, pasta, dos*

king, song; that is, with a VELAR NASAL, whose IPA symbol is [ŋ]: [páŋ], [atúŋ]. Other speakers (for instance in Mexico City, Buenos Aires and Madrid) pronounce the same words with final [n], the final sound in English *kin, son*: *pan* [pán], *atún* [atún]. Everyone pronounces *panes* [pánes] 'loaves of bread', *atunes* [atúnes] 'tuna fishes' with [n]. In English, replacing final [n] with [ŋ] may give rise to a difference in meaning, as in *kin* vs *king*. In Spanish this is never the case; the velar nasal sound [ŋ] is an allophone of the phoneme /n/, which some speakers use in word-final position. For speakers who pronounce /pán/ as [páŋ], but /pánes/ as [pánes], the two sounds [n] and [ŋ] are allophones of /n/ in complementary distribution, since the two sounds occur in different contexts: [ŋ] occurs word-finally and [n] before a vowel.

We have considered several cases in Spanish where allophones are found in complementary distribution. It is also possible for allophones to be in FREE or STYLISTIC VARIATION. This is the case when the same speaker may pronounce the same phoneme in exactly the same phonological context in more than one way depending, for instance, on the degree of formality in the interaction. In many Spanish dialects, both in southern Spain and in large areas of Latin America, the phoneme /s/ has another allophone, [h], before a consonant and at the end of a word, so that *este* /éste/ 'this' may be pronounced [éhte] and *los amigos* /los amígos/ 'the friends' can be realized as [lohamíɣoh]. This phenomenon, which is known as ASPIRATION of /s/, is one of the main aspects of dialectal variation in the Spanish-speaking world (see 9.2.5.2). For many, if not most, speakers of Spanish who aspirate /s/ at the end of a word or before a consonant, this is in fact a variable rule. These speakers may pronounce *los ata* 's/he ties them' as [loháta] on one occasion and say [losáta] a few seconds later. In general, the less formal the context the greater the likelihood that /s/ will be aspirated (or left unpronounced).

1.5 Phonology and phonetics

Traditionally the study of the sounds used in human communication is divided into two subdisciplines, phonology and phonetics. The discipline of phonology is primarily concerned with the contrastive units of speech (phonemes) and the patterns in which they are arranged and distributed in different languages. For instance, when we say that /s/ and /z/ are two different phonemes in English and that, furthermore, this pair of segments differs in a feature (the voiceless vs voiced contrast) which is also used systematically to distinguish a whole series of pairs of consonants in this language (/f/ and /v/, /θ/ and /ð/, /p/ and /b/, /t/ and /d/, etc.), we are doing phonology.

The field of phonetics, on the other hand, deals with the physical aspects of speech sounds. The description of the gestures with the tongue, lips and other articulators involved in the production of different speech sounds is known as ARTICULATORY PHONETICS. With the help of appropriate technology (nowadays mostly software programmes), it is also possible to study the physical characteristics of the sound waves of the different consonants and vowels used in the languages of the world. This is the realm of ACOUSTIC PHONETICS.

Although, in practical terms, it is difficult to study phonology without at the same time being concerned with phonetic aspects and vice versa, phonology and phonetics remain two separate fields, each with its specialized journals, academic positions and so on. In general, phonologists are mostly concerned with providing models of speakers' mental representations of the sound system of their language (which very often lends phonological analysis a markedly speculative character). For this purpose they employ abstract symbolic systems, which have reached a high level of sophistication.[4] The emphasis in much phonological theorizing is on issues such as simplicity, elegance and economy in the formalism used in the description. Phoneticians, on the other hand, are more concerned with developing experimental methodologies that may provide them with more accurate knowledge of all aspects of speech, and employ statistics to deal with the variable nature of actual pronunciation. In recent years, a school of thought known as Laboratory Phonology has attempted to bridge the gap between the two disciplines of phonetics and phonology.[5] The present writer is particularly sympathetic towards these endeavours.

In this book, phonological and phonetic aspects will be presented together. In our presentation of Spanish pronunciation, we will incorporate the results

---

[4] For Spanish, good examples are Alarcos (1965), as a representative of the school known as European or Praguean Structuralism and J. Harris (1969, 1983), representing Generative Phonology.
[5] The Laboratory Phonology perspective is summarized in Pierrehumbert, Beckman and Ladd (2001). See also Bybee (2001) for a largely compatible view.

1.5 Phonology and phonetics

of many decades of work on Spanish phonology and phonetics, although, on the one hand, we will avoid all unnecessary phonological formalism and, on the other, we will not discuss the details of specific experiments in Spanish phonetics.

As indicated in previous sections, we will use two types of representation: phonemic transcriptions, representing the contrastive units of the language, and phonetic transcriptions, which will be broader or narrower depending on the aspects that we want to emphasize but, naturally, will never include every detail of pronunciation, since that is simply not do-able with an alphabet.

Some linguists include MORPHOPHONOLOGICAL RULES and alternations in the domain of phonology, whereas other linguists are of the opinion that these phenomena are better treated as part of morphology, a separate branch in the study of language that deals with the structure of words. Examples of morphophonological rules in Spanish are plural formation (e.g. *palo-s* 'stick-s' vs *sol-es* 'sun-s') and the vowel/diphthong alternations shown in examples such *puedo/podemos* 'I can / we can', *puerta/portal* 'door/doorway', etc. In this book the main morphophonological rules of Spanish will be considered in Chapter 12, separately from purely phonological phenomena, as already noted in the preface.

A widespread assumption among linguists is that the division of labour between phonology and phonetics (or between phonologists and phoneticians) is based on a parallel distinction between two kinds of structure in the object of study, the sounds of human language: a phonological structure and a phonetic structure. In this view, the units of the phonological level would be contrastive, categorical and learned, whereas the phonetic level would contain noncontrastive, gradual and universal entities. Many noncontrastive aspects of pronunciation, in this view, would be a consequence of the physical properties of the systems involved in oral communication, the articulatory and auditory systems. These aspects would thus be expected to be automatic and universal.

As we already know, some subphonemic, allophonic, aspects of pronunciation are clearly language-specific (i.e. are found in language A but not in language B). These phenomena would fall within the purview of phonology to the extent that they can be understood as giving rise to distinct phonetic categories. For instance, the allophonic phenomenon of aspiration of /s/ found in some Spanish dialects can be conceptualized as transforming the expected sound (if the process did not exist) [s] into a different sound [h], a distinct allophonic category. This can be interpreted as the operation of a phonological rule /s/ → [h] applying in certain contexts and certain styles. Similarly, the fact that in Spanish the consonants /b/, /d/ and /g/ are realized as the approximant consonants [β], [ð], [ɣ], respectively, is a language-specific phenomenon of allophony that could be expressed by means of a rule replacing one symbol by another and would thus fall within the domain of phonology. Other more specific details of pronunciation, which in this view are seen as physiologically conditioned (hence universal) and as not producing distinct allophonic categories, are relegated to the domain of phonetics. For instance, in the production of the phoneme /k/ the tongue is further back when followed by a vowel articulated more towards the back of the mouth, and is more fronted before front vowels. The reader can verify this by observing the position of the tongue in the production of /k/ in *car key*. The same effect can be observed in the Spanish example *caqui* /káki/ 'khaki'. To the extent that this is an automatic, universal effect, it would fall outside of phonology and within universal phonetics.

Some phonologists distinguish three levels of representation: an underlying phonological level, consisting of phonemes, or sometimes other more abstract entities; a surface phonological level, broadly similar to a broad phonetic transcription, where the main allophones – those that are judged to constitute distinct phonetic categories – are represented; and a phonetic level, which would include noncategorical allophonic details, assumed to be largely predictable and universal, and whose study is beyond the scope of the discipline of phonology.

This distinction between the phonological and the universal/automatic phonetic levels, however, now appears less clear than some years ago. Let me clarify with an example. In many languages vowels tend to be somewhat longer before voiced consonants than before voiceless consonants. In English, for instance, the vowel of *mad* is longer than that of *mat* and the vowel of *bid* is longer than the vowel of *bit*. This is a predictable, noncontrastive, feature: the greater length of the vowel in *mad* and *bid* is predictable from the fact that the following segment is /d/ and not /t/. Furthermore, we still have the 'same' vowel. It is not the case that this results in a contrast between short and long vowels in English. The effect is gradual, not categorical. Lengthening of vowels before voiced consonants (or shortening before voiceless consonants) is also found in other languages and it is possible to find a physical explanation for this phenomenon. From all of this, we may conclude that this is a phonetic effect: noncontrastive, automatic, gradual and universal. However, it turns out that although in French, another language that has been studied in this respect, vowels are also longer before voiced than before voiceless consonants, the difference in duration between vowels in these two contexts is systematically smaller in French than in English (Mack 1982; Keating 1984). Therefore, we have to conclude that speakers of English and French must learn to produce the appropriate difference in duration between vowels in these two contexts in their particular language. The effect has a physical basis, but the details of its implementation are language specific and are part of what speakers need to learn in order to acquire a native 'accent'. Going back to the other example above, differences among languages are also likely to be found in the degree to which /k/ coarticulates with following vowels (in fact in the coarticulation of velars we find differences even among Spanish dialects) even if the presence of some degree of coarticulation is to be expected in any language.

In more general terms, there is very little evidence for a level of universal phonetics, which would allow someone to have a perfect, native-like, pronunciation once he or she had mastered the phonemes and phonological rules of the language. This is perhaps bad news for some users of this book but it is probably better to be upfront about the difficulties involved in acquiring native-like pronunciation in a second language. The fact is that it is rarely if ever the case that two analogous sounds are pronounced in exactly the same way in two different languages. Sometimes the difference is rather obvious, as in the case of English /t/ and Spanish /t/ (see Chapter 8). In other cases, the difference is more subtle, but generally it is still there. Acquiring a native accent in a second language involves learning to control many fine details of pronunciation in which the language you are learning differs from your native one. Most of this learning must be unconscious and can only be obtained by exposure to native speech.

The good news, on the other hand, is that most of these details of pronunciation do not affect communication in any significant manner. All phonemic contrasts and the most important allophonic details of Spanish pronunciation will be explained in this book, and salient differences with respect to English will be emphasized. This includes both those differences where transfer from English may affect comprehension and most of those which may result in a strong foreign accent. Mastery of this information should prove beneficial to readers interested in improving their pronunciation of Spanish.

1.6 The International Phonetic Alphabet: advantages and shortcomings

The community of researchers interested in the study of the sounds of speech communication, through the International Phonetic Association, has developed an alphabet, known as the International Phonetic Alphabet or IPA, whose goal is to allow for the transcription of the sounds of any language in a way that will be unambiguous and readily understandable to all phoneticians, whether or not they know the language in question.

The existence of this alphabet is very convenient. In principle, it permits anyone who has mastered this alphabet to read IPA transcriptions in any language with a certain degree of accuracy, that is, making all distinctions that are linguistically relevant to native speakers of the language. It also allows for the ready comparison of the sound systems of different languages and dialects. For these reasons, in this book the alphabet that we are using for our transcriptions is the IPA, with some minor modifications noted immediately below.[6]

In works dealing only or mainly with one language, authors sometimes modify certain aspects of the IPA that may be particularly inconvenient for the language under study. Here we will also deviate from the IPA in a couple of minor respects. Firstly, IPA uses the symbol [r] to represent an alveolar trill as in *perro* and a different symbol [ɾ] to represent the alveolar flap of *pero*. For the transcription of Spanish this is especially confusing, since, given the conventions of Spanish orthography, a transcription such as [pero] immediately suggests the word *pero* 'but', instead of *perro* 'dog', which is what it is intended to represent. To avoid this problem we will add a diacritic, a bar above, to the symbol for the trill. We thus transcribe *perro* 'dog' as [pér̄o] and *pero* 'but' as [péɾo], reserving the symbol [r] for a rhotic of unspecified character.[7]

The other modification of the IPA that we adopt is that word-stress will be indicated with an acute accent on the stressed vowel, [kása] 'house', instead of using a vertical line immediately before the stressed syllable, [ˈkasa], as required by strict application of the IPA norms. For Spanish this makes things much more clear, especially concerning stress contrasts in sequences of vowels.

To indicate GLIDES (as in the bolded sounds in *pienso* 'I think', *peine* 'comb', *suelo* 'floor', *aula* 'classroom'), the IPA alphabet offers two choices. One is to use the symbols [j] and [w]: [pjénso], [péjne], [swélo], [áwla]. The second choice, which we adopt here, is to indicate the fact that the sounds in question form a syllable with an adjacent vowel by means of a subscript diacritic: [pi̯énso], [péi̯ne], [su̯élo], [áu̯la].[8]

A separate problem is that the IPA sometimes has distinct symbols for differences in pronunciation that are not contrastive in the language under study. In these cases a choice must be made among two or more alternatives. For instance, in Spanish the pronunciation of *y* in words such as *yeso* and *mayo* (and also of *ll* for most speakers) can range from a sound similar to that in English *Yale* to a sound that resembles that in English *jail*, even leaving aside more radically different pronunciations of this phoneme, as are found, for instance, in Argentinian Spanish. The IPA provides at least four symbols [j],

---

[6] Rather than using some other phonetic alphabet, such as that of the *Revista de Filología Española*, which was specifically created for the transcription of Spanish and emphasizes the differences that one may find among Spanish dialects.
[7] Following a proposal to the International Phonetic Association in Whitley (2003).
[8] In the system of the *Revista de Filología Española* different symbols are used for prevocalic and postvocalic glides: [pi̯énso], [su̯élo] vs [péi̯ne], [áu̯la].

[ʝ], [ɟ] and [d͡ʒ], signifying differences in degree of constriction. In Spanish, the sounds represented by these four IPA symbols are all in 'stylistic variation'. Whereas for the transcription of individual tokens either by the same or by different speakers all four symbols may indeed be employed, when we are only interested in representing the phoneme or in offering a 'typical' phonetic transcription, one of the symbols must be chosen. We will transcribe *yeso* as [jéso] when no particular dialect is being considered.

The case where the language makes more contrasts along a certain phonetic dimension than those for which there are separate IPA symbols is less problematic, since it can be solved by using diacritic marks added to the basic IPA symbols.

Finally it is important to keep in mind that when comparing languages we can never really speak of strictly identical sounds, only of analogous sounds (Pierrehumbert, Beckman and Ladd 2001).

EXERCISES

1. Do all Spanish varieties have the same number of phonemes? Explain in detail.

2. Provide minimal pairs for the following phonemic oppositions in Spanish: /p/-/b/, /t/-/d/, /k/-/g/, /n/-/ɲ/, /ɾ/-/r/.

3. Is it possible to find minimal pairs contrasting /n/ and /ŋ/ in Spanish? Explain.

4. In Spanish the bolded letter is essentially the same sound in *lado, palo, mal, sol*. In English on the other hand, we find quite different sounds in *light, low*, on the one hand, and *ball, pal*, on the other. Is this a phonemic contrast in English? How would you explain the difference between English and Spanish in this respect?

5. Provide an exhaustive list of cases where the same phoneme is written in more than one way in standard Spanish orthography, giving examples.

6. Give five minimal pairs demonstrating that the position of the word-stress is phonemic in Spanish.

7. Are the sounds [b] and [β] in phonemic contrast in Spanish?

2 Variation in Spanish pronunciation

2.1 Variation in pronunciation: dialects, sociolects, styles

In all languages there is variation among speakers in some of the words they use, the grammatical constructions that they employ and, importantly for us, in their pronunciation. From the way people speak we can often tell where they come from. An individual's way of speaking may also give us information about social variables such as his or her educational background, socioeconomic class, age, gender and ethnicity.

The distinct ways of speaking a language in the regions and countries where it is spoken natively are known as the geographical varieties or DIALECTS of the language. Thus, in the case of Spanish, we may speak of a Mexican dialect, a Caribbean dialect, a Chilean dialect, an Andalusian dialect and a Northern-Central Peninsular dialect, among others, to refer, respectively, to the Spanish of Mexico, the Caribbean, Chile, Andalusia and north-central Spain. It is important to realize, nevertheless, that the dialects of a language are not discrete entities with sharp boundaries; rather, these are merely convenient labels that we may use to try to capture the geographical variation that is found within the language. We will return to this point in the next section.

It is also important to note that, as a technical term used in the field of Linguistics, the term 'dialect' does not have any negative connotation. It is a completely neutral term that simply refers to a geographically defined variety of a language. All such varieties are dialects of the language. Their scientific study is known as Dialectology. Spanish dialectologists are then those scholars concerned with describing the ways in which the Spanish language varies in different parts of the Spanish-speaking world and investigating the possible sources of this variation. Although dialectal variation may affect all aspects of the language, from syntax and morphology to lexicon, in this book we will be concerned only with those aspects of dialectal variation that have to do with pronunciation.

Geography, though, is not the only source of variation in language. Inside the same region or even within a single town we also find linguistic variation among speakers. Socially defined varieties within the same community are known as SOCIOLECTS. These include the specific ways in which different age, ethnic, occupational and other social groups differ in their language. We all know that certain pronunciations (and other linguistic features) are more typical of some age groups or some social classes, etc. In these cases we will speak of sociolectal variants. For example, in some parts of Spain, the consistent contrast between *y* /j/ and *ll* /ʎ/ in pronunciation is nowadays a sociolectal variant associated with the oldest age groups, not used by the younger generations.

In addition to different speakers having different linguistic habits, we are all aware that we do not speak in the same manner on all occasions. Certain ways of speaking are more colloquial and certain other ways more formal. To give one example, many Spanish-speakers tend to pronounce the final *-d* in words such as *ciudad*, *verdad*, etc., when reading and in other formal situations, but not when chatting with their friends. All native speakers of a language have control over a range of styles. Learning the stylistically appropriate usage of different pronunciations is in fact one of the greatest challenges for second-language learners. In the case of Spanish, this difficulty is compounded by the fact that pronunciations that are considered 'colloquial' in some areas are acceptable in more formal discourse in other areas. For instance, 'dropping' the /-d-/ in participles such as *cantado*, *hablado* is much more acceptable in formal situations in Spain than in Mexico or Argentina. To give another example, most Mexicans pronounce all their 's's, but in Puerto Rico or Venezuela such 's'-ful pronunciation is found only in the most formal styles. That is, what is a perfectly colloquial pronunciation for a Mexican speaker may be considered overly formal in, say, Venezuela.

In the next sections we will examine the main features of pronunciation that characterize the Spanish of the different geographical areas where it is spoken. We will consider first the Spanish of Spain; that is, Peninsular and Canary Island Spanish. After that, we will present the most important phonological traits of the main dialects of Latin American Spanish.

2.2 Main geographical varieties of the Spanish language in Spain

Simplifying greatly, we may distinguish two main dialects of the Spanish language in the Iberian peninsula: Northern-Central Peninsular Spanish and Southern Peninsular Spanish or 'Andalusian' in a broad sense (including, besides Andalusia, Murcia and the southern part of Extremadura). However, as already indicated, a fact to be kept in mind is that dialects do not have well-defined boundaries, like those of political entities. It does not make much sense for instance to ask where the geographical boundaries of the Andalusian dialect are or to what extent they coincide with those of Andalusia. Regarding the pronunciation of Spanish in Spain, it is more correct to speak of northern-central and southern features than of two distinct dialectal areas with a clear boundary.

To refer to Northern-Central Peninsular Spanish the term 'Castilian Spanish' is sometimes used, meaning Spanish as spoken in the historical regions of Old and New Castile (corresponding to the greatest part of the present-day regions of Castilla-León, Madrid and Castilla-La Mancha). It is important to bear in mind that, on the one hand, the main features of this dialect spread over areas which are not Castilian in any historical or modern political sense, such as Aragon, and, on the other, many Southern Peninsular features are abundantly found in the speech of the southernmost area of Castilla-La Mancha. For other complications with the term 'Castilian' see 2.8.

2.2.1 Northern-Central Peninsular Spanish

As we will discuss in more detail below, the Peninsular standard variety is based on the speech of educated speakers from the northern-central area. This does not mean, however, that all pronunciation traits found in this geographical area are accepted as part of the formal standard.

A northern-central feature, which is part of the standard language of Spain, but not found in parts of Andalusia, in the Canary Islands, or anywhere in Latin America, is the phonological contrast between /θ/ and /s/ as in *roza* / r̄óθa/ 's/he rubs against' vs *rosa* / r̄ósa/ 'rose'. In the standard Peninsular variety, the sound [θ] only occurs where the spelling has *z* (as in *zona* 'zone', *zurdo* 'lefthanded', *zapato* 'shoe') and in *ce*, *ci* (*centro* 'centre', *cine* 'cinema').

Besides the Peninsular standard use of /θ/ corresponding to *z* and *c(e)*, *c(i)* in the spelling, however, many speakers in large areas of northern-central Spain also have the sound [θ] in two other contexts: in their pronunciation of the group -*ct*- as in *recta* 'straight line', *dictar* 'to dictate', pronounced [r̄éθta], [diθtár], and also for syllable- or word-final -*d*, as in *admirar* [aθmirár] 'to admire', *red* [r̄éθ] 'net', *virtud* [birtúθ] 'virtue', *verdad* [berðáθ] 'truth' (alternating with the deletion of the consonant in word-final position in words with more than one syllable, [birtú], [berðá], see 8.2.4). These pronunciations, although common in parts of the Castilian area even among professionals and other educated speakers, are not part of the standard and are avoided by some other speakers of the same dialect.

Two other features of the Northern-Central Peninsular dialect that, to Latin American ears, are very salient, are a strong, STRIDENT POST-VELAR pronunciation of /x/ (in *ajo* 'garlic', *mujer* 'woman', etc.) and also a more strident pronunciation of /s/ than in most of Latin America (see 3.2.2).

Until recently, the distinction between /ʎ/ and /ʝ/ was found over large northern and central areas of the Iberian Peninsula (as well as isolated points in the south) and was considered part of the educated Peninsular norm. Nowadays, however, very few speakers in this area make this contrast with any consistency among the younger generations.

Although Northern-Central Peninsular Spanish is often considered a conservative variety, the deletion of /-d-/ in participles in -*ado*, such as *hablado* [aβláo], *cantado* [kantáo], etc., and in a few other lexical items with the same ending, such as *lado* 'side', is common in this geographical variety even among educated speakers in semi-formal situations, whereas the same phenomenon is stigmatized as uneducated in most of the Latin American areas where it is also found. The simplification of syllable-final clusters as in *texto* [tésto] 'text', *excusa* [eskúsa] 'excuse', *construir* [kostruír] 'to build', is also widespread in the speech of educated speakers of this dialect, whereas in Mexico and some other Latin American countries the orthographic consonant clusters are more commonly pronounced without simplification by educated speakers.

A non-phonological feature of Northern-Central Peninsular Spanish, absent from all of Latin America and parts of Andalusia, is the distinction between informal *vosotros* and formal *ustedes* for 'you plural' with their associated verbal forms.

2.2.2 Southern Peninsular Spanish

Andalusian and the other Southern Peninsular varieties are usually considered to be more innovative or radical in their pronunciation than northern and central Peninsular dialects of Spanish. In simple terms, what this means is that they show more articulatory weakening or reduction of certain consonants and deviate to a greater extent from the pronunciation suggested by the standard spelling. Some southern features of pronunciation are the following:

(a) The lack of contrast between /s/ and /θ/. For instance, *rosa* 'rose' and *roza* 's/he rubs' receive the same pronunciation (see 3.6).
(b) The ASPIRATION (pronunciation as [h]) or loss of /s/ word finally and before a consonant, as in *este* [éhte] 'this', *las casas* [lahkása] 'the houses'.
(c) The weaker pronunciation of /x/, as an aspiration [h], *mujer* [muhé].

(d) The VELARIZATION of final /n/, as in *pan* [páŋ] 'bread'(with the nasal of English *thing*) or its loss, with nasalization of the preceding vowel, [pã].

(e) The NEUTRALIZATION or lack of distinction between /r/ and /l/ before another consonant, e[r] *niño* 'the boy', and neutralization or loss of these consonants in word-final position, *cantar* [kaṇtá] 'to sing', *comer* [komé] 'to eat', *hospital* [ohpitá] 'hospital'.

(f) The deletion of intervocalic /-d-/ as in *comido* [komío] 'eaten', *cadena* [kaéna] 'chain', *callada* [kajá] 'quiet, *fem.*'

(g) The weakening of /t͡ʃ/, which is variably realized as [ʃ] (the initial sound of English *sheep*) in part of the southernmost area of Andalusia, *muchacho* [muʃáʃo] 'boy'.

Not all these southern features of pronunciation have the same geographical extension or the same social consideration. For instance, although not part of the Northern-Central Peninsular standard, some limited aspiration of /s/ is found in the speech of speakers from Madrid and some other central areas in informal contexts. As mentioned above, intervocalic /-d-/ is commonly deleted in northern and central regions of Spain as well, but usually only in participles in *-ado* (extensive weakening of /-d-/, as in Andalusia, on the other hand, is also found among rural speakers in parts of Asturias and Cantabria, on the northern fringe of the Peninsula). Thus, a speaker from, say, Burgos, will often delete the /-d-/ in *asado* [asáo] 'roasted, *masc.*', but not in *asada* 'roasted, *fem.*' or in *comido* 'eaten', whereas an Andalusian will delete this consonant in all three of these examples. The velarization of /n/ is generally not found in the central and eastern area of Spain, but is common along the western part of Spain, all the way to Galicia and Asturias.

2.2.3 Canary Island Spanish

The Spanish spoken in the Canary Islands presents all the southern features (a)–(f) mentioned above. This is understandable if we take into account that the Islands were colonized from Seville and, for centuries, preserved more contact with southern than with northern Spain. In addition to these features, the phoneme /t͡ʃ/ orthographically represented by *ch* has a more PALATAL character (more retracted) than in Peninsular Spanish; a pronunciation also found in Cuba and other parts of the Caribbean (see 9.1). Another feature has to do with the VOICED pronunciation of /p t k/ between vowels, as will be discussed in more detail in 8.2.2. The general auditory impression of Canary Island Spanish is very similar to that of Caribbean Spanish. This is because of many shared features at both the segmental and the intonational levels.

2.3 Main geographical varieties of the Spanish language in Latin America

In the Americas, the Spanish language is spoken natively from the southwestern United States to Tierra del Fuego. Over these vast territories the language is not totally uniform, as one might expect. Differences are, nevertheless, relatively small; certainly much smaller than those found, for instance, within the small territory where the Basque language is spoken. One feature that is common to all Latin American Spanish, in opposition to Northern-Central Peninsular Spanish, is the absence of the contrast between /s/ and /θ/. All of Latin American Spanish has a single phoneme /s/ instead of the two phonemes of Northern-Central Peninsular Spanish.[1]

As indicated above, some differences between Peninsular and Latin American Spanish have to do with the social consideration of certain variable phenomena and, consequently, the likelihood of their appearance in the formal speech of educated speakers. Pronunciations of the type *cantao, hablao* (for *cantado, hablado*) do not raise any eyebrows in Spain, and may be found in the speech of politicians and university professors (although they are still avoided by radio announcers). In most of Latin America, on the other hand, these pronunciations are considered 'vulgar' or 'uneducated'. Conversely, in many Latin American countries, the reduction of the hiatus in *golpear* 'to hit', *golpeó* 's/he hit', pronounced as if they were spelled *golpiar, golpió*, is common in the speech of speakers of all educational levels, whereas in Spain this is often considered a 'vulgar' or 'rural' pronunciation.

Regarding geographical variation within Latin American Spanish, what we said before about the difficulty of establishing dialectal boundaries applies here as well. Again, it is more sensible to speak of the geographical extension of different features.

Although most of the phonological traits found in Latin American Spanish are also found in parts of Spain, a few are not. In addition, some Latin American areas are characterized by intonational patterns that do not have a Peninsular counterpart. The main phonological variables (i.e., aspects of variation in pronunciation) within Latin American Spanish are the following:

(a) Aspiration of /s/. Word- and syllable-final /s/ is consistently preserved in the highlands of Mexico and Guatemala, in the Central Valley of Costa Rica, and in the Andean region of Colombia, Ecuador, Peru and Bolivia. In most of the rest of Latin America this consonant is weakened (aspirated or deleted) to different extents, this phenomenon reaching particularly high frequency in Caribbean dialects.

---

[1] Some use of the /s/-/θ/ opposition, although not in a totally consistent manner, has been reported for Cuzco, Peru (see Caravedo 1992).

(b) Velarization of /n/. Word-final /n/ is pronounced as [n] in Mexico, most of Colombia, Chile and Argentina. In most other areas it is pronounced as VELAR [ŋ]. In Yucatán, Tucumán and a small area of Colombia, on the other hand, we find final [m], *pan* [pám] 'bread'.
(c) Neutralization of syllable-final /l/ and /r/. In Latin America this phenomenon is found basically in the Caribbean (Cuba, Puerto Rico, Dominican Republic, Venezuela); e.g.: *mejor* [mehól] 'better'.
(d) Deletion of intervocalic /-d-/. As mentioned, in Latin America this phenomenon is generally stigmatized. Nowadays it is found mostly in Caribbean regions, in informal styles.
(e) Contrast between /ʎ/ and /j/. This phonological contrast is made only in the Andean region of Colombia, Ecuador, Peru and Bolivia, as well as in Paraguay, where, for instance, *cayó* 's/he fell' and *calló* 's/he became silent' are pronounced differently.
(f) Pronunciation of /j/. The pronunciation of this phoneme shows considerable variation, ranging from a SEMIVOWEL (similar to the initial sound of Eng. *yes*) to a more constricted consonant sound, which may be a FRICATIVE, an AFFRICATE (similar to the initial sound of Eng. *John*) or a STOP. In Argentina and Uruguay it is pronounced with the STRIDENT FRICATIVE sound of Fr. *jamais* (Eng. *pleasure*), but younger speakers in the Buenos Aires area favour a pronunciation [ʃ] (as in Eng. *ship*).
(g) Pronunciation of /r̄/. In several Latin American areas, including the Caribbean (Cuba, the Dominican Republic and Puerto Rico), Guatemala, Costa Rica and the Andean region, we find types of /r̄/ that are different from that usually described for the standard language (see 11.3.2).
(h) Pronunciation of /x/. In Latin America, the phoneme /x/ is not pronounced as stridently as in northern areas of Spain. Realizations vary from a sound similar to English [h], found in the Caribbean and most of Central America, among other areas, to a stronger (VELAR) realization in central Mexico, Argentina and Chile, which is still less strident than the Northern Peninsular variant.
(i) Pronunciation of /t͡ʃ/. This phoneme is weakened to [ʃ] in Northern Mexico, Panama and parts of Chile. Other variants are a very fronted realization [t͡s] in Chile and a very palatalized realization in parts of Cuba and Puerto Rico (like in the Canary Islands) (see 9.1).

With the caveats expressed above in mind, for practical purposes it is useful to divide Latin America into dialectal areas. We may distinguish the following regions: Mexico, Central America, the Caribbean, the Andean region, Paraguay,

2.3 Main geographical varieties in Latin America

Chile and the River Plate region (other slightly different classifications are also possible, see, e.g., Dalbor 1997:22–3; Lipski 1994:3–33). Again, these are not regions with clearly traceable boundaries. If we say, for instance, that the Spanish of Mexico has feature 'f', what we mean is that this feature is 'typical' of Mexican Spanish, but this does not imply that this feature is found over the whole area of the country or that it is not found in parts of other countries as well. Country-by-country descriptions can be found in Canfield (1981), Lipski (1994) and, with some limited grouping, Alvar (1996a:vol. II).

2.3.1 Mexico (and the USA)

The Spanish of Mexico, in opposition to most other Latin American varieties, is characterized by the consistent pronunciation of word- and syllable-final /s/ and other final consonants: *estos* [éstos] 'these' (except in Veracruz and some other small coastal and northern regions, where there is aspiration). Educated Mexican speakers pronounce all syllable-final consonants with greater faithfulness to their orthographic representation than most Peninsular speakers of the same educational level. Thus, whereas, as we mentioned, speakers of the Peninsular standard will normally simplify the syllable-final clusters in *texto* [tésto] 'text', *construir* [kostruír] 'to build', etc., educated Mexicans pronounce the sequences suggested by the orthography: [téksto], [konstruír] (Lope Blanch 1996:81). On the other hand, unstressed vowels tend to be reduced in colloquial styles in Mexican Spanish, especially before /s/: *p's no* (*pues no* 'well, no'), *buenas noch's* (*buenas noches* 'good night') (Lope Blanch 1966).

Mexican Spanish has taken a sizeable number of loanwords from the main indigenous language of central Mexico, Nahuatl, and, with them, has acquired the word-initial consonant group /tl/, found in toponyms such as *Tlaxcala* and also in common nouns of Nahuatl origin, like *tlapalería* 'paint shop', *tlecuil* 'hearth', etc. For speakers from Spain and other Spanish-speaking countries this is a rather difficult initial cluster to pronounce, but it is perfectly normal in Mexican Spanish.

Like in many other Latin American areas, vowel sequences of the type /ea/, /oe/, etc., are commonly pronounced as DIPHTHONGS, *golpear* [golpiár], *poeta* [pu̯éta]. As a curiosity, we may mention here that in a couple of cases a difference in meaning has been created depending on whether the original vowel sequence is maintained or is pronounced as a diphthong. Thus, Mexicans distinguish *cohete*, pronounced [koéte] (three syllables) 'space rocket' from *cuete* [ku̯éte] (two syllables) 'fire cracker' (both *cohete* [koéte] in standard Peninsular Spanish). A similar, although not identical, case is that of *maestro (de escuela)* 'school teacher', pronounced [maéstro], vs *maestro (albañil)*

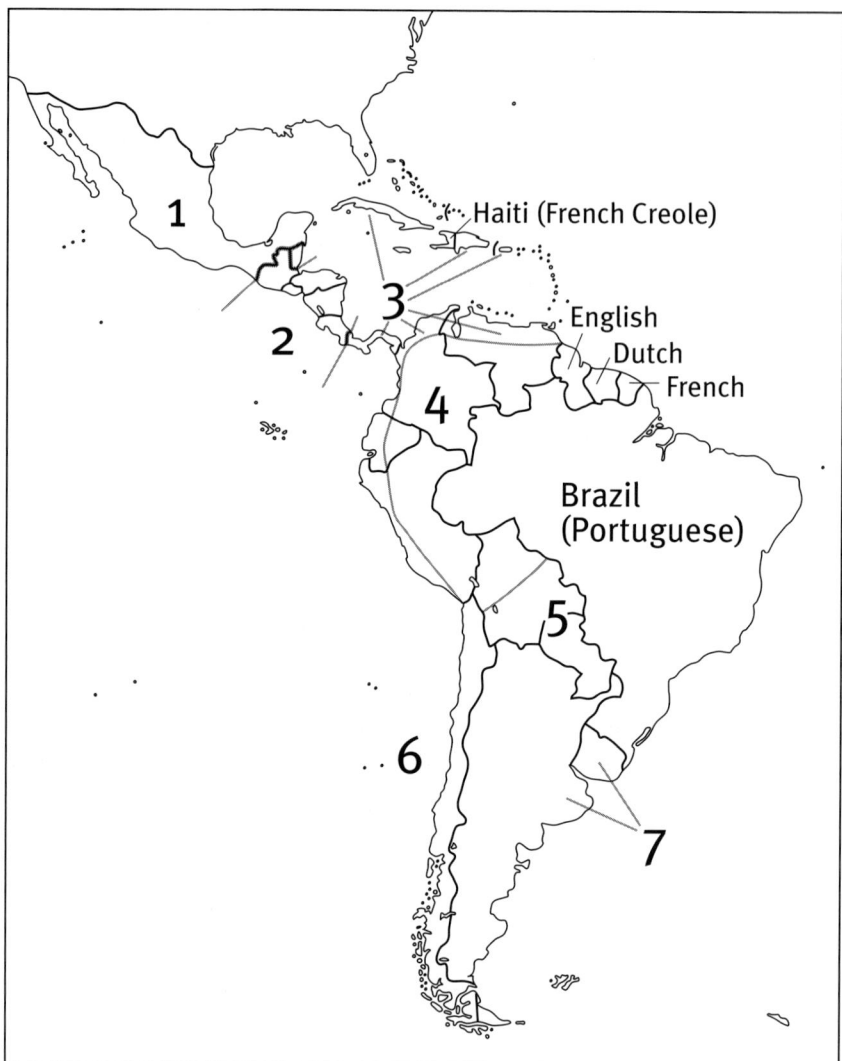

Figure 2.1. Main dialectal areas of Latin American Spanish: (1) Mexican; (2) Central American (Guatemala, El Salvador, Honduras, Nicaragua, Costa Rica); (3) Caribbean (Cuba, Dominican Republic, Puerto Rico, Panama, coast of Venezuela and Colombia); (4) Andean (highlands of Colombia, Ecuador, Peru and Bolivia); (5) Paraguayan (Paraguay and lowlands of eastern Bolivia); (6) Chilean; (7) River Plate (Argentina and Uruguay).

'mason', which is pronounced [máistro]. As we can see, in these examples the more learned or school-based meaning of the word has preserved a conservative pronunciation, whereas the more advanced pronunciation is related to other meanings less connected to technical or school contexts.

As a regional feature within Mexico, we may note that in parts of northern Mexico, /t͡ʃ/ is pronounced as [ʃ], *mucho* [múʃo].

Regarding the orthography of place names and other words of Nahuatl, Maya or other indigenous origin, it should be noted that the value of the letter *x* in such words is highly ambiguous. It can represent the phoneme /x/, as in *México* and *Oaxaca*. It can also, however, have the Old Spanish value of /ʃ/ as in *Xola*, a sound otherwise not found in modern Spanish. Finally in some toponyms it is simply /s/ as in *Xochimilco* [sot͡ʃimílko] and *Tlaxcala* [tlaskála].

As for the Spanish spoken in the United States, the contemporary presence of the Spanish language in this country is largely the result of immigration from Latin America, and it has the features of the areas of origin of the immigrants (mostly Mexico in the southwest, but Cuba in Miami and primarily Puerto Rico and the Dominican Republic in New York, for instance). One should remember, however, that the American Southwest was once part of Mexico. In parts of the state of New Mexico and in southern Colorado, we indeed find Spanish speakers whose Spanish-speaking ancestors have lived in the area since colonial times. Their Spanish represents a continuation of northern Mexican Spanish in some respects, but has also developed some distinctive features, as a consequence of its relative isolation. A feature that Traditional New Mexican Spanish shares with the varieties of northern Mexico is a very weak articulation of orthographic *y*, *ll* (like in Eng. *yes*), and the deletion of this palatal segment between /i/ or /e/ and another vowel, *anillo* [anío] 'ring', *silla* [sía] 'chair', *cabello* [kaβéo] 'hair' (Canfield 1981: 80; Alvar 1996b: 93). A local trait, which clearly distinguishes Traditional New Mexican Spanish from central Mexican, is the aspiration of /s/, which occurs not only syllable finally but even at the beginning of a word, as in *la semana* [lahemána] 'the week' (as also happens in some areas of northern Mexico, see Brown and Torres Cacoullos 2003). Naturally, bilingual speakers in the USA show some influence from English, to a greater or lesser degree depending on the speaker.

2.3.2 Central America

The Central American area has very questionable dialectal unity. Nevertheless, even if the area is not linguistically uniform, it is possible to speak of Central American Spanish in opposition to Mexican Spanish, on the one hand, and to Caribbean Spanish, on the other; that is, as a group of varieties that differ from both Mexican and Caribbean Spanish in some specific traits. The Central American dialectal area would include most of Central America south of Mexico except for Panama, whose speech is more of the Caribbean type. A non-phonological feature of Central American Spanish is the use of three forms for 'you, singular', *tú, vos* and *usted*, with complex sociolinguistic rules governing their use.

In most of Central America, there is a weak [h] in *mujer, ajo*, etc. (as in Caribbean Spanish but unlike most of Mexico, where a sound with greater friction, [x], is found). In addition, /s/ also tends to be aspirated in much of the region (also as in the Caribbean dialect and unlike in central Mexico), but aspiration of /s/ is not found in some highland areas of Central America, such as central Guatemala and the Central Valley of Costa Rica. As in Traditional New Mexican Spanish, aspiration affects word-initial /s/ in Honduras and El Salvador. Final /n/ is velar in all of Central America (also unlike central Mexico). Typical of Costa Rican Spanish is a type of /r̄/ that resembles English /r/. The group /tr/, in *tres, atrás*, etc., is also pronounced in Costa Rica with a COARTICULATION that recalls that given to this cluster in English *tree* (a feature also found in parts of Chile and some other areas). This coarticulation also affects the cluster /dɾ/, in *vendrá*, etc.

In parts of Central America (and Colombia), the consonants /b d g/ are often pronounced as stops after all consonants, unlike in the most common Spanish pattern (see 8.2).

2.3.3 Caribbean

Caribbean Spanish, which includes the Spanish spoken in the Dominican Republic, Cuba, Puerto Rico, Panama, and the coasts of Venezuela and Colombia, is generally considered the most 'innovative' or 'radical' among the geographical varieties of Latin American Spanish. The consonant weakening phenomena which were mentioned above as Southern Peninsular (and Canary Island) features, are found in this area with greater intensity than anywhere else in Latin America. In addition, there are also a couple of specifically Caribbean developments.

Most of the consonant-weakening phenomena of Caribbean Spanish are subject to sociolinguistic variation, with higher degrees of weakening being associated with more colloquial styles. Thus, whereas practically all Caribbean speakers aspirate preconsonantal and word-final /s/ to a certain extent (except, perhaps, for some radio announcers), this is a highly variable process and the highest indices of aspiration and deletion of /s/ are found in the most colloquial styles. The same speaker will pronounce, for instance, *los animales* 'the animals' as [lohanimále] on some occasions and as [losanimáleh] or [losanimáles] other times. The more [s]'s are pronounced, the greater the perceived level of formality (see 9.2.5.2).

The neutralization of /ɾ/ and /l/ before a consonant and word finally is widespread throughout this dialectal area. This is a feature that many speakers find difficult to avoid, even in careful style, for instance in Puerto Rico, where the resulting sound is generally [l], *puerta* [pu̯élta] 'door'. In parts of the Dominican Republic (El Cibao region) these consonants are vocalized in preconsonantal position: *parte* [pái̯te] 'part' (see 11.4).

The deletion of intervocalic [-d-] is found in colloquial styles, *pescado* [pehkáo] 'fish', but, like in most of Latin America and unlike in Spain, it is strongly stigmatized as 'vulgar' or uneducated.

The velar pronunciation of final /n/ is general and is not corrected in formal speech. Sometimes the weakening goes further, resulting in a nasalized vowel, *pan* [pã] 'bread', as also happens in Andalusia and the Canary Islands.

The phoneme /x/ is realized as [h]. In fact, one might as well speak of a phoneme /h/ instead of /x/ for Caribbean (and Central American) Spanish.

Some Puerto Rican speakers, but by no means all, have a DORSAL pronunciation of /r̄/ which recalls Parisian French /r/ somewhat (similar pronunciations are also found in parts of Cuba and the Dominican Republic). The consideration of this feature is not uniform among Puerto Ricans. Whereas some Puerto Ricans are of the opinion that this is a 'rural' feature, which should be avoided in educated speech, other Puerto Ricans see it as a marker of local origin which makes their speech distinctively Puerto Rican, a sign of Puerto Ricanness of which they are proud (see 11.3.2).

The weakening of /t͡ʃ/ to [ʃ] is spreading in Panama, whereas in Cuba we frequently find a palatal [c] of the Canary Island type and in Puerto Rico different allophonic variations of /t͡ʃ/ coexist.

Caribbean Spanish intonation includes a CIRCUMFLEX contour in pragmatically unmarked yes/no questions, a feature that it shares with Canary Island Spanish (see 14.9).

2.3.4 Andean Region

The speech of the highlands of Colombia, Ecuador, Peru and Bolivia is characterized by two conservative features: lack of weakening of /s/ (like in Mexican Spanish) and maintenance of the contrast between /ʎ/ and /j̦/, although this second feature is now in the process of being lost in many places. These conservative traits are found in the interior, mountainous areas of these countries. In the coastal area of Colombia, Ecuador and Peru we find some degree of aspiration of /s/ and no distinction between /j̦/ and /ʎ/, instead. In the interior lowlands of eastern Bolivia, the phenomenon of /s/ aspiration reappears again.

Aside from sharing these two conservative features, there is considerable diversity even within the properly Andean region. The Spanish of the Bolivian highlands and the Peruvian and Ecuadorian Andes, an area of intense contact with the indigenous Quechua and Aymara languages, differs substantially from that of central Colombia in its rhythm and intonation. Interestingly, in the Andes of Ecuador, Peru and Bolivia, we find the same phenomenon of deletion of unstressed vowels in contact with /s/ noted above for central Mexico. In this same area we also find an assibilated pronunciation of /r̄/ (which is somewhat stigmatized as a sign of rural origin).

Minimally, thus, in the territory that comprises the countries of Colombia, Ecuador, Peru and Bolivia we can distinguish four major dialectal subareas: (a) the coastal regions, (b) the interior region of Colombia, (c) the Ecuadorian, Peruvian and Bolivian highlands and (d) the lowlands of eastern Bolivia (this last dialectal area having more in common with Paraguay).

2.3.5 Paraguay

Paraguay is unique in Latin America in its nation-wide bilingualism. Besides Spanish, an indigenous native language, Guaraní, is widely spoken and respected as a symbol of national identity. Paraguayan Spanish preserves the phonemic contrast between /ʎ/ and /j/, with even greater vitality than in the Andean region (even though Guaraní lacks the palatal lateral /ʎ/). The phoneme /j/ is normally given an AFFRICATE pronunciation [d͡ʒ] (somewhat like in Eng. *John*) in all contexts. In Paraguay, syllable- and word-final /s/ is weakened, unlike in the core Andean region, but like in the other Southern Cone countries. A distinctive trait of the Spanish of Paraguay and neighbouring areas, possibly due to Guaraní influence (and to which we will return later), is the frequent occurrence of a GLOTTAL STOP word initially and between vowels in hiatus.

2.3.6 Chile

The Spanish of Chile has several distinctive traits. Syllable- and word-final /s/ is often aspirated. The group /tr/ is given a similar assibilated pronunciation to that found in Costa Rica (and some other areas, including La Rioja, in Spain). Before the vowels /e/ and /i/, the consonants /k g x/ have an advanced PALATAL pronunciation, so that, for instance, the Chilean pronunciation of *gente* 'people' sounds somewhat as if it were written *giente* to speakers of other Spanish dialects. The phoneme /t͡ʃ/ is variably realized as [ʃ] in some areas of Chile, whereas in other areas of Chile it advances its point of articulation to [t͡s].

2.3.7 River Plate

The Spanish variety spoken in an area of Argentina and Uruguay including the capital cities of Buenos Aires and Montevideo receives the name of River Plate or Porteño Spanish.[2] The most striking phonological feature of River Plate Spanish is the pronunciation of the consonant represented by orthographic *y* and *ll* with a sound similar to that of French *jamais* (found in English as the last sound in the French borrowing *rouge* and in words such as *measure*). This is part of the national standard of Argentina. The younger speakers in the Buenos Aires area are further changing this sound to [ʃ] (as in English *sheep*) (see 9.3).

In Buenos Aires /s/ is regularly aspirated before another consonant, *este* [éhte], *mismo* [míhmo], but not in other contexts. In other parts of Argentina, but not in the Buenos Aires standard, word-final /s/ is also aspirated before a vowel or pause: *estos otros* [éhtoh ótroh].

Outside of the phonological realm, a salient characteristic of Argentinian Spanish is the use of *vos* instead of *tú* for 'you, *singular*': *vos cantás* 'you sing', *vos decís* 'you say', *vos sos* 'you are'. While VOSEO is by no means an exclusively Argentinian phenomenon, since it is found over most of Central America and large parts of South America (parts of Colombia, Venezuela, Ecuador, Bolivia, Paraguay, Chile, etc.), what is different is its social consideration. In most *voseo* areas, *vos* is replaced by *tú* in more formal situations and when speaking to outsiders. In Argentina, instead, the use of *tú* has completely disappeared from everyday usage.[3] This is all confirmation of Argentinians' confidence and pride in their national standard (which is based on the speech of the Buenos Aires middle class).

2.4 More on the limitations of dialectal classification

The classification of Spanish varieties into major dialectal areas that we have presented in the sections above hides substantial diversity within each of the areas, both of sociolectal nature and geographical. Speakers within most, if not all, of these areas are acutely aware of internal regional differences. These differences are especially salient to natives of the area in question. Thus, whereas, for instance, the Northern-Central Peninsular Spanish spoken in Santiago de Compostela, Bilbao, Burgos, Madrid, Zaragoza and Barcelona may appear rather homogenous to outsiders, including Latin Americans, generally speakers from northern-central Spain have no trouble distinguishing among these

---

[2] The name *River Plate* makes reference to the Río de la Plata, the broad estuary where both Buenos Aires and Montevideo are located. *Porteño* refers to these two major ports.
[3] In Montevideo the form *tú* is preserved as an intermediate treatment between informal *vos* and formal *usted*, but generally with verbal *voseo* forms: *tú podés* 'you can'.

Figure 2.2. Grey: areas without weakening of preconsonantal and final /s/ (highlands of Mexico and Guatemala, Central Valley of Costa Rica, Andean region). Everywhere else there is greater or lesser aspiration of /s/. Vertical lines: area where the palatal lateral phoneme /ʎ/ has been preserved (Andean region and Paraguay).

geographical varieties.[4] Similarly, for many Andalusians it is inconceivable that anybody may speak of an Andalusian dialect, since they perceive great differences in the way the language is pronounced in the different provinces

---

[4] We are referring to the varieties of Spanish found in this part of the Peninsula, not to other languages such as Galician, Basque and Catalan, that, together with Spanish, are also spoken in parts of this area.

of Andalusia. In the same way, in Colombia, Venezuela, Argentina, Mexico, Peru, the Dominican Republic, etc., there is often much awareness of regional differences within each country.

In some areas, natives may in fact be able to tell the speech of one village from that of the next village. In the case of locally unusual developments this is sometimes reflected in local sayings. A couple of examples from Extremadura, in central-western Spain, may suffice as illustration. The village of Fuente del Maestre, in Extremadura, for instance, is an island of SESEO within an area of Spain where /s/ and /θ/ are distinguished. This local phonetic peculiarity is noted in the saying *Todoh loh de La Fuente / son conosidoh / porque disen aseite, / sebá y tosino* 'All those from La Fuente are well known because they say [aséi̯te] (= *aceite* 'oil'), [seβá] (= *cebada* 'barley') and [tosíno] (= *tocino* 'bacon')' (Álvarez Martínez 1996). In areas of Extremadura where historical /h/ from Latin /f-/ is still aspirated, they use the saying *Quien no diga jierro, jumo, jacha, jigo y jiguera no es de mi tierra* (using orthographic *j* to represent [h]) 'Anybody who does not say [hi̯éro] (= *hierro* 'iron'), [húmo] (= *humo* 'smoke'), [hát͡ʃa] (= *hacha* 'axe'), [híɣo] (= *higo* 'fig') and [hiɣéra] (= *higuera* 'fig tree') is not from my land.' It is important, however, to keep in mind that, in formal interactions and when speaking to outsiders, many speakers, if not all, will shift towards variants more in accordance with the standard language of the country – the Peninsular standard in this case. Essentially the same situation is found in Latin America. Speakers use local pronunciations and other local linguistic variants to show solidarity within the group, but they also recognize the existence of a national or regional standard (even a pan-Latin-American standard).

A final caveat to end this section. Traditionally, dialectal classifications are based on the speech of rural areas. In the large cities of the Spanish-speaking world there is usually much more internal diversity than in rural areas, as these cities have often attracted immigrants from other parts of the country and elsewhere. In Mexico City and Lima, for example, one may find speakers of geographical varieties of Spanish from all over the respective country. In Madrid and Barcelona, it is not at all uncommon to hear Andalusian Spanish, and, increasingly, a visitor may also hear a number of Latin American varieties in these cities, as a result of recent immigration from Latin America.

2.5 Other varieties of Spanish

Although, for practical reasons, the description in this book is limited to the socially most important varieties of Spanish spoken in Latin America and Spain, there are other geographical varieties of Spanish spoken outside of these two major geographical areas which we can only briefly mention here.

First of all, outside of Latin America and Spain, Spanish is an official language in Equatorial Guinea, a former colony of Spain. Equatorial Guinea is the only Spanish-speaking country in Africa. In this country, Spanish is mostly spoken as a second language by people who in many cases are multilingual (see Casado-Fresnillo 1995). Lipski (1985b) reports a general tendency to neutralize the tap/trill contrast.

In the Philippines, also a former Spanish colony, Spanish is no longer an official language and is spoken natively by only about 3 per cent of the population, normally in a situation of bi- or multilingualism. It is interesting to note that many Filipino speakers of Spanish maintain the /j̞/ - /ʎ/ contrast. Some of them also possess the /s/ - /θ/ distinction of Northern-Central Peninsular Spanish (see Quilis 1995).

A very special case is that of Sephardic Spanish or Judeo-Spanish, spoken by the descendants of the Spanish Jews who, after being expelled from their country in the fifteenth and sixteenth centuries, established communities in the Balkans, North Africa and elsewhere (see T. Harris 1994; Penny 2000:174–193). Having been preserved for five centuries, nowadays Judeo-Spanish is in a situation of general decline. Perhaps the greatest number of speakers is now found in Israel, but, for the most part, the language is not being transmitted to the new generations. Judeo-Spanish is strikingly different from all other contemporary dialects of Spanish in its pronunciation. Having evolved in isolation from the rest of the Spanish dialects, Judeo-Spanish did not participate in the radical changes that affected some of the Spanish consonants in the sixteenth and seventeenth centuries. Thus, Sephardic Spanish maintains the contrast between /z/ and /s/ of Old Spanish, as in /káza/ 'house' vs /pása/ 's/he passes', which has disappeared from all other Spanish dialects. Corresponding to /x/ in the rest of the modern Spanish dialects, we find /ʒ/ in some words and /ʃ/ in others, also as in Old Spanish, as in /óʒo/ 'eye' (Modern Spanish *ojo* /óxo/) and /deʃítes/ 'you said' (Modern Spanish *dijiste* /dixíste/). See 9.2.4.

Not properly 'dialects of Spanish' are the CREOLE languages Papiamentu, Palenquero and Chabacano. Creole languages have their origin in a simplified contact variety or pidgin which at some point was acquired as a native language and continued developing as any other natural language from that point on. The three Creole languages mentioned above derive their lexicon mostly, but by no means exclusively, from Spanish, but in their morphology and syntax they are quite different languages from Spanish. Papiamentu is spoken in the Dutch Antilles (Aruba, Curaçao and Bonaire). Palenquero is the language of El Palenque de San Basilio, on the Pacific coast of Colombia, a community founded by a group of runaway slaves. Chabacano (Caviteño and Zamboagueño) is a Spanish-based Creole of the Philippines (it is also known as Philippine Creole Spanish in the specialized literature).[5]

2.6 The Ibero-Romance languages

The overview of Spanish dialects that we have presented above has not included mention of linguistic varieties spoken in Spain such as Asturian, Aragonese, Galician and Catalan. This is because these are not really dialects of the Spanish language. Rather, these are sister languages or co-dialects of Spanish. Asturian, Aragonese, Galician, etc., represent independent evolutions from Latin in their respective regions, whereas Mexican, Argentinian, Andalusian, etc., all have their source in the specific evolution of Latin that took place in the original Castilian area, around the city of Burgos, in the early middle ages, which later spread over much of the Peninsula and the Spanish colonies in the New World as the Kingdom of Castile expanded its territory.

More information on the historical development of the Ibero-Romance varieties and their influence on the regional Spanish of bilingual areas is presented in Appendix C.

2.7 The notion of standard language. Is there a standard Spanish pronunciation?

Languages, such as English and Spanish, that are used in the educational system, the media, government, commerce, etc., have a standard form. This is the variety of the language for which grammars and dictionaries are written. In the case of English, there is some small amount of national variation in the recognized standard. As is well known, the American standard differs from the British standard in a few details of spelling (*center* or *centre*, *color* or *colour*, *organize* or *organise*, etc.), some vocabulary and a few grammatical constructions. Differences in pronunciation are somewhat greater among national or regional standards of English. Regarding Spanish, the Real Academia Española, which has affiliated academies in all Spanish-speaking countries, is charged with the mission of ensuring the standardization of the language.[6] The success of the Academy's efforts to fix the standard and maintain the unity of the language is more evident in some aspects than in others. The clearest success in standardization is found in the orthography. The Real Academia's orthographic rules

---

[5] Both Palenquero and Papiamentu perhaps were originally Portuguese-based Creoles, which were re-lexified with Spanish vocabulary (see McWhorter 2000).
[6] As reflected in its motto: 'Limpia, fija y da esplendor'.

are accepted throughout the Spanish-speaking world. We do not even find anything like the small differences that exist between British and American spelling. In other nonorthographic aspects, on the other hand, we do find some variation.

One may say that each Spanish-speaking country has its own national standard, which is generally based on the linguistic usage of the upper-middle class of the national capital: what in Spanish is sometimes called *la norma culta* or educated norm of the capital. In the written language, differences in vocabulary and grammar are sometimes noticeable in genres such as journalistic writing and realistic novels, but essentially nonexistent in academic and scientific prose. As in English, differences among national standard pronunciations are greater. Experience has shown, however, that, for practical purposes such as the teaching of Spanish as a foreign language and speech synthesis, it is sufficient to distinguish a Peninsular standard from a Latin American standard pronunciation. Furthermore, these two standard pronunciations differ only in a few points. At the level of phonemes, there is only one difference: as we already know, Latin American standard pronunciation has a single phoneme /s/ corresponding to both phonemes /s/ and /θ/ of the Peninsular standard. This difference is an important one. Whereas in Spain standard speakers are expected to observe the /θ/ vs /s/ contrast, in Latin America the use of the sound /θ/ contrasting with /s/ marks one's pronunciation as definitely foreign. There are other differences of phonetic detail, which have already been mentioned and will be explained in later chapters, such as the fact that standard Peninsular /x/ is pronounced with more friction than its standard Latin American counterpart and that northern Peninsular /s/ also has a more sibilant sound. The contrast between a lateral phoneme /ʎ/ corresponding to orthographic *ll*, as in *calle* 'street' and a different palatal phoneme /j/ corresponding to *y*, as in *mayo* 'May', which until recently was taught as part of the Peninsular standard, as well as forming part of the standard of some South American countries, including Colombia and Paraguay (but not Mexico or Puerto Rico, for instance), is no longer considered worth emphasizing. This is because the contrast has been lost in the speech of the younger generations in most of the urban areas of both Spain and South America where it had been preserved until now. Both in Spain and in most of the South American countries where the lateral palatal /ʎ/ is still found, this is now considered a regional, old-fashioned, rural or even pretentious pronunciation, and is not expected in the speech of a second-language speaker.

The Peninsular standard pronunciation is based on the speech of educated speakers from Madrid and the area of Castile to the north of the capital, including cities such as Burgos and Valladolid. Some features of colloquial

Madrid speech, such as the weakening of /s/ before some consonants (as in *esquina, espera*) and the deletion of /d/ in participles in -*ado*, are not part of the formal standard (but are not really stigmatized in Spain either). The educated Madrid pronunciation is accepted as the standard one even in areas of Spain, like Andalusia, where the local pronunciation is quite different. Some educated Andalusian speakers (although not all) in cities such as Seville and Granada will, for example, make the /s/ - /θ/ contrast as in the Peninsular standard, even though the local Spanish pronunciation that they learned from their parents does not have this contrast. It is interesting to note that in the Canary Islands, on the other hand, the national standard pronunciation, although recognized as such, is strictly an external norm and is not taken by most native Canarians as a model to be carefully imitated.

As for Latin American Spanish, the general Latin American standard pronunciation is modelled on the educated speech of speakers from highland cities such as Mexico City and Bogotá, which lacks weakening of syllable-final /s/ and other consonants. The fact is that educated speakers from quite distant geographical points in Latin America can sometimes sound very much alike in their formal style (even if the popular speech of the respective areas is rather more distinctive). This type of pronunciation, without weakening of final consonants, is regarded as 'correct' or 'neutral' throughout Latin America, whereas the Peninsular standard is seen as 'correct' but foreign. It is, in fact, possible to speak of a general Latin American norm of pronunciation.

This does not mean, however, that there are no other more local norms that enjoy prestigious status at the national or regional level. In particular, the standard Argentinian pronunciation, used on radio and television in this South American country, has some very distinctive features, including the sound /ʒ/ (as in English *measure* or French *jamais*) corresponding to orthographic *y* and *ll* (e.g. *yo me llamo* /ʒó me ʒámo/ 'I am called') and the frequent aspiration or weakening of /s/ before a consonant, as in *este, espera* (but not in other contexts), in addition to some very characteristic intonational contours. For most Argentinians this is their real model of pronunciation.

2.8 What's in a name: Castilian or Spanish? *¿Castellano o español?*

The language with which we are primarily concerned in this book was in its origin the result of the particular evolution of Latin that took place in the old Kingdom of Castile, one among many Ibero-Romance varieties. For the medieval period, the language is thus properly called Castilian (or Old Castilian), as distinct from Leonese, Aragonese, Catalan, Galician-Portuguese, Mozarabic, etc. The term 'Old Spanish' is often used in the scholarly literature as a concept that includes Old Castilian and also its closest relatives, such as Leonese, Aragonese, Navarrese Romance and even Mozarabic (but not Galician-Portuguese or Catalan).

As the language of Castile spread out from its small place of origin and became the dominant language of Spain, it also started to receive the name of 'Spanish' from the sixteenth century onwards. We thus end up with two names for the same language, Castilian and Spanish; *castellano y español*.

Nowadays, in bilingual areas of Spain the term *castellano* is preferred in opposition to the local language. Most people thus speak of *castellano* as opposed to *catalán, gallego, asturiano* or *euskera* (*vasco*). The existence of two names for the language, however, allows for the possibility of using one or the other name for ideological purposes. For instance, a Catalan nationalist may use Catalan vs Spanish, as a way to emphasize that for him or her Catalonia is a different nation from Spain. A Spanish nationalist may also have ideological reasons for using one term or the other. In monolingual areas of Spain, both terms *castellano* and *español* are used. The term *español* is especially common when the language is set in opposition to English, French and other foreign languages.

In Latin America, which name is used depends very much on the established tradition of the region or the country. In Mexico and Puerto Rico, for example, the normal name for the language is *español*. In other countries, including, for instance, Peru and Argentina, on the other hand, the language is usually called *castellano*. It is likely that in the period immediately after the wars of independence, the name *español* was purposely avoided in some newly independent republics to emphasize its breaking away from Spain; whereas the alternative name *castellano* was seen as more politically neutral. Nowadays, however, what we have is simply different traditions in different Latin American countries, without any particular ideological connotations attached to either of the two terms. Mexicans call their language *español*, Argentinians and Peruvians call their language *castellano*. That's all. Nothing is meant by using one name or the other.

In English, the term 'Castilian Spanish' is sometimes used to refer to the Peninsular standard variety of the language, as opposed primarily to Latin American Spanish. In the Spanish-speaking countries this usage is not at all common. The difference between the English and Spanish usage in this respect can be a source of confusion. Once I inspected a software product that contained some recorded sentences in some of the major languages of the world. For Spanish three dialects were listed, including 'Castilian'. But the 'Castilian' phrases were actually in Argentinian Spanish! Obviously the speaker who recorded the sentences had indicated that he spoke *castellano*.

In this book we will use 'Castilian Spanish' to refer specifically to the Spanish varieties spoken in the historical regions of Old and New Castile (corresponding to the present-day regions of Madrid, and most of Castilla-León and Castilla-La Mancha) as well as to the standard pronunciation of Spanish in Spain. Most of the time, this term will be equivalent to Northern-Central Peninsular Spanish, since many similar traits are found throughout this area. Strictly speaking, however, the two terms are not identical. For instance, the Spanish spoken in Catalonia (in contact with the Catalan language) is a variety of Northern-Central Peninsular Spanish, but is not Castilian Spanish in our usage. Occasionally the terms 'Castilian Spanish' and 'Standard Peninsular Spanish' will need to be differentiated as within the Castilian area we find pronunciations that are not part of the Peninsular Standard language (see section 2.7 above).

EXERCISES

1. The underlined segments in the following words may receive different pronunciations depending on the dialect. Explain.

   <u>c</u>esta, co<u>s</u>ta, ma<u>y</u>o, <u>ll</u>ega, ra<u>z</u>a

2. List the main phonological features that distinguish the following Spanish dialects:

   Caribbean, Mexican, Northern-Central Peninsular, River Plate

3. Here you have a semi-narrow phonetic transcription of the same text in two Spanish varieties, Madrid (M) and Buenos Aires (BA). List the main systematic differences between the two dialects that you can observe in this text. The text is a Spanish version of 'The north wind and the sun', a text that is frequently used in publications of the International Phonetic Association to illustrate phonetic transcription.[7]

   El viento norte y el sol
   El viento norte y el sol porfiaban sobre cuál de ellos era el más fuerte, cuando acertó a pasar un viajero envuelto en ancha capa.

---

[7] Quilis and Fernández (1985:190–2) also provide a Standard Peninsular transcription of this text. Martínez Celdrán *et al.* (2003) provide two more transcriptions of the same text, representing a conservative Standard Peninsular variety and Buenos Aires Spanish (but without using the same level of phonetic detail or even the same symbols in both).

M:
[elβi̯ento nórte i̯elsól porfi̯áβan soβrekṷál déi̯os éra elmás fṷérte | kṷando aθertó apasár úm bi̯axéro embṷél̯to enántʃ a kápa]
BA:
[elβi̯ento nórte i̯elsól porfi̯áβan soβrekṷál déʒos éra elmáh fṷérte | kṷando asertó apasár úm bi̯axéro embṷél̯to enántʃ a kápa]
Convinieron en que quien antes lograra obligar al viajero a quitarse la capa sería considerado más poderoso.
M:
[kombini̯éron eŋke ki̯en án̯tes loɣrára oβligár alβi̯axéro a kitárse lakápa sería konsiðeráðo más poðeróso]
BA:
[kombini̯éron eŋke ki̯en án̯teh loɣrára oβligár alβi̯axéro a kitárse lakápa sería konsiðeráðo máh poðeróso]
El viento norte sopló con gran furia, pero cuanto más soplaba, más se arrebujaba en su capa el viajero; por fin el viento norte abandonó la empresa.
M:
[elβi̯ento nórte sopló koŋgrám fúri̯a| pero kṷan̯tomás sopláβa más seareβuxáβa ensukápa elβi̯axéro || porfín elβi̯ento nórte aβan̯donó laemprésa]
BA:
[elβi̯ento nórte sopló koŋgrám fúri̯a| pero kṷan̯tomás sopláβa más seareβuxáβa ensukápa elβi̯axéro || porfín elβi̯ento nórte aβan̯donó laemprésa]
Entonces brilló el sol con ardor, e inmediatamente se despojó de su capa el viajero; por lo que el viento norte hubo de reconocer la superioridad del sol.
M:
[en̯tónθes βri̯ó elsól konarðór | ei̯mmeði̯átamén̯te seðespoxó ðesukápa elβi̯axéro | porlokelβi̯ento nórte úβo ðerekonoθér lasuperi̯oriðá ðelsól]
BA:
[en̯tónseh βriʒó elsól konarðór | ei̯mmeði̯átamén̯te seðehpoxó ðesukápa elβi̯axéro | porlokelβi̯ento nórte úβo ðerekonosér lasuperi̯oriðá ðelsól]

4 Identify the following linguistic varieties (see Appendix C2):

(a) Chistavino (b) Mozarabic (c) Chabacano (d) Mirandês (e) Aranese (f) Judeo-Spanish (g) Palenquero

3 Consonants and vowels

3.1 Consonants and vowels

In the study of the sounds of a language it is customary to make a distinction between vowels and consonants, as these two types of sounds differ both in their articulation and in their distribution. Consonants are produced by blocking or obstructing in some manner the flow of air coming out from the lungs. Vowels are produced without such an obstruction. For the analysis and classification of vowels and consonants different parameters are usually employed.

3.2 Description and classification of consonantal sounds

In the production of consonant sounds an articulatory organ, known as the active articulator (e.g. the lower lip, the tip of the tongue, the dorsum of the tongue), is displaced to make contact or form a constriction with another articulatory organ, the passive articulator (e.g. the upper lip, the upper front teeth, the alveolar area, the hard palate, the velum). The main articulators used in the production of the speech sounds of the Spanish language (and also of English) are identified in Fig. 3.1.

For the classification and description of consonants three parameters are employed: manner of articulation, place of articulation and activity of the vocal folds.

3.2.1 Manner of articulation

This feature refers to the type of obstruction that is created in the articulation of the consonant. Regarding manner of articulation, the following classes of consonants can be distinguished:

a) Plosives (oral stops). These are consonants in whose articulation the flow of air is completely stopped before it is released. To this class belong the sounds

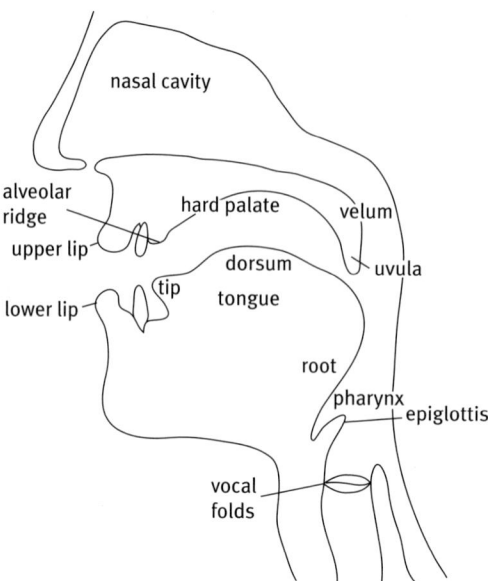

Figure 3.1.   Articulators.

[p t k], as in *pan* [pán] 'bread', *tan* [tán] 'so', *can* [kán] 'dog', as well as the allophones [b d g] of the phonemes /b d g/, as in *cambio* [kámbi̯o] 'change', *anda* [án̪da] 's/he walks', *vengo* [béŋgo] 'I come' (see 8.1).

The phoneme /ɟ/, as in *yeso* /ɟéso/ 'plaster', also has a plosive allophone [ɟ] in some dialects, including Castilian, where a plosive realization of this phoneme is frequent in phrase-initial position and after some consonants: [konʲɟéso] 'with plaster' (see also below, under affricates, and 9.3).

If we pronounce a sequence containing a plosive, such as [apa], slowly we can notice that there is a moment when the flow of air is completely blocked. The term ORAL STOP, which is also given to these segments, refers to this aspect of their articulation, whereas the term PLOSIVE makes reference to the explosion produced when the occlusion is released.

b) Fricatives. In the production of these consonants the flow of air is not completely interrupted. Instead, it escapes through a narrow constriction between the articulators, producing turbulence or friction. Examples in Spanish are [f] as in *feo* [féo] 'ugly', [s] as in *ese* [ése] 'that' and [x] as in *ajo* [áxo] 'garlic'. As we already know, the phoneme /s/, besides its allophone [s], has two other common allophones in syllable-final position, [z] as in *mismo* [mízmo] 'same' and, in 'aspirating' dialects, [h], as in Car., Andal., etc., *este* [éhte] 'this' ([h] also occurs instead of [x] in some dialects). Both [h] and [z] are also fricative sounds.

3.2 Description and classification: consonantal sounds

Also fricatives are [θ] in Cast. *hace* [áθe] 's/he makes' (Eng. ***thick***) and [ʒ] in Arg. *yeso* [ʒéso] 'plaster', *mayo* [máʒo] 'May', *ella* [éʒa] 'she' (Eng. ***pleasure***). The sound [ʃ], as in Eng. ***sheep***, is also a fricative. This sound is become increasingly common in Argentina, where it competes with [ʒ], corresponding to the spellings *y* and *ll* (by a DEVOICING process): Arg. *yeso* [ʃéso], *mayo* [máʃo], *ella* [éʃa]. In other dialects, including those in parts of Chile, northern Mexico and New Mexico, Panama and southern Spain, on the other hand, the fricative sound [ʃ] is found where other dialects have the affricate [t͡ʃ], corresponding to the spelling *ch*: e.g. Chile, *macho* [máʃo] 'male' (common [mát͡ʃo]).

Notice that, unlike plosives like [p] and [t], whose prolongation produces only a longer period of silence, fricative sounds can be continued: [fff], [sss], [xxx], [ʒʒʒ]. See 9.2.

c) Approximants. If the constriction made by the articulators is not narrow enough to produce friction, we speak of approximant consonants, referring to the fact that the active articulator merely approximates or approaches the passive articulator. English [ð] as in *gather* is a fricative, the intervocalic sound in Spanish *cada* 'each', on the other hand, is an approximant and can be realized with very little constriction. This could be indicated by adding a subscript diacritic for greater aperture in a comparative analysis: Sp. *cada* [káð̞a], Eng. *gather* [gæðə(ɹ)]. More generally, between vowels and in several other contexts, the Spanish phonemes /b d g/ have approximant allophones, as we already know. For simplicity, we will use the symbols [β ð ɣ] without diacritics: *sabe* [sáβe] 's/he knows', *lava* [láβa] 's/he washes', *pide* [píðe] 's/he asks', *lago* [láɣo] 'lake'. See 8.1 and 8.2.

The consonant [j̞], as in *mayo* [máj̞o] 'May' has a very variable degree of constriction and, depending on the dialect, may be better classified as a fricative or as an approximant (leaving aside realizations with full occlusion, for which we are using the symbol [ɟ], and also leaving aside the strident fricatives [ʒ], [ʃ] of Argentinian and some other dialects).

d) Affricates. These are consonants whose articulation includes two phases: occlusion and fricative release. Spanish has only one affricate phoneme /t͡ʃ/ as in *chapa* [t͡ʃápa] 'plate, sheet'. As mentioned above, in some dialects (parts of Chile, Panama, etc.) the occlusion is weakened in colloquial speech, resulting in the fricative [ʃ]. See 9.1.

The sound [ɟ], mentioned above as a plosive allophone of /j/, can be realized with some affrication, in which case we may transcribe it as [ɟ͡j].

Other common affricates found in other languages are [t͡s] (as in German ***Zeit*** 'time', Basque ***beltz*** 'black', ***abertzale*** 'patriot'), [d͡z] (as in Italian ***mezzo*** 'half') and [d͡ʒ] (as in both the initial and the final consonant of English ***judge***; in Arg. Sp. it occurs as an allophone of /ʒ/ after a nasal or lateral, as in *cónyuge*). Both phases of the affricate must share the same place of articulation. A sequence such as /ks/, as in *taxi*, is not an affricate.

e) Nasals (nasal stops). These consonants, like plosives, are produced with complete occlusion through the oral channel, but they allow the flow of air to escape through the nasal cavity. This is accomplished by the lowering of the velum. Properly, these consonants are, thus, nasal stops. Spanish has three nasal stop phonemes /m/, /n/ and /ɲ/, as in *cama* [káma] 'bed', *cana* [kána] 'grey hair', *caña* [káɲa] 'cane' (see 10.1). It is easy to verify that in the pronunciation of [m] the lips are completely closed, like for [p] and [b], but we can still produce the sound [mmm] because of airflow through the nasal cavity. Another nasal consonant that we have already introduced in previous chapters is the velar nasal [ŋ] (as in Eng. *king*), which occurs in all dialects before a velar consonant, as in *tengo* [téŋgo] 'I have', and, in so-called 'velarizing' dialects (e.g. Caribbean), also word finally, as in *pan* [páŋ]. The assimilation of nasals to the point of articulation of immediately following consonants results in yet other allophonic nasal sounds, as we will see immediately below and, in more detail, in 10.2.

f) Laterals. These are consonants produced with contact between the articulators along the central axis of the mouth, allowing airflow through one or both sides. All Spanish dialects have a lateral phoneme /l/ as in *lado* [láðo] 'side', *palo* [pálo] 'stick', *mal* [mál] 'badly', for which contact is with the tip of the tongue against the alveolar region, with free passage of air through the sides of the tongue.

In addition, conservative speakers in parts of Spain and the Andean region have another lateral phoneme /ʎ/, corresponding to orthographic *ll*, with articulatory contact in the palatal area, as in *pollo* [póʎo] 'chicken' (most commonly [pójo]). See 11.2.

g) Rhotics. These are 'r-sounds'. In Spanish there are two rhotic phonemes, a trill /r̄/, as in *carro* [kár̄o] 'cart, car', and a tap /ɾ/ as in *caro* [káɾo] 'expensive'. In Spanish these consonants are called *vibrantes*. The tap [ɾ] (*vibrante simple*) is produced with a single rapid contact of the tip of the tongue against the alveolar region. The trill [r̄] (*vibrante múltiple*) is produced with two or more such rapid gestures. See 11.3.

If we consider only the prototypical allophone of each phoneme for classificatory purposes, we can classify the phonemes of Spanish by their manner of articulation as in Table 3.2.[1]

---

[1] As explained elsewhere, of these, /θ/ is found only in Castilian Spanish, /ʒ/ basically in Argentinian, and /ʎ/ is a phoneme only for conservative speakers in the Andean region, Paraguay and parts of Spain. The consonant /j/ has a marginal status as a phoneme, since for the most part it can arguably be taken to represent realizations of the phoneme /i/ under certain conditions (see 9.3).

3.2 Description and classification: consonantal sounds

Table 3.1 Manner of articulation.

Plosives	[p]	*pan* [pán] 'bread'
	[t]	*tan* [tán] 'so'
	[k]	*can* [kán] 'dog'
	[b]	*con barro* [kombáro] 'with mud'
	[d]	*con dos* [kon̪dós] 'with two'
	[g]	*con gana* [koŋgána] 'willingly'
	[ɟ]	*enyesa* [enʲɟésa] 's/he plasters'
Fricatives	[f]	*feo* [féo] 'ugly'
	[θ]	Cast. *cena* [θéna] 'supper'
	[s]	*sal* [sál] 'salt'
	[z]	*mismo* [mízmo] 'same'
	[ʝ]	*playa* [pláʝa] 'beach'
	[x]	*ajo* [áxo] 'garlic'
	[h]	Andal., Car., etc., *este* [éhte] 'this'; Car., etc, *ajo* [áho] 'garlic'
	[ʃ]	Arg. (innov.) *playa* [pláʃa] 'beach'; NMex. *mucho* [múʃo] 'much'
	[ʒ]	Arg. (conserv.) *playa* [pláʒa]
Approximants	[β]	*sabe* [sáβe] 's/he knows', *lava* [láβa] 's/he washes'
	[ð]	*cada* [káða] 'each'
	[ɣ]	*lago* [láɣo] 'lake'
Affricates	[t͡ʃ]	*hacha* [át͡ʃa] 'axe'
Nasals	[m]	*cama* [káma] 'bed'
	[n]	*cana* [kána] 'grey hair'
	[ɲ]	*caña* [káɲa] 'cane'
	[ŋ]	*tengo* [téŋgo] 'I have', Andal., Car., etc., *pan* [páŋ] 'bread'
Laterals	[l]	*lado* [láðo] 'side'
	[ʎ]	Conserv. Cast. & And. *llora* [ʎóra] 's/he cries'
Rhotics	[ɾ]	*toro* [tóɾo] 'bull'
	[r̄]	*torre* [tór̄e] 'tower', *reto* [r̄éto] 'challenge'

'Prototypical' does not necessarily mean 'most common', since for /b d g/ the continuant or approximant allophones have a wider distribution than the plosive allophones.

In this book we will use some additional, more inclusive, terms. The term LIQUID is used to refer to both laterals and rhotics. It is useful to have a name for this class of consonants. In Spanish, for instance, the only consonant

Table 3.2 Consonantal phonemes of Spanish classified by manner of articulation. Phonemes in parentheses are found only in some dialects.

Plosives	/p/ /t/ /k/ /b/ /d/ /g/
Fricatives	/f/ (/θ/) /s/ (/ʒ/) /ʝ/ /x/
Affricates	/t͡ʃ/
Nasals	/m/ /n/ /ɲ/
Lateral	/l/ (/ʎ/)
Rhotic	/r̄/ /ɾ/

clusters found word (and syllable) initially are those that contain a liquid as a second member: /pɾ/, /pl/, etc. Liquids and nasals together form the class of SONORANT consonants, as opposed to the OBSTRUENT class, which includes plosives, fricatives and affricates.

3.2.2 Place of articulation

The feature of place is used to classify consonant sounds with respect to the articulators that are involved in their production.

a) Bilabial. The plosive consonant [p] as in *pan* [pán], is produced by making contact with both lips. We say that it is a bilabial consonant. Also bilabial are [b] as in *sin boca* [simbóka] 'without mouth' and *un vaso* [úm báso] 'a glass', and the approximant consonant [β] as in *la boca* [laβóka] 'the mouth', *tu vaso* [tuβáso] 'your glass' (both allophones of the phoneme /b/). The nasal consonant [m], as in *mes* [més] 'month', has a bilabial place of articulation as well. Nasals take a bilabial place of articulation before bilabial consonants, as shown in the example *un vaso* /ún báso/ [úm báso].

b) Labiodental. In the production of the fricative consonant [f] the active articulator is again the lower lip, which moves to make contact with the upper tooth range (passive articulator). By its point of articulation this sound is a labiodental. English and most other European languages have another labiodental fricative, [v], which functions as a distinct phoneme. English has a contrast between the voiceless labiodental fricative /f/ and the voiced labiodental fricative /v/. In Spanish, on the other hand, the voiced sound [v] only occurs as an allophone of the phoneme /f/ before a voiced consonant, in rare words such as *afgano* /afgáno/ [avɣáno] 'Afghan'. A labiodental nasal [ɱ] occurs before [f], as in *énfasis* [éɱfasis] 'emphasis'.

c) Interdental. In interdental consonants the tip of the tongue or apex is protruded between the upper and lower teeth. Northern-Central Peninsular

3.2 Description and classification: consonantal sounds

Spanish has an interdental fricative [θ], which functions as a distinctive phoneme in this dialect, as in *servicio* /serbíθio/ [serβíθi̯o] 'service' (LatAm. [serβísi̯o]), *ceniza* [θeníθa] 'ashes' (LatAm. [senísa]).

English has two phonemic interdental fricatives, voiceless /θ/ and voiced /ð/, as in **th**ought and **th**ough, respectively. As mentioned, in Spanish there is an approximant [ð], more exactly [ð̞], as an allophone of /d/. In the production of the Spanish voiced approximant [ð] the apex approaches the rim of the upper teeth. This articulation is properly described as apico-dento-interdental (see Navarro Tomás 1977:99).[2]

d) Dental. In dental consonants the passive articulator is the base of the upper front teeth. In the Spanish dental plosives [t] and [d] (which have a more fronted articulation than the corresponding English sounds), the active articulator is the apex. More completely, then, these consonants are apico-dental. The sonorants /n/ and /l/ become dental before a dental consonant: *un tío* /ún tío/ [ún̪ tío] 'an uncle', *un día* /ún día/ [ún̪ día] 'a day', *el tío* /eltío/ [el̪tío] 'the uncle'.

e) Alveolar. In alveolar consonants the passive articulator is the alveolar ridge, the raised area where the roots of the upper front teeth are inserted. Spanish [n], [l], [ɾ] and [r̄] are normally articulated as apico-alveolar consonants; that is, with contact involving the apex and the alveolar ridge.

English /t/ and /d/ are also apico-alveolar consonants. In a narrow comparative analysis we could transcribe, e.g., Sp. *ten* /tén/ 'have!' as [t̪én], with a dental diacritic under the first consonant to specify that its point of articulation is different from that of Eng. *ten* /tɛn/ [tʰɛn] (an independent difference is that Eng. /t/ is aspirated in this position). In general, in this book we will use the dental subscript only under consonants which normally have a different (alveolar) point of articulation in Spanish, but become dental by assimilation; but not for [t] and [d] which always represent dental consonants in Spanish.

Another alveolar consonant is [s]. In different Spanish dialects this sound has somewhat different articulations. In Northern-Central Peninsular Spanish we find an apico-alveolar consonant, with the tip of the tongue raised towards the alveolar ridge. In most of Latin America and Southern Spain, on the other hand, the apex is curved down towards the lower teeth in the production of this sound and the constriction is made with the predorsum or blade of the tongue. This predorso-alveolar or lamino-alveolar articulation is also the most common

---

[2] A more exact match of English /ð/ occurs in Castilian Spanish in contexts where /θ/ is voiced, as in *juzgado* /xuθgádo/ [xuðɣáð̞o] 'tribunal', see 9.2.5.1.

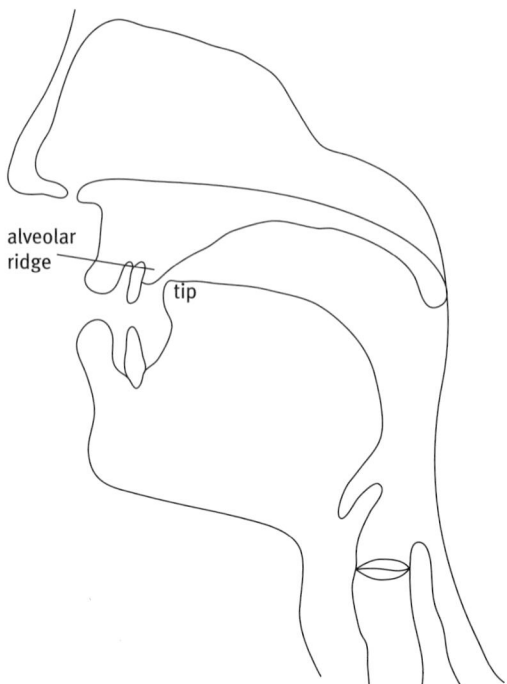

Figure 3.2a. Apical /s/. The tongue tip approaches the alveolar region behind the upper teeth. This articulation is typical of Northern-Central Peninsular Spanish.

one in English. In general we will use the symbol [s] for both articulations. When necessary (comparing dialects), we can add a diacritic: [s̺] apico-alveolar; [s̻] predorso-alveolar. The difference between these two articulations of /s/ is illustrated in Fig. 3.2a–b.

f) Prepalatal (or postalveolar). The fricatives [ʃ] (as in Eng. *she*) and [ʒ] (as in Eng. *measure*, Fr. *jamais* 'never', Arg. *yo* 'I'), and the corresponding affricates [t͡ʃ] (as in Sp. *choza* 'hut', Eng. *church*) and [d͡ʒ] (as in Eng. *jail*, Arg. *cónyuge* 'spouse'), are articulated with a constriction formed between the front part of the dorsum and an extensive area of the front of the mouth between the alveolar ridge and the hard palate. In the IPA table this place of articulation is called postalveolar. An alternative name, which we will use since it appears to be more appropriate for Spanish, is prepalatal. (A third name for this place of articulation is palato-alveolar.)

g) Palatal. The most common pronunciation in Spanish of the phoneme /ʝ/, spelt *y, ll* (*yo, mayo, llama, ella*), involves the raising of the dorsum towards the hard palate (the roof of the mouth). If there is full contact we obtain the voiced palatal plosive [ɟ] or affricate [ɟ͡ʝ]. Without full contact, we will obtain a

3.2 Description and classification: consonantal sounds

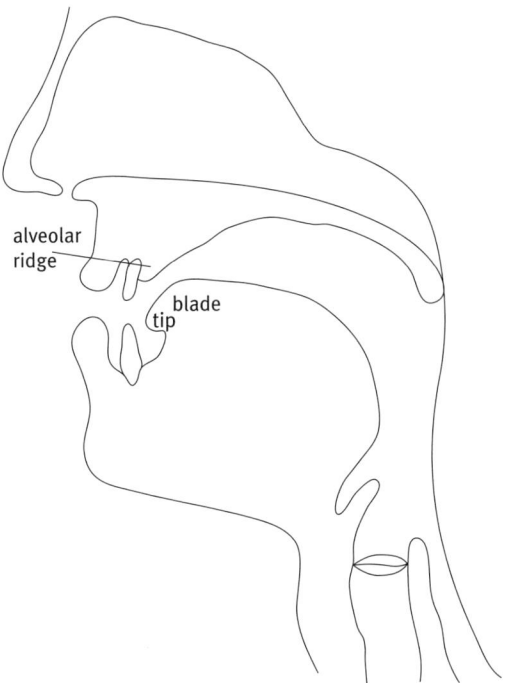

Figure 3.2b. Predorsal (laminal) /s/. The tongue tip is curved behind the lower teeth and the narrowing of the air passage is produced with the tongue blade (predorsum). This is the most common articulation of /s/ in Latin American Spanish (and also in English).

palatal fricative [ʝ] or, with even less constriction, a palatal approximant or glide (see 9.3 for the distribution of these allophones). That is, the voiced consonant /ǰ/ (with allophones [ɟ], [ɟ͡ʝ], [j]), has a more retracted place of articulation than the voiceless affricate *ch* /t͡ʃ/ in most dialects of Spanish.

The nasal *ñ* /ɲ/ is also a palatal consonant, and so is the lateral *ll* /ʎ/ of LLEÍSTA dialects (see 11.2.2).

h) Velar. The plosives [k] and [g] are articulated with the back part of the dorsum making contact against the back of the mouth (the velum). The exact place of contact is more fronted before /i/ and /e/ and more retracted before /o/, /u/. For [ɣ], as in *lago* /lágo/ [láɣo] 'lake', the articulation is in the same velar region as for [g] and [k], but the postdorsum only approximates the velum, without making full contact.

The most common pronunciation of the phoneme we are representing as /x/ is as a velar fricative, as in *ajo* [áxo] 'garlic', which is somewhat more fronted in *gente* [xénte] 'people', etc. This pronunciation is commonly found in, for instance, Mexico, Peru and Argentina. In northern Spain, the place of

Table 3.3 Place of articulation.

Place of articulation	active articulator	passive articulator	examples
Bilabial	lower lip	upper lip	[p] [b] [β]
Labiodental	lower lip	upper front teeth	[f] [v] [ɱ]
Dental	apex	upper front teeth	[t] [d]
Interdental	apex	edge of upper front teeth	[θ]
Alveolar	apex/predorsum	alveolar ridge	[n] [l] [ɾ] [r̄] [s]
Prepalatal	predorsum	postalveolar region	[ʃ] [t͡ʃ] [ʒ] [d͡ʒ]
Palatal	dorsum	hard palate	[j] [ɟ] [ɲ] [ʎ]
Velar	postdorsum	velum	[k] [g] [ɣ] [x]
Glottal	glottis (vocal folds)		[h] [ʔ]

articulation is slightly more retracted, postvelar or even uvular, which gives the sound a more strident quality.[3]

i) Glottal (laryngeal). The obstruction in the production of a consonant can also take place in the glottis (the space between the vocal folds). English has a glottal stop [ʔ], as in a common pronunciation of /t/ in words like *button*, and a glottal fricative [h], which is an independent phoneme. Spanish does not have a glottal stop, but a glottal or laryngeal fricative [h], occurs in some Spanish dialects. This sound has two main sources in Spanish. First of all, a laryngeal fricative [h] is commonly found instead of a velar [x] in many dialectal areas, including Central America, the Caribbean, Colombia and parts of southern Spain: *ajo* [áho]. Secondly [h] is an allophone of /s/ in dialects with aspiration: *este* [éhte] 'this', *es tonto* [éh tón̩to] 'he is silly'.

3.2.3 Activity of the vocal folds: voiced and voiceless consonants

The third parameter that is used in the classification of consonantal sounds is the activity of the vocal folds during the production of the consonant. The vocal folds or vocal cords are a pair of sets of cartilages and muscles on either side of the larynx. The space between the vocal folds is known as the glottis.

When the vocal cords are brought together, subglottal pressure increases, forcing them apart as the air flows out. As air pressure drops, however, other

---

[3] Uvular sounds have a constriction formed with the back of the tongue and the uvula. This is the place of articulation of French *r*.

3.2 Description and classification: consonantal sounds

forces act to bring the vocal cords together again, thus starting a rapid process of vibration. This results in a voiced sound (see, for instance, Laver 1994:191–4; Hayward 2000:222–6). If, on the other hand, the vocal folds are separated, they will not produce vibration, and the result will be a voiceless sound. If we place our fingers over our throat (on the spot where our Adam's apple is located) and we alternate between producing [zzzzz] (as in English *zoo*) and [sssss], we will notice vibration in the production of [z] but not when saying [s]: [z] is voiced; [s] is voiceless. We can do the same experiment with other pairs of fricative or approximant segments such as [ʃ] and [ʒ], [f] and [v], or [x] and [ɣ]. The contrast between [p] and [b], [t] and [d], and [k] and [g] is also one of voice.

Both in Spanish and in English the use of voice as a distinctive feature is limited to the obstruents. Sonorant consonants and vowels are normally voiced. Nevertheless devoicing of vowels at the end of an utterance is common in the speech of some speakers. In Andalusian Spanish, the 'aspiration' of /s/ may also result in a voiceless copy of a following nasal or lateral, as in Andal. /mísmo/ [mím̥mo] 'same', /ísla/ [íl̥la] 'island' (notice the use of the subscript to indicate devoicing). The fact remains, however, that a phonological contrast between voiced and voiceless segments with the same manner and point of articulation is found only among the obstruents.

In English the contrastive use of the feature of voice is more systematic than in Spanish, since in addition to the contrast between the two stop series, voiceless /p t k/ and voiced /b d g/, found in both languages, English also has a contrast between the voiceless fricatives /f θ s ʃ/ and the corresponding voiced segments /v ð z ʒ/, as well as between the voiceless affricate /t͡ʃ/ and its voiced counterpart /d͡ʒ/.

Spanish lacks contrasts between voiced and voiceless fricatives and affricates with the same place of articulation. Except for palatal /j/, whose phonemic status is unclear (see 9.3),[4] voiced fricatives occur only as allophones of voiceless segments in the context of a following voiced consonant. Thus, to repeat, whereas in English, /v/ and /z/ are contrasting phonemes (*fat* vs *vat*, *sue* vs *zoo*), in Spanish the voiced alveolar fricative [z] is only an allophone of /s/, as in /mísmo/ [mízmo] 'same', and the voiced labiodental fricative [v] is an allophone of /f/ as in /afgáno/ [avɣáno] 'Afghan'.

Among the plosives, both English and Spanish make a phonological contrast between a voiceless /p t k/ and a voiced /b d g/ series at the same three places of articulation. Whereas the phonological contrast is the same in the two languages, at the phonetic level, concerning its actual realization, the nature of the contrast is quite different. Thus, in English, in certain positions the /p t k/ vs

---

[4] And /ʒ/ which, for the most part, replaces it in Argentinian Spanish.

Consonants and vowels

Table 3.4 Main consonant sounds of Spanish.

		bilabial	labiodental	interdental	dental	alveolar	prepalatal	palatal	velar	glottal
plosive	v'less	p			t				k	
	voiced	b			d			ɟ	g	
fricative	v'less		f	θ		s	ʃ		x	h
	voiced		v			z	ʒ	ʝ		ɦ
approx.	voiced	β			ð				ɣ	
affricate	v'less						t͡ʃ			
	voiced						d͡ʒ			
nasal		m	ɱ	n̪	n̥	n	nʲ	ɲ	ŋ	
lateral				l̪	l̥	l	lʲ	ʎ		
rhotic	tap					ɾ				
	trill					r̄				

/b d g/ contrast mainly involves the presence vs absence of aspiration, whereas in Spanish voiceless plosives are not aspirated (see 8.3).

3.3 The Spanish consonant inventory

We can now classify the main consonant sounds of Spanish using the three features of place of articulation, manner of articulation and voice (whether they are voiced or voiceless). This is shown in Table 3.4. It should be kept in mind that no single Spanish dialect possesses all these sounds. A few additional symbols will be introduced in later chapters.

If we consider only the main or prototypical allophone of each phoneme, we obtain the distribution in Table 3.5, where phonemes found only in some dialects are in parentheses.

We can obtain a simpler, more systematic, table, valid for most Spanish dialects, by grouping certain places of articulation. In Table 3.6 the following articulations are grouped together:

labial includes bilabial and labiodental
dental includes dental and interdental
(pre)palatal includes prepalatal and palatal

For comparison, the consonantal phonemes of English are shown in Table 3.7.

3.4 Description and classification of vowels: the Spanish vowel system

For the description of vowels, the main features that are used refer to the position of the tongue body and the shape of the lips.

Depending on whether the tongue is raised, in neutral position or lowered, we have high, mid or low vowels.

3.4 Description and classification of vowels

Table 3.5 The consonantal phonemes of Spanish.

		bilabial	labiodental	interdental	dental	alveolar	prepalatal	palatal	velar
plosive	v'less	p			t				k
	voiced	b			d				g
fricative	v'less		f	(θ)		s			x
	voiced						(ʒ)	(j)	
affricate	v'less						t͡ʃ		
nasal		m				n		ɲ	
lateral						l		(ʎ)	
rhotic	tap					ɾ			
	trill					r̄			

Notes: /θ/ only in Peninsular Spanish
/ʎ/ only in some Peninsular and South American varieties
/ʒ/ only in Argentinian Spanish
/j/ of questionable status as a phoneme

Table 3.6 The consonantal phonemes of Spanish (rearranged).

		labial	dental	alveolar	(pre)palatal	velar
plosive	voiceless	p	t			k
	voiced	b	d			g
affricate	voiceless				t͡ʃ	
fricative	voiceless	f	(θ)	s		x
	voiced				(j)	
nasal		m		n	ɲ	
lateral				l	(ʎ)	
rhotic	tap			ɾ		
	trill			r̄		

Considering the horizontal dimension, we have front, central and back vowels: in the articulation of front vowels the tongue body moves towards the front of the mouth, for back vowels the tongue is retracted, and for central vowels it occupies an intermediate position.

The third feature that is commonly used in the classification of vowels is whether the lips are rounded or spread in the production of the vowel.

Spanish has a simple and cross-linguistically rather common vocalic system. There are five vowel phonemes /i/, /e/, /a/, /o/, /u/, classified as shown in Table 3.8. As we can see, lip rounding is redundant in Spanish with respect to the back/non-back position of the tongue: the back vowels /u/, /o/ are articulated

Table 3.7 The consonantal phonemes of English.

		labial	dental	alveolar	prepalatal	velar	glottal
plosive	voiceless	p		t		k	
	voiced	b		d		g	
affricate	voiceless				t͡ʃ		
	voiced				d͡ʒ		
fricative	voiceless	f	θ	s	ʃ		h
	voiced	v	ð	z	ʒ		
nasal		m		n		(ŋ)[5]	
lateral				l			
rhotic approxim.				ɹ			

Table 3.8 The vowel phonemes of Spanish.

	Front	Central	Back
High	i		u
Mid	e		o
Low		a	
	Non-round		Round

with rounded lips (are rounded vowels), the non-back vowels /i/, /e/, /a/ are not rounded.

The vowels of Spanish and the organization of vowel systems will be considered in more detail in 7.1. Other features used in the classification of vowels such as nasalization, contrasts in voice quality and tenseness/laxness are also introduced there.

3.5 Glides

Glides differ from vowels in being non-syllabic. They occur next to a vowel (either preceding or following it) in the same syllable. Most commonly, glides are high. In Spanish there is a front or palatal glide [i̯] and a back or labiovelar glide [u̯]. Some authors distinguish between semiconsonants [j], [w], if they

---

[5] The phonemic status of /ŋ/ in English is open to debate. Since this segment only occurs in postvocalic position and, in addition, word-final [ŋg] is not found, some linguists have proposed that [ŋ] is the phonetic realization of the phonological sequence /ng/ in certain positions. If we accept this analysis, something special must then be said regarding contrasts such as *finger* [ŋg] vs *singer* [ŋ] and *longer* [ŋg] 'comparative of long' vs *longer* [ŋ] 'someone who longs'.

precede the vowel, as in *viejo* [bjéxo] 'old', *pues* [pwés] 'then', and semivowels, if they follow the vowel, as in *peine* [péi̯ne] 'comb', *deuda* [déu̯ða] 'debt'. We will not follow this tradition and will use the same symbols [i̯], [u̯] in both cases.

As argued in 5.4, in Spanish glides are best considered allophones of the corresponding high vowels, and not independent phonemes: high vowels are usually realized as glides when non-stress-bearing and adjacent to a different vowel; e.g. *baile* /báile/ [bái̯le] 'dance', *patio* /pátio/ [páti̯o] 'yard', *lidiar* /lidiár/ [liði̯áɾ] 'to fight', *duelo* /duélo/ [du̯élo] 'mourning; duel', *cuida* /kuída/ [ku̯íða] 's/he cares for', etc. There are, nevertheless, some exceptions; e.g.: *dueto* [du.éto] 'duet', *huída* [u.íða] 'flight', etc., with two vowels in HIATUS, where the first one is an unstressed high vowel. We will make use of phonemic syllable boundaries in these exceptional words: *dueto* /du.éto/, *huida* /u.ída/, *guiar* /gi.áɾ/. The reason for representing the phonological contrast as, for instance /du.éto/, with marked syllabification, vs /duélo/, with regular syllabification – and not as /duéto/, with a high vowel, vs /du̯élo/, with a phonemic glide – is that the former choice accounts better for the general patterns of the language. In this context (unstressed high vowel followed by another vowel) diphthong formation is indeed the rule. Only in a minority of words do the high vowels /i u/ fail to become glides in this context. It is thus more economical to mark these words as having an exceptional syllabification than to recognize the existence of phonemic glides (see 5.4).

We can also find mid glides [e̯], [o̯], in colloquial speech, as in bisyllabic *línea* [líne̯a] 'line', *poeta* [po̯éta] 'poet', for more careful trisyllabic [líne.a], [po.éta]. There is no question about the allophonic nature of these mid glides.

3.6 Dialectal differences in phoneme inventory

There are few differences in the number of phonemes among Spanish dialects. These have been pointed out in previous sections and will be repeated here.

Perhaps most famously, Northern-Central Peninsular Spanish has a contrast between a voiceless interdental fricative /θ/ and a voiceless apico-alveolar fricative /s/, as demonstrated by pairs like *cima* [θíma] 'summit' and *sima* [síma] 'abyss'. This contrast is not made in any Latin American dialect and is also lacking in the Canary Islands and parts of southern Spain. In Spanish dialectology, the existence of a single phoneme /s/ (generally articulated as predorso-alveolar) instead of the /θ/-/s/ contrast is known as SESEO. In parts of Andalusia (as well as in small parts of Central America) the only phoneme that exists instead of the two of Castilian has a dental articulation which makes it perceptually more similar to Castilian /θ/ than to Castilian

/s/. This phenomenon is known as CECEO. The existence of the contrast in Castilian Spanish is referred to as *distinción* /s/-/θ/.

Traditionally, the standard pronunciation of Spanish in both Spain and several South American countries (but not, for instance, in Mexican Spanish) included a phonemic contrast between the palatal lateral /ʎ/, corresponding to orthographic *ll*, and a palatal non-lateral /ʝ/, corresponding to orthographic *y* when followed by a vowel, e.g. *calló* [kaʎó] 's/he became silent' vs *cayó* [kaʝó] 's/he fell'. The maintenance of this phonological contrast is known as LLEÍSMO, opposed to YEÍSMO which is the merger of both phonemes in a single phoneme /ʝ/. Nowadays the *lleísta* pronunciation is rapidly losing ground. This contrast is still practised by some speakers in northern and central Spain as well as in part of Colombia, Ecuador, Peru, Bolivia and Paraguay, but in most of these areas urban and younger speakers tend to be *yeísta*.

The pronunciation of both orthographic *ll* and *y* as /ʒ/, as in standard Argentinian Spanish, is known as *yeísmo rehilado* (= strident) or *žeísmo*. As mentioned before, *žeísmo* is giving ground to the newer phenomenon of *šeísmo* in the Buenos Aires area, as the common realization of this phoneme is becoming [ʃ] in the speech of the younger generations. In Argentinian Spanish, a clear contrast is made between words with orthographic prevocalic *ll* and *y*, on the one hand, which are realized with [ʒ] ~ [ʃ] (phonemic /ʒ/), and, on the other hand, words spelt with prevocalic *hi-*, *-i-*, realized as [i̯] ~ [j] (phonemic /i/), as in *yerba* [ʒérβa] 'mate leaves' vs *hierba* [i̯érβa] 'grass, weed'. This contrast is much less secure or nonexistent in other dialects (see 9.3 for details).

EXERCISES

1. For the following examples, give the phonetic symbol for the sound represented by the underlined letter and indicate its manner of articulation.

   Example: *sa<u>b</u>e* [β] approximant

   <u>m</u>esa, es<u>qu</u>ina, <u>c</u>esto, <u>r</u>ojo, <u>p</u>oco, li<u>g</u>a, ba<u>rr</u>o, sua<u>v</u>e, <u>ll</u>ega, a<u>r</u>o, pon<u>g</u>o, le<u>ch</u>e

2. For the following examples, give the phonetic symbol for the sound represented by the underlined letter and indicate its place of articulation.

   Example: *sa<u>b</u>e* [β] bilabial

   <u>d</u>eja, hi<u>j</u>o, <u>b</u>oina, <u>ch</u>ico, en<u>c</u>aje, <u>s</u>uelo, <u>c</u>ielo, ni<u>ñ</u>a, <u>m</u>ano, <u>f</u>aro, <u>ll</u>uvia, <u>y</u>egua

3. Indicate whether the underlined letter represents a voiced or a voiceless sound and provide the corresponding phonetic symbol.

   me<u>t</u>a, mie<u>d</u>o, suel<u>d</u>o, lo<u>r</u>o, ve<u>l</u>o, mar<u>c</u>a, <u>a</u>rco, ca<u>m</u>po, <u>f</u>iera, ma<u>y</u>o, o<u>ch</u>o

Exercises

4 Provide the phonetic symbol and describe the underlined segments (main allophones). Where dialects may vary, choose a specific dialect consistently.

Example: *sabe* [β] voiced bilabial approximant

roca, vela, lago, cinco, envase, año, perro, tengo, lejos, erguido, valle, vergel

5 Indicate whether the underlined letter represents a vowel, a glide or a consonant.

hielo, pienso, pinto, treinta, reímos, reino, Juan y Pedro, soy, hoyo, yeso

6 Provide the phonetic symbol and an example for the following definitions.

Example: voiced bilabial approximant [β] *sabe*

high front vowel
alveolar lateral
alveolar rhotic tap
voiceless velar fricative
palatal nasal
labiodental nasal
voiced velar approximant
voiceless interdental fricative
voiceless prepalatal affricate
labiovelar glide
voiced alveolar fricative
alveolar rhotic trill

4 Acoustic characterization of the main classes of Spanish speech sounds

4.1 Introduction

The communicative value of the articulatory gestures that we have described in the previous chapter lies primarily in the distinct ways in which they modify the air flow, producing different sound waves.[1] These sound waves, rapid changes in air pressure propagated like waves in a pond, impact the auditory organs of the listener, who will interpret them as carrying a certain message if she or he knows the language (and probably as meaningless speech sound otherwise).

In this book, the sounds of Spanish are described mostly from an articulatory perspective. Nevertheless we will also make some reference to the acoustic properties of the main types of speech sounds. Whereas, in the past, the study of speech sound waves required complex and expensive equipment, nowadays there are very inexpensive (or even free) software programmes that readers of this book can use to analyse their own pronunciation or other records of speech. Speech analysis programmes provide a visual display of sound waves and permit filtering and analysis of the waves. Here we will point out the main cues that allow us to identify and analyse the major classes of segments of the Spanish language. Some additional information on individual sounds and classes of sounds will be given in later chapters.[2]

---

[1] Primarily, but not entirely. The visual cues provided by the movements of the lips are also very important in perception, as demonstrated by the so-called 'McGurk effect' (McGurk and MacDonald 1976).

[2] A detailed exposition of acoustic phonetics is beyond the scope of this book. Some excellent references are Laver (1994), Ladefoged (1992, 1996), Johnson (2003) and Hayward (2000). For a spectrographic analysis of Spanish sounds, see Quilis (1981) and Martínez Celdrán (1998), and for American English, Olive *et al.* (1993).

4.2 Vowels and voiceless plosives

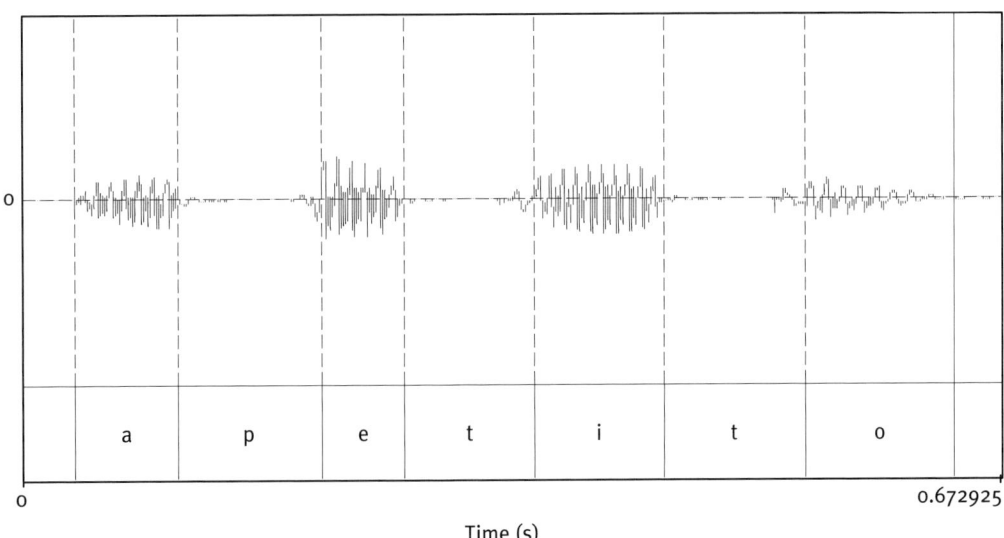

Figure 4.1.   Waveform of a production of *apetito*.

4.2 Vowels and voiceless plosives

The two maximally different types of speech sounds are vowels and voiceless plosives. In Fig. 4.1[3] we have the waveform of a production of *apetito* /apetíto/ 'appetite'. In this representation, the horizontal dimension corresponds to time, whereas the amplitude of the wave (its displacement from the horizontal zero line, which represents normal air pressure), shows the amount of acoustic energy or intensity at a given point (increase or decrease in air pressure, above or below the zero line respectively). The general amplitude of the wave will depend on how loudly or how softly we speak (or how close we are to the microphone), but different sounds also differ in their relative amplitude. In general; vowels produce waveforms with greater amplitude than other neighbouring segments.

Observe first the portions corresponding to the three voiceless plosives. In the articulation of voiceless plosives or oral stops, the articulators come together and completely block the passage of air for an instant. This moment of silence is reflected in the absence of energy corresponding to the moment of occlusion for the three plosives in Fig. 4.1.

In the production of vowels, as in that of other voiced sounds, the air flow from the lungs causes the vocal cords to vibrate; that is, to open and close rapidly

---

[3] All figures in this chapter have been produced with the software program PRAAT (developed by Paul Boersma and David Weenink, www.praat.org).

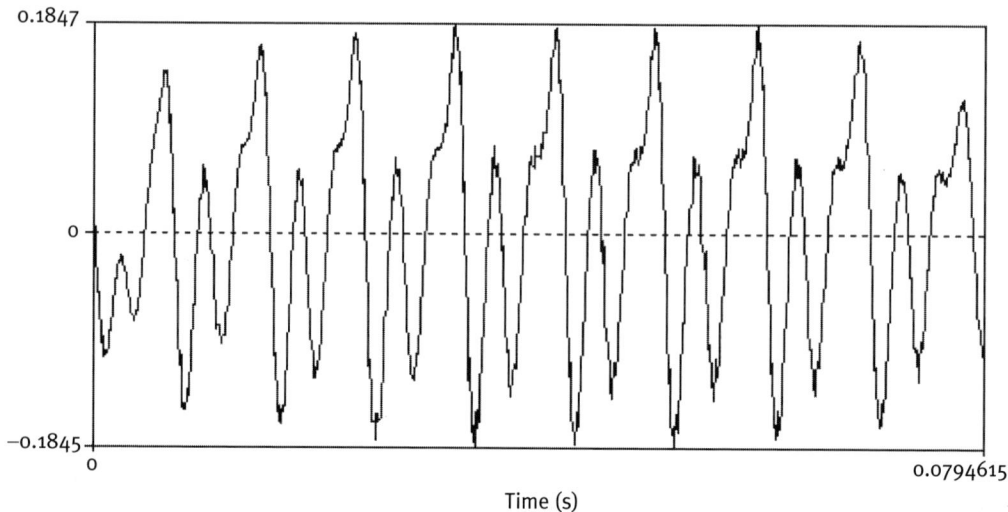

Figure 4.2.   Quasi-periodic waveform of /i/ from /apetíto/.

(see 3.2.3). In the articulation of vowels, the flow of air then passes unimpeded through the oral cavity and is modulated in different ways depending on the size of the front and back cavities created by the positioning of the tongue.

The complex vibration of the vocal cords can be compared to that produced when we pluck a cord of a guitar. In Fig. 4.1 the vocalic portions are visible as quasi-periodic waves; that is, as waves with a repeated pattern. This can be better observed in Fig. 4.2, which displays just the third vowel in Fig. 4.1, /i/.

The number of repetitions or cycles of a periodic wave per unit of time is known as its frequency. Frequency is given in cycles per second or hertz (abbreviated Hz). In Fig. 4.3, we have a sound wave of another vowel, /a/. The duration of this segment is given in the lower part of the figure as 0.100175 seconds, or just a little over a tenth of a second. If we count peaks of amplitude we see that from point to point the wave repeats itself almost exactly ten times in this time interval. In one second, there would be 100 cycles. We will say that the fundamental frequency of this wave is about 100 cycles per second or 100 Hz. Differences in fundamental frequency translate into differences in perceived pitch. The higher the fundamental frequency of a wave, the higher the pitch. The fundamental frequency of a periodic sound wave depends on the rate of repeated opening and closing of the vocal cords.

We can observe in Fig. 4.2 and Fig. 4.3 that superimposed on the larger cycle (the fundamental frequency) of the vowel's wave there are other periodic components with higher frequencies. These are known as harmonics and

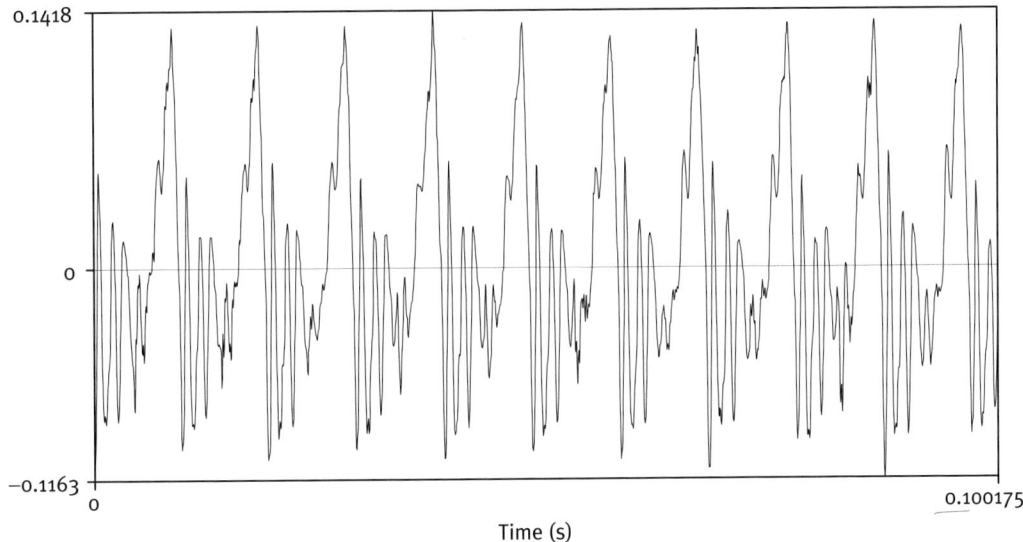

Figure 4.3. Waveform of the vowel /a/ produced with a fundamental frequency of about 100 Hz. In the figure there are ten cycles in a tenth of a second.

are always integral multiples of the fundamental frequency. The amplitude of harmonics above the fundamental frequency reveals the quality of the vowel. Notice that the vowels /i/ (Fig. 4.2) and /a/ (Fig. 4.3) have different patterns of harmonics, visible as different patterns of peaks and valleys within each cycle.

In addition to inspecting waveforms, we may obtain information about speech sounds by analysing spectrograms. A spectrogram is a representation of the speech signal that gives us more detail by allowing us to observe the distribution of energy at different frequencies. This allows us, for instance, to distinguish more clearly one vowel from another. Figure 4.4 is a spectrogram produced from the waveform in Fig. 4.1. In a spectrogram, as in a waveform, the horizontal axis indicates time; the vertical axis, on the other hand, indicates frequency and darker colour indicates greater intensity at the corresponding frequencies. In Fig. 4.4 we can observe that the energy of vowels is concentrated in certain bands of frequencies. These darker horizontal bands are known as FORMANTS (each formant is a bundle of harmonics). As we will see in Chapter 7 each vowel has a characteristic distribution of formants. For instance, the first formant is higher for /a/ than for any other vowel.

For the oral stops in /apetito/ we can observe that the spectrogram is completely blank during the occlusion. The release of the consonantal hold

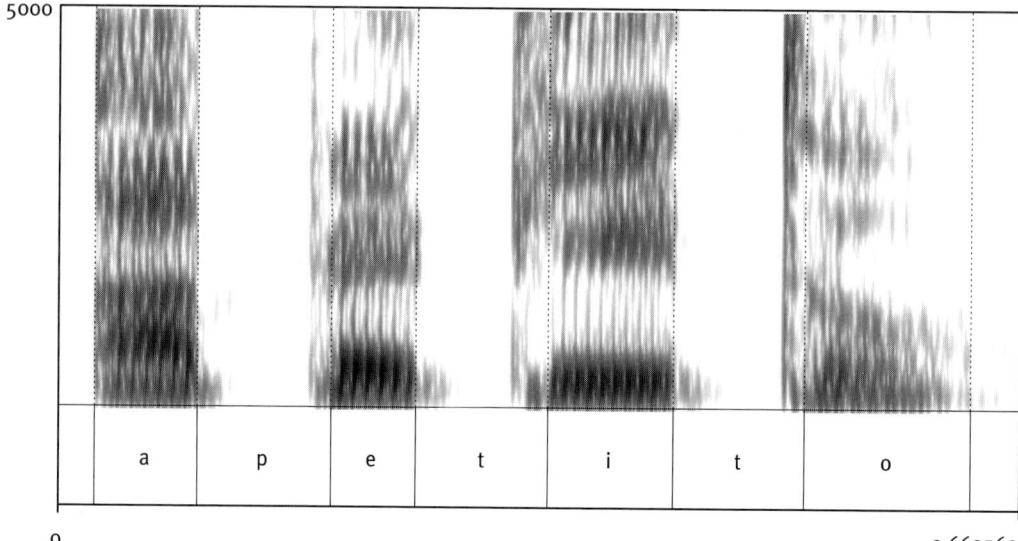

Figure 4.4. Spectrogram of *apetito*. Vowels are characterized by the presence of formants (darker horizontal bars). Each voiceless plosive contains a period of silence followed by nonperiodic energy during the release.

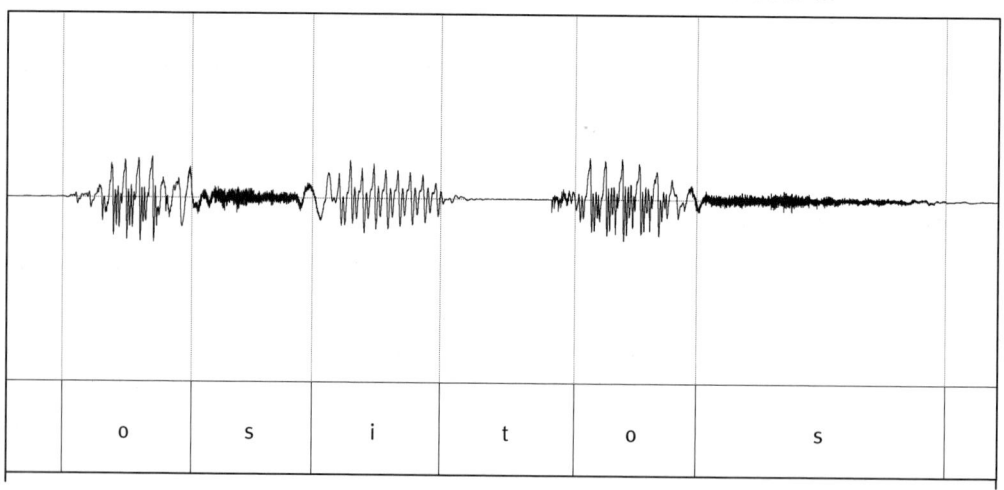

Figure 4.5. Waveform of /osítos/.

4.3 Fricatives and affricates

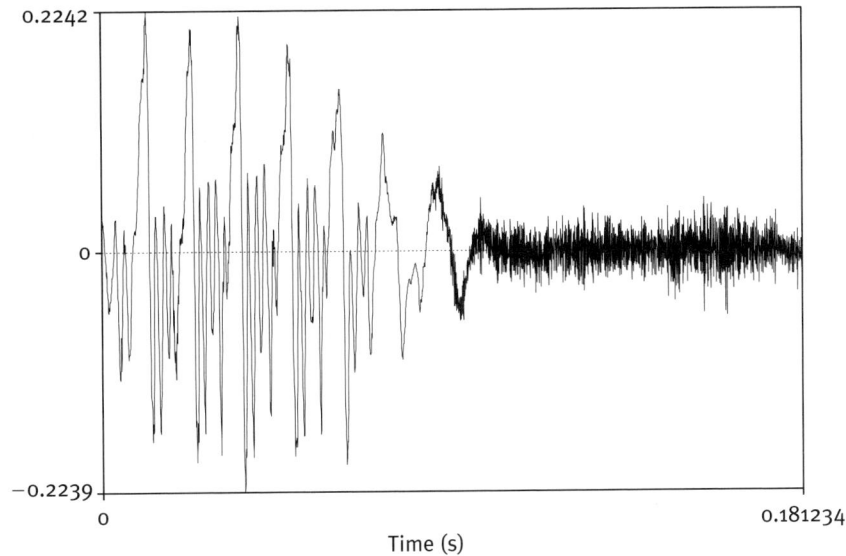

Figure 4.6.   Waveform of /-os/ from Fig. 4.5.

is marked by a vertical line followed by a short interval of aperiodic energy or noise right before the vowel formants begin. The centre of energy of this bar as well as the shape of the transitions at the edges of the formants of adjacent segments give us information about the place of articulation of the consonant.

4.3 Fricatives and affricates

The 'visual signature' of fricatives is very different from that of both oral stops and vowels. In voiceless fricatives, the acoustic energy does not have its source in the vibration of the vocal cords but in the narrowing of the passage of air in the oral cavity created by the articulators, which produces turbulence. Fricatives have a nonrepetitive or aperiodic sound wave whose centre of energy is at different frequencies depending on its place of articulation. In Fig. 4.5 we have the waveform of a production of *ositos* /osítos/ 'little bears'. Notice how different the portions of the waveform corresponding to the two instances of the fricative /s/ are from both of the vocalic portions and the portion corresponding to the occlusion of the plosive /t/.

In Fig. 4.6 part of the final two segments /-os/ of /osítos/ has been enlarged so the difference between the periodic wave of /o/ and the aperiodic wave of /s/ can be observed better.

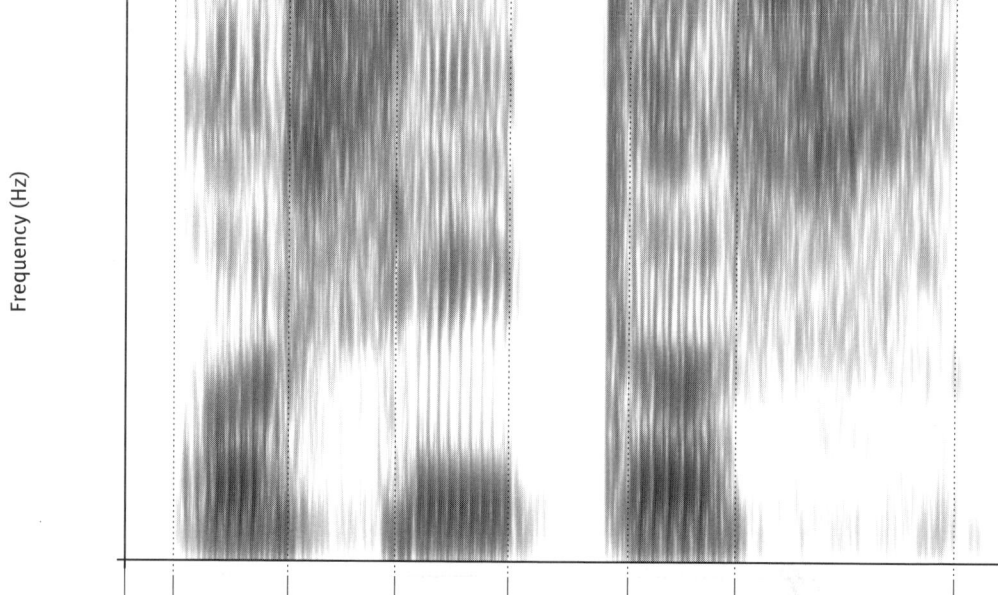

Figure 4.7. Spectrogram of /osítos/.

Figure 4.7 is a spectrogram of /osítos/ obtained from the same signal as Fig. 4.5. Notice that for /s/ the energy is distributed in a random fashion (without format bands) in the upper part of the spectrogram.

Affricates combine occlusion with fricative release. The two phases can be observed in the spectrogram of *hacha* /átʃa/ 'axe' in Fig. 4.8.

4.4 Voiced plosives and approximant allophones of /b d g/

The voiced plosive phonemes of Spanish /b d g/, as we know, are realized without complete occlusion, as approximants, in many positions, including between vowels. Their degree of constriction can vary substantially. The more

4.4 Voiced plosives and allophones of /b d g/

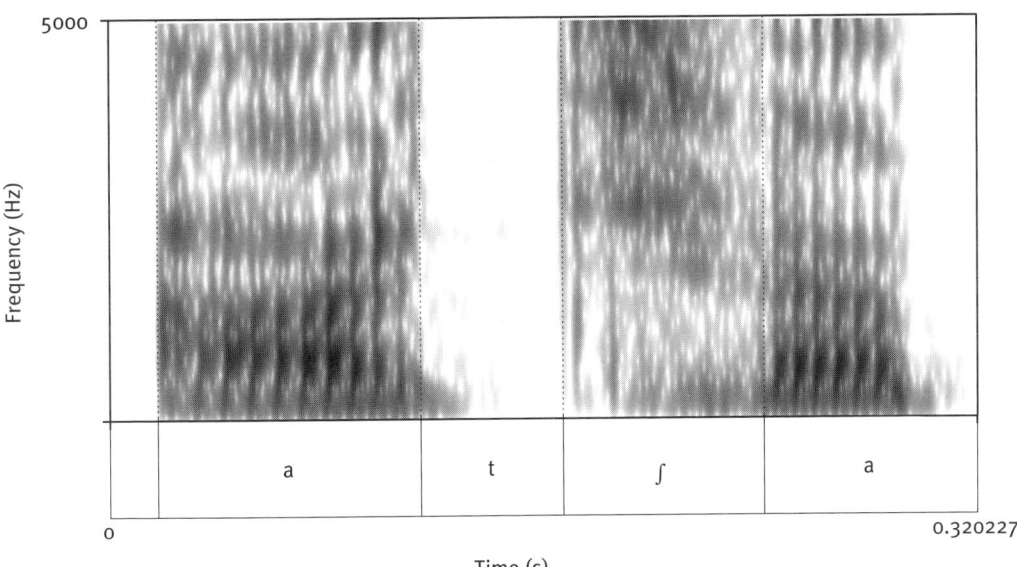

Figure 4.8. Spectrogram of *hacha* /át͡ʃa/. Notice the two distinct phases of the affricate: occlusion + fricative release.

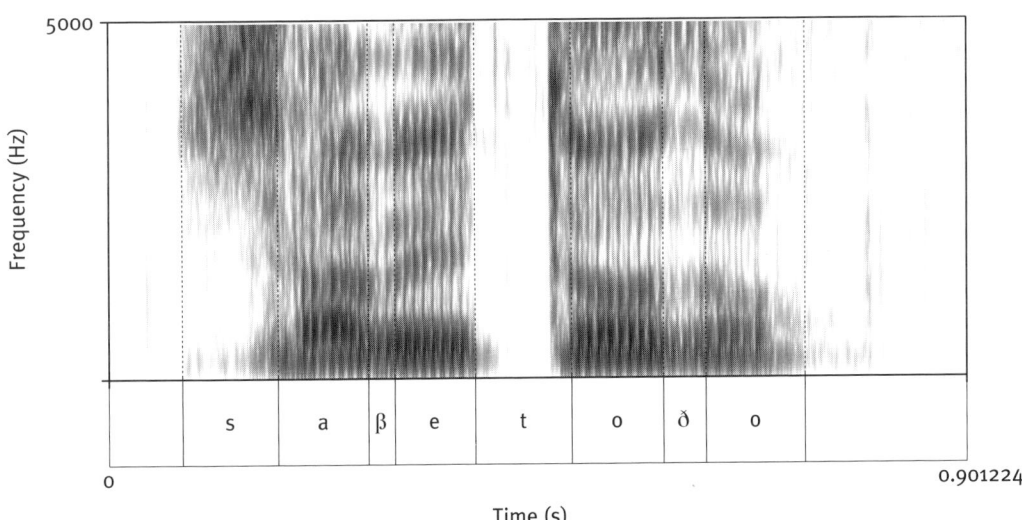

Figure 4.9. Spectrogram of *sabe todo* /sábe tódo/ 's/he knows everything'.

open their articulation, the more their spectrogram will resemble that of vowels. In Fig. 4.9 we have a spectrogram of a production of *sabe todo* /sábe tódo/.

The spectrographic characteristics of voiced plosives in intervocalic position can be illustrated with an English example, since they normally do not occur in Spanish. In Fig. 4.10 we can compare a rendition of Spanish *ave* /ábe/

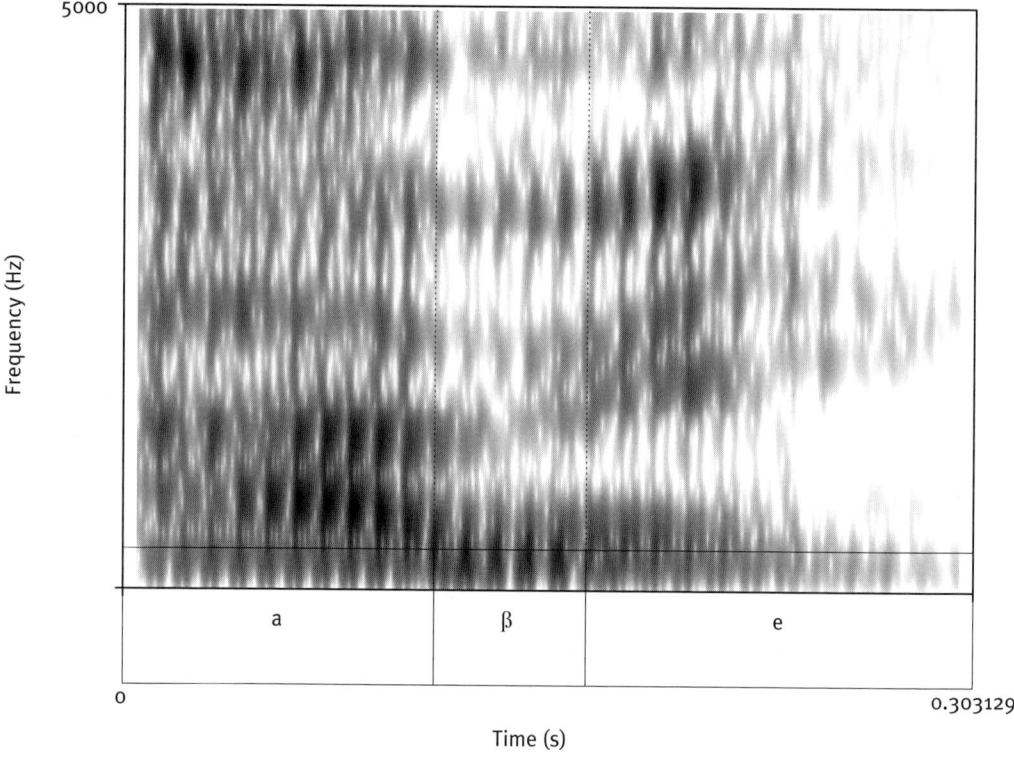
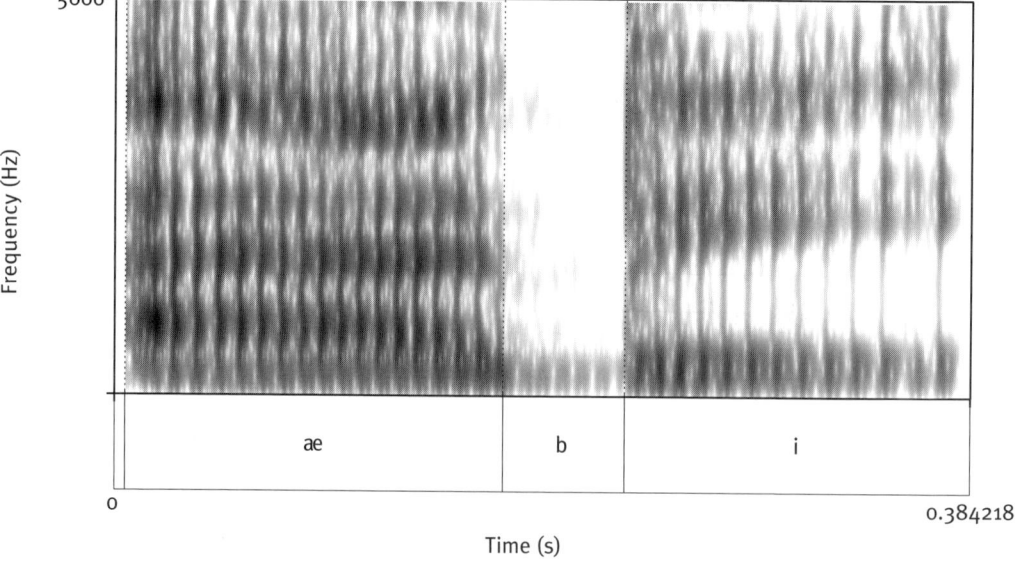

Figure 4.10. (a) Spectrogram of *ave* /ábe/ [áβe] 'bird'. Voiced bilabial approximant.
(b) Spectrogram of Eng. *abbey* [æbi]. Voiced bilabial oral stop.

4.4 Voiced plosives and allophones of /b d g/

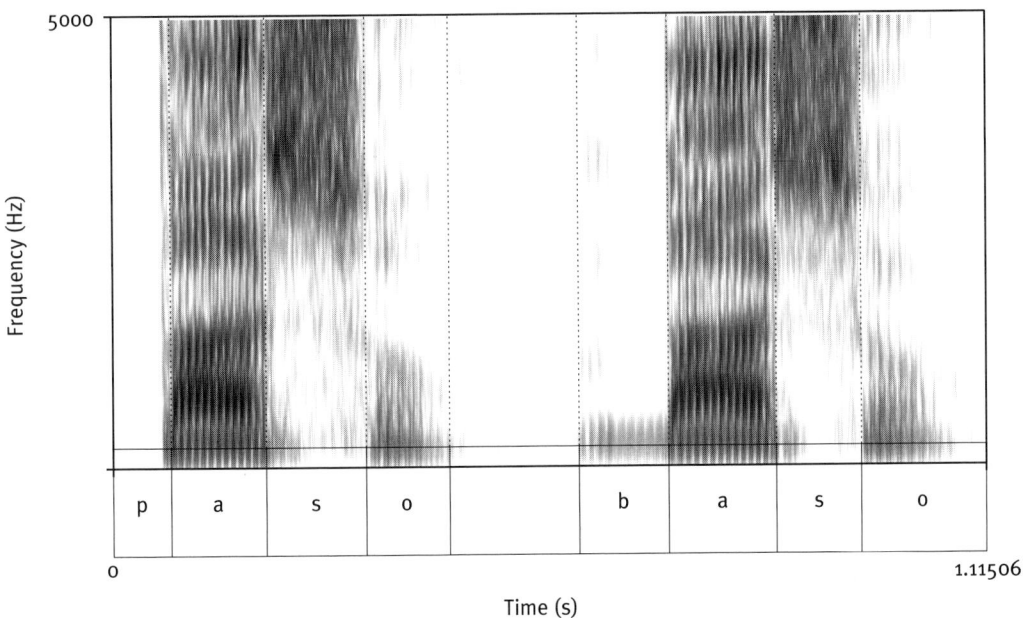

Figure 4.11.   Spectrogram of *paso* /páso/ 'step' and *vaso* /báso/ 'glass'.

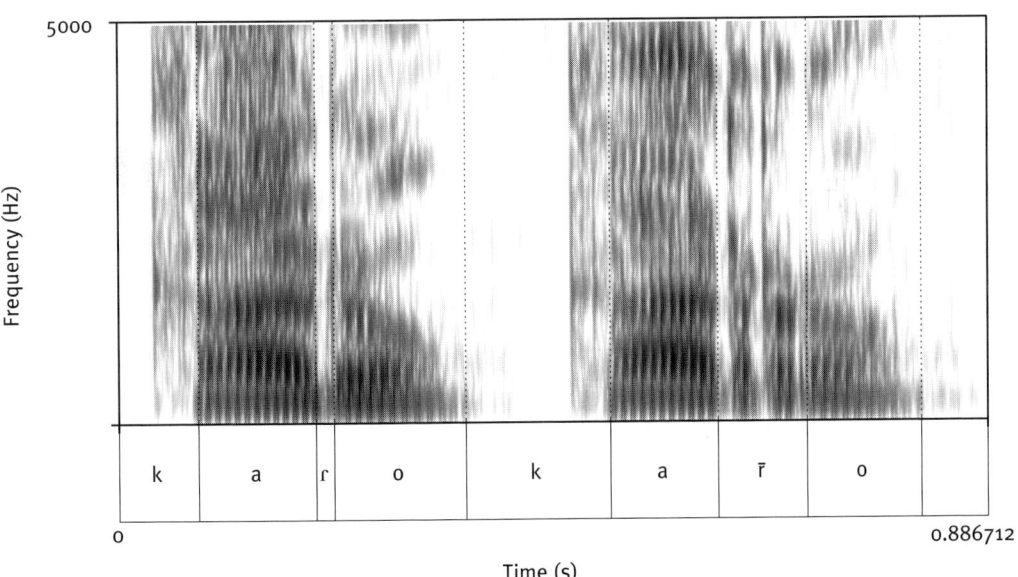

Figure 4.12.   Spectrogram of *caro* /káɾo/ and *carro* /káɾ̄o/. Notice the single brief intervocalic occlusion in *caro* and the three brief occlusions in this production of *carro*.

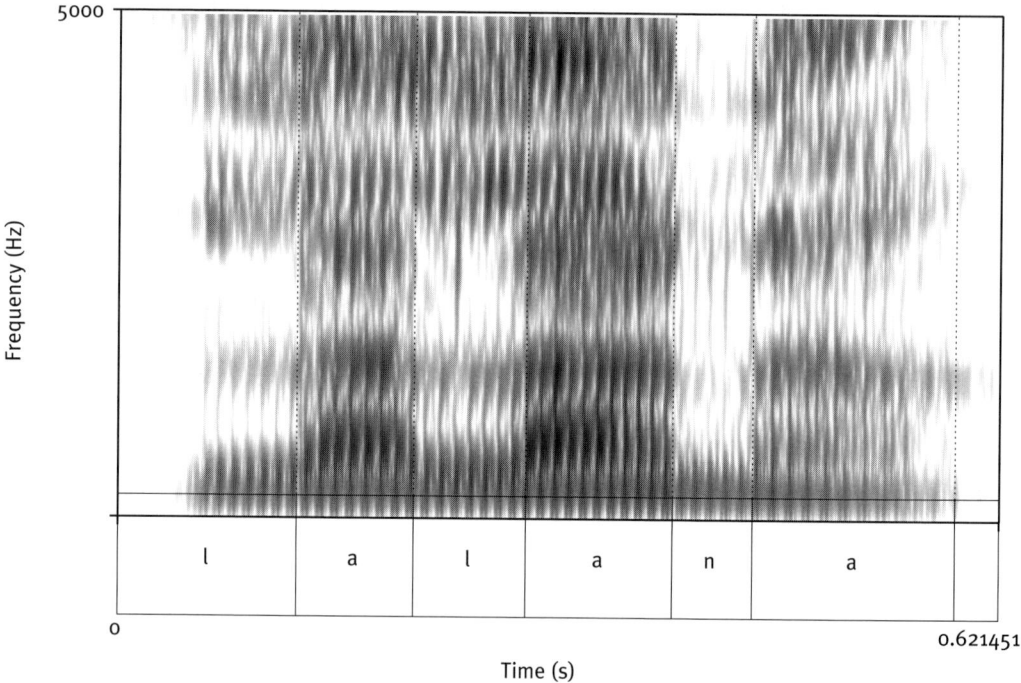

Figure 4.13.   Spectrogram of *la lana* 'the wool'.

'bird', which contains an intervocalic approximant consonant, with a rendition of *abbey* produced by a native English speaker. Notice that in English *abbey* the only energy observable in the portion of the spectrogram corresponding to /b/, which is an oral stop or plosive, is found in the lower part of the spectrogram. This is known as a voice bar and indicates that the segment is voiced. All voiced segments have this low band of energy.

In Fig. 4.11, *paso* /páso/ 'step' and *vaso* /báso/ 'glass' are compared. In this utterance-initial context, /b/ is an oral stop. Notice that /b/ has a voice bar, indicating vibration of the vocal folds during the occlusion, which is absent in /p/. On the other hand, the release of /p/ is marked by a very brief aspiration (much briefer than that of English /p/ in the same position).

4.5 Sonorant consonants

The brief contact with the tip of the tongue in the rhotic tap results in a spectrogram similar to that of a voiced stop, but very short. The sequence of brief contacts in the trills produces a series of such blank spots except for the voice bar. This is illustrated in Fig. 4.12 with spectrograms of *caro* /káɾo/ 'dear' and *carro* /káro̱/ 'cart, car'.

Nasals and laterals also have formants, although less intense than those of adjacent vowels. In Fig. 4.13, we can see a spectrogram of an utterance of *la lana* 'the wool'.

Some more details will be given as we study specific sounds and classes of sounds in later chapters.

EXERCISES

1. If you have access to a computer, obtain a speech analysis programme (several are freely available on the internet for download, including PRAAT and Wavesurfer) and a microphone and try to reproduce the figures in this chapter recording your own speech.

5 The syllable

5.1 Introduction

Consonants and vowels are phonologically grouped in units called syllables. The concept of the syllable is an important one in the sound structure of Spanish, as many phonological processes in this language are best seen in the light of syllable structure (A. Alonso 1945; J. Harris 1983).

In practical terms, the correct division of words at the end of a line of text requires the proper identification of syllable boundaries. The Spanish poetic tradition is also based on counting syllables in lines of poetry. All of this demands agreement on the part of the users of the language on how many syllables a given utterance has and where exactly the syllable boundaries lie. The structure of the Spanish language makes universal agreement on both of these points considerably easier to achieve than in English. As we will see, the only real difficulties are found in the syllabification of sequences of vocoids (vowels and glides).[1]

5.2 Syllable structure

A syllable is formed by a set of segments grouped together around a nucleus or peak of sonority, which in Spanish is always a vowel. Minimally, thus, a syllable may consist of a vowel alone as in *a* 'to', *o* 'or', *y* 'and' and the first syllable of *a-re-na* 'sand' and *hu-ma-no* 'human'(recall that orthographic *h* is always silent). The vowel constitutes the nucleus of the syllable and may be preceded and/or followed by less open (less sonorous) segments within the syllable. The nucleus may be preceded by an onset consonant, as in *tú* 'you', *sí* 'yes', or by a consonant cluster, as in the first syllable of *pla-ne-ta* 'planet'. Onset clusters

---

[1] We will use the term 'vocoid' to refer to vowels and glides indistinctly.

5.2 Syllable structure

Table 5.1 Structure of the syllable: examples.

	Rhyme		
Onset	Nucleus	Coda	
	á		*a* 'to'
	ái̯		*hay* 'there is'
t	ú		*tú* 'you'
m	á	s	*más* 'more'
tɾ	é	s	*tres* 'three'
pl	á	n	*plan* 'plan'
b	ái̯	s	*vais* 'you-pl go'
b	i̯é	n	*bien* 'well'
b	u̯éi̯		*buey* 'ox'
b	i̯ái̯	s	*(cam)biáis* 'you-pl change'

may have at most two consonants in Spanish. Furthermore, the structure of these clusters is very constrained: onset clusters always consist of a plosive or /f/ followed by /l/ or /ɾ/. A consonant may also follow the nucleus as a coda, as in *tres* 'three', *plan* 'plan'. Only rarely do we find coda clusters in Spanish, as in the first syllable of *pers-pi-caz* 'perspicacious' and in the last syllable of *bí-ceps* 'biceps'. In Spanish coda clusters the second consonant is always /s/.[2]

Nucleus and coda together are said to constitute the syllable rhyme. The basic binary division of subsyllabic constituents is thus between onset (optional) and rhyme. The rhyme, in its turn, consists of an obligatory nucleus and an optional coda.

The nucleus in Spanish, in addition to a vowel, may contain a glide as a 'satellite' either before or after the nuclear vowel, as in *prue-ba* 'test', *hay* 'there is', *vein-te* 'twenty'. That is, we find both single vowels and diphthongs in the nucleus. Less commonly we may also have a triphthong, with both a prevocalic and a postvocalic glide as in *buey* 'ox' and in the last syllable of *cam-biáis* 'you-pl change'. This is summarized in Table 5.1 with examples showing possible syllable structures.

To understand the structure of the syllable and syllabification it is helpful to refer to the notion of SONORITY.[3] The phonemes of a language can be arranged along a scale of sonority from most open or vowel-like to most closed or

---

[2] Except for some family names like *Sanz*, *Sainz*, with /nθ/ in Peninsular Spanish. In the pronunciation of foreign words the tendency is to simplify coda clusters. For instance, in *Nueva York* the last consonant may be left unpronounced.

[3] This concept has a long tradition in phonology. See Clements (1990) for discussion.

Table 5.2 Sonority scale in Spanish.

6	low vowel	a
5	mid vowels	e o
4	high vowels	i u
3	liquids	l (ʎ) ɾ r̄
2	nasals	m n ɲ
1	obstruents	f (θ) s x j t͡ʃ b d g p t k

consonant-like. The Spanish phonemes can be ordered according to the scale of sonority in Table 5.2 (similar scales have been proposed for other languages, with small differences in the number of levels that it is useful to distinguish).

To be a syllable peak a segment must have a sonority level of 4 or higher in this scale. High vocoids (sonority 4) may be either syllable peaks or satellites (that is, glides, as in *pie* [pi̯é] 'foot'). Mid vowels (sonority 5) are always syllable peaks in careful pronunciation, but may become glides in less careful speech (e.g. *lí-ne-a* → *lí-ne̯a* 'line', see 5.5.3). The low vowel /a/ (sonority 6) can only be a syllable peak.

A syllable has a single peak of sonority. This property defines what a syllable is. Within the syllable, the peak (nuclear vowel) is the most open or sonorous element. Around the vowel other segments are grouped in terms of decreasing sonority, from most vowel-like in the centre to least vowel-like in the periphery. Thus, in onset clusters the more sonorous, more vowel-like liquids (sonority 3) are closer to the nucleus than obstruents (sonority 1). In sequences of segments like *tre-* and *pla-*, for instance, there is a constant increase of sonority from the first element in the onset of the syllable to the nuclear vowel. Sequences like *rte-*, *lpa-*, on the other hand, cannot possibly be TAUTOSYLLABIC (= in the same syllable), since they show a decrease of sonority from the first segment to the second, followed by an increase from the second to the third. We may also conclude that between consonants in an onset cluster there must be a sonority difference of 2, since obstruent + nasal groups are not found in Spanish.[4]

Glides (nonsyllabic allophones of high vowels) are more sonorous than all consonants and are closest to the nuclear vowel. In, for instance, the first syllable of *plie-gue* 'fold' we have a uniform increase in sonority: from the most closed segment, the plosive /p/, to the most open, the vowel /e/. In the first syllable of *trans-portar* 'to transport' we have a sonority increase up to the vowel and a decrease in the rhyme; see Table 5.3.

---

[4] Notice that in *neumático* 'pneumatic', for instance, the etymological /p/ has been deleted even in the standard orthography.

5.3 Syllabification rules: consonants

Table 5.3 Examples of syllables showing sonority curve.

p	l	i	e		t	r	a	n	s
1	3	4	5		1	3	6	2	1

5.3 Syllabification rules: consonants

5.3.1 The CV rule

For the division of words and phrases into syllables, a first general rule is that a consonant is always syllabified with a following nucleus. A sequence of the type VCV (vowel-consonant-vowel) is always syllabified as V-CV: *a-la* 'wing', *a-mo* 'I love'. This rule has no exceptions in Spanish.[5] Remember, in this respect, that orthographic *rr* represents a single consonant /ɾ̄/. Thus *perro* 'dog' is [pé.ɾ̄o][6] and orthographically as well we would have *pe-rro* as the proper syllable division at the end of a line. This also applies of course to the orthographic digraphs *ch* and *ll*: *co-che* [kó.t͡ʃe] 'car', *va-lla* [bá.ja] 'fence'. A phonology/orthography mismatch is presented by the letter *x* when it stands for /ks/, as in, for instance, *taxi* 'taxi', *examen* 'exam'. Phonologically we have [ták.si], [ek.sá.men]. For orthographic purposes, the division at the end of a line would be as in *ta-xi*.

5.3.2 Consonant clusters

A sequence of two consonants is syllabified as an onset cluster only if it is one of those groups that are possible word initially. As already mentioned, these are always of the form plosive or /f/ + /ɾ/ or /l/ (*muta cum liquida* in classical terminology). Consequently, we have *o-tro* 'other', *la-bro* 'I till', *co-pla* 'song' but *ar-te* 'art', *cuen-ta* 'bead'.

The same principle applies for the syllabification of word-internal sequences of three or four consonants. Grouped with a following nucleus as onset we can have at most two consonants, a *muta-cum-liquida* cluster: *com-pro* 'I buy', *en-tra-da* 'entry', *cons-truc-ción* 'construction'. A useful way to think about this is that, when we divide a word into syllables, each syllable must have the structure

---

[5] Some speakers pronounce *an-he-lo* 'longing' *ad-he-rir* 'to adhere' with a syllable break between consonant and following vowel induced by the presence of orthographic *h* (which is silent). This is a minority pronunciation, which the Spanish Academy condemns as incorrect (RAE 1973:45). The normal syllabification of these words is *a-nhe-lo* [a.né.lo] *a-dhe-rir* [a.ðe.ɾíɾ].

[6] Representations within brackets in this chapter are generally very broad phonetic transcriptions with either all or only relevant syllable boundaries indicated by a single dot. Other times, simple orthographic forms with indication of syllabification by hyphens will be employed.

Table 5.4 Onset clusters.

/pɾ/ *pron-to* 'soon', *siem-pre* 'always'	/pl/ *plu-ma* 'feather', *so-plo* 'I blow'
/bɾ/ *bro-ma* 'joke', *a-bro* 'I open'	/bl/ *blan-co* 'white', *pue-blo* 'town'
/tɾ/ *tram-pa* 'trick', *vien-tre* 'belly'	/tl/ *tle-cuil* (Mex.) 'hearth', *a-tlas* (∼ *at-las*)*
/dɾ/ *dra-ma* 'drama', *ce-dro* 'cedar'	–
/kɾ/ *cre-ma* 'cream', *lu-cro* 'lucre'	/kl/ *cli-ma* 'climate', *bi-ci-cle-ta* 'bike'
/gɾ/ *gra-mo* 'gram', *lo-gro* 'I achieve'	/gl/ *glo-ria* 'glory', *é-glo-ga* 'eclogue'
/fɾ/ *fru-ta* 'fruit', *su-fro* 'I suffer'	/fl/ *flor* 'flower', *in-flo* 'I inflate'

* See text.

of a well-formed, free-standing Spanish word.[7] In this respect, it is important to keep in mind that, unlike in English, in Spanish words cannot start with *sC* clusters. Consequently, these sequences are always divided between two syllables inside words: *mos-ca* 'fly', *cons-ta* 'it consists'.

Examples of all possible onset clusters are given in Table 5.4. Notice that although almost all plosive + liquid sequences create onset clusters, there is one exception, namely the sequence */dl/. Word-initially, this sequence is not found in Spanish words. In the few examples that have this sequence word-internally the two consonants are separated (HETEROSYLLABIC): *ad-lá-te-re* 'lackey'. The exclusion of this onset cluster is no doubt motivated by the great phonetic similarity between the two consonants /d/ and /l/. As for initial /tl-/, this group does not occur in words of Latin origin, but it is found in Mexican Spanish, including a relatively large number of toponyms, such as *Tlalnepantla*, and also common nouns borrowed from the Nahuatl language like *tlapalería* 'paint store' and *tlecuil* 'hearth'. We find dialectal variation in the syllabification of word-internal /tl/. In all of Latin America, the Canaries and the northwest of the Peninsula, this sequence is syllabified as an onset cluster (unlike in English): *a-tlas* 'atlas', *a-tlán-ti-co* 'Atlantic', *a-tle-ta* 'athlete'. In most of Spain, on the other hand, this is not a possible onset cluster and we have *at-las*, *at-lán-ti-co*, *at-le-ta* (with possible weakening of /t/ in syllable-final position).

5.3.3 Codas

Final and word-internal consonants not syllabifiable as onsets are attached as codas to a preceding nucleus. As already mentioned, codas either contain

---

[7] Although this principle is not fully respected in the case of intervocalic /ɾ/ (e.g. *ca-ro*), since this segment is excluded from word-initial position.

5.3 Syllabification rules: consonants

Table 5.5 Possible codas. Frequent codas are in boldface.

	Word-medial	Word-final
Plosive	a**p**-to 'apt'	clu**b** 'club'
	a**b**-do-men 'abdomen'	ver-da**d** 'truth'
	é**t**-ni-co 'ethnic'	dé-fi-ci**t** 'deficit'
	a**d**-jun-to 'adjunct'	fra**c** 'tuxedo'
	a**c**-to 'act'	
	si**g**-no 'sign'	
Fricative	a**f**-ga-no 'Afghan'	che**f** 'chef'
	me**z**-cla 'mixture'	na-ri**z** 'nose'
	ba**s**-to 'rough'	ja-má**s** 'never'
		bo**j** 'box bush'
Nasal	ca**n**-to 'I sing'	pa**n** 'bread'
		ál-bu**m** 'album'
Liquid	a**l**-to 'tall'	sa**l** 'salt'
	ca**r**-ta 'letter'	ma**r** 'sea'
Plosive + /s/	a**bs**-ten-ción 'abstention'	bí-ce**ps** 'biceps'
	a**ds**-cri-bir 'ascribe'	ro-bo**ts** 'robots'
	e**x**-tra /éks.tɾa/ 'extra'	tó-ra**x** /tó.ɾaks/ 'thorax'
Fricative + /s/		che**fs** 'chefs'
Nasal + /s/	i**ns**-truc-tor 'instructor'	ye**ns** 'yens'
		Sa**nz** /-ns/ ~ Cast. /-nθ/ (a surname)
Liquid + /s/	pe**rs**-pi-caz 'perspicacious'	pó-s-te**rs** 'posters'
		va**ls** 'waltz'

only one consonant or at most a group of two consonants, where the second one is always /s/ (in a few surnames also /θ/ in Peninsular Spanish). Very few consonants are common in the coda. Those are in boldface in Table 5.5.

The affricate /t͡ʃ/ is not found in coda position, except word finally in a few recent borrowings, e.g. *match*, and in a common pronunciation of Catalan surnames ending in orthographic *-ch*, e.g. *Blanch*.[8] For the treatment of internal coda /t͡ʃ/ in adapted borrowings, cf. LatAm. *guachimán* from *watchman*.

As can be deduced from the examples in Table 5.5, most of the attested codas are in fact quite rare. The only common codas are those in boldface in the table. That is, commonly we may have only the codas in Table 5.6.

---

[8] Although this orthography is intended to represent /-k/ in Catalan.

Table 5.6 Common codas.

Word-medial	/-s/, (/-θ/), /-N/*, /-l/, /-ɾ/
Word-final	/-d/, /-s/ (/-θ/), /-n/, /-l/, /-ɾ/

* /N/ is a nasal with the same point of articulation as the following consonant.

It is evident that in Spanish there is a clear imbalance between onset and coda position in terms of distribution of consonants. The coda allows for only a restricted number of contrasts among consonants. We may note the following processes of neutralization in the coda, which are studied in the corresponding chapters. Some of these processes are common to the language as a whole, others are restricted by dialect or style (A. Alonso 1945):

a) Plosives. Syllable-final plosives are included in Table 5.5 (possible codas) but the only one among them in Table 5.6 (common codas) is word-final /-d/. Coda plosives are subject to many neutralizations. Typically there is no contrast between voiced and voiceless consonants in this position, in spite of the orthography. Other reductions of coda plosives also take place. Final /-d/ is also commonly reduced or deleted. See 8.2.

b) Fricatives. The fricative /s/ (and /θ/) is aspirated or deleted in coda position in a great number of dialects. Fricatives may also assimilate in voice to a following voiced consonant. Coda /f/ is only found in a few words, where it is subject to the same processes. Coda /x/ is only common in *reloj*, pronounced [r̄eló] by many speakers (there are a few other less common examples: *boj* 'box bush', *carcaj* 'quiver'). See 9.2.3.

c) Affricates. The affricate /t͡ʃ/ is not found in coda position (except for unadapted borrowings).

d) Nasals. There is no contrast among nasals in the coda. Word-finally we find only /n/, which assimilates in place to a following consonant. Word-medially, nasals always agree in place with a following consonant. Notice the morphophonological alternation in *presumir* 'presume' but *presunción* (not *presumción*) 'presumption'. See 10.2.

e) Liquids. Regarding the rhotics, there is no tap/trill contrast in coda position. In addition, both in Caribbean and in Andalusian areas the contrast between /l/ and /ɾ/ is also neutralized in this position. See 11.4.

As for coda clusters it must be said that, first, clusters other than those in Table 5.5 are not found in Spanish. This results in some morphophonological alternations when non-permissible clusters would be created, as in *esculpir* 'to sculpt', *escultor* (not *esculptor) 'sculptor', *escribir* 'to write', *escritor* (not *escribtor) 'writer'. Secondly, in word-medial coda clusters with /s/, it is common for the consonant before the /s/ to be deleted: *extra* [éstra] 'extra', *transporte* [traspórte] 'transportation', *obstáculo* [ostákulo] 'obstacle'. Depending on the geographical area, this simplification may be common in all styles or restricted to only colloquial or careless speech.

5.3.4 Adaptation of word-initial consonant sequences in borrowings

Spanish does not allow /sC-/ onsets. Regularly, native words which originally had this word-initial sequence in Latin have added a word-initial /e/ (e.g. SPĪNA > *espina* 'thorn'). This EPENTHESIS is still a productive process: in borrowings from English and other languages with word-initial /sC-/ a vowel /e/ is systematically inserted at the beginning of the word. This initial vowel is added in orthographically adapted borrowings: *eslogan* 'slogan', *estrés* 'stress', *estándar* 'standard'. But even when not added in the orthography, this vowel is always present in normal Spanish pronunciation: *stop* [estóp], *un snob* [ún eznóβ].

Other word-initial groups such as *ps-*, *pn-*, *mn-*, *pt-*, *x-* (for /ks-/), mostly in loanwords from Greek, are simplified by deletion of the first consonant. In some cases (but not always), the official orthography reflects the pronunciation by having eliminated an original word-initial consonant, optionally or obligatorily: *salmo* 'psalm', *pseudo* ~ *seudo* 'pseudo', *psicología* ~ *sicología* 'psychology', *neumático* 'pneumatic', *nemónico* 'mnemonic', *pterodáctilo* [teroðáktilo] 'pterodactyl', *xenófobo* [senófoβo] 'xenophobic'.

5.4 Syllabification rules: vocoids (vowels and glides)

The only real complications regarding syllable structure in Spanish have to do with the syllabification of sequences of vocoids. These can be syllabified as HIATUS – that is, in different syllables, as in *vía* [bí.a] 'way', *leo* 'I read' [lé.o] – or, as a DIPHTHONG, in the same syllable, as in *pie* 'foot' [pi̯é] (one syllable). Sequences of vocoids can be quite complex in Spanish as we see in examples like *cambiáis* [kam.bi̯áis̯] 'you-pl change', *huías* [u.í.as] 'you fled', with three vocoids in a row, and *instruíais* 'you-pl instructed', with four (syllabified as [ins.tru.í.ai̯s]). (These complications are purposely avoided in the orthographic rules for word-division, according to which sequences of orthographic vowels cannot be separated at the end of a line, whether they form a diphthong or a hiatus – RAE 1999:88.)

For the most part, the syllabification of sequences of two vocoids is predictable according to the following rules:

a) If both vocoids are nonhigh (mid or low: /a e o/), the sequence is syllabified as a hiatus.

/ea/	*teatro* [te.á.tɾo] 'theatre'	
/ee/	*leemos* [le.é.mos] 'we read', *dehesa* [de.é.sa] 'prairie'	
/eo/	*beodo* [be.ó.ðo] 'drunkard'	
/oa/	*boato* [bo.á.to] 'pomp', *toalla* [to.á.ʝa] 'towel'	
/oe/	*poeta* [po.é.ta] 'poet'	
/oo/	*mohoso* [mo.ó.so] 'mouldy', *loo* [ló.o] 'I praise'	
/ae/	*saeta* [sa.é.ta] 'arrow', *área* [á.ɾe.a] 'area'	
/ao/	*ahora* [a.ó.ɾa] 'now', *caos* [ká.os] 'chaos'	
/aa/	*albahaca* [al.βa.á.ka] 'basil', *Saavedra* [sa.a.βé.ðɾa]	

b) If the sequence contains a stressed high vocoid /í ú/ preceded or followed by a nonhigh vowel /a e o/, it is syllabified as a hiatus.

/ía/	*tía* [tí.a] 'aunt', *María* [ma.ɾí.a]
/íe/	*sonríe* [son.r̃í.e] 's/he smiles'
/ío/	*frío* [fɾí.o] 'cold'
/úa/	*púa* [pú.a] 'barb'
/úe/	*evalúe* [e.βa.lú.e] 's/he evaluate, subjunct.'
/úo/	*búho* [bú.o] 'owl', *dúo* [dú.o] 'duo'
/aí/	*caída* [ka.í.ða] 'fall', *ahí* [a.í] 'there'
/eí/	*leído* [le.í.ðo] 'read', *leí* [le.í] 'I read'
/oí/	*bohío* [bo.í.o] 'hut', *oí* [o.í] 'I heard'
/aú/	*aúlla* [a.ú.ʝa] 's/he howls'
/eú/	*reúne* [r̃e.ú.ne] 's/he gathers'
/oú/	–[9]

Sequences of rising sonority, of the type /ía/, where the stressed high vowel comes first, are found mostly at the end of words. In word-internal position they are uncommon and tend to become diphthongs (according to rule (d) below) by displacement of the stress. Both possibilities are acceptable for words such as *período* [pe.ɾí.o.ðo] or *periodo* [pe.ɾi̯ó.ðo] 'period', *policíaco* [í.a] or *policiaco* [i̯á] 'police-related' (and other words ending in *-iaco*).

c) Sequences of two identical high vowels – which are very rare – are syllabified as hiatus, regardless of stress.

---

[9] This sequence is not found within word boundaries. A possible example across a prefix boundary (not listed in the dictionary of the RAE) would be *coúso* [ko.ú.so] 'joint use'. Another example is found in the compound *austro-húngaro* 'Austro-Hungarian'.

5.4 Syllabification rules: vocoids

/ii/   *tiito* [ti.í.to] 'uncle, *dim.*', *chiita* [tʃi.í.ta] 'Shiite', *antiitaliano* [a.n̪ti.i.ta.li̯á.no] 'anti-Italian', *nihilista* [ni.i.lís.ta] 'nihilist'

/uu/   *duunviro* [du.um.bí.ɾo] 'duumvir'

Otherwise, the general rule is syllabification of the sequence as a diphthong. Two subcases can be distinguished:

d1) Sequences where unstressed /i u/ is adjacent to /a e o/ are generally syllabified as diphthongs. In Spanish we have both rising diphthongs, where the sequence rises in sonority or aperture, from a closer to a more open position (glide + vowel), and falling diphthongs, with the opposite configuration (vowel + glide).

Rising diphthongs

/ia/   *italiano* [i.ta.li̯á.no] 'Italian', *feria* [fé.ɾi̯a] 'fair'
/ie/   *pienso* [pi̯én.so] 'I think', *pie* [pi̯é] 'foot'
/io/   *idioma* [i.ði̯ó.ma] 'language', *patio* [pá.ti̯o] 'yard'
/ua/   *cuando* [ku̯án.do] 'when', *recua* [r̄é.ku̯a] 'mule train'
/ue/   *prueba* [pɾu̯é.βa] 'test', *tenue* [té.nu̯e] 'tenuous'
/uo/   *cuota* [ku̯ó.ta] 'quote', *fatuo* [fá.tu̯o] 'fatuous'

Falling diphthongs

/ai/   *vainilla* [bai̯.ní.ja] 'vanilla', *hay* [ái̯] 'there is'
/ei/   *veinte* [béi̯n̪.te] 'twenty', *rey* [r̄éi̯] 'king'
/oi/   *boina* [bói̯.na] 'beret', *hoy* [ói̯] 'today'
/au/   *jaula* [xáu̯.la] 'cage', *taurino* [tau̯.ɾí.no] 'related to bullfighting'
/eu/   *neutro* [néu̯.tɾo] 'neutral', *Europa* [eu̯.ɾó.pa] 'Europe'
/ou/   *bou* [bóu̯] 'type of fishing boat'[10]

In its preference for rising diphthongs over hiatus in this context, Spanish clearly differs from English. Notice, for instance, that in Spanish there are diphthongs in *Vie-na, In-dia-na, San-Die-go*, whereas in English the sequences in these words are heterosyllabic, *Vi-en-na, In-di-a-na, San-Di-e-go*.

d2) Sequences where two different high vocoids are in contact are also generally diphthongs.

/i u/ *viuda* [bi̯ú.ða] 'widow', *ciudad* [θi̯u.ðáð] ~ [si̯u.ðáð] 'city'
/ui/ *cuida* [ku̯í.ða] 's/he cares for', *ruido* [r̄u̯í.ðo] 'noise', *fui* [fu̯í] 'I went'

---

[10] This sequence is rare. Besides the example given in the text, which is a borrowing from Catalan, it is found in surnames and toponyms of Catalan and Galician-Portuguese origin such as *Masnou*, *Sousa* and *Bousoño*.

Table 5.7 Gliding rule.

/i /, /u / → [i̯], [u̯] if adjacent to a different V and not stress-bearing

Examples:
/péine/ [péi̯ne] (falling diphthong), /piérna/ [pi̯érna] (rising diphthong)

These tautosyllabic sequences of high vocoids are generally pronounced as rising diphthongs (glide + vowel) (Navarro Tomás 1977:67; Quilis 1993:179). Notice, for instance, that *viuda* rhymes with *suda*, and not with *vida*, which indicates that the nuclear vowel is /u/; whereas *cuida* rhymes with *vida*.

The descriptions in (a)–(d) can be stated in a more concise manner: all nonhigh and high but stressed vocoids are syllable peaks. Sequences where a nonstress-bearing high vocoid is in contact with another vocoid are diphthongs (except for the rare sequences /ii/, /uu/). That is, the occurrence of glides can be predicted from the Gliding rule in Table 5.7.

Sequences of vocoids that do not present the context for the Gliding rule are realized as hiatus (separate syllables) in careful pronunciation. According to this rule, diphthongs and hiatus sequences would be in complementary distribution in Spanish.

There are, however, some contrasts between glide and high vowel or, equivalently, diphthong and hiatus, in the same context (see Hualde 1997; Hualde and Prieto 2002; Aguilar 1999; among others). This is because the Gliding rule in Table 5.7 (which captures the statements in (d1) and (d2)) has some lexical exceptions. Consider the contrasting pairs in Table 5.8 (only the relevant syllable divisions are indicated).

The examples on the right column of Table 5.8 are always pronounced with a diphthong. This is what is expected, since they present the context for the Gliding rule. The examples on the left column may also be pronounced with a diphthong, depending on the style or dialect but, crucially, they also have a possible pronunciation in hiatus. These words are exceptions to the general gliding of unstressed high vowels in contact with a different vowel.

Since words of the *dueto* type (left column in Table 5.8), with a possible hiatus, are considerably less frequent in the lexicon than those of the *duelo* type, with an obligatory diphthong, we will refer to them as containing an exceptional hiatus and we will indicate their anomalous syllabification in their phonological representation: /du.éto/ 'duet', /pi.é/ 'I chirped', /u.ímos/ 'we fled', etc. Except for this group of words with exceptional hiatus, syllabification in Spanish is predictable. In particular, glides can be considered allophonic variants of high vowels when adjacent to another vowel and not bearing the

5.4 Syllabification rules: vocoids

Table 5.8 Examples of pairs contrasting in syllabification of sequences of vocoids.

Exceptional hiatus (exceptions to Gliding rule)		Diphthong (by Gliding rule)
dueto [du.éto] 'duet'	vs	*duelo* [du̯élo] 'mourning; duel'
pié [pi.é] 'I chirped'[11]	vs	*pie* [pi̯é] 'foot'
riendo [r̄i.éndo] 'laughing'	vs	*siendo* [si̯éndo] 'being'
mi diana [miði.ána] 'my target'	vs	*mediana* [meði̯ána] 'medium, *fem.*'
reiré [r̄e.iré] 'I will laugh'	vs	*reiné* [r̄ei̯né] 'I ruled'
huimos [u.ímos] 'we flee'	vs	*fuimos* [fu̯ímos] 'we were; we went'
enviamos [embi.ámos] 'we send'	vs	*envidiamos* [embiði̯ámos] 'we envy'

stress on their own. What needs to be lexically marked as exceptional is that some high vocoids constitute nuclei of separate syllables in contexts where they should be syllabified together with another vowel and realized as glides (RAE 1973:58; Hualde 1997; J. Harris and Kaisse 1999, etc.).

To summarize:

- Sequences of two vowels are syllabified as hiatus if both are nonhigh (e.g. *poeta*) or if at least one is high but stressed (e.g. *caída*). Sequences containing unstressed high vowels in contact with a different vowel, on the other hand, are regularly syllabified as diphthongs (e.g. *baile, duelo, siendo*), but this rule has a few lexical exceptions (*dueto, riendo*).

This is shown in Table 5.9, where phonological representations of regular and exceptional words are given.

All of this pertains to syllabification in careful style or at the lexical level. As we will see in 5.5.3, many sequences syllabified as hiatus in this style can be reduced to diphthongs in more colloquial pronunciation.

5.4.1 Lexical distribution of exceptional hiatus

As just explained, the glides [i̯ u̯] are positional variants of the high vowels /i u/ when adjacent to a different vowel and not bearing the stress on themselves.

As also just mentioned, this rule has, nevertheless, some exceptions and that is why we find pairs that contrast in syllabification such as *du-e-to* 'duet' (with an

---

[11] According to the most recent orthographic norms (RAE 1999) this word may be written either *pié* or *pie*. The accent mark is now optional on account of the fact that for many Latin American speakers this word is pronounced with a diphthong (exactly like 'foot') and is thus monosyllabic (according to another orthographic rule monosyllables do not need an accent mark). The form *pié*, with an accent mark, reflects the pronunciation in hiatus prevalent in Peninsular Spanish, Mexican and some other Latin American dialects.

Table 5.9 Examples of syllabification of vowel sequences.

Orthography	Phonological representation	Syllabification
poeta	/poéta/	[po.é.ta]
caída	/kaída/	[ka.í.ða]
baile	/báile/	[bái̯.le]
duelo	/duélo/	[du̯é.lo]
dueto	/du.éto/	[du.é.to]
siendo	/siéndo/	[si̯én.do]
riendo	/r̃i.éndo/	[r̃i.én.do]

exceptional hiatus) vs *du̯e-lo*, and *pi-é* 'I chirped' vs *pi̯e* 'foot' (and *pí-e* 'I chirp, subjunct.') and the other examples in Table 5.8. It turns out that the exceptions to the Gliding rule are not randomly distributed in the lexicon. In this section we will consider the contexts that favour the presence of exceptional hiatus.

An important caveat is that the lexical distribution of exceptional hiatus is subject to a great deal of dialectal and even idiolectal variation. Hiatuses are much more common in Castilian Spanish than in most South American dialects, for instance. Even within the same geographical area, speakers do not always agree on which words presenting the context for the Gliding rule can be pronounced with a hiatus instead of a diphthong. For a given speaker there may also be differences in the strength of his or her intuitions regarding the syllabification of particular words. (The consequences of this variation for the application of the orthographic rules of accentuation are explained in 13.10.3.) Nevertheless, when it is found, the occurrence of exceptional hiatus is limited to some specific contexts.

1) First of all, a sequence in the context of the Gliding rule may be exceptionally syllabified as a hiatus if in a morphologically related word the high vowel of the sequence bears the stress (and it is thus necessarily in hiatus), as in the following examples:

a. Rising sonority (type /i.a/)

porf[i.á]*ban*	'they disputed'	cf. *porfían*	'they dispute'
env[i.á]*mos*	'we send'	cf. *envía*	's/he sends'
esp[i.á]*ndo*	'spying'	cf. *espía*	's/he spies'
g[i.á]*r*	'to guide' (*guiar*)	cf. *guía*	's/he guides'
r[i.á]*da*	'high waters'	cf. *río*	'river'
d[u.é]*to*	'duet'	cf. *dúo*	'duo'
d[i.ú]*rno*	'diurnal'	cf. *día*	'day'

b. Falling sonority (type /a.i/)

r[e.i]ré	'I will laugh'	cf. reír	'to laugh'
[o.i]ré	'I will hear'	cf. oír	'to hear'
h[u.i]ríamos	'we would flee'	cf. h[u.í]r	'to flee'
pr[o.i]bír	'to prohibit' (prohibir)	cf. prohíbe	's/he prohibits'

All the examples above allow a syllabification in hiatus for some (but not all) speakers.

It should be noticed that, although hiatus is possible in the verb forms above and many similar ones, it is totally impossible in other verbs with orthographically identical sequences such as camb[i̯á]ban 'they changed' (cf. cambia [kámbi̯a] 's/he changes'), envid[i̯á]mos 'we envy' (cf. envidia [embíði̯a] 's/he envies'), limp[i̯á]ndo 'cleaning' (cf. limpia 's/he cleans'), r[e̯i]naré 'I will reign' (cf. reinar 'to reign'), where the verbal paradigm does not include forms with stress on the high vowel.

Very few of these hiatus words have sequences of falling sonority (type /a.i/). A hiatus in the infinitive in verbs with monosyllabic roots (reír, oír, huir) may be transferred to the future and conditional, but not to other forms of the verb. Thus, the hiatus of the infinitive oír 'to hear' affects the pronunciation of the future [o.i]ré 'I will hear' and the conditional [o.i]ría, but not the subjunctive [o̯i]gamos 'we hear', which follows the pattern of [ói̯]go 'I hear'.

2) Secondly, we may have a hiatus with unstressed high vowel if there is a morphological boundary between the two vocoids. This is the case in compounds, especially when the second vowel in the sequence is stressed as in boquiancho [boki.ántʃo] 'wide-mouthed', less commonly if the stress is further away, as in boquiabierto [boki̯abi̯érto] 'open-mouthed'.[12] Across a prefix boundary, we may have hiatus in b[i.é]nio 'biennium' (cf. v[i̯é]nto 'wind', V[i̯é]na 'Vienna', etc., representing the regular pattern). The presence of a suffix boundary accounts for the possibility of exceptional hiatus in certain words. Especially following /u/, derivational suffixes such as -oso, -al, -ario may give rise to exceptional hiatuses: virt[u.ó]so 'virtuous', respet[u.ó]so 'respectful', man[u.á]l 'manual', punt[u.á]l 'punctual', est[u.á]rio 'estuary', sant[u.á]rio 'sanctuary', also jes[u.í]ta 'Jesuit'. Infinitives ending in -uar (evaluar, puntuar, etc.) and -uir (construir, influir, etc.) also allow a hiatus.[13]

---

[12] Pensado (1999:4457) cites the contrasting examples barbihecho [baɾβi.étʃo] 'clean shaven', where stress and morpheme boundary coincide, vs barbiespeso [baɾβi̯espéso] 'with a thick beard'.

[13] However, after a velar, hiatus with /u/ is strongly dispreferred. Thus, although most adjectives in -ual are in the exceptional hiatus class, this does not apply to ling[u̯á]l. Similarly, the ending -uente allows for a hiatus pronunciation in examples such as congr[u.é]nte 'congruous', but not in consec[u̯é]nte 'consequent', where it directly follows a velar consonant. As mentioned in the text, infinitives in -uar also have exceptional hiatus: act[u.á]r 'to act' (cf. actúa 's/he acts'), eval[u.á]r 'to

3) There are a few other exceptional words that do not meet either of the two morphological conditions above. These cases are, however, severely constrained:

a. They are always sequences of increasing sonority (e.g. /i.a/, but not /a.i/).
b. They (almost) always occur at the beginning of the word (Initiality condition).[14]
c. The stress is either on the second vowel in hiatus or on the following syllable (Stress condition).
d. Most of these words have one of the two sequences /i.a/, /i.o/.

Again, the exemplification here follows what seem to be the most common patterns in Castilian Spanish, but they do not necessarily coincide with the intuitions of all speakers from this area, let alone other dialects.

The Initiality condition can be observed in the following examples:

b[i.ó]logo 'biologist'   but   rad[i̯ó]logo 'radiologist'
d[i.á]na 'target'   but   med[i̯á]na 'middle', Ind[i̯á]na
l[i.á]na 'liana'   but   ital[i̯á]na 'Italian, fem.'

As for the Stress condition, it is reflected in the fact that many Castilian speakers syllabify for instance *di-álogo* 'dialogue' and *di-alogo* 'I converse' but *di̯alogó* 's/he conversed' (stressed vowel is in boldface for clarity), or *di-ámetro* 'diameter' but *di̯ametral* 'diametral'. This condition may also operate in cases of morphologically conditioned hiatus so that the hiatus of *du-o* 'duo' is preserved in *du-al* 'dual', *du-eto* 'duet' and *du-alismo* 'dualism', but not in *du̯alidad* 'duality', where the stress is further away. Exceptional hiatus is never found after the stress (e.g. in words like *radio, historia*).

Let us keep in mind that these are necessary but not sufficient conditions. A given speaker may pronounce, for instance *li-ana, pi-ano, pi-ojo* with lexical hiatus vs *vi̯aje* [bi̯áxe] 'trip', with obligatory diphthong. The conditions above tell us only where exceptional hiatus may be found, not that under those conditions we will necessarily have a hiatus.

The relative lexical frequency of diphthong vs hiatus in words meeting both the Initiality condition and the most strict Stress condition in Castilian Spanish is illustrated in Table 5.10 (which is based on a dictionary search and thus excludes verb forms other than the infinitive). In the case of sets of words transparently related by derivation, generally only one word with the same

evaluate' (cf. *evalúa* 's/he evaluates'), and many others. But this does not apply to infinitives in /-kuár/: *evacuar, adecuar, licuar* and *oblicuar*, which obligatorily have a diphthong (Quilis 1993:183). With these verbs there is often insecurity or fluctuation in stress pattern. Thus the RAE offers both *adecúa* and *adecua* 's/he makes suitable'.

[14] With very rare exceptions. One of them is *embrión* [embri.ón] 'embryo'.

Table 5.10 Lexical distribution of exceptional hiatus and diphthong in words with an initial stressed sequence (Castilian Spanish).

Hiatus	Diphthong
/i.á/	/iá/
ciática criada crianza diablo diábolo diácono diáfano dial diálisis diálogo diámetro diana diantre diáspora diástole fiable fiambre fiasco grial guiar hiato liana liar miaja miasma piano piara piastra quiasmo riacho riada tiara triángulo triásico viable vianda viario viático	viaje*
/i.ó/	/ió/
biólogo, bio-, bióxido bi-, biombo criollo dióxido fiordo guión ion lioso miope piojo prior prioste quiosco Rioja	diócesis dios iota viola
/i.ú/	/iú/
diurno	triunfo viudo
/i.é/	/ié/
bienio cliente diedro riel riera trienio	bien Bierzo bies ciego cielo cien ciénaga ciencia cieno cierne cierre cierto ciervo cierzo Diego diente diéresis Diesel diestra dieta diez diezmo fiebre fiel feltro fiemo fiera fierro fiesta griego grieta hierba hierro liebre liendre lienzo miedo miel miembro mientes mientras miércoles mierda mies niebla nieto nieve pie piedra piel piélago pienso pierna pieza pliegue prieto quiebra quien quieto riego rienda siega siembra siempre sien siena sierpe sierra siervo siesta siete tiembla tiempo tiento tierno tierra tieso tiesto vieira viejo viento vientre viernes
/u.á/	/uá/
dual truhán zuavo	cuádriga cuadro cuádruple cuajo cual cuan cuanto cuáquero cuarta cuarzo cuasi cuate gua guaba guagua guaira gualdo guanche guano guante guapo guarda guardia guarro guasa guata Juan quark quasar suave
/u.é/	/ué/
cruento dueto fluencia	bueno buey checa cruel* cuesco cuesta cuestión cueva cuévano duelo duende dueño fuego fuelle fuente fuera fuero fuerte grueso güero hueco huelga huella huérfano hueso huerta huésped huevo juego juerga jueves juez luego luengo mueble mueca muela muelle muérdago muermo muerte muesca muestra nuera nuestro nueve nuevo nuez prueba pueblo puente puerco puerro puerta puerto puesto rueca rueda ruedo ruego sueco suegra suela suelo sueldo suelto sueño suero suerte suéter suevo trueno trueque tuerca tuerto tueste tuétano vuelco vuelo vuelta vuestro zueco
/u.í/	/uí/
druida fluir fruir gruir huir luir pruina suizo	buitre juicio muy ruido* ruin* ruina*

root is given in the table. As we can see, even though hiatus with unstressed high vowels is exceptional, there are specific contexts where it is very frequent in Castilian. In other Spanish dialects, however, most of the hiatus words given in the table have a regular diphthong.[15]

5.4.2 Historical origin of diphthong/hiatus contrast

Classical Latin did not have rising diphthongs. These diphthongs have one of two main possible origins in Spanish:

1) First of all, original heterosyllabic sequences have been reduced to diphthongs. Historical phonologists speak of an 'anti-hiatus tendency' which has produced the reduction of most historical hiatuses with unstressed high vowels to diphthongs in Spanish and other ROMANCE languages (Quilis 1993:184; Lloyd 1987:320; Penny 2002:60).[16] This has also affected sequences originally separated by a consonant which was later deleted:

PRETI-U(M) > prec̯io 'price'
ITALI-A > Ital̯ia 'Italy'
RUGĪTU(M) > ru-ido > ru̯ido 'noise'
CRŪDĒLE(M) > cru-el > cru̯el 'cruel'

Contraction (= Gliding rule) is the general solution. However, this process has exceptionally been blocked in some words, for morphological reasons (paradigm effects or presence of certain morphological boundaries) and in a 'strong position' (in initial position and under the Stress condition: in, or immediately before, stressed sequences). These are the words that present exceptional hiatus nowadays. The 'strength' of these positions may derive from general rhythmic patterns of the language, according greater relative duration to stressed and immediately pretonic positions (see Hualde and Chitoran 2003).

2) By a general process of ' breaking' , the stressed low-mid vowels /ɛ/, /ɔ/ of Vulgar Latin (corresponding to the short mid vowels of Classical Latin, see 12.3) gave rise to the diphthongs /ie/ [i̯e] and /ue/ [u̯e] in Spanish:

T[ɛ]RRA > t[i̯é]rra 'land'
P[ɔ]RTA > p[u̯é]rta 'door'

---

[15] There are also some Castilian speakers for whom some of the words given here as having a diphthong in the most common Castilian pronunciation can be syllabified in hiatus. These are marked with a following asterisk in the table, e.g. *cruel**.

[16] In many instances rising diphthongs were later eliminated by palatalization of the preceding vowel with absorption of the glide, as in VĪNEA > vin̯ia > viña 'vineyard'.

5.5 Resyllabification and contraction

Table 5.11 CV resyllabification across word boundaries.

[pó.ko.s‿a.mí.ɣos]	*pocos amigos*	'few friends'
[kó.me.n‿a.kí]	*comen aquí*	'they eat here'
[má.l‿i.ta.li̯á.no]	*mal italiano*	'bad Italian'
[sa.βé.r‿ál.ɣo]	*saber algo*	'to know something'
[klú.β‿es.pa.ɲól]	*club español*	'Spanish club'
[t͡ʃé.f‿ar.xen.tí.no]	*chef argentino*	'Argentinian chef'

Among words with this historical derivation, we do not find any cases of exceptional hiatus. Since, on the other hand, most instances of *ie*, *ue* result from breaking, this explains why hiatus is rare with these sequences. We may have an exceptional hiatus in a word like *cli-ente* 'client' which had a hiatus in Latin, but never in words where *ie*, *ue* derive from single vowels.

The tendency to reduce sequences in hiatus to diphthongs still operates in casual speech, with greater or lesser intensity depending on the dialect (see section 5.5.3 below).

5.5 Resyllabification and contraction processes

5.5.1 (Re-)syllabification of consonants across word and prefix boundaries

A word-final consonant is normally resyllabified together with a following word-initial vowel in connected speech, as shown in the examples in Table 5.11.

Examples such as *las alas* 'the wings' and *la salas* 'you salt it' are thus homophonous (in dialects without aspiration, see below), since in the first example the final /s/ of the article is resyllabified as an onset.[17]

Word-final consonants preceding a vowel may nevertheless undergo weakening processes in this position. In particular /s/ may be aspirated and /n/ may be velarized in this phonological context in dialects with these phenomena: *poco*[h] *amigos* 'few friends', *come*[ŋ] *aquí* 'they eat here'. Aspiration of word-final /s/ is, however, less frequent before a word-initial vowel, in the

---

[17] This resyllabification process explains nonstandard forms such as *amoto* 'motorcycle' (standard *moto*) and *arradio* 'radio' (standard *radio*). Nouns such as *moto* and *radio* are unusual in that they are feminine nouns ending in *-o*. (This is because they are etymologically shortened forms: *la motocicleta*, *la radiofonía*. In many Latin American countries *radio* is masculine.) Some speakers interpret sequences such as *una moto*, *una radio* as *un amoto*, *un arradio* and then produce *el amoto*, *el arradio* with the definite article.

Table 5.12 Resyllabification of C#V vs no resyllabification of C#C.

Resyllabification	No resyllabification
[klúβ‿espaɲól] *club español* 'Spanish club'	[klúβ.latíno] *club latino* 'Latin club'
	[klúβ.r̄ománo] *club romano* 'Roman club'
[t͡ʃéf‿arxentíno] *chef argentino* 'Argentinian chef'	[t͡ʃéf.lusitáno] *chef lusitano* 'Lusitanian chef'
	[t͡ʃéf.r̄úso] 'Russian chef'

resyllabification context, than before a word-initial consonant. In Buenos Aires Spanish, for instance, word-final /s/ is preserved as [s] only occasionally before a consonant (in 11 per cent of the instances, at the same rate as word-internal /s/ in preconsonantal position, in a study by Terrell 1978, cited in Bybee 2000) but almost systematically before a vowel (88 per cent of the cases in the same study, see 9.2.4).

As for word-final /n/, it may become [ŋ] in velarizing dialects even if followed by a vowel. Thus, in such dialects, the two-word example *e*[ŋ] *aguas* 'in waters' may contrast with *e*[n]*aguas* 'petticoat', and *e*[ŋ] *ojos* 'in eyes' may also form a minimal pair with *e*[n]*ojos* 'troubles', although these facts have been disputed.

Regarding word-final *r*, it is always realized as the tap /ɾ/ when resyllabified. As explained in 11.3, in syllable-final position we have an indistinct, neutralized segment [r] = [ɾ] ~ [r̄] (usually a tap, but possibly a trill) and this is what we find in, for instance, *sabe*[r] *poco* 'to know little', where the word-final consonant is not resyllabified. In contexts of resyllabification, on the other hand, we find a clear tap [ɾ] as the only option, as in *sabe*[ɾ] *algo* 'to know something'.[18]

Resyllabification across word boundaries only affects C–V sequences. In contrast, a word-final consonant is not resyllabified with a word-initial consonant even if this would result in a well-formed *muta-cum-liquida* group. That is, onsets are not maximized across word boundaries.

The sequences /b.l/, /f.l/ in the examples in Table 5.12 are clearly different from word-internal /bl/, /fl/ clusters (see section 5.6 below). The difference is even greater in the case where the word-initial segment is a rhotic, since word-initial rhotics are always trills.

---

[18] Except in the Spanish of bilingual Basque speakers.

5.5 Resyllabification and contraction

Table 5.13 No resyllabification of C + glide across word boundaries.

Resyllabification	No resyllabification
[las̪.íxas] *las hijas* 'the daughters'	[laz.ɟérβas] *las hierbas* 'the herbs'
[kon̪.úmo] *con humo* 'with smoke'	[koŋ.gu̯ékos] *con huecos* 'with holes'

Word-initial glides count as consonants, not as vowels, for the purposes of the resyllabification rule. That is, there is no resyllabification of word-final consonants before word-initial glides.

Consequently with this syllabification, the non-resyllabified word-final consonants in the examples on the right-side column in Table 5.13 may undergo the assimilation and weakening processes found in the preconsonantal coda context. As for the syllable-initial glide (phonemically /i/ /u/) it undergoes fortition, to different degrees depending to the dialect (see 9.3). Thus in *las hierbas* /las iérbas/ 'the herbs, the grasses' the glide may strengthen to a palatal fricative or plosive and we may find voice assimilation of /s/, [lazɟérβas] or its weakening [lahɟérβah], depending on the dialect. In the example *con huecos*, the nasal assimilates in place as in the position preceding a velar consonant, and the initial glide is normally reinforced as [gu̯] in this context: [koŋgu̯ékos].

The morphological boundaries of transparent prefixes such as *sub-* and *des-* behave as word boundaries for syllabification purposes, allowing resyllabification of the final consonant of the prefix before a vowel (*su-ba-tó-mi-co* 'subatomic', *de-sar-me* 'disarmament'), but not before a consonant or glide (*sub-lin-gual* 'sublingual', *des-hie-lo* 'thawing'). This results in interesting contrasts in pronunciation, which are examined in 5.6.

In a minority of aspirating dialects (e.g. in some Andalusian varieties), the /s/ of the prefix *des-* can be aspirated before a vowel [dehárme] 'disarmament'. This also applies to forms like *nosotros* 'we' [nohótro], analysable as *nos+otros*. As for orthographic syllable division, the academic rules give both options as acceptable: *de- sarme* or *des- arme*, *no- sotros* or *nos- otros* (RAE 1999:88).

5.5.2 Syllable contraction across word boundaries

In connected speech, it is frequent in Spanish for sequences of vocoids to be grouped in a single syllable across word boundaries (Navarro Tomás 1977:147–58). This is especially common when a word ending in an unstressed vowel

Table 5.14 Syllable contraction across word boundaries.

mi hermano	/mi ermáno/	[mi̯ermáno]	'my brother'
tu abuelo	/tu abuélo/	[tu̯aβu̯élo]	'your grandfather'
esta historia	/ésta istória/	[éstai̯stóri̯a]	'this story'
la unión	/la unión/	[lau̯ni̯ón]	'the union'
se acaba	/se akába/	[se̯akáβa]	'it ends'
no entiendo	/no ɴtieɴdo/	[no̯eɴti̯éṉdo]	'I don't understand'
este ornamento	/éste orɴaméɴto/	[éste̯orɴaméṉto]	'this ornament'
una hormiga	/úna orɴmíga/	[únao̯rmíɣa]	'an ant'
cámara oscura	/kámara oskúra/	[kámarao̯skúra]	'dark chamber'

is followed by another word beginning with an unstressed vowel, as in the examples in Table 5.14. This affects both sequences containing unstressed /i u/, which are syllabified as tautosyllabic when occurring within a word, and sequences of non-high vowels, which are heterosyllabic in citation form.

As shown in the examples, both high and mid vowels may become glides by this process of contraction. The higher of the two vowels in the sequence is the one that tends to undergo greater shortening, producing a glide percept. If the two vowels have the same height (i.e. both are high or both are mid), the first of the two becomes a glide. In the case of mid vowels, they may become true high glides [i̯], [u̯], in colloquial speech in some dialects; e.g. *se acaba* [si̯akáβa].

Unstressed /e/ may also be elided in casual style in contact with another vowel if (a) word final, *est(e) individuo* 'this guy', *nombr(e) antiguo* 'old name', *tien(e) orgullo* 's/he has pride', *los qu(e) utilizan* 'those who use', or (b) word-initial in a closed syllable, *casi (e)stamos* 'we are almost there', *ya (e)ntraron* 'they came in already' (Monroy Casas 1980:70–8; Quilis 1993:172, fn. 21).

In the case of two identical vowels, they may be reduced to the duration of a single vowel so that, for instance, *estaba hablando* /estába ablándo/ is often produced [estáβaβláṉdo]; that is, identical to *estaba blando* 'it was soft'. Even three identical unstressed vowels in a row may be contracted to the duration of a single vowel, as in *iba a Alicante* /íba a alikánte/ [iβalikáṉte] 'I / s/he was going to Alicante' (Monroy Casas 1980:65). More exactly, these sequences of identical vowels are subject to gradient reduction in duration; in some cases the total duration of the sequences is not longer than that of a single vowel in the same context. Additional examples:

te esperamos	/te esperámos/	[tesperámos]	'we await you'
lo ocultamos	/lo okultámos/	[lokul̯támos]	'we hide it'
estaba aquí	/estába akí/	[estáβakí]	'it was here'

5.5 Resyllabification and contraction

It is possible to have contraction also if one of the two vowels is lexically stressed, in which case its stress may be reduced (i.e., not associated with a pitch accent, see Chapter 14):

ha estado	/á estádo/	[áestáðo] ~ [a̯estáðo]	'has been'
está aquí	/está aquí/	[estákí] ~ [estakí]	'is here'
pedí otra	/pedí ótra/	[peði̯ótra]	'I asked for another'

Syllable contraction is particularly likely between words with a close syntactic link, such as determiners and nouns, clitic pronouns and verbs, etc. The Spanish poetic tradition takes the possibility of these processes into account for counting syllables in a line of verse. For instance, the line *te ofrecemos nuestra vida* 'we offer you our life' will usually count as eight syllables:

teo-fre-ce-mos-nues-tra-vi-da   = 8 syllables

Nevertheless, in accordance with the optionality of applying contraction in normal speech, the possibility of syllabifying without contraction and counting nine syllables in this example is in no way excluded.

5.5.3 Reduction of word-internal vowel sequences in colloquial speech

In rapid or colloquial speech, word-internal heterosyllabic sequences can undergo the same processes of reduction as the identical sequences across word boundaries, especially in intonationally weak positions. Reduction to a single syllable may affect sequences containing only mid and low vowels (which, as we know, in careful speech are always in hiatus), sequences of identical vowels, and also words with exceptional hiatus with a high vowel, as shown in the examples in Table 5.15 (in regular orthography with indication of syllabification).

Because of this reduction process, in colloquial speech the lexical contrast between, for instance, *va riendo* [bár̄i.éndo] 's/he goes about laughing', with exceptional hiatus, and *barriendo* [bar̄i̯éndo] 'sweeping' may thus be neutralized.[19] This also applies to contrasts between single vowels and sequences of identical vowels as in *azar* 'chance' vs *azahar* 'orange blossom'; *pasemos* 'we pass, *subjunct.*' vs *paseemos* 'we take a walk, *subjunct.*', etc.

The likelihood of word-internal reduction depends on the dialect and, to a certain extent, on the specific word. In many Latin American dialects reductions are common even in careful speech. Castilian has a greater tendency to preserve

---

[19] Example from Alarcos Llorach (1965:155).

Table 5.15 Reduction of heterosyllabic sequences of vowels in colloquial speech.

Careful speech	Reduction	
1. Different nonhigh vowels		
to-a-lla	t*o*a-lla	'towel'
al-mo-ha-da	al-m*o*(h)a-da	'pillow'
pe-le-a-mos	pe-l*e*a-mos	'we fight'
2. Identical vowels		
al-ba-ha-ca	alb[a]ca	'basil'
cre-e-mos	cr[e]mos	'we believe'
3. Exceptional hiatus		
en-vi-a-mos	en-v*i̯*a-mos	'we send'
li-a-ba	l*i̯*a-ba	'I tangled'

lexical hiatuses, both those with nonhigh vowels and exceptional ones with high vowels:

	Castilian careful	e.g. Colombian	
pelear	pel[e.a]r	pel[i̯a]r	'to fight'
enviar	env[i.a]r	env[i̯a]r	'to send'
cambiar	camb[i̯a]r	camb[i̯a]r	'to change'

As shown in the examples, in careful Castilian speech, there is a hiatus both in *pelear* 'to fight' with a sequence /ea/ and in *enviar* 'to send', which has an exceptional hiatus /i.a/ (cf. *envía* 's/he sends'). (As mentioned, words with exceptional hiatus also allow a syllabification with a diphthong, but crucially not vice versa, so that, in Castilian, the word *enviar* can be pronounced as either [em.bi.ár] or [em.bi̯ár], but *cambiar* can be only be [kam.bi̯ár].) In the same style, however, Colombians and other Latin Americans will often produce these sequences as a diphthong, and the three words in our example may 'rhyme'.

As for sequences of identical vowels, although they tend to be reduced to the duration of a single vowel in non-affected speech in many words, e.g. *alcohol* [alkól] 'alcohol', Navarro Tomás (1977:153–4) notices that some less frequent words such as *mohoso* 'mouldy', and *loor* 'praise', are rarely reduced in the Castilian pronunciation that is the object of his description.

The most extreme case of reduction involves stressed high vowels in hiatus. These sequences can sometimes become tautosyllabic phrase-internally when they do not receive intonational prominence. For instance, *serían las tres y media*

5.5 Resyllabification and contraction

Table 5.16 Contraction in sequences of three or more vocoids.

Careful speech	Sequence	Reduction	
al-go-aus-te-ro	/o-au/	al-goaus-te-ro	'somewhat austere'
á-re-a-es-tre-cha	/e-a-e/	á-reaes-tre-cha	'narrow area'
im-pe-rio-in-glés	/io-i/	im-pe-rioin-glés	'English empire'
Vic-to-ria-Eu-ge-nia	/ia-eu/	Vic-to-riaeu-ge-nia	'Victoria Eugenia'
pe-tró-le-o-ar-gen-ti-no	/e-o-a/	pe-tró-leoar-gen-ti-no	'Argentinian petrol'

'it may have been three thirty' may be pronounced [serián lastrés‿i méðia]. Historically, this process can be seen to have operated in the evolution of words such as VIGINTĪ > v[e.í]nte > v[éi̯]nte 'twenty', RĒGĪNA > r[e.í]na > r[éi̯]na 'queen'. Nowadays the adverb *ahí* 'there', together with a pronunciation in hiatus [a.í], also has a diphthong pronunciation [ái̯], especially when not phrase-final: *ahí está* 'there it is'. The adverb *ahora* 'now', besides its careful form [a.óra], presents a colloquial form [áora] or [áu̯ra], depending on the dialect. As noted in 2.3.1, in Mexican Spanish some reduced forms have acquired a specialized meaning. Thus, whereas *maestro* [ma.éstro] is the regular word for 'teacher', the reduced form [mái̯stro] is used for 'master bricklayer'.

5.5.4 Sequences of three or more vocoids

Some sequences of three or more vocoids can also be reduced to a single syllable (and be counted as a single syllable in poetry). The syllables resulting from this contraction process can be much more complex than those present lexically; that is, in citing words and in careful speech. Recall that in careful speech the only possible diphthongs are those containing [i̯] or [u̯] and that there is at most one such glide on either side of the nuclear vowel. Examples of complex sequences are given in Table 5.16.

As explained in section 5.2, a syllable has a single sonority peak, with decreasing sonority on both sides of the peak. It follows that only groups of vocoids with a single sonority peak are reducible to a single syllable. If we consider the degree of aperture (low–mid–high) of the vowels involved, it is easy to see that all the groups in the examples in Table 5.16 satisfy the criterion of presenting a uniform sonority curve, Table 5.17.[20]

---

[20] Within the sonority curve, we may, however, have 'flat areas', as in the example *petróleo Argentino*, where the peak /a/ is preceded by two mid vowels. What is not possible is to go up, down and up again in sonority within a single syllable. Recall also that in sequences of two unstressed mid vowels the first one is weaker.

Table 5.17 Sonority curves in sequences of vocoids reducible to a single syllable.

Low	a	a	a	a
Mid	o	e e	o	e
High	u	i i	i	u
	alg**o au**stero	*á***rea e**strecha	*imper***io in**glés	*Victor***ia Eu**genia

Table 5.18a Sequences not reducible to a single syllable.

Careful speech	Sequence	Reduction (2 syllables)	
una-u-otra	/a-u-o/	*una-u̯o-tra*	'one or the other'
sale-y-entra	/e-i-e/	*sale-yen-tra*	'it leaves and enters'
rey-antiguo	/ei-a/	*re-yan-ti-guo*	'ancient king'

Table 5.18b Sonority curves in sequences not reducible to a single syllable.

Low	a		a
Mid	o	e e	e
High	u	i	i
	una **u** otra	sal**e y** entra	r**ey a**ntiguo

On the other hand, it is not possible to have reduction to a single syllable when there is more than one sonority peak, as in the examples in Table 5.18.

As can be seen, in these sequences not reducible to a single syllable, the sonority goes down from a peak and up again, resulting in two peaks of sonority in the sequence.

5.6 Contrasts in syllabification

In Spanish, we find contrasts of syllabification in two cases. First of all, the presence of a transparent prefix boundary acts as a barrier for the syllabification of two types of sequences of segments that are tautosyllabic when occurring in other word-internal contexts: (a) sequences of plosive or /f/ and liquid, and (b) consonant plus glide sequences. Examples are given in Table 5.19.

Table 5.19 Contrasts in syllabification.

(a) plosive, /f/ + liquid groups		
sublingual /sub.liŋuál/ 'sublingual' vs	*sublime* /sublíme/ 'sublime'	
subregión /sub.r̄exión/ 'subregion' vs	*sobrino* /sobríno/ 'nephew'	
(b) consonant + glide groups		
deshielo /des.iélo/ [dezjélo] vs 'thawing'	*desierto* /desiérto/ [desi̯érto] 'desert'	
deshuesa /des.uésa/ [dezɣu̯ésa] vs 's/he debones'	*resuena* /r̄esuéna/ [r̄esu̯éna] 'it resonates'	

Besides examples like *deshielo* with an obvious morphological decomposition that explains their syllabification, we also find the consonant [j] in postconsonantal position in a few examples without a transparent prefix boundary, like *cónyuge* 'spouse' (vs *boniato* 'sweet potato') and *abyecto* 'abject' (vs *abierto* 'open'). As discussed in 9.3, these cases can be analysed as containing an anomalous syllable boundary (historically they also derive from prefixation).

In addition, as we saw above, there is a lexical contrast between sequences where unstressed high vowels are realized regularly as glides and lexical exceptions where the Gliding rule does not apply. The spectrograms in Fig. 5.1 illustrate the contrast between diphthong (*italiana*) and exceptional hiatus (*la liana*).

5.7 Syllable contact

Words are made of one or more well-formed syllables. It follows that the phonological structure of words can be derived in part from the structure of the syllable. There are, nevertheless, some additional constraints and generalizations that affect possible sequences of segments across syllable boundaries within the word. We refer to these generalizations as 'syllable-contact' rules. One such rule is that in Spanish there are no sequences of identical consonants (geminates) within word domains, unlike in Latin or in Italian. There are no words like *[ál.la], *[és.so], *[áp.pa], etc. There are very few exceptions to this rule, with /bb/ (*obvio* 'obvious', *subvención* 'subvention'), and with /nn/ (*perenne* 'perennial', and the scientific term *pinnípedo* 'seals and related animals'). If we include the productive prefix *in-* within the word domain, then there are a few more examples with /nn/ as well as the assimilated sequence [mm], e.g. *innombrable*

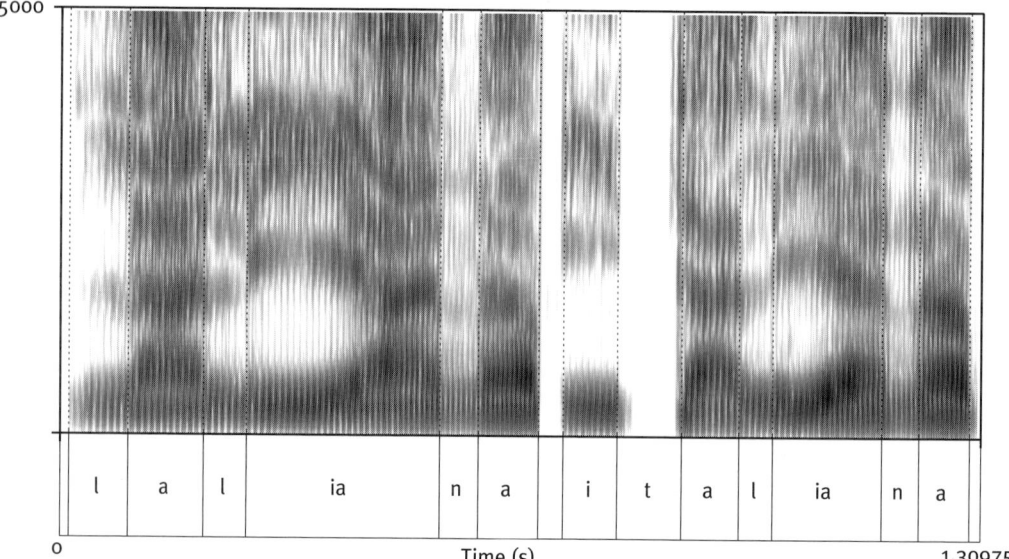

Figure 5.1. Spectrogram of the examples *la liana* 'the liana', with exceptional hiatus [i.á], and *italiana* 'Italian, *fem.*', with a diphthong [iá]. Notice the much greater duration of the hiatus sequence of *liana*, which contains a clearly segmentable high vowel [i] before [a].

'unnamable', *inmortal* [immoɾtál] 'immortal'. No other word-internal geminates are found. The prefix *des-* regularly becomes *de-* before *s-* as in *desalar* 'to desalinate'. (For the realization of these sequences across word boundaries, see next section.)

There is a tendency for coda consonants to have greater sonority than immediately following syllable-initial consonants. This is only a tendency, since /s/ may be commonly followed by more sonorous segments in the next syllable, as in *isla* 'island', *mismo* 'same', etc. A fact that is in accordance with this syllable-contact tendency, however, is the rarity of plosives in word-internal codas.

Furthermore, in sequences of two plosives across syllable boundaries, there is a restriction that affects their point of articulation. In such sequences, the second consonant is always a dental and the first one cannot be dental. We thus find the sequences /pt/, /kt/, as in *apto* 'apt', *acto* 'act', but not the reverse sequences */tp/, */tk/. The only exceptions are found in recent borrowings from English (*fútbol* 'football', *básquetbol* 'basket ball', *rugby*) and across prefix boundaries, transparent (*adposición* 'adposition', *subcomisión* 'subcommittee') or opaque (*adverbio* 'adverb', *advertir* 'warn').

5.8 Identical consonants across word barriers

Table 5.20 Identical consonants across word barriers.

a) Groups reducible to the duration of a single consonant
/ss/ → ~ [s]   *ojos secos* 'dry eyes', *los sacos* 'the bags'
/θθ/ → ~ [θ]   *paz cercana* 'approaching peace', *luz cegadora* 'blinding light'
/dd/ → ~ [ð]   *edad de oro* 'golden age', *ciudad destruida* 'destroyed town'
/rr̄/ → ~ [r̄]   *vender ropa* 'to sell clothes', *Mar Rojo* 'Red Sea'

b) Groups usually realized as a longer consonant
/nn/ → [n:]   *avión nuevo* 'new aeroplane', *comen nabos* 'they eat turnips'
/ll/ → [l:]   *papel liviano* 'light paper', *mal lago* 'bad lake'

Another restriction is that word-internal nasals are always homorganic with following segments. There are no words with sequences such as */mt/.[21] The only exceptions are found with the sequence /mn/, which occurs in examples such as *himno* 'hymn', *columna* 'column' and *alumno* 'student'.

5.8 Sequences of identical consonants across word boundaries

Across word boundaries, when two identical consonants (or nearly identical, in the case of /rr̄/) are found, the group tends to be reduced in duration (Navarro Tomás 1977:175–6; Quilis 1993:375–6). The amount of reduction, however, is not the same for all such groups. In particular, the groups /ss/, /θθ/, /dd/ and /rr̄/ are much more likely to be reduced to the duration of a single consonant than the groups /nn/ and /ll/ (Table 5.20).[22]

The consonants which can undergo the greatest reduction in groups of two identical segments are thus those with a continuant realization (including /d/, which is realized as continuant [ð] in this context, see 8.1). The noncontinuant consonants /n/ and /l/ (which are produced with full contact between the articulators), on the other hand, are more distinctly produced as long or geminated when occurring in sequences across word boundaries. This also applies to the examples of word-internal /nn/ discussed in the section above.

In a controlled reading experiment reported in Hualde (2004), although a statistically significant difference in duration was found between /s/ and /ss/ (e.g. *sabe siempre* 's/he always knows', *tenga sólo* 'I have only' vs *sabes siempre* 'you always know', *tengas sólo* 'you have only') and between /r̄/ and /rr̄/ (e.g. *salí*

---

[21] When they arose historically, these sequences underwent either nasal assimilation as in COMITE > *comde > conde 'count', LIMITE > *limde > linde 'limit', or consonant epenthesis, as in NŌMINE > *nomne > *nomre > nombre 'name', depending on the specific sequence (see, e.g., Penny 2002:87–90).

[22] In Table 5.20, the symbol '~' is to be interpreted as 'approaches the duration of'.

rápido 'I left quickly', *dormí roncando* 'I slept snoring' vs *salir rápido* 'to leave quickly', *dormir roncando* 'to sleep snoring'), this difference was of only about 20 ms on average in both cases, and much smaller than the difference between /n/ and /nn/ (e.g. *dará nada* 's/he will give nothing', *come nueces* 'it eats walnuts' vs *darán nada* 'they will give nothing', *comen nueces* 'they eat walnuts'), which was of over 50 ms on average.[23]

EXERCISES

1. Divide the following examples in to syllables:

    *destrucción, extraordinario, balaustrada, estropeáis
    boina, mohíno, feísimo, peine, bohío, caíais, muestreo*

2. Syllabify the following phrases, first with careful syllabification and then applying all possible contractions, as in the model. Indicate semivowels (glides) with the half-moon diacritic.

    *poeta italiano   po-e-ta-i-ta-li̯a-no   po̯e-tai̯-ta-li̯a-no
    puedo estar
    pierde aceite
    fuente hermosa
    viene Emilio*

3. One of the rules of orthographic accent in Spanish is that all words stressed on the antepenultimate syllable bear an accent mark. Syllabify the following examples employing careful or 'citation-form' syllabification (which is the one that is taken into account for the orthographic accent rules) and explain why they have an accent mark or why they do not:

    petróleo, monopolio, área, baila, imperio, línea, continuo

4. In the Spanish poetic tradition, metrically equivalent lines of verse have the same number of syllables up to the last stressed syllable in the line. For instance, the most common traditional line has seven syllables up to the last stress. If the line ends with a word with penultimate stress, this results in eight syllables to the end of the line. If the final syllable of the line is stressed, then the line will have exactly seven syllables. If the line ends with a word with antepenultimate stress, on the other hand, the line will have nine syllables (= seven up to the last stress). It is traditional to use the unmarked penultimate stress pattern as point of reference. For instance, the measure

---

[23] The average duration of /n/ was 73 ms and that of /nn/, 125 ms. Notice that this is still less than twice the duration of /n/. For the other segments tested, average values across tokens and speakers were /s/ = 102 ms vs /ss/ = 123 ms, /ɾ/ = 56 ms, /rr̄/ = 79 ms.

that we are discussing is referred to as *octosílabos* or 'eight-syllable' lines, which is the number of syllables to the end when the line ends with stress on the penultimate syllable of the line. The following stanzas from the beginning of 'Canción del Pirata' by José de Espronceda (1808–42) contain 'eight-syllable lines' (= seven syllables up to the last stress), which means that the fourth and eighth lines should have exactly seven syllables (traditionally said to count as 7 + 1 empty beat), since they end in a stressed syllable:

> *Con diez cañones por banda,*
> *viento en popa, a toda vela,*
> *no corta el mar, sino vuela*
> *un velero bergantín.*
> *Bajel pirata que llaman,*
> *por su bravura, el Temido,*
> *en todo el mar conocido*
> *del uno al otro confín.*

Count the syllables in these lines, indicating all contractions that must be made to obtain the correct number of syllables. The first four lines are counted for you; follow the model for the remaining four:

Con | diez | ca | ño | nes | por | b**a**n | da = 8
 1   2   3   4   5   6   7

vien | to‿en | po | pa‿a | to | da | v**e** |la = 8
  1   2   3   4   5 6   7

no | cor |ta‿el | mar | si |no | v**ue** |la = 8
 1   2   3   4   5 6   7

un | ve | le | ro | ber |gan|t**í**n = 7 + 1
 1   2   3   4   5   6   7

Now count the syllables in this stanza, from the same poem:

> *¿Qué es mi barco? mi tesoro,*
> *¿qué es mi dios? la libertad,*
> *mi ley, la fuerza y el viento,*
> *mi única patria, la mar.*

The word *riela* in the first line of the following stanza, also from the same poem, has an exceptional hiatus; count the syllables:

> *La luna en el mar riela,*
> *en la lona gime el viento*
> *y alza en blando movimiento*
> *olas de plata y azul.*

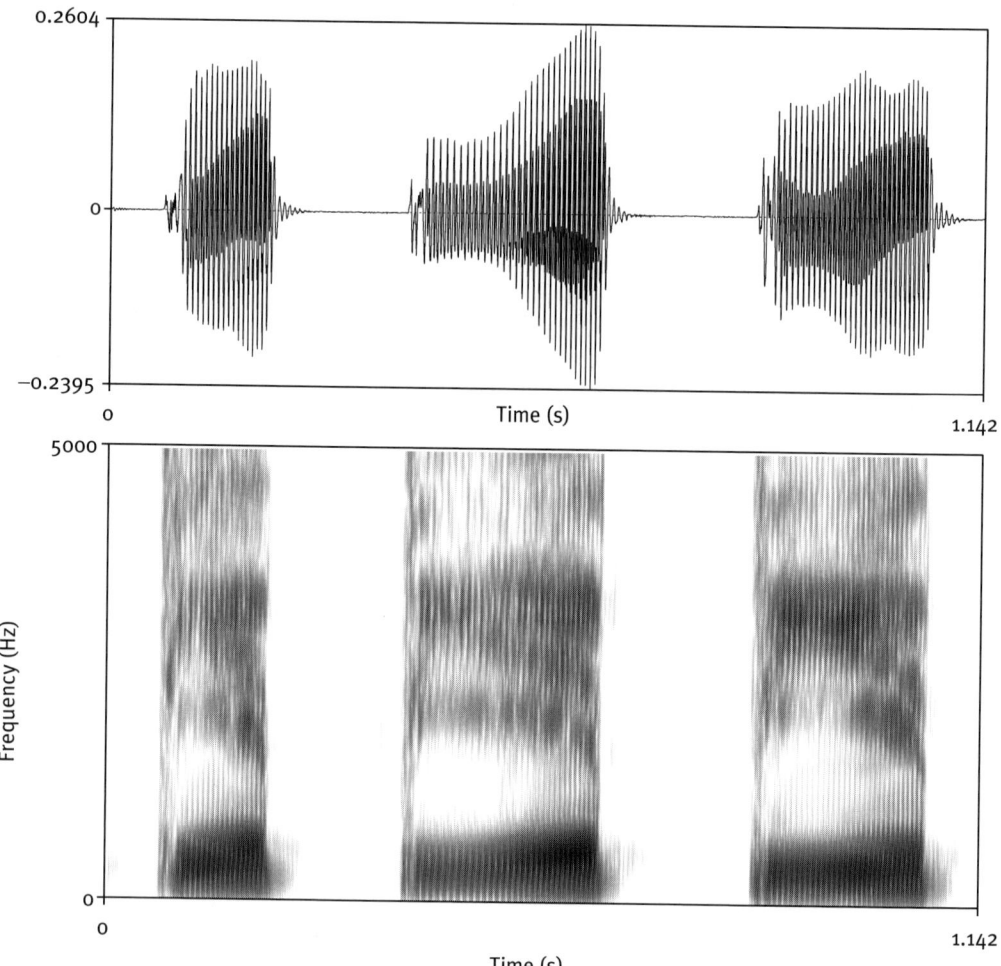

Figure 5.2. Waveforms and spectrograms of the contrasting triplet *pie* 'foot', *pié* 'I chirped' and *píe* '(that) I/s/he chirp'.

> The following two stanzas by Luis de Góngora (1561–1627) also contain 'eight-syllable' lines; count the syllables:
>
> *Ciego que apuntas y atinas,*
> *caduco dios, y rapaz,*
> *vendado que me has vendido,*
> *y niño mayor de edad,*
> *por el alma de tu madre*
> *– que murió, siendo inmortal,*
> *de envidia de mi señora –,*
> *que no me persigas más.*

> *Diez años desperdicié,*
> *los mejores de mi edad,*
> *en ser labrador de amor*
> *a costa de mi caudal.*
> *Como aré y sembré, cogí.*
> *Aré un alterado mar,*
> *sembré una estéril arena,*
> *cogí vergüenza y afán.*

5. Consider Fig. 5.2, which contains waveforms and spectrograms for the contrasting triplet *pie* [pi̯é] 'foot', *pié* [pi.é] 'I chirped' and *píe* [pí.e] 'I /s/he chirp, *subjunct*.', in that order. What differences do you observe?

6 Main phonological processes

6.1 Introduction

In this chapter, we will define the main types of phonological processes, providing examples both from present-day Spanish and from the historical evolution of the language. By phonological process, we mean any phenomenon that affects the realization of phonemes in specific contexts in a significant way. In the case of the most important types of phonological process, such as neutralization and assimilation, we will consider the analytical solutions provided by different phonological schools.

6.2 Neutralization of phonemic contrasts

We have defined phonemes as contrastive sounds in a language. However, there are cases where two sounds that are generally found in phonemic opposition fail to contrast in some specific environment. To give an example from English, it is clear that in English /p/ and /b/ are distinct phonemes, as it is easy to come up with minimal pairs that prove the existence of this phonemic contrast. The contrast is found word initially (*pit* vs *bit*), word medially (*rapid* vs *rabid*) and word finally (*lap* vs *lab*). Following word-initial /s/, on the other hand, there is no such contrast. We have words like *spot, speak, spate* and many others with this sequence but not **sbot, *sbeak, *sbate*. Furthermore, if a word written *sbot* actually existed it would be pronounced exactly the same as *spot*. There is no possible /p/ vs /b/ contrast in this context in English. We say that, in English, the /p/ vs /b/ contrast is neutralized after initial /s/. (This also applies to /t/ vs /d/ and /k/ vs /g/).

An important generalization about Spanish phonology is that many phonological contrasts that obtain in the onset of the syllable are neutralized in the coda (A. Alonso 1945).

6.2 Neutralization of phonemic contrasts

Starting with the nasal consonants, in syllable-initial position we find three phonemes which contrast in place of articulation: bilabial /m/, alveolar /n/ and palatal /ɲ/ (as in *cama* 'bed', *cana* 'grey hair' and *caña* 'cane'). This contrast is, however, not found in the coda. In word-internal codas, there is no possible contrast in place among nasals. Nasal consonants in this position always have the same place of articulation as the following consonant: *campo* [kámpo] 'field', *énfasis* [éɱfasis] 'emphasis', *tanto* [tán̪to] 'so much', *ansia* [áns̪i̯a] 'anxiety', *ancho* [án̠ʲt͡ʃo] 'wide', *hongo* [óŋgo] 'fungus', etc. That is, for instance, [kampo] is a possible Spanish word, but neither *[kanpo] nor *[kaɲpo] are possible Spanish words; these could only be anomalous pronunciations of [kámpo]. Similarly, we have [tan̪to] but not *[tamto], etc.[1] The contrasts among the nasal phonemes are neutralized in this position. This neutralization in place of articulation also extends to word-final nasals. Word-finally, we find only [n] (or [ŋ] in velarizing dialects). A look at a Spanish dictionary will reveal that (except for a few unassimilated borrowings) there are not any other nasals but -*n* at the end of Spanish words (unlike in English where we have the three-way contrast in place illustrated by, for instance, *sum* vs *sun* vs *sung*). Like in the word-internal coda context, word-final nasals also assimilate in place to a following consonant.

Regarding the plosives, the contrast between two members of the voiceless/voiced pairs /p/-/b/, /t/-/d/, /k/-/g/ is again robust in the onset of the syllable, but much less so in the coda. A common pattern is the neutralization of the contrast in voice for each point of articulation. For instance, in spite of the orthographic difference, the *p* in the coda of the first syllable of *apto*, *óptico*, *óptimo*, etc., is not pronounced differently from the *b* of *obtener*, *obstáculo*, etc. In both sets of words we have [β] in a neutral style and [p] in emphatic pronunciation (other intermediate realizations are also possible): *apto* [áβto] ∼ [ápto], *obtiene* [oβti̯éne] ∼ [opti̯éne]. A possible word *abto* would not be different from *apto* in its pronunciation. This is a neutralization in voice. (Other neutralizations among obstruents in this position take place in different dialects, see 8.2.)

The rhotics (*r* segments) present a special case in Spanish, as the contrast between tap /ɾ/ and trill /r̄/ is limited to the word-internal intervocalic position. But leaving other contexts aside (see 11.2), there is neutralization in coda position, as with the other sets of segments mentioned in the preceding paragraphs. There is no possible contrast between, e.g., [páɾte] and [pár̄te]; rather, these are two realizations of the same word *parte* pronounced with lesser or greater emphasis, or in different dialects. We may say that what we have in

---

[1] Except for the group /mn/, as in *alumno* 'student'.

Table 6.1 The nasal archiphoneme (European Structuralism).

orthography	phonological representation	phonetic representation
campo 'field'	/káNpo/	[kámpo]
énfasis 'emphasis'	/éNfasis/	[émfasis]
tanto 'so much'	/táNto/	[tán̪to]
ansia 'anxiety'	/áNsia/	[ánsi̯a]
ancho 'wide'	/áNt͡ʃo/	[ánʲt͡ʃo]
anca 'haunch'	/áNka/	[áŋka]
pan 'bread'	/páN/	[pán] ([páŋ])

this preconsonantal position is a nondistinct rhotic which in a broad phonetic transcription we may represent simply as [r]: [párte].

Another process of neutralization of importance in Spanish dialectology is the neutralization of liquids, found in southern Spain and the Caribbean. In these varieties, there is no contrast between rhotics and liquids in the coda. That is, words such as *harto* 'full' and *alto* 'tall' are homophonous.[2]

6.2.1 Neutralization and phonological schools

A theoretical problem that arises in situations of neutralization of phonemic distinctions is that of ascribing the occurring pronunciations to one phoneme of the language or another. For instance, is the bilabial nasal [m] of *campo* [kámpo] 'field' an instance of the phoneme /m/ or of /n/ (or perhaps of /ɲ/, since there is no possible contrast)? And what about the labiodental nasal [ɱ] of *énfasis* [émfasis] 'emphasis', and the velar nasal of *tengo* [téŋgo] 'I have'?

Within the phonological school known as European Structuralism (which has its roots in the Prague Circle, active in the first decades of the twentieth century), the general solution in cases of neutralization is to postulate an ARCHIPHONEME. An archiphoneme represents the result of the neutralization of two or more phonemes in a given context. For instance, in the case at hand, we would postulate a nasal archiphoneme /N/ (archiphonemes are represented with capital letters by convention). We would say that, in Spanish, in the coda of the syllable, the three nasal phonemes labial /m/, alveolar /n/ and palatal /ɲ/ are replaced by a nasal archiphoneme /N/, whose place of articulation is not contrastive or pertinent, as in Table 6.1 (see

---

[2] In *lleísta* dialects (i.e. those with a phoneme /ʎ/), the contrast between the alveolar lateral /l/ and the palatal lateral /ʎ/ (e.g. *ola* /óla/ 'wave' vs *olla* /óʎa/ 'cooking pot') is also neutralized in the coda.

6.2 Neutralization of phonemic contrasts

Alarcos Llorach 1965; Quilis 1993; among others). It is important to keep in mind that the nasal archiphoneme is not a fourth nasal phoneme, but, rather, the result of the neutralization of the three nasal phonemes.

Within generative approaches that incorporate the principle of UNDER-SPECIFICATION, the phonological solution is similar to that offered by the European Structuralist analysis: in the coda we have a nasal with a phonologically unspecified place of articulation, which receives a surface specification by rule (see, for instance, J. Harris 1984).

In most other phonology approaches, archiphonemes are not employed and all surface realizations are necessarily assigned to one of the recognized phonemes of the language instead. In our example one of the nasal phonemes of Spanish would have to be chosen in the phonologization of nasals in the coda.

The solution that we will adopt in our phonological representations is to write /n/ in word-final position (e.g. *pan* /pán/ [pán] ~ in velarizing dialects [páŋ]), since, when resyllabified, word-final nasals are clearly realizations of /n/: *pa*[n] *amargo* 'bitter bread'. As for the word-internal preconsonantal position, we will write /N/, which is to be understood as a nasal whose actual place of articulation is determined by the following consonant; e.g. /káNpo/, /éNfasis/, etc.

Let us now consider the other main cases of neutralization in Spanish that we mentioned in the section above.

In standard Castilian Spanish (as described in Navarro Tomás 1977; Quilis 1993; etc.) and other dialects where the contrast between voiced and voiceless plosives is neutralized in the coda, the archiphonemes /P T K/ are postulated in a Praguean structuralist analysis: *técnica* /téKnika/ [téɣnika] ~ [téknika] 'technique', *digno* /díKno/ [díɣno] ~ [díkno] 'worthy'. Again, in a generative analysis with underspecification, a similar solution could be adopted: a plosive unspecified for the feature of voice.

Regarding the rhotics, at the phonological level, the European structuralist solution would be to postulate an archiphoneme /R/ representing the neutralization of tap and trill in coda position: *parte* /páRte/ 'part', *amor* /amóR/ 'love'. In this book, instead, we will represent word-final rhotics as taps in phonemic representations. This is justified by the fact that this is the way they are realized when resyllabified, as in *da*[ɾ] *otro* 'to give another one'. As with the nasals, the choice of phoneme is less obvious in the case of word-internal preconsonantal rhotics. We will assign word-internal preconsonantal rhotics also to the phoneme /ɾ/ because this corresponds to the most common realization, with the understanding that there is a rule of variable strengthening applying to coda /ɾ/, both word internally and word finally (not when resyllabified):

Main phonological processes

Table 6.2 Consonantal phonemes of conservative Castilian Spanish.

	labial	dental	alveolar	(pre)palatal	velar
plosives	p	t			k
	b	d			g
fricatives	f	θ	s		x
affricates				ʝ	
				t͡ʃ	
nasals	m		n	ɲ	
laterals			l	ʎ	
rhotic tap			ɾ		
rhotic trill			r̄		

/párte/ [párte] ~ [párte], /amór/ [amór] ~ [amór̄], but *amor herido* /amór erído/ [amóreríðo] 'wounded love' (without possible strengthening in this case).

In addition to the neutralization of the two rhotics in coda position, in other environments, aside from the word-internal intervocalic context, there is no contrast either, because only one of the two rhotics occurs. In particular, word initially only the trill is found. There is [r̄áta] 'rat', but *[ɾáta] is not a possible Spanish word. In fact, in discourse, it is possible to find minimal pairs such as *a Roma* [ar̄óma] 'to Rome' vs *aroma* [ɾóma] 'aroma'. (The distribution of the rhotics is described in detail in 11.3.) In standard European structuralist analyses, we would also have an archiphoneme /R/ in this case, /Ráta/, obligatorily realized with a trill in this position, [r̄áta] (Alarcos Llorach 1965:98, 183–4; Canellada and Kuhlmann Madsen 1987:13). In other structuralist analyses, however, it is postulated that in this case we are dealing with the DEFECTIVE DISTRIBUTION of a phoneme (the tap simply does not occur word initially), and phonemically we would have /r̄áta/, without postulating an archiphoneme in this case (Quilis 1993:42).

We will finish this section by presenting a complete phonemic analysis of the Spanish consonant system following the postulates of European structuralism. The conservative (*lleísta*) variety of Castilian Spanish described by Navarro Tomás, Alarcos Llorach, Quilis and other authors has the consonantal phonemic inventory shown in Table 6.2.

If we consider only consonants in coda position, on the other hand, we see that the set of contrastive segments in this position is much smaller. In terms of archiphonemes, we have the inventory in Table 6.3.

Some Spanish dialects have somewhat different inventories and would also have different sets of archiphonemes, since the neutralization rules applying

Table 6.3 System of phonologically contrastive consonants in the coda in conservative Castilian Spanish (phonemes and archiphonemes – European structuralist analysis).

	labial	dental	alveolar	velar
plosives	P	T		K
fricatives	f	θ	s	x
nasal			N	
lateral			L	
rhotic			R	

to consonants in the coda are not identical in all dialects. In particular, in Andalusian and Caribbean dialects where *alto = harto*, one would postulate a single liquid archiphoneme in the coda, representing the neutralization of /l/, /ɾ/ and /r̄/ in a Praguean analysis.

6.3 Assimilation

ASSIMILATION is a process by which a segment acquires some features from another segment, becoming more similar to it. Assimilation may involve both consonants and vowels as both triggers and targets. Most assimilations are anticipatory phenomena; that is, they result in a segment anticipating some aspect of the articulation of a following segment (as in the labialization of the nasal in *u*[m] *pato* 'a duck'). Less commonly, however, we also find assimilations in the opposite direction (perseverative assimilation).

6.3.1 Consonant-to-consonant assimilation

In Spanish phonology, there are two important processes of assimilation affecting sequences of consonants. First of all, as mentioned in the previous section (and discussed in more detail in Chapter 10), nasals assimilate in place of articulation to an immediately following consonant, as in *un perro* [úm pér̄o] 'a dog'. Laterals also assimilate in place, but to a more reduced set of following consonants than nasals do (not to labials or velars, see 11.2): *el toro* [el̪tóɾo] 'the bull'.

The second important process is the assimilation in voice of fricatives. In many Spanish dialects, fricatives become voiced before voiced consonants: *isla* [ízla] 'island'. This process is optional and it is also often incomplete; that is, the fricative may become only partially voiced.

The most radical type of assimilation is total assimilation in all features, where a segment becomes identical to the trigger of the assimilation. In some varieties of Cuban and Chilean Spanish, liquids in the coda assimilate totally to certain following consonants, as in *pulga* [púgga] 'flea'. In Andalusian, /s/ in the coda may assimilate to a following segment in place and manner, but retaining features of aspiration or voicelessness, as in *costa* [kóʰtta] 'coast', *isla* [íl̥la] 'island', *mismo* [mím̥mo] 'same' (9.2.5.2.).

The fact that the prefix *in-* appears as *i-* before liquids, as in *ilegal* 'illegal', has its origin in a process of total assimilation in Latin, *in+legalis* > *illegalis* (with a geminate /ll/ in Latin).

All the examples that we have given are of coda consonants assimilating to consonants in the onset of a following syllable. Cross-linguistically this is the most common type of assimilation between consonants.

6.3.2 Consonant-to-vowel assimilation

The most common process whereby a consonant assimilates to a vowel is palatalization. Palatalization generally involves either dental/alveolar or velar consonants becoming palatal or prepalatal before a front glide or a front vowel (the palatalization of labials is more rare). In the history of Spanish and the other Romance languages, processes of palatalization of both dental/alveolar and velar consonants are pervasive. Many alveolar or dental consonants palatalized before a glide as in Lat. SENIŌRE > *señor*. Velars palatalized, not only before glides, but also before the front vowels /i/, /e/, as in Lat. GEMMA > Sp. *yema* 'yolk'. These several palatalization processes are discussed at length in textbooks on the history of the Spanish language (see, for instance, Penny 2002:61–72). Brazilian Portuguese has a conspicuous phenomenon of palatalization of dentals as a synchronic process of allophony. In Standard Brazilian Portuguese /t/ is realized as [t͡ʃ] and /d/ as [d͡ʒ] before /i/, as in *tia* [t͡ʃía] 'aunt', *dia* [d͡ʒía] 'day'. In modern Spanish the most noticeable phenomenon of allophonic palatalization is found in Chilean, where the velar fricative /x/ becomes a palatal fricative [ç] before a front vowel or glide: *mujer* [muçéɾ] 'woman', *gente* [çén̪te] 'people'.

The palatalization of dentals and alveolars results from the temporal overlap of the consonantal gesture made with the tip or blade of the tongue with the raising and fronting of the body of the tongue involved in the production of the following vowel. Velars, on the other hand, share their active articulator with vowels, since they involve a constriction with the dorsum. Velars thus require some degree of coarticulation with following vowels. In probably all languages the constriction produced by velar consonants is somewhat more fronted before a front vowel and more retracted before a back vowel (cf. Eng. *car key*). When this coarticulation is increased beyond a certain point, it will result in distinctive palatal allophones, as it is the case in Chilean Spanish with the velar fricative /x/.

Although in most cases the palatalization of consonants is triggered by a following segment, palatalization by preceding vowels (perseverative assimilation) is not unattested. In modern Basque dialects alveolar nasals, laterals and sometimes other alveolar and dental obstruents are palatalized after /i/. For instance, *mutila* 'the boy', *mina* 'the pain', *ditut* 'I have them' are pronounced [mutiʎa], [miɲa], [dicut] in many Basque dialects (IPA [c] = voiceless palatal stop) (see, e.g., Hualde 1991b, 2003b). If we compare Portuguese *noite* 'night', *oito* 'eight', *leite* 'milk', *muito* 'much', *feito* 'done' with the corresponding Spanish cognates *noche, ocho, leche, mucho, hecho*, we will notice that, at a certain point in the evolution of Spanish, /t/ palatalized after a front glide.[3]

6.3.3 Vowel-to-vowel assimilation

Whereas assimilation processes involving consonants generally take place under strict adjacency, vowel-to-vowel assimilation often takes place at a distance, across consonants. In the evolution of Spanish a front glide in a following syllable (known as YOD in historical linguistics) often affected the quality of the stressed vowel, raising it. To give just one example, the presence of this yod in the following syllable is the reason for the difference in the root vowel that we now find in *llover* 'to rain' vs *lluvia* 'rain'.

The raising of the stressed vowel triggered by a final high vowel is known in Romance linguistics as METAPHONY. In many Italian dialects (although not in Standard Italian) metaphony is pervasive in inflectional paradigms. Robust patterns of metaphony are also found in Asturian co-dialects of Spanish, where masculine singular nouns and adjectives ending in -*u* have a higher stressed vowel than other forms of the morphological paradigm; e.g.: [gétu] 'he-cat' vs [gáta] 'she-cat', [gátos] 'cats' (see 7.4.2).

In the cases of vowel-to-vowel assimilation just mentioned only one vowel undergoes assimilation (the stressed vowel in our examples). Sometimes, however, a vowel triggers assimilation in height, backness/frontness or some other feature in all vowels in a given domain, such as the word. In such cases one speaks of VOWEL HARMONY. Vowel harmony is common in many languages of the world including Turkish, Hungarian, Finnish and many Bantu languages.[4] In the Spanish context, some obsolescent Cantabrian dialects present a vowel harmony process where mid vowels in all pretonic syllables in the word domain,

---

[3] To give another example, in German the distribution of the voiceless velar fricative [x] (*ach-Laut*) and the voiceless palatal fricative [ç] (*ich-Laut*) is determined by the preceding vowel, not by the following vowel, unlike in Chilean Spanish.

[4] In contrast, consonant harmony is a quite rare phenomenon and is generally limited to sibilants.

including clitics, become high when the stressed vowel is high; e.g. [koxeɾé] 'I will take' vs [kuxiɾía] 'I would take' for standard *cogeré* vs *cogería* (Penny 1969a, 1978; see 7.4.2). In Eastern Andalusian as well, some authors have noted the existence of a process of vowel harmony (see 7.4.1). In Eastern Andalusian, final mid vowels have a more open quality in words where a final /s/ has been lost, e.g. *pino* [píno] vs *pinos* [pínɔ] and this open quality may be transmitted to other mid vowels throughout the word, e.g.: *monótono* [monótono] vs *monótonos* [mɔnɔ́tɔnɔ].

6.3.4 Vowel-to-consonant assimilation

The assimilation of vowels to consonants is usually less apparent than the assimilation of consonants to vowels, generally remaining at the level of small phonetic effects. The opening of the mid vowels /e/, /o/, and the fronting of /a/ before weakened /s/ in Eastern Andalusian are a cases of vowels assimilating to consonants. In other dialects of Spanish as well, certain consonants have an effect on the allophony of mid vowels (see 7.1).

In English some coda consonants, including /r/, /l/ and /ŋ/, have a noticeable effect on the quality of preceding vowels. In addition, vowels are considerably longer before voiced than before voiceless consonants, which also results in changes in vowel quality (as in *mat* vs *mad*, *bit* vs *bid*, etc.). These effects are much less noticeable in Spanish.

A common vowel-to-consonant assimilation phenomenon is the nasalization of vowels in contact with nasal consonants. In English vowels may present considerable nasalization before a nasal, *can't* [kæ̃ʔ]. In Spanish as well, vowels have some degree of nasalization in contact with nasals, especially when the vowel is both preceded and followed by a nasal consonant, as in the second vowel in *semana* 'week', and before a nasal in the coda, as in *canto*. In Andalusian and Caribbean dialects coda-nasals produce considerable nasalization of preceding vowels. In fact, in these dialects the nasalization of the vowel is often the only remnant of a final nasal, e.g. *están* [ehtã] 'they are'. Processes of this type (nasalization of vowel with subsequent deletion of the triggering consonant) gave rise to phonemic nasalized vowels in languages such as Portuguese and French.

6.4 Dissimilation

Dissimilation is the opposite process from assimilation: it refers to cases where a segment becomes more different from another neighbouring segment. In Latin, the adjective-forming suffix - ĀLIS, as in ANNĀLIS 'yearly', CAPITĀLIS 'capital', NAVĀLIS 'naval', AEQUĀLIS 'equal, even', etc., dissimilated to -ĀRIS after another /l/, especially if immediately preceding, as in SINGULĀRIS 'alone, single'. The distribution of adjectival *-al* and *-ar* in Spanish is still to a great extent determined by this dissimilatory rule: *terrenal, celestial, temporal,* etc., vs *angular, regular, similar,* etc. Consider, for instance, the adjectives referring to points of articulation: *labial, dental, palatal* vs *alveolar, velar, uvular*.

Also included under dissimilation is the deletion of one of two identical or similar segments in a word domain. Cross-linguistically, dissimilation is a rare phenomenon and in modern Spanish we do not find any systematic phenomena of dissimilation, although some isolated morphophonological cases can be mentioned, in addition to the *-al* ~ *-ar* alternation inherited from Latin.

A morphologically conditioned instance of dissimilation is the deletion of *-s* in first person plural verb forms when followed by the clitic pronoun *nos*; e.g.: *vamos* 'let's go' but *vámonos* (not **vámosnos*) 'let's leave'.

From a synchronic point of view, the occurrence of the clitic sequence *se lo* (*se la*, etc.) where we would expect **le lo* can be understood as a dissimilation; e.g.: *le di el libro a Juan* 'I gave the book to Juan', *se lo di a Juan* 'I gave it to Juan' (not **le lo di*), although the historical origin of this rule is quite different (see Penny 2002:136).

6.5 Weakening and deletion

Most phonological evolution consists of the reduction of articulatory gestures (including assimilation as a type of reduction). The ultimate stage in the reduction of a segment is its complete deletion. For instance, in the evolution from Lat. AMĪCA [ami:ka] to Sp. *amiga* [amíɣa] we can distinguish two weakening or lenition phenomena, first the voicing of the intervocalic plosive and then the reduction in the magnitude of the oral consonantal gesture, where the articulators only approximate instead of producing full occlusion: [amí:ka] > [amíga] > [amíɣa]. If we compare the French cognate *amie*, we observe that in this language there has been a further step, the deletion of the segment.

Reductions first appear in the most colloquial styles, from there they may be extended to formal styles and then eventually may become part of the standard pronunciation. When the older pronunciation finally disappears we say that there has been a sound change. Continuing with the lenition of the Latin voiceless stops, we see that nowadays in many Spanish dialects in the case of participles in *-ado* (ultimately from Lat. -ĀTUM) a colloquial pronunciation in [-ao] or even [-au̯] competes with a more formal pronunciation in [-aðo]. Illustrating with an example, the evolution has been Lat.

AMĀTUM > [amátu] > [amádo] > [amáðo] > [amáo] > [amáu̯], where the last three pronunciations are found in northern Spain corresponding to different degrees of formality/colloquialness and pronunciations further to the left in this chain are no longer possible.

A well-studied case in Spanish is the weakening of syllable- and word-final /s/. In many Spanish dialects where the weakening of /s/ to [h] or zero is very frequent in colloquial styles, speakers have a much higher rate of conservation of [s] in their formal styles. In the Dominican Republic, where the weakening of /s/ is particularly advanced, both pronunciations with [s] and with [h] are considered somewhat formal, since the most colloquial pronunciation completely eliminates this segment. In French, the same process of /s/ weakening was brought to completion some centuries ago as we can see when we compare Spanish words such as *fiesta* 'party', *espina* 'thorn', *pasta* 'dough', *escuela* 'school', *esposa* 'wife' and many others with their French cognates, respectively for these examples, *fête, épine, pâte, école, épouse*.

From the perspective of the synchronic phonological analysis of a language, we are concerned with two main types of weakening processes (and this also applies to all other types of diachronic processes). First, we are interested in cases where there is synchronic variation (free or stylistic variation). As a case in point, the weakening of /s/ is part of the synchronic phonology of Spanish, since, for instance, all of [espína] ~ [ehpína] ~ [epína] are found in some dialects, but not of French, where there is no trace of the historical /s/ in any pronunciation of *épine*. (In French we are dealing with a completed sound change, only relevant for the history of the language.)

Secondly, we are concerned with cases where evolutionary weakening of phonemes in certain contexts (but not in others) has resulted in distinct allophones in complementary distribution. An example is the weakening of /b d g/ in Spanish.

6.6 Strengthening

Fortition, the strengthening of articulatory gestures, is a comparatively rare phenomenon. From a historical point of view the trilling of word-initial rhotics in Spanish is a fortition.

As discussed above, the approximantization (spirantization)[5] of /b d g/ is essentially a lenition (or weakening) process. Nevertheless, in parts of Central

---

[5] The term *spirantization* is often found as the name of this phenomenon. *Spirant* is an alternate name for fricative. Since the relevant allophones of /b d g/ in Spanish are not really fricatives but, rather, approximants, *spirantization* is not an appropriate label.

America and Colombia, plosives, and not approximants, are regularly found in many contexts where other Spanish varieties have approximants (after all consonants and even glides) and in this case we are most likely dealing with a fortition. In addition, in the particular case of Latin [u̯] we find historical fortition. Consider, for example, the evolution Lat. VACCA [u̯ákka] > Sp. *vaca* /báka/ 'cow', pronounced with a plosive, [báka], in utterance-initial position.

The most important fortition process in the phonology of Spanish is the strengthening of syllable-initial glides. In the case of the palatal glide this can produce fricative or plosive realizations, depending on the dialect, as in *hielo* 'ice', *deshielo* 'thawing'. Regarding the labiovelar glide, its fortition results in neutralization with the sequence /gu/ *whisky* ~ *güisqui*, *huevo* [u̯éβo] ~ [gu̯éβo] 'egg' (see 9.3).

6.7 Epenthesis

Epenthesis is the insertion of a segment. The epenthesized segment may be a consonant or a vowel. In American English a transitional plosive is inserted in nasal + fricative sequences so that, e.g., *prince* may be homophonous with *prints*, and *sense* with *cents* (cf. also *Thompson* from *Thom* + *son*, *some*[p]*thing*, etc.). The origin of this epenthetic plosive can be explained as a retiming of articulatory gestures. Specifically, if the velum is raised before the oral occlusion of the nasal stop is released, the result will be the perception of a homorganic oral stop (see Browman and Goldstein 1986, 1991, 1992). In Spanish, an epenthetic plosive inserted as a transitional element between nasal or lateral and rhotic has been grammaticalized in the future and conditional of irregular verbs, e.g. *pondré* 'I will put' (*poneré* > *ponré* > *pondré*), *tendré* 'I will have', *saldré* 'I will leave').[6]

The most significant phenomenon of epenthesis in modern Spanish is a process of vowel epenthesis: the insertion of /e/ before word-initial /s/ followed by a consonant (*sC* → *esC*), observable in the adaptation of borrowings (e.g. *estrés* 'stress') and in the English pronunciation of many Spanish speakers (see 5.3.4).

Spectrographic analysis shows that, in onset clusters including a rhotic, very frequently there is a short vowel between both consonants (known as *svarabhakti*, a term from Sanskrit). This *svarabhakti* element has a similar

---

[6] Historically we find epenthesis of an oral stop between /m/ and a following rhotic as well in words such as, e.g., Lat. NŌMINE > *nomne* (by posttonic vowel deletion) > *nomre* (by dissimilation) > *nombre* (by epenthesis) and several other examples: HOMINE > *hombre* 'man', HUMERU > *hombro* 'shoulder', FAMINE > *hambre* 'hunger' and FĒMINA > *hembra* 'female'.

formant structure to the following vowel and has occasionlly been reinterpreted as a full vowel, as in OSp. *corónica* (from *crónica*) 'chronicle' and nonstandard variants like *tíguere* for *tigre* 'tiger' (Quilis 1993:337–42).

6.8 Metathesis

METATHESIS is the transposition or interchange of two segments (saying *methatesis* would be an instance of metathesis). Sometimes metathesis takes place to avoid sequences that are dispreferred in the language. For instance, from Lat. SPATULA we should have Sp. *espadla by regular evolution. The sequence /dl/ was avoided by metathesizing the two consonants in Sp. *espalda* 'back'. In Golden Age Spanish the same metathesis of /dl/ to /ld/ applied regularly in *vos(otros)* imperatives followed by clitic pronouns: *comedlos* → *comeldos* 'eat them'. This morphophonological rule of metathesis is no longer in use; instead the problematic or uncommon sequence /dl/ is avoided by replacing these imperatives with the corresponding infinitive forms in pronunciation; e.g., *comedlos* is most commonly pronounced exactly as *comerlos* 'to eat them'.

We saw above that the sequence /nr/ underwent internal epenthesis in future forms such as *ponré* > *pondré* 'I will put'. Another, competing, solution to the sequence /nr/ that we find in earlier stages of the language is the metathesis of this sequence, *porné*. Although, in the case of these verb forms, metathesis is not the solution that finally prevailed, we have historical metathesis of /nr/ to /rn/ in words such as Lat. GEN(E)RU > *yerno* 'son-in-law', TEN(E)RU > *tierno* 'tender' (cf. Fr. *gendre*, *tendre*, as well as Sp. *engendrar* 'to engender', with epenthesis).

As a nonstandard phenomenon, in Aragon and other regions we find metathesis of a rhotic from a word-internal onset group to the onset of the initial syllable when this also results in an allowable *muta-cum-liquida* group, as in *probe* for *pobre* 'poor', *Grabiel* for *Gabriel*, etc. (A metathesis in the opposite direction is found in the evolution Lat. CRUSTA > *costra* 'crust', Lat. CREPĀRE > *quebrar* 'to break'). The common nonstandard form *naide* for *nadie* 'nobody' shows metathesis of a glide.

6.9 Consequences of the overlap of articulatory gestures

Processes apparently as different as assimilation, epenthesis and deletion may have their origin in a retiming in the coordination of articulatory gestures (Browman and Goldstein 1986, 1991, 1992).

6.9 Overlap of articulatory gestures

a

oral gestures	alveolar fricative	dorsovelar approximant
vocal folds	open	vibrating
	s	ɣ

b

oral gestures	alveolar fricative		dorsovelar approximant
vocal folds	open	vibrating	
	s	z	ɣ

Figure 6.1. Partial voice assimilation of /s/ as anticipation of the laryngeal gesture. Panel a: exact coordination of oral and laryngeal gestures. Panel b: anticipation of vocal fold vibration.

Let us consider, to begin with, the assimilation in voice of fricatives. As mentioned above, in Spanish, /s/ and other fricatives become completely or partially voiced before a voiced consonant. In a sequence of consonants such as /sɡ/ (in, e.g., *rasgo*) we have two gestures in the oral cavity: first a narrowing of the articulatory channel is made in the alveolar region, producing friction, and then the dorsum is raised towards the back of the mouth for the approximant [ɣ]. In the larynx, the vocal folds are first abducted or separated, for a voiceless consonant, and then are brought together and initiate vibration. If the two oral gestures are perfectly synchronized with the two laryngeal gestures (Fig. 6.1a), we will have a sequence [sɣ]. If the coordination is, however, not perfect and the voicing is initiated before the dorsal gesture, we will have some partial voicing of the sibilant, which may also be complete if the overlap is increased, see Fig. 6.1b.

It is also easy to see how the assimilation in place undergone by nasals results from the retiming of the coordination between oral gestures and the raising of the velum to close the passage of air through the nasal cavity. For example, if in a group /nb/ (as in *con barcos* /kon bárkos/ 'with boats') the velum is still lowered when the labial occlusion is attained, the result will be the perception of [m]; that is, a sequence [ñmb]. Perceptual hiding and reduction of the apico-alveolar occlusion will result in [mb]. Notice that the labial occlusion may also (partially) overlap with the apico-alveolar gesture. If hidden in perception the gesture may become deleted in production in historical change. See Fig. 6.2.

As a final example, consider now the historical epenthesis of oral stops in sequences of nasal + tap, as in /nómɾe/ > /nómbɾe/ 'name' and /tenɾé/ >

Figure 6.2.

a

oral gestures	apico-alveolar occlusion	
		labial occlusion
nasal cav. (velum)	[OPEN]	[CLOSED]
	n	b

b

oral gestures	apico-alveolar occlusion		
		labial occlusion	
nasal cav. (velum)	[OPEN]		[CLOSED]
	n	m	b

c

oral gestures	apico-alveolar occlusion			
		labial occlusion		
nasal cav. (velum)	[OPEN]			[CLOSED]
	n	n͡m	m	b

Nasal assimilation. Panel a: perfect coordination of oral gestures (apical and labial occlusion) and opening and closing of passage to the nasal cavity. Panel b: second occlusion is attained before velum is raised. Panel c: further overlap of labial with apical gesture. This may produce perceptual deletion of apical gesture.

Figure 6.3.

a

oral gestures	labial occlusion	apico-alveolar tap
nasal cav. (velum)	[OPEN]	[CLOSED]
	m	ɾ

b

oral gestures	labial occlusion		apico-alveolar tap
nasal cav. (velum)	[OPEN]	[CLOSED]	
	m	b	ɾ

Intrusive plosive. Panel a: first a labial occlusion is produced with an open nasal port. Then, an apico-alveolar tap gesture is coordinated with the raising of the velum, simultaneously closing passage of air through the nasal cavity. Panel b: closing the nasal port before the labial closure is released produces the percept of an intrusive labial oral stop [b].

/tendré/ 'I will have'. In spite of the fact that epenthesis may seem a very different kind of phonological process, in a case like this its best explanation is also as a retiming of articulatory gestures (Ohala 1974; Browman and Goldstein 1991). In, for instance, /mr/, the closing of the passage to the oral cavity while the labial occlusion is still in place will produce an epenthetic /b/ sound. This is illustrated in Fig. 6.3.

EXERCISES

1. In Catalan only voiceless oral stops can occur in word-final position; that is the contrast between voiced and voiceless plosives is neutralized in this position. This is shown in the following examples for all three places of articulation (as in Spanish, voiced plosives are realized as continuants between vowels):

    (i) masc.   fem.
        tip   [típ]   tipa   [típə]   'satiated'
        llop   [ʎóp]   lloba   [ʎóβə]   'wolf'
        gat   [gát]   gata   [gátə]   'cat'
        mut   [mút]   muda   [múðə]   'mute'
        ric   [r̃ík]   rica   [r̃íkə]   'rich'
        amic   [əmík]   amiga   [əmíɣə] 'friend'

    In a possible Praguean structuralist analysis, the six plosive phonemes of Catalan would be replaced by the three archiphonemes /P T K / in final position in phonological representations, thus capturing the fact that there is no possible opposition between voiced and voiceless plosives in this context. This Praguean phonological description would contain a statement to the effect that the word-final archiphonemes /P T K / are phonetically realized as the voiceless members of the neutralized pairs (unlike coda plosives in Spanish which may be realized with variable voicing):[7]

    (ii) Praguean analysis
        a. Phonological representations (phonemes and archiphonemes)
            /tipə/, /ʎobə/, /gatə/, /mudə/, /r̃ikə/, /əmigə/
            /tiP/, /ʎoP/, /gaT/, /muT/, /r̃iK/, /əmiK/
        b. /P T K/ are realized as voiceless.

    In a generative analysis on the other hand, the nature of the underlying final consonant in the masculine would be determined by the consonant that appears in morphologically related forms, such as the feminine. In this

---

[7] Except before a voiced consonant, where they undergo assimilation in voice and sometimes other features, as in *amic dolent* [əmiɣðulén] 'bad friend'. For the purpose of this exercise we may leave this context aside. We also leave aside the phonemic analysis of the neutral vowel [ə].

analysis, surface forms are obtained by the application of a rule of final devoicing:

(iii) Generative analysis:
   a. Phonological representations
      /tipə/, /ʎobə/, /gatə/, /mudə/, /r̄ikə/, /əmigə/
      /tip/, /ʎob/, /gat/, /mud/, /r̄ik/, /əmig/
   b. Devoicing rule: Plosive → Voiceless in context Word-final.

In a third, less abstract analysis, all the masculine forms in the left column of (i) would end in voiceless plosive phonemes /p t k/, whereas, as in the other two analyses, some of the feminine words have intervocalic voiceless plosives and some others have voiced plosives. This is essentially the phonemic analysis that standard Catalan orthography embodies. This analysis would be complemented with a phonological generalization or constraint against word-final voiced plosives and a lexical statement to the fact that in many sets of morphologically related words the voiceless phonemes /-p -t -k/ alternate with /-b- -d- -g-/ in intervocalic position but in many other words they do not:

(iv) Phonemic analysis implied in Catalan orthography
   a. Phonological representations
      /tipə/, /ʎobə/, /gatə/, /mudə/, /r̄ikə/, /əmigə/
      /tip/, /ʎop/, /gat/, /mut/, /r̄ik/, /əmik/
   b. Constraint: There are no word-final voiced plosives
   c. In some sets of morphologically-related words final /-p -t -k/ correspond to /-b- -d- -g-/

Compare these three analyses. Do you find one of these analyses more appealing than the others? Why?

2   The Spanish word *candado* 'lock' derives from Lat. CATENĀTUM. You may assume the following diachronic derivation: CATENĀTU(M) > *cadenado* > *cadnado* > *candado*. What kind of process does the last step exemplify? Consider now the historical derivation of *primero* 'first': Lat. PRIMĀRIU(M) > *primairo* > *primeiro* > *primero*. Do the historical evolutions of these two words have anything in common?

3   A common pronunciation of the borrowing *pub* in Spain is [páf]. How do you explain this adaptation?

4   In many Basque dialects the definite article is -*a* in certain contexts and -*e* in other contexts. The two forms of the article are in complementary distribution,

Exercises

as illustrated in the following examples (in Basque orthography). Can you define the context for the alternation? What kind of phonological process is this?

stem		def. singular	
gizon	'man'	gizona	'the man'
lagun	'friend'	lagune	'the friend'
azal	'skin'	azala	'the skin'
min	'pain'	mine	'the pain'
eder	'beautiful'	ederra	'the beautiful one'
etxe	'house'	etxea	'the house'
mendi	'mountain'	mendie	'the mountain'
baso	'forest'	basoa	'the forest'
esku	'hand'	eskue	'the hand'
txakur	'dog'	txakurre	'the dog'
enbor	'log'	enborra	'the trunk'
mutil	'boy'	mutile	'the boy'

5   Provide an explicit account for the assimilation of the nasal in the example *sin cartas* 'without letters' in terms of articulatory gestures.

7 Vowels

7.1 The Spanish vowel system from a typological perspective

Spanish has a simple, symmetrical, five-vowel system. These vowels can be arranged in the shape of a triangle, as in Table 7.1. In the height dimension there are two high vowels /i u/, two mid vowels /e o/, and one low vowel /a/. Along the frontness/backness dimension, there are two front vowels /i e/, one central vowel /a/, and two back vowels /u o/.

Five is the most common number of vowel phonemes cross-linguistically and, among these, symmetrical systems, as in Spanish, are in the majority (Disner 1984).

The back vowels of Spanish are redundantly rounded. In this as well, Spanish presents the typologically most common situation. The reason for these two features to co-occur is clear when we consider that both the retraction of the tongue body and the rounding and protrusion of the lips have the effect of enlarging the front cavity of the mouth and thus contribute to the same acoustic effect. Nevertheless these two gestures do not necessarily go together. Languages like French and German have front rounded vowels, as in Fr. *tu* /ty/ 'you', *feu* /fø/ 'fire',[1] and Japanese has a five-vowel system /i e a o ɯ/, where four of the vowels have approximately the same quality as in Spanish, but the fifth is a high back unrounded vowel.

A simpler symmetrical inventory is the three-vowel system /i a u/ found, for instance, in the Andean languages Quechua and Aymara. Often in languages with this type of inventory the high vowels have an allophonic range that includes mid vowels. This is the case in many dialects of Quechua and in Aymara where [e], [o] can be realizations of the phonemes /i/, /u/, respectively, for instance in contact with an uvular consonant. The bilingual Spanish of

---

[1] In Spain, the Gascon dialect of the Arán Valley has the high front round vowel phoneme /y/, as in *luna* /lyna/ 'moon'.

7.1 Spanish system – typological perspective

Table 7.1 The vowel phonemes of Spanish.

	Front	Central	Back
High	i		u
Mid	e		o
Low		a	
	Nonround		Round

Table 7.2 A seven-vowel symmetrical system (late Latin / early Romance).

	Front	Central	Back
High	i		u
Higher-mid	e		o
Lower-mid	ɛ		ɔ
Low		a	

native speakers of Quechua and Aymara sometimes displays some fluctuations between [e] and [i] and between [o] and [u]. This is understandable from the point of view of the native system of these speakers, where these are not pairs of vowels in phonemic contrast.

Seven-vowel symmetrical systems are not uncommon either, although not as common as Spanish-type five-vowel systems. The modern Spanish vowel system derives from an earlier seven-vowel system, as in Table 7.2, which developed in the late Latin / early Romance period in most central and western Romance areas. When compared with modern Spanish, this system had an additional contrast in height, distinguishing higher-mid vowels /e o/ from lower-mid vowels /ɛ ɔ/ in stressed syllables.[2] In nonfinal unstressed syllables the system was already that of modern Spanish.

This seven-vowel system is still found in Standard Italian and, with additions, also in Portuguese and Catalan. In Spanish the lower-mid vowels systematically became the diphthongs [i̯e], [u̯e] by 'breaking,' e.g.: tɛrra > tierra 'land', pɔrta > puerta 'door'. Consequently with this evolution, the vowels /e o/ of modern Spanish are more similar in quality to the higher-mid vowels of Catalan and Portuguese than to their lower-mid vowels. Nevertheless, depending on the phonetic context, the Spanish mid vowel phonemes have somewhat higher or lower allophones. For instance, the vowel /e/ tends to be higher or closer before

---

[2] The seven-vowel system of late Latin was itself a development of an earlier system with ten different vowels with five different qualities and a distinction of length: /iː i eː e aː a o oː u uː/.

Table 7.3 A nine-vowel symmetrical system.

Higher-high	i					u
Lower-high		ɪ			ʊ	
Higher-mid			e		o	
Lower-mid				ɛ	ɔ	
Low				a		

Table 7.4 Vowel system of conservative General American English.

Higher-high	i beet						u food
Lower-high		ɪ bit				ʊ foot	
Higher-Mid			e bait			o boat	
Lower-Mid					ʌ but		
				ɛ bet		ɔ bought	
Low				æ bat		ɑ cot	

a palatal consonant, as in *pecho*, and it is especially open in contact with a trill and before /x/, as in *perro*, *lejos*. But even in this context /e/ is not as open as the typical realization of the phoneme /ɛ/ of other Romance languages (or the lower-mid vowel in English *bed*). The same considerations apply to the back mid vowel.

By adding one more contrast in height we can have a nine-vowel triangular system, as in Table 7.3.

The English vowel system has rather a quadrilateral shape, since a front/back contrast is also made between two low vowels /æ/ and /ɑ/. By adding also a central unrounded vowel in the mid range, we obtain the vowel system of conservative varieties of General American English, as in Table 7.4, where for each vowel phoneme a representative example is given.

To these, RP British English adds another central vowel /ɜ/ in words like *bird*. On the other hand, many North American dialects have lost the distinction between /ɔ/ and /ɑ/, not making any contrast between *caught* and *cot* or the names *Dawn* and *Don*.

7.1 Spanish system – typological perspective

What we have said so far allows us to see, in general terms, how the Spanish and English vowel systems are organized, how vowel phonemes are distributed in the vowel space in English and Spanish. But it is important to keep in mind that we cannot directly equate vowels for which we have provided the same symbol in the two languages when we consider their phonetic realization. It is rarely if ever the case that two vowel phonemes are exactly identical in two different languages that are not in contact. Regarding the comparison that we want to establish here, the fact is that, even though English has more than twice as many vowels as Spanish, no English vowel exactly corresponds to any Spanish vowel. A more detailed comparison will be provided in the next section.

The three features of height, frontness/backness and lip rounding are not the only ones that languages use for contrasting vowel phonemes. In some languages, including the Romance languages French and Portuguese, vowels can be contrastively nasalized. To give an example, in French *beau* /bo/ 'beautiful', with an oral vowel, contrasts with *bon* /bõ/ 'good', with a nasalized vowel. In Spanish (and in English), instead, nasalization is an allophonic feature: vowels are partially nasalized in contact with nasal consonants. If in a vowel – nasal stop sequence such as /an/ the velum is lowered, allowing air to flow through the nasal cavity, before the oral occlusion is formed, the result will be the partial nasalization of the vowel, [ãn], as explained in 6.9. Diachronically, a common source of phonemic nasalized vowels is the weakening of syllable-final consonants, leaving the nasalization of the preceding vowel as residue (this is the origin of the nasalized vowels of French and Portuguese). This path of development is observable in Caribbean and Andalusian dialects where a word like /pán/ 'bread' may be produced as [pãŋ] ∼ [pã]. In principle this may result in contrastively nasalized vowel phonemes in these Spanish dialects if [pã] eventually becomes the only common pronunciation. In Guaraní (which is a national language of Paraguay, together with Spanish) in words where the stressed vowel (the last vowel of the word) is nasalized, nasalization affects all vowels and other segments, through a harmony process. This language thus has a contrast between oral and nasalized vowels limited to the (final) stressed position which results in a contrast between oral and nasal word domains.

Besides normally voiced vowels, some languages (including some indigenous languages of Mexico) possess vowels with creaky and/or breathy voice. In Spanish and English, creaky voice or devoicing of vowels is an allophonic phenomenon found in utterance-final position in the speech of some speakers as a result of intonational dropping to a very low tone.

There are also languages with a contrast between vowels produced with a retracted and with an advanced tongue root. A number of African languages have vowel harmony processes involving this feature.

The relative tenseness or laxness of the articulation is sometimes used as a feature in the classification of vowels. Some phonologists use tenseness/laxness in English, instead of vowel height, as the feature for distinguishing between the two members of the pairs /i/-/ɪ/, /e/-/ɛ/, /o/-/ɔ/, /u/-/ʊ/, where the first vowel in each pair is tense and the second one is lax (e.g. /i/ is a high, front, tense vowel and /ɪ/ a high, front, lax vowel).

Finally, duration is frequently used as a contrastive feature in vowel systems. Classical Latin had a contrast between five short and five long vowels: /i e a o u/ and /iː eː aː oː uː/ (which eventually, in most of central and western Romance, developed into the seven-vowel system we saw above). Japanese also uses contrastive vowel length and so do many other languages of the world. In the pairs of English mid and high vowels in the paragraph above, the first member of each pair normally has greater duration, and some phonologists in fact interpret the contrast as being fundamentally a matter of vowel length, as opposed to height or tenseness. Spanish does not have contrastive vowel length, but can have sequences of identical vowels, as in *cree* 's/he believes', *moho* 'mould', *azahar* 'orange bloom' (vs *azar* 'chance'), etc.; cf. *pasé* 'I passed', *pasee* 'I/she/he stroll, subjunct.', *paseé* 'I strolled' (Lorenzo 1972; Monroy Casas 1980:60–4).

7.2 Spanish and English vowels contrasted

As just mentioned, none of the five Spanish vowels is exactly identical to any English vowel. A problem for a detailed comparison is that there are considerable differences among English varieties in the pronunciation of vowels. It can be said that, whereas in Spanish, with its simple vowel system, dialectal differences in phonology affect mostly the pronunciation of certain consonants, in English, most of the variation is in the way that vowels are pronounced. Therefore the comparison we make here will not necessarily apply to all English dialects.

Whereas Spanish has two high vowels /i u/, English has four /i ɪ u ʊ/ (*beet, bit, boot, foot*). English /i u/ are longer than the corresponding Spanish vowels and are also slightly diphthongal, compare Sp. *sí* [sí] 'yes', *su* [su] 'his/her/their' (pure, non-diphthongized vowels) with Eng. *see* [siʲ], *Sue* [suᵘ] (longer, with some degree of diphthongization). The English vowel /i/ has been described as starting at a slightly lower position than Spanish /i/ and gliding up to approximately the position of this Spanish vowel (Stockwell and Bowen 1965:95).

Regarding /u/, a change that appears to be in progress in many English varieties is the fronting of this vowel, which becomes somewhat centralized, [ʉᵘ].

7.2 Spanish and English vowels contrasted

Comparison of the vowel charts (based on average formant values) offered in Ladefoged (2001:43–4) for a conservative style of American English from recordings made in the 1950s and for contemporary Californian English is very revealing in this respect: younger speakers have a much more centralized (less back) articulation of /u/. Another recent study comparing the acoustic characteristics of English vowels produced by four (presumably young) speakers of General American English and of Spanish vowels produced by four speakers from Madrid (Bradlow 1995) also reveals a considerably fronted realization of English /u/ when compared with Spanish /u/.[3]

Regarding the mid vowels, an important difference between the two languages is that English /e o/ (*bait, goat*) tend to diphthongize to [eɪ], [oʊ], becoming more or less clear diphthongs depending on the dialect. In General American English /e/ is quite consistently a clear diphthong [eɪ], but /o/ is not always so clearly diphthongal (Olive *et al.* 1993:33). In British RP, on the other hand, the vowel we are noting /o/ is actually [əʊ], with a centralized and only slightly rounded nucleus (Roach 2000:23). In contrast, Spanish /e o/ are pure monophthongs. In fact, Spanish has a phonological contrast between /e/ and /ei/: *ves* [bés] 'you see', *veis* [béi̯s] 'you-*pl.* see'; *pena* [péna] 'pain', *peina* [péi̯na] 's/he combs'; *le* [le] (dative clitic), *lee* [lée] 's/he reads', *ley* [léi̯] 'law'. English /e/ [eɪ] (*pain, bay, café*) is thus intermediate in its degree of diphthongization between the Spanish monophthong /e/ (*pena, ve, café*) and the Spanish diphthong /ei/ (*peina, ley, carey*). On the other hand, English /e/ (*bait*) contrasts in this language with a lower, non-diphthongizing vowel /ɛ/ (*bet*). Spanish does not have this contrast and some realizations of Spanish /e/, for instance in contact with /r̄/ and /x/ (*perro, lejos*), may be closer to English /ɛ/ than to English /e/.

The Spanish mid back vowel /o/ is also always realized as a pure vowel, unlike its English counterpart, and contrasts with /ou/, even if the diphthong /ou/ is rare in Spanish; compare Sp. *gota* 'drop', *bote* 'boat', *cono* 'cone' with English *goat, boat, cone*.

Finally, in the low region, English has a contrast between a front low vowel /æ/ (*man, bad, bat*) and a back low vowel /ɑ/ (General American *cod, pot*; British RP *card, part*). Spanish has a single low vowel /a/ which is closer to American English /ɑ/ than to American English /æ/, but less retracted, occupying a central position between front and back.

---

[3] Since, in this variety of English, /i/ appears to be more peripheral than Spanish /i/, Bradlow (1995:1919) concludes that 'the vowels of English are articulated with a fronted tongue position relative to the tongue position for the Spanish vowels'. This, however, may not apply to other English varieties.

Table 7.5 The vowels of Spanish and American English compared.

		Spanish	English
High vowels	Front	/i/: short, nondiphthongal	Contrast between two phonemes /i/ (*beat*): long, slightly diphthongal and /ɪ/ (*bit*): short, lower, more centralized
	Back	/u/: short, nondiphthongal and more retracted than Eng. /u/	Contrast between two phonemes /u/ (*food*): long, slightly diphthongal and /ʊ/ (*book*): short, lower Both often more centralized than Sp. /u/
Mid vowels	Front	/e/: pure vowel, contrasts with diphthong /ei/ – *pena* vs *peina*. Slightly higher or lower allophones depending on the context.	Contrast between two phonemes /e/ (*bait, made*): higher, realized as a diphthongizing vowel [eɪ̯], with a shorter offglide than the Sp. diphthong /ei/ [ei̯]. /ɛ/ (*bet*): lower, shorter, nondiphthongal
	Back	/o/: pure vowel, contrasts with diphthong /ou/ – *Sosa* vs *Sousa*. Slightly higher and lower allophones depending on the context.	Contrast between two/three phonemes /o/ (*boat, go*): higher, often realized as a diphthongizing vowel [oʊ̯], with a shorter offglide than Sp. diphthong /ou/ [ou̯]. /ɔ/ (*dog, dawn*): lower, shorter. In many North American varieties neutralized with /ɑ/. /ʌ/ (*cut*): central, unrounded.
Low vowels		/a/: central	Contrast between two phonemes /æ/ (*mad*): front /ɑ/ (*pod*): back

For other English vowels there are not any similar phonemes in Spanish. Table 7.5 summarizes the comparison between Spanish and American English vowels.

Besides differences in vowel inventory, another very important difference between Spanish and English has to do with the reduction of vowels in unstressed syllables in the latter language. In English only a subset of vowels are allowed in unstressed syllables and reduction to a neutral vowel [ə] (schwa) in unstressed position is widespread. This is reflected in numerous alternations, e.g. *t*[ɛ]*l*[ə]*gr*[æ]*ph, t*[ə]*l*[ɛ]*gr*[æ]*pher; object* (noun) [ˈɑbd͡ʒɪkt] vs *object* (verb) [əbˈd͡ʒɛkt] (transcriptions based on Kenyon and Knott 1953). In Spanish, on the other hand, there are only very slight differences in quality

7.3 Acoustic characterization of Spanish vowels

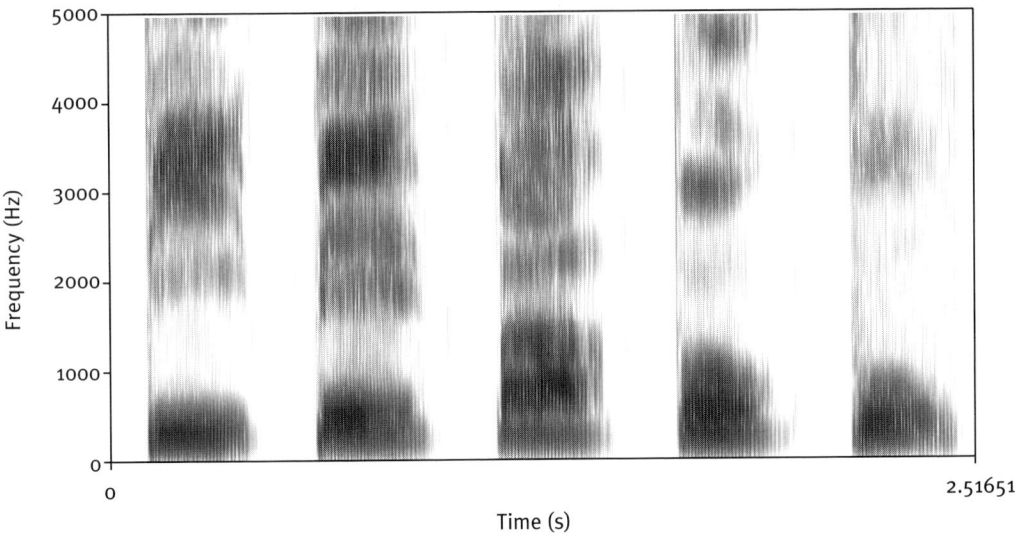

Figure 7.1.   Spectrogram of /pipepapopu/.

between stressed and unstressed vowels (Quilis and Esgueva 1983). We have, for instance, essentially the same vowel qualities in *número* [número] 'number', *numero* [numéro] 'I number' and *numeró* [numeró] 's/he numbered'. In this resistance to reduction in unstressed position, Spanish differs from its close relatives Catalan and Portuguese – cf. Sp. *a la casa* [alakása] vs Cat. *a la casa* [ələkázə] 'to the house' – and, on the other hand, resembles Standard Italian.

7.3 Acoustic characterization of Spanish vowels

As mentioned in 4.2, the spectrogram of vowel sounds is characterized by the presence of dark horizontal bars, known as FORMANTS, indicating greater energy at certain frequency levels. The first two of these formants (F1 and F2) provide information that can be used to uniquely identify the five Spanish vowels. Figure 7.1 shows a spectrogram of /pipepapopu/ produced by the author. In this figure, F1 goes up from /i/ to /a/ and then down: i < e < a > o > u. F2, on the other hand, is highest for /i/ and progressively declines: i > e > a > o > u.

In Table 7.6 we show the average formant values for the five Spanish vowels that Quilis and Esgueva (1983) obtained in a spectrographic study in which they analysed data from sixteen male speakers from both Spain and Latin America producing several tokens of each vowel (both stressed and unstressed

Table 7.6 Spanish vowels. Average values in Hz for F1 and F2 (based on data for sixteen male speakers in Quilis and Esgueva 1983:244).

	F1	F2
/i/	264.5	2317.5
/e/	435.8	1995.01
/a/	657.28	1215
/o/	474.5	888.4
/u/	293.5	669.08

and always in contact with labial consonants) included in words inserted in a carrier phrase.[4]

As we can see from Table 7.6, the height of the first formant or F1 correlates inversely with vowel height. That is, the lower the vowel the higher its F1 value: F1 is highest for /a/ and lowest for the high vowels. The second formant or F2, on the other hand, correlates directly with palatality or frontness. The more fronted the vowel, the higher its F2 value: F2 is highest for /i/ and lowest for /u/.

By plotting formant values in a chart we obtain the vowel triangle. This is what we have done in Fig. 7.2 where the values in Table 7.6 have been plotted, with F1 along the vertical or y axis and F2 on the horizontal or x axis. The x axis uses a logarithmic scale, since this reflects human perception more accurately. Notice that in order to obtain the correct orientation for the triangle the point of origin of the coordinates has been placed on the upper right corner.

7.4 Dialectal phenomena involving vowels

Vowel qualities are remarkably stable among Spanish dialects. There is nothing in Spanish like the differences in vowel quality that we find across geographical and social varieties of English. This is no doubt in part due to the simplicity and symmetry of the system.[5] Speakers with a low educational level may show

---

[4] This source also provides data for six female speakers. Bradlow (1995) offers similar data for four male speakers of Madrid Spanish for stressed vowels preceded by a labial and followed by a dental. Martínez Celdrán (1995, 1998:41–3) offers formant values for five male speakers. Ladefoged (2001:35–6, 41–2) charts the formants of the five Spanish vowels in stressed position produced in the context /m_s/ (*masa, mesa, misa, mosca, musa*), apparently from a single speaker.

[5] But this is not a determining factor. Within Basque dialects, for instance, there is much variation affecting vowels, in spite of the fact that most Basque dialects also have a simple five-vowel phoneme system.

7.4 Dialectal phenomena involving vowels

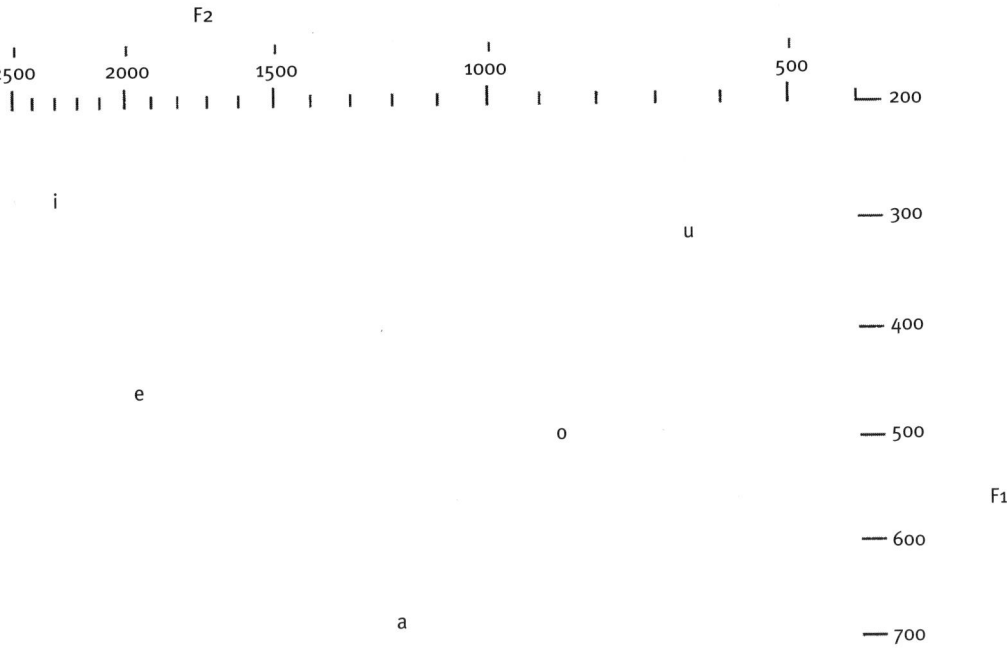

Figure 7.2. Formant chart of Spanish vowels, based on data from Table 7.6, adapted from Quilis and Esgueva (1983), average for sixteen male subjects.

some departures from the norm, especially in the distribution of mid and high vowels in pretonic syllables – e.g. *cevil* for standard *civil*, *midicina* for *medicina* 'medicine', etc. – and dialectally we may also find some other differences with respect to the standard in specific words – e.g. *escuro* for *oscuro* 'dark', *semos* for *somos* 'we are', etc. – but these nonstandard forms are only sporadic developments and are generally shunned by educated speakers.[6]

A phenomenon worth mentioning is the shortening and deletion of unstressed vowels, especially before /s/: *buenas noch(e)s* 'good night', *p(ue)s no* 'well, no', *mil pes(o)s* 'a thousand pesos', *un caf(e)cito* 'a little coffee', where the vowel in parentheses may be perceptually deleted. This phenomenon has been reported primarily in Mexican and Andean Spanish, two areas where, on the other hand, syllable-final /s/ does not undergo weakening.[7]

---

[6] In some cases, the forms that have become established in the modern standard are different from the most common ones in Old Spanish. This is the case with most infinitives in *-ir*, where high vowels have been generalized in the root, against an earlier preference for mid vowels, as in *sufrir* (OSp. *sofrir*) 'to suffer', *escribir* (OSp. *escrevir*) 'to write', *cubrir* (OSp. *cobrir*) 'to cover', etc. (see Penny 2002:189–90).

[7] See Canellada and Zamora Vicente (1960), Lope Blanch (1966), Lipski (1994).

7.4.1 Eastern Andalusian vowels

In Eastern Andalusian varieties, spoken in the province of Granada and neighbouring areas, word-final /s/ is very commonly deleted in popular speech. A number of Spanish dialectologists, including linguists who are native speakers of these varieties, have reported that, even though the /-s/ is not pronounced, morphological distinctions are preserved because final vowels have a different quality according to whether they are before a 'silent /-s/' or in absolute word-final position. In particular, the final mid vowels /e/ /o/ are reported to have very open allophones [ɛ] [ɔ] before 'silent /-s/' and much higher allophones when truly word-final. This allows for the singular/plural distinction to be maintained: *libro* [líβro̝][8] 'book' vs *libros* [líβrɔ] 'books'; *libre* [líβre̝] 'free, sg.' vs *libres* [líβrɛ] 'free, pl.' As Alvar (1991:235) puts it: 'en Almería, Jaén y Granada, en el singular *niño* o *pobre* se pronuncian con una vocal final muy cerrada, con lo que el singular queda así marcado, mientras que los equivalentes regionales de *niños* o *pobres* tienen una vocal final muy abierta (por supuesto falta la -s), con lo que la marca de abertura sirve para indicar el plural'.[9] The low vowel acquires a more fronted or palatalized character in the plural, somewhat like Eng. /æ/: *libra* [líβra] 'pound' vs *libras* [líβræ] 'pounds'. This phenomenon is apparently peculiar to Eastern Andalusia and is not found in Western Andalusia, the Canary Islands, the Caribbean, or other areas where /-s/ is also frequently deleted.

In Eastern Andalusian, the open or closed quality of the final vowel is, furthermore, transmitted to the stressed vowel and even to the pretonic, especially when they are all mid vowels, e.g. *lobos* [lɔ́βɔ] 'wolves' vs *lobo* [ló̝βo̝] 'wolf'; *peroles* [pɛrɔ́lɛ] 'pots'. This is thus an example of vowel harmony since all vowels in the word may be affected by the quality of the final vowel (see 6.3.3).[10]

---

[8] The subscript under the final vowel is the IPA diacritic for a raised vowel.
[9] 'In Almería, Jaén and Granada, in the singular *niño* or *pobre* are pronounced with a very close final vowel, with which the singular is thus marked, whereas the regional equivalents of *niños* or *pobres* have a very open final vowel (of course the -s is lacking), so that the openness feature indicates plural number.'
[10] Alonso *et al.* (1950:212) find that harmonization is particularly noticeable when all the vowels in the word share the same basic quality: 'Cuando en la palabra van varias vocales idénticas, la cerrazón del singular o la abertura del plural se extienden a toda la palabra, con extraordinaria diferenciación' ('When the word contains several identical vowels, the closeness of the singular or the openness of the plural extend to the whole word, with extraordinary differentiation'). Since the pioneering work of Navarro Tomás (1939) and Alonso *et al.* (1950), this phenomenon has attracted considerable attention on the part of phonologists, phoneticians and dialectologists; see (in alphabetical order) Alarcos Llorach (1958, 1983), Alvar (1955), Gómez Asencio (1977), Hualde and Sanders (1995), Llorente (1962), López Morales (1984), Martínez Melgar (1986, 1994), Morillo-Velarde (1985), Rodríguez-Castellano and Palacio (1948), Salvador (1957–8, 1977), Sanders (1998), Villena Ponsoda (1987).

7.4.2 Metaphony and pretonic vowel raising in Asturian and Cantabrian dialects

In some varieties spoken in rural areas of the regions of Asturias and Cantabria, in northern Spain, we find some interesting phenomena affecting vowels. Recall from Chapter 2 (section 2.6) that these varieties are not properly dialects of Spanish, but, rather, closely related co-dialects: they represent independent developments from Latin, even if later on they were influenced by Standard Spanish. The vowel assimilations in question are nowadays confined to a few areas of Asturias and Cantabria and seem to be, furthermore, a receding phenomenon. We can distinguish two main types of vowel assimilation and harmony processes in this area: (1) metaphony, the raising (and sometimes centralization) of the stressed vowel (and sometimes other vowels as well) in words ending in a high vowel; and (2) raising of pretonic mid vowels in words where the stressed vowel is high. The specific facts are somewhat different in different local varieties. Pretonic vowel raising appears to be particularly prevalent in Cantabrian dialects, such as the Pasiego dialect, where it interacts with metaphony in complex ways.

Metaphony, as just mentioned, is triggered by final unstressed high vowels. The local varieties of central Asturias (as well as Standard Asturian, which is based on the varieties of this area) have a contrast between mid and high vowels in unstressed final position (in inflectional endings) which is much more robust than that of Standard Spanish (where the inventory in unstressed inflectional endings is basically limited to /e a o/). A contrast between final mid and high vowels is also found in Eastern Asturian and Cantabrian varieties, although in these dialectal areas it is often most noticeable through the concomitant presence of metaphony. This contrast is, in part, inherited from Latin and, in part, the product of analogical extension (see Neira Martínez 1991). The unmarked masculine singular ending is *-u*, but the plural ending is *-os*, reflecting an inherited contrast in Latin that has been lost in Spanish: *llobu* (< Lat. LUPU(M)) 'wolf' vs *llobos* (< Lat. LUPOS) 'wolves'[11] (examples are from a dialect with the contrast in final syllables but without metaphony).[12] Exceptionally, however, some nouns that tend to be used mostly in the singular end in *-o*: *agosto* 'August', *ganao* 'cattle', *oso* 'bear' (this is an innovation in Asturian). In some examples,

---

[11] In general, the shape of nouns and adjectives in Spanish and the other Ibero-Romance languages reflects the Latin accusative form.

[12] There are some central Asturian dialects with an *-o/-u* contrast but without metaphony. Standard Asturian, as developed by the Academia de la Llingua Asturiana, does not display metaphony and has forms like those given in the text. From a historical point of view it appears that these dialects have lost the metaphonic process, which appears to be ancient and connected with similar phenomena in Portuguese and in Italian dialects (Menéndez Pidal 1954; D. Alonso 1958, 1962; Blaylock 1965; Penny 1994, 2000:98–102).

Table 7.7 Metaphony in Lena Asturian.

Nouns masc. sg. count	masc. pl.	fem. sg.	
/gétu/	/gátos/	/gáta/	'cat'
/pélu/	/pálos/		'stick'
/benténu/	/benténos/	/benténa/	'window'[13]
/sébanu/	/sábanos/	/sábana/	'sheet'
/péʃaɾu/	/páʃaɾos/	/páʃaɾa/	'bird'
/nínu/	/néna/	/nénas/	'child'
/píɾ̄u/	/péɾ̄a/	/péɾ̄os/	'dog'
/koɾdíɾu/	/koɾdéɾos/	/koɾdéɾa/	'lamb'
/tsúbu/	/tsóbos/	/tsóba/	'wolf'
/kúbu/	/kúbos/		'pail'
/kabrítu/	/kabrítos/	/kabríta/	'kid, young goat'

Adjectives masc. sg.	fem. sg.	mass	
/blénku/	/blánka/	/blánko/	'white'
/éltu/	/álta/	/álto/	'tall'
/síku/	/séka/	/séko/	'dry'
/túntu/	/tónta/	/tónto/	'stupid'
/ísti/	/ésta/	/ésto/	'this'

for the same Standard Spanish form where the noun can have either a count or a mass interpretation, we find two forms in Central Asturian: a form ending in -*u* as a count noun and another form ending in -*o* as a mass noun, e.g. *pelu* 'a hair' vs *pelo* 'hair (mass)'. Adjectives with two forms in Spanish, e.g. *blanco/blanca* 'white', have three forms in Central Asturian: *blancu/blanca/blanco*, where the third form is used in agreement with mass nouns, regardless of gender (this is also an innovation) – *el gatu blancu* 'the white cat', *la casa blanca* 'the white house' vs *el ganao blanco* 'the white cattle', *la farina blanco* 'the white flour' (cf. Sp. *la harina blanca*).

Final -*u* is thus a feature of masculine singular count nouns and agreeing modifiers and pronouns. In part of the area with this -*u*/-*o* contrast, forms in -*u* are further characterized by the metaphony of the stressed vowel and, in some varieties, also other vowels in the word domain. Metaphony is also found

---

[13] In the case of nouns with masculine and feminine forms referring to inanimates, the masculine often refers to a smaller object than the feminine.

7.4 Dialectal phenomena involving vowels

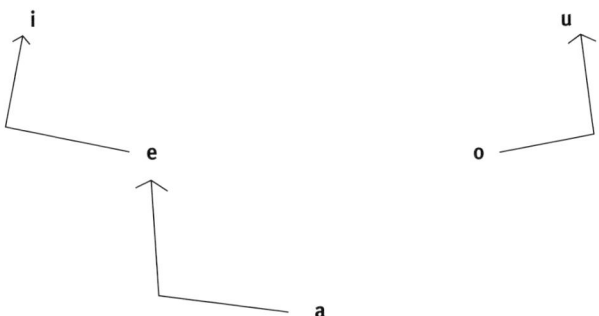

Figure 7.3. Raising of stressed vowels in metaphony contexts in Lena Asturian: /a/ rises to /e/; /e/ rises to /i/; /o/ rises to /u/.

in words ending in the other high vowel, -*i*, but the contrast between final -*e* and -*i* is less robust.

Since the specific facts are somewhat different in different local varieties it is better to consider several varieties separately.

a) Metaphony in Lena (Central Asturian)

In Lena, metaphony takes the form of one-degree raising affecting the mid and low vowels: the mid vowels rise to high and the low vowel /a/ rises to /e/. High vowels are not affected in Lena. Examples are given in Table 7.7 (data from Neira 1955).[14]

If we compare the forms ending in a high vowel with other forms in their inflectional paradigm (or with their cognates in Castilian Spanish), we can see that in these items there is a step-wise raising of the stressed vowel, as schematized in Fig. 7.3.

b) Metaphony in other Asturian dialects: Alto Aller and Nalón Valley

As we have just mentioned, metaphony in the dialect of Lena can be characterized as the replacement of a vowel phoneme by another, higher, phoneme in metaphonic contexts.[15] In other areas, however, metaphonic raising is accompanied by centralization in words ending in -*u*, which is itself centralized. Thus, whereas Menéndez Pidal, describing the dialect of Lena, tells us that in that dialect Standard Spanish *palo* 'stick' is pronounced *pelu* and Spanish *pelo* 'hair' becomes *pilu*, Rodríguez-Castellano (1952) describes the vowels that appear in metaphonic contexts in the dialect of Alto Aller as 'open and mixed', different from the clear vowels of words without metaphony: 'las vocales resultantes de esta inflexión no son sonidos de timbre claro y preciso, a la manera castellana, sino que presentan en todos los casos un matiz oscuro y mixto muy

---

[14] The facts were first described by Menéndez Pidal (1899, 1906).
[15] As described by Menéndez Pidal and later by Neira, a native speaker of the dialect.

Table 7.8 Raising of /a/ under metaphony in Asturian.

Lena	Nalón Valley	Standard Spanish	
[blḯŋku]	[blɔ́ŋku]	*blanco*	'white, *masc. sg.*'
[pélu]	[pɔ́lu]	*palo*	'stick'
[gétu]	[gɔ́tu]	*gato*	'cat'
[péʃaru]	[pɔ́ʃaru]	*pájaro*	'bird'

característico' (1952). He insists that for native speakers of this dialect the stressed vowel of a word like [pḯlü] 'stick' (pl. [pálos]) is not confused with the [e] of, for instance, the mass noun [pélo] 'hair' (the dieresis is the IPA diacritic for centralization).

In the Nalón Valley as well, the final and stressed vowel of words with metaphony are centralized, at least in the speech of the older generations in García Alvarez's (1960) study, so that, for instance, for Spanish *caldero* 'pot' these speakers produce [kaldïrü], with both raising and centralization of the stressed vowel. A difference with respect to both Lena and Alto Aller is that in the Nalón Valley the raising of the stressed low vowel /a/ produces a back vowel.[16]

c) Pretonic vowel raising and metaphony in Pasiego (Cantabria)

In the Cantabrian dialect spoken in Montes de Pas (described and analysed in Penny 1969a, 1969b),[17] there is a harmony process affecting pretonic vowels that interacts with metaphony. In words where the stressed vowel is high, preceding mid vowels also become high. Thus, contrasting with [koxeré] 'I will take' (Standard Sp. *cogeré*), [koxerás] 'you will take', etc., we find [kuxiría] 'I would take' (for Standard Sp. *cogería*), [kux̯iéra] 'I took (*subjunct*)' (for Standard Sp. *cogiera*), etc., where the stressed syllable contains a high vowel or a prevocalic high glide. Similarly, we have [melokompró] 's/he bought it for me' (like Standard Sp. *me lo compró*), but [miludi̯ó] 's/he gave it to me' (cf. Standard Sp. *me lo dio*).

In words ending in /-u/, which is centralized, centralization affects all vowels in the word domain including proclitics. In addition, pretonic mid vowels are raised to high when the stressed vowel is high, either inherently or as a result of metaphony, as shown in the examples in Table 7.9.

---

[16] The isogloss or boundary between the areas with anterior and posterior raising of /a/ is given in Rodríguez-Castellano (1955).

[17] Penny (1978) describes another Cantabrian dialect where the harmony facts are somewhat different, that of Tudanca. In Hualde (1989, 1998) these two dialects are compared with each other and with Asturian varieties.

Table 7.9 Metaphony and pretonic vowel raising in Pasiego (Cantabria).

Standard Spanish	Pasiego	
por el camino	[pül kämĭnü]	'by the road'
el cordero	[ïlkürð̆ïrü]	'the lamb'
contento	[küntĭntü]	'happy, *masc. sg.*'
redondo	[r̃ïð̆ŭndü]	'round, *masc. sg.*'

In an example like [küntĭntü] 'happy, *masc. sg.*' (fem. [konténta]) metaphony feeds the application of pretonic raising: /konténtü/ → /köntĭntü/→ [küntĭntü], whether we see this as two steps in a synchronic (morpho-) phonological process or in diachronic terms.

It is unfortunate that, to my knowledge, there are no published instrumental studies of these vowel-harmony phenomena.

EXERCISES

1. Bradlow (1995), analysing data from four male speakers of Madrid Spanish, obtained the formant values in Table I for stressed vowels in CVCV words (where each value is an average of 20 tokens: 4 speakers × 5 repetitions). Plot these values in a formant chart. Compare this chart with Fig. 7.2. To make the chart you may use a program such as PlotFormant (which was used to produce Fig. 7.2) or Microsoft Excel®, or you can make a drawing manually, using graph paper.

   Table I Madrid Spanish vowels.

Phonemes	F1	F2
/i/	286	2147
/e/	458	1814
/a/	638	1353
/o/	460	1019
/u/	322	992

2. Bradlow (1995) also obtained formant values for the eleven vowel phonemes of General American English in CVC words, as given in Table II (each value is again an average of 20 tokens: 4 speakers × 5 repetitions). Make another

formant chart with these values and compare it with the chart you made for Spanish in Exercise 1. Do you find any surprising mismatches between the position of these American English vowels in the vowel quadrilateral and the labels used in their description (back/front, high/mid/low)? (For a larger study of American English vowels, see Hillenbrand *et al.* 1995.)

Table II General American English vowels.

Phonemes	F1	F2
/i/	268	2393
/ɪ/	463	1995
/e/	430	2200
/ɛ/	635	1796
/æ/	777	1738
/ʌ/	640	1354
/ɑ/	780	1244
/ɔ/	620	1033
/o/	482	1160
/ʊ/	481	1331
/u/	326	1238

3   The great Spanish phonetician Tomás Navarro Tomás (1977) distinguished two allophones for the Spanish vowel /e/ in complementary distribution (also for /o/): an open allophone in words such as *perro*, *guerra*, *remo*, *teja*, *lejos* and a different, close, allophone of this vowel in, for instance, *pecho*, *peña*, *sello*, *pesca*, *vengo*. Other Spanish phoneticians have disagreed with Navarro Tomás's description, denying the existence of distinct allophones in complementary distribution (see Quilis 1993:145; Martínez Celdrán 1984:288–301). Record three repetitions of each of the examples in a carrier phrase (e.g. *digo___ para ti* 'I say___for you') and measure F1 and F2 for /e/ using a program for speech analysis. Which hypothesis do your data support? Do you find open and close allophones in complementary distribution? Do you find any tendencies in specific contexts? (For all experiments involving recording data from human subjects you should follow the rules and procedures established at your institution.)

4   In Eastern Andalusian a pair of words such as [píno] 'pine tree' and [pínɔ] 'pine trees' can be distinguished solely by the quality of the final vowel. Because of the existence of these 'minimal pairs' some authors have concluded that in

this Spanish dialect there is a (partial) *desdoblamiento* or 'doubling' of the system of vowel phonemes. Penny (2000:125–6), for instance, proposes a system with eight vowel phonemes: /i e ɛ æ a ɔ o u/ for Eastern Andalusian (see also references in note 10). Do you agree with this point of view? Consider also the possible contrasts in the same dialect shown in Table III.

Table III

pino caído	[pínokaío] 'fallen pine'	*pinos caídos*	[pínɔʰkkaíɔ] 'fallen pines'
pino grande	[pínoɣránde] 'big pine'	*pinos grandes*	[pínɔxrándɛ] 'big pines'
pino enano	[pínŋenáno] 'dwarf pine'	*pinos enanos*	[pínɔ.enánɔ] 'dwarf pines'

8 Plosives

8.1 Voiceless and voiced plosives: main allophones

Spanish has two series of plosive or oral stop phonemes, voiceless /p t k/ and voiced /b d g/, at the same three places of articulation, bilabial, dental and velar. In spite of the phonological labels that we are adopting, it is important to stress that the voiced 'plosives' are most commonly realized as approximants. The voiceless plosives may, on the other hand, be realized as voiced in certain contexts, in some styles and dialects, as we will explain below. The characterization of the phonemes, therefore, does not necessarily apply to all of their allophonic variants.

In what is taken to be the standard pronunciation, the phonemes /p t k/ are realized as unaspirated voiceless plosives /p t k/, whereas each of the phonemes /b d g/ has two allophones in complementary distribution: voiced plosives /b d g/ are found after pause, after nasals and, in the case of /d/, also after a lateral. Elsewhere these consonants are produced as the approximant allophones [β ð ɣ]. Stated differently, the plosive allophones /b d g/ occur after pause and after a HOMORGANIC sonorant (since, whereas nasals assimilate in place to all following consonants, /l/ only assimilates to consonants produced with the front of the tongue; that is, to dental /d/, but not to labial /b/ or velar /g/). See Table 8.1.

The allophonic distribution just described is somewhat idealized and does not take certain facts of variation into account. We will now proceed to a more detailed description of the /p t k/ vs /b d g/ contrast in Spanish by phonological context, considering also details of variation.

8.2 The voiced/voiceless contrast by phonological context

8.2.1 Utterance-initial plosives

In the production of plosives the formation and release of the oral occlusion must be coordinated with the activity of the vocal folds. If the vocal folds are

8.2 Voiced/voiceless – phonological context

Table 8.1 Spanish voiceless and voiced plosives.

/p/	[p]		*pan* [pán] 'bread', *sopa* [sópa] 'soup'
/t/	[t]		*tan* [tán] 'so', *lata* [láta] 'can'
/k/	[k]		*can* [kán] 'dog', *aquí* [akí] 'here'
/b/	[b]	after pause, after nasal	*van* [bán] 'they go', *ambos* [ámbos] 'both'
	[β]	elsewhere	*se van* [seβán] 'they leave', *desván* [dezβán] 'attic', *calvo* [kálβo] 'bald', *árbol* [árβol] 'tree'
/d/	[d]	after pause, after nasal, after lateral	*dan* [dán] 'they give', *andan* [án̪dan] 'they walk', *caldo* [kál̪do] 'broth'
	[ð]	elsewhere	*lo dan* [loðán] 'they give it', *los dan* [lozðán] 'they give them', *arde* [árðe] 'it burns'
/g/	[g]	after pause, after nasal	*ganso* [gánso] 'goose', *tango* [táŋgo] 'tango'
	[ɣ]	elsewhere	*hago* [áɣo] 'I do', *rasgo* [r̄ázɣo] 'trait', *algo* [álɣo] 'something', *orgullo* [orɣújo] 'pride'

Table 8.2 Voice Onset Time contrasts.

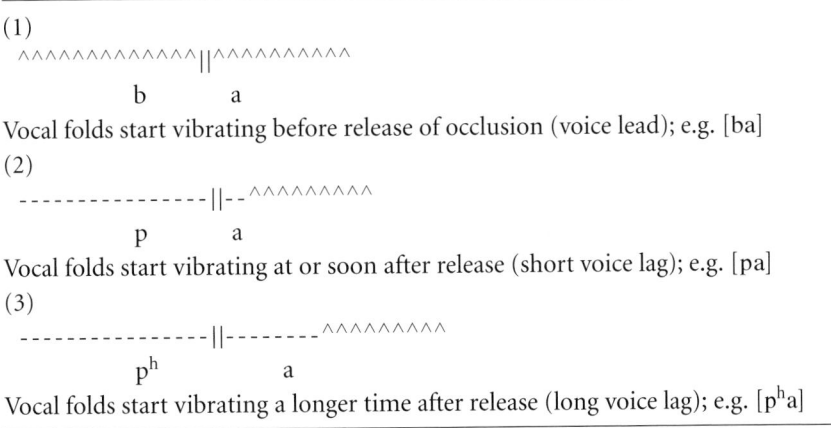

(1)

∧∧∧∧∧∧∧∧∧∧∧||∧∧∧∧∧∧∧∧∧

          b   a

Vocal folds start vibrating before release of occlusion (voice lead); e.g. [ba]

(2)

----------------||--∧∧∧∧∧∧∧∧

          p   a

Vocal folds start vibrating at or soon after release (short voice lag); e.g. [pa]

(3)

----------------||--------∧∧∧∧∧∧∧∧

        p^h   a

Vocal folds start vibrating a longer time after release (long voice lag); e.g. [pʰa]

brought together and are vibrating before the occlusion is released, we will have a voiced plosive. If the onset of voicing is timed to occur at the moment of the release or slightly after, the result is a voiceless stop. Finally, if there is a considerable lapse between the release of the occlusion and the moment at which the vocal folds start vibrating for the following vowel or liquid, aspiration will result between the release of the occlusion and the onset of voicing and we will have a voiceless aspirated plosive.

In Table 8.2 these three coordinations of gestures are schematized. The examples are for plosives with a labial occlusion, but the same applies to the other

Plosives

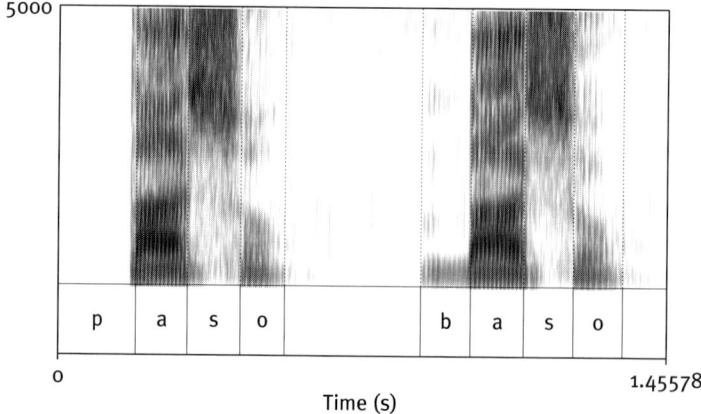

Figure 8.1. Spectrograms paso /páso/ - vaso /báso/. Notice the very brief aspiration at the release of /p/ and the presence of a voice bar (energy in the lowest frequencies) during the occlusion of /b/.

places of articulation. In some languages (e.g. Thai) each of these coordinations of glottal and oral gestures corresponds to a different phoneme: /b/, /p/ and /pʰ/, which differ along the dimension of Voice Onset Time or VOT (Lisker and Abramson 1964). Spanish uses only the first two of these phonetic segments: voiced [b] (with voice lead) and voiceless unaspirated [p] (with short voice lag), corresponding respectively to /b/ and /p/. As we will see later, the facts of English are rather different. English makes use of all three phonetic categories (voice lead, short voice lag and long voice lag), even though, as in Spanish, there are only two phonological categories, /b/ and /p/. In particular, utterance initially, category (2) in Table 8.2 (short voice lag) corresponds to phonemic /p/ in Spanish but is an allophonic realization of phonemic /b/ in English.

In utterance-initial position, the difference between /b d g/ and /p t k/ is fundamentally a matter of VOT. In Spanish, the vocal folds start vibrating for the production of /b d g/ during the occlusion, whereas for /p t k/ the onset of voicing is at or shortly after the release.[1] In Fig. 8.1 this is reflected in the presence of a voice bar in /báso/ [báso] 'glass' and its absence in /páso/ [páso] 'step'. Waveforms of the initial syllables of these examples, [pa] and [ba] are shown in Fig. 8.2. In addition to this difference in VOT, the voiceless plosives

---

[1] Castañeda (1986) obtained the following average VOT values in milliseconds for Peninsular Spanish (negative values indicate voicing before the release of the consonant, which is taken to be the zero point for VOT): /p/ = 6.5, /t/ = 10.4, /k/ = 25.7, /b/ = −69.8, /d/= −77.7, /g/= −58. The values reported in Williams (1977) for four Latin American dialects are similar, but not identical, indicating perhaps the existence of some small but systematic differences in VOT across Spanish dialects (Rosner *et al.* 2000).

8.2 Voiced/voiceless – phonological context

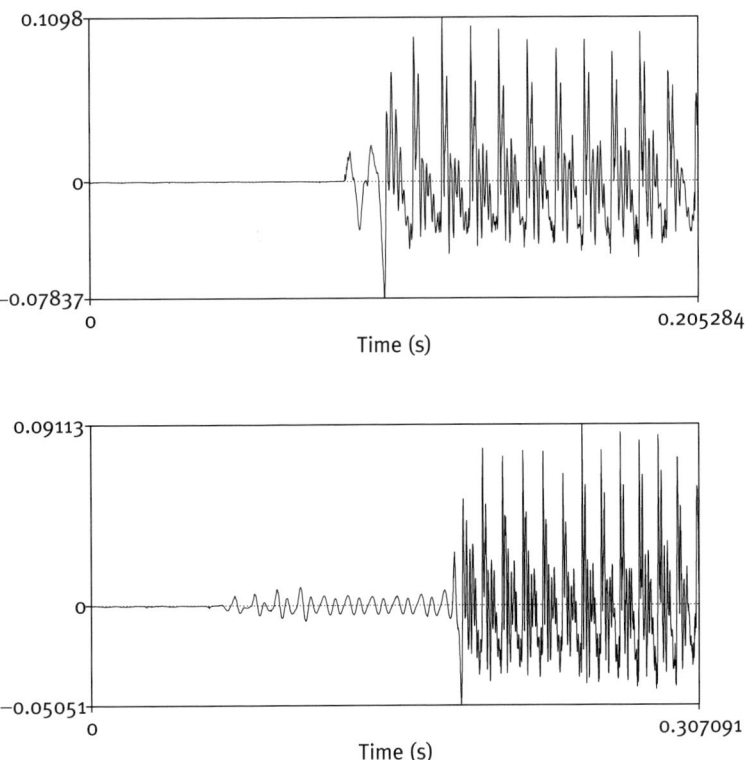

Figure 8.2. Waveforms. Upper panel /pa/, lower panel /ba/.

/p t k/ have a more abrupt release than the voiced plosives /b d g/ (Williams 1977).

Sporadically utterance-initial /b d g/ are produced without full occlusion.

8.2.2 Intervocalic plosives

As we already know, an important feature of Spanish pronunciation is that in intervocalic position /b d g/ are not realized as stops but rather as approximants [β ð ɣ], without full closure and with only approximation of the articulators. Navarro Tomás in his *Manual* calls these allophones 'fricatives' and this term has been adopted by other Spanish phoneticians and phonologists. However, spectrographic analysis clearly shows that these segments lack the aperiodic energy or noise that defines fricative articulations. What the spectrogram of these segments shows is the presence of formant structure creating a transition between the two flanking vowels. The term approximant consonant is therefore more appropriate (Martínez Celdrán 1991a).

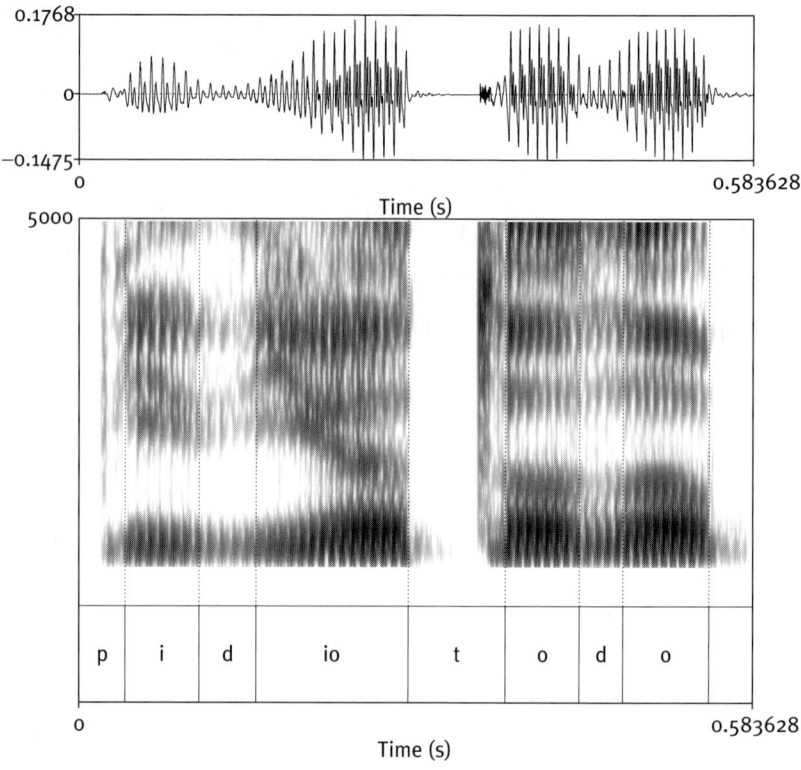

Figure 8.3.   Waveform and spectrogram of /pidió tódo/ [piði̯ó tóðo] 's/he asked for all'. In this particular instance, the second /d/ was produced with less constriction.

Spectrographic analysis also shows considerable variation in the actual amount of periodic energy in Spanish [β ð ɣ], reflecting variation in the degree of constriction. The more open the articulators, the stronger the formant structure, the more vowel-like the spectrogram of these segments will be (see Fig. 8.3). Recent research has started to investigate the factors that contribute to the observable variation. One of them is stress: /b d g/ have more open, vowel-like, articulations after a stressed vowel than in the onset of a stressed syllable. The place of articulation of the surrounding vowels also appears to have an effect, at least for /g/, with more open articulation between low vowels than between high vowels (Cole et al. 1998; Ortega-Llebaria 2003). Between vowels, thus, the contrast is between /b d g/, realized as the voiced approximants [β ð ɣ], and /p t k/, usually realized as the voiceless plosives [p t k]. There is, therefore, both a contrast in voicing (voiced vs voiceless) and a contrast in manner of articulation (approximant vs plosive). In addition there is a difference in duration, with /p t k/ having greater duration than /b d g/. Another example is given in Fig. 8.4.

8.2 Voiced/voiceless – phonological context

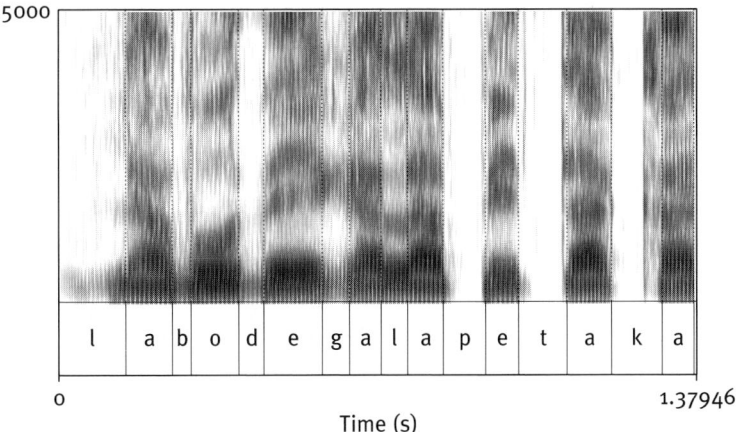

Figure 8.4.   Spectrogram of /la bodéga la petáka/ [laβoðéɣalapetáka] 'the cellar, the cigarette box'.

In the previous paragraph we have said that /p t k/ are 'usually' realized as voiceless plosives. The reason for the hedge 'usually' is that in certain styles and dialects phonological /p t k/ are actually often realized with voicing throughout the occlusion in intervocalic position. The phenomenon is particularly pervasive in Canary Island and Cuban Spanish: *Paco* [págo], *zapato* [sabádo] 'shoe' (Trujillo 1980; Oftedal 1985; Marrero 1988; Quilis 1993:222–4). The voicing of intervocalic /p t k/ is also found in many Peninsular areas in a stylistically restricted way: it is rather frequent in conversational speech, but not in more careful styles, such as reading a text (Torreblanca 1976 for Toledo, Machuca Ayuso 1997 for Barcelona, Lewis 2001 for Bilbao). On the other hand, Colombian Spanish does not participate in this weakening process (Lewis 2001).

Naturally, the question that arises is how the phonological contrast between intervocalic voiced and voiceless plosives is maintained if the 'voiceless' plosives can actually be realized as voiced. Part of the answer is that, since intervocalic phonological /b d g/ are always realized as approximants, there can still be a manner contrast between /b d g/ [-β- -ð- -ɣ-] and /p t k/ [-b- -d- -g-]. This is, however, not the complete answer, for voiced approximant realizations of intervocalic /p t k/ have also been reported. Machuca Ayuso (1997) found that over 40 percent of the conversational tokens of /p t k/ that she analysed were voiced plosives [b d g], but, in addition, about 9 per cent were voiced approximant realizations. One difference even in the case of these maximally weakened instances of phonological /p t k/, though, is that their duration is still greater than that of phonological /b d g/.

144 **Plosives**

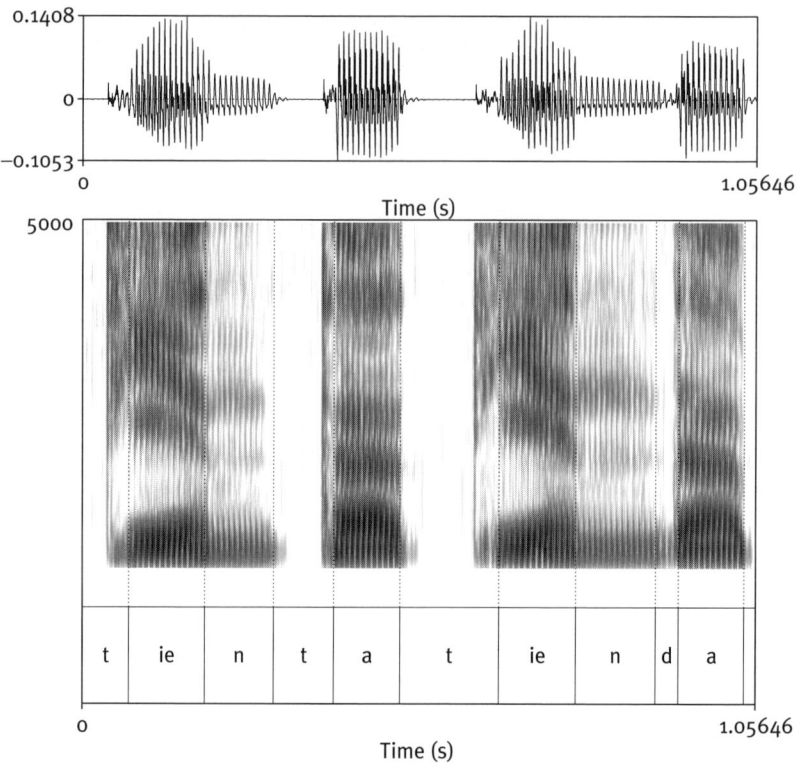

Figure 8.5. Waveform and spectrogram /tiéNta/ [t̪i̯én̪ta] 's/he tempts' vs /tiéNda/ [t̪i̯én̪da] 'shop; tent'. Notice the much greater duration of the occlusion in the postnasal /t/ compared with /d/.

8.2.3 Postconsonantal plosives

As indicated above, in the standard distribution of allophones of /b d g/, the voiced plosives /b d g/ occur after a homorganic sonorant consonant (i.e., in the groups [mb], [n̪d], [l̪d], [ŋg]) and the approximant allophones [β ð ɣ] occur in all other postconsonantal contexts. In contexts where /b d g/ are realized as plosives, the contrast between the two series of phonemes is one of voicing and not of manner (e.g. *tromba* [trómba] 'whirlwind' vs *trompa* [trómpa] 'trunk', *saldo* [sál̪do] 'sale' vs *salto* [sál̪to] 'jump', *tienda* [t̪i̯én̪da] 'shop' vs *tienta* [t̪i̯én̪ta] 's/he tempts', *manga* [máŋga] 'sleeve' vs *manca* [máŋka] 'one-armed, fem.'). The contrast in voicing is manifested in spectrograms as presence vs absence of energy in the lower area of the spectrogram (the voice bar). An equally salient difference when we compare voiced and voiceless plosives in this context, however, is the much greater duration of the occlusion for voiceless stops (Martínez Celdrán 1991b; Zampini and Green 2001) (see Fig. 8.5).

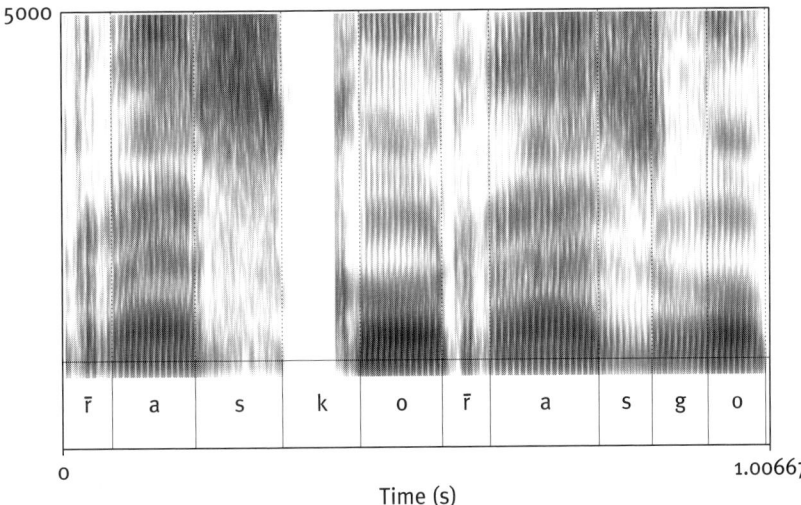

Figure 8.6. Spectrogram /r̄ásko/ [r̄ásko] 'I scratch' vs /r̄ásgo/ [r̄ázɣo] 'trait'.

Duration is thus an important phonetic cue for the contrast in those postconsonantal contexts where /b d g/ are usually realized as plosives.

In other postconsonantal contexts there is a contrast in manner (e.g. *rasgo* [r̄ázɣo] 'trait' vs *rasco* [r̄ásko] 'I scratch', *pardo* [párðo] 'brown, dark' vs *parto* [párto] 'I leave, I divide' (see Fig. 8.6).

A major deviation from this allophonic pattern is found in Central American and Colombian areas where the tendency is to pronounce plosives after all consonants and even glides; e.g. CA/Col. *carbón* [kaɾbón] (standard [kaɾβón]) 'coal', *verde* [béɾde] (standard [béɾðe]) 'green' (Fernandez 1982; Canfield 1981). In colloquial styles of Cuban Spanish voiced plosives are also produced after liquids, which assimilate to the place of articulation of following consonants; e.g. Cu. *el verde* [ebbédde] 'the green one' (Guitart 1976:24). Some variation in the realization of postconsonantal /b d g/ is also found in other areas of Latin America, with phonetic plosives in some of the postconsonantal contexts where approximants occur in the standard distribution (Quilis 1993:221).

It is important to realize that the complementary distribution between two allophones, e.g. [b] and [β], is a simplification of reality. What we have is a continuum of phonetic realization where at one extreme we have complete closure and at the other extreme complete deletion of the consonant. Different phonological contexts favour different ranges of closure degree, and dialects may also differ in this respect, especially in postconsonantal environments. The most general statement, valid for all Spanish dialects, regarding the distribution of allophones of /b d g/, would be the following: between vowels continuant allophones (of variable degrees of constriction) occur; after a nasal we find plosives; in other positions there is variation including both continuant and noncontinuant realizations.

8.2.4 Syllable-final plosives

We must distinguish word-internal from word-final codas. In word-internal syllable-final position, the contrast between the phonologically voiced and phonologically voiceless plosives is neutralized. In spite of the orthographic difference, in standard pronunciation we find the same set of realizations, ranging from a voiceless plosive in emphatic pronunciation to a voiced approximant in more relaxed conversational speech; compare, e.g., *óptimo* 'optimal' and *obtiene* 's/he obtains', both [p ~ β]; *étnico* 'ethnic' and *admirar* 'to admire', both [t ~ ð]; *acné* 'acne' and *agnóstico* 'agnostic', both [k ~ ɣ]. The two pronunciations indicated do not cover the whole range: it is also possible to find voiced plosives as well as partially voiced continuant or noncontinuant realizations; e.g. *apto* [ápto] ~ [áb̥to] ~ [abto] ~ [áβto] 'apt'. The voiced approximant realization can be taken as the standard nonemphatic variant (both for orthograhic *p, t, c*, and for *b, d, g*).

For many speakers of northern varieties of Peninsular Spanish the facts are slightly more complicated. For these speakers, the neutralization of voiced and voiceless plosives in word-internal codas takes place as stated above only for labials and dentals. In the case of the velars, however, these speakers variably or consistently pronounce syllable-final *g* as the voiceless fricative [x] (causing neutralization with the phoneme /x/), but this pronunciation is not extended to words with orthographic *c* in this position; e.g. *digno* [díxno] 'worthy', *signo* [síxno] 'sign', *magno* [máxno] 'great', *zigzag* [θixθáx] 'zigzag' vs *acto* [ákto] ~ [áɣto] 'act', *pacto* [pákto] ~ [páɣto] 'pact', *dicto* [díkto] ~ [díɣto] 'I dictate', *doctor* [doktór] ~ [doɣtór] 'doctor, physician'. In this same dialectal area it is also frequent for syllable-final *c* to be pronounced as [θ], but this pronunciation is somewhat stigmatized and thus less common; e.g. *dicto* [díθto] 'I dictate' (cf. Martínez Martín 1983:189–97; Quilis 1965:23). Both the pronunciation of coda *g* as [x] and of coda *c* as [θ] seem to be orthographically motivated, since the letters *g* and *c* may also have these respective values in other positions.

In Caribbean dialects, all word-internal coda plosives may be realized as a velar consonant or as a glottal stop [ʔ] in emphatic pronunciation: *admitir* [aɣmitír] 'to admit', *submarino* [sukmaríno] (Guitart 1976:23, 48; Zamora and Guitart 1982:109–15).

8.2 Voiced/voiceless – phonological context

In earlier centuries, word-internal coda plosives were probably on their way out of the language. Before the Spanish Academy was established we often find forms like *dino* for *digno* 'worthy', *afeto* for *afecto* 'affect', *lecion* for *lección* 'lesson', *conceto* for *concepto* 'concept', etc. The Academy, however, decided to keep many of these etymological consonants in the orthography[2] and nowadays they are generally pronounced by educated speakers when present in the orthography, with few exceptions. In Castilian Spanish, nevertheless, deletion of the coda consonant, even in careful educated speech is normal in some cases such as the ending *-cción* – e.g. *dirección* [direkθi̯ón] ~ [direɣθi̯ón] ~ [direθi̯ón] 'direction, address' (probably because of the existence of other words like *contaminación* 'pollution') – and *x* before a consonant, e.g. *experimento* [esperiméṉto] 'experiment', *extraño* [estráɲo].[3] Educated Mexican is more conservative in this respect than Castilian. In rural speech of many areas, both in Spain and Latin America, on the other hand, the vocalization and deletion of coda plosives is very common, e.g. *doctor* [dou̯tór] ~ [dotór] 'doctor', *perfectamente* [perfétaméṉte] 'fine'.

Word finally, the only plosive in native words is /d/. The most common realization of this phoneme, in educated speech, is as the approximant [ð], just like other instances of postvocalic /d/ – *salud* [salúð] 'health' – but the reduction and deletion of the consonant is also common, especially in colloquial styles, [salúð̞] ~ [salú]. In Standard Castilian deletion of final /d/ in colloquial speech is possible with words of more than one syllable (*salud* 'health', *verdad* 'truth', *Madrid*) but not with monosyllables (*sed* 'thirst', *red* 'net', *vid* 'vine'), and only before pause or a consonant-initial word (not in, e.g., *salud envidiable* 'enviable health').[4] In Andalusian, deletion is also possible and common in monosyllables and may even be found in the prevocalic context (but in Andalusian word-internal intervocalic /-d-/ is also subject to deletion).

In north-central Spain a voiceless fricative realization of /-d/ is not uncommon: [salúθ] (see, for instance, Martínez Martín 1983). For many speakers of this area *pez* [péθ] 'fish' rhymes with *sed* [séθ] 'thirst', *red* [r̄éθ] 'net', although a difference surfaces in the plural: *peces* [péθes] 'fishes' vs *redes* [r̄éðes] 'nets'.[5] The interdental voiceless fricative realization is less common (but not impossible) if a vowel-initial word follows: *se*[ð] *enorme* (~*se*[θ] *enorme*) 'enormous thirst'. Naturally (partially) devoiced dental approximants

---

[2] Not all, however. An interesting case in modern Spanish is the pair *respecto* 'respect, adverb' (*con respecto a* 'regarding, with respect to') vs *respeto* 'respect, noun'. Both variants are allowed in cases like *septiembre* ~ *setiembre* 'September'.
[3] This phonological simplification is the source of frequent hypercorrected misspellings like *expléndido* for *espléndido* 'splendid', *extricto* for *estricto* 'strict', etc.
[4] Except for *usted* 'you', which can be said to have *usté* as an alternative variant in all contexts.
[5] Humoristically, one sometimes finds the spelling *Madriz* for *Madrid*.

Plosives

Table 8.3 Pronunciation of word-final orthographic -d, -t, -g, -c, -k, -b, -p in educated Castilian Spanish.

Letter	Common pronunciations	Notes
-d	[ð ~ θ ~ 0] *salud* [ð ~ θ] *sed*	Deletion only in words of two or more syllables. Partial neutralization with /θ/.
-t	[t] *déficit*	
-g	[ɣ ~ x] *zigzag*	Partial neutralization with /x/ and /k/.
-k, -c	[k ~ ɣ ~ 0] *coñac* [k] *bloc*	Deletion only in words of two or more syllables.
-b	[β ~ b ~ 0] *club* [f] *pub* /páf/	Only in a few borrowings. Word-specific pronunciations.
-p	[p] *stop*	Only in a few borrowings.

(*se*[ð̥]) are also found as an intermediate realization. Interestingly, a devoiced or partially devoiced continuant pronunciation of final /-d/ has also been reported for Central Mexico, a dialect that lacks the phoneme /θ/ (J. Harris 1969:40). Both in Catalan-speaking areas and in parts of South America, -*d* is realized as [t]: [salút] (in South America in somewhat emphatic speech, in Catalonia in all styles in the speech of many speakers).

Final -*t* is found in borrowings from Classical Latin and other languages like *cénit* 'zenith' and *déficit* 'deficit' and Catalan names like *Bonet*. Whether /t/ neutralizes with /d/ in word-final position depends on the pronunciation of final /-d/ in the specific dialect. In standard Castilian Spanish there is no neutralization: /-t/ [t] as in *cénit* [θénit] contrasts with /-d/, realized as a (voiced or voiceless) continuant as in *red* [r̄éð] ~ [r̄éθ]. That is, final /d/ partially neutralizes with /θ/, not with /t/, whereas in word-internal codas /t/ and /d/ neutralize. In the Spanish of Catalonia and those South American varieties where word-final -*d* can be [t], on the other hand, /t/ and /d/ neutralize in this position.

Word-final -*b* and -*p* are only found in a few recent borrowings, which often have idiosyncratic pronunciation. Thus in much of Spain *club* is usually pronounced [klúβ] (~ [klúb]), with a more reduced form [klú] before pause or consonant (and perhaps an emphatic form [klúp], also before pause or consonant, not before a vowel) but *pub* has a variant [páf] – that is, /páf/.

As for the velars, we find partial neutralization in Castilian. Both -*g* and -*k* or -*c* can be pronounced as [k ~ g ~ ɣ] but, in addition, -*g* can be pronounced as [x], as in *zigzag* [θixθáx], *bulldog* [buldóx].

Table 8.4 Word-final plosives before a vowel in Castilian Spanish.

/-d/	[ð] ~([θ])	salu[ð] enorme (salu[θ] enorme) 'enormous health'
/-t/	[t]	défici[t] enorme 'enormous deficit'
/-g/	[ɣ] (~[x])	zigza[ɣ] extraño (zigza[x] extraño) 'strange zigzag'
/-k/	[k]	coña[k] extraño 'strange brandy'
/-b/	[β]	clu[β] americano 'American club'
/-p/	[p]	lapto[p] americano 'American laptop'

We may conclude that in Castilian Spanish, word finally, unlike what happens in word-internal codas, there is no complete neutralization between voiced and voiceless plosive phonemes, since a difference usually surfaces before a vowel in a following word and may also surface in other phrasal contexts. On the other hand, /-d/ may neutralize with /-θ/ and /-g/ with /-x/, at least for some speakers, including educated speakers. This is summarized and exemplified in Table 8.4. In Mexican Spanish devoiced pronunciations of /-d/ and /-g/ are also found, although with different consequences for the system of phonological contrasts.

8.3 Spanish and English plosives in contrast

In English, word-initial /p t k/ are realized as aspirated [pʰ tʰ kʰ]; that is, with long VOT lag: *pot* [pʰɑt], *top* [tʰɑp], *cop* [kʰɑp]. Voiceless aspirated plosives also occur word internally on the onset of stressed syllables: *appeal* [əpʰiɫ]. On the other hand, these phonemes are not aspirated after the stress, as in *rapid*, or after initial /s/ as in *spot* [spɑt], *stop* [stɑp], a position where the /p t k/ and /b d g/ series are actually neutralized (*sbot, *sdop).

As for English /b d g/, utterance initially these phonemes may be realized with voicing during the occlusion (voice lead) [b d g], as in Spanish, but they are also very frequently realized as voiceless unaspirated, [b̥ d̥ g̊]. Voiced and voiceless unaspirated plosives are in free variation in this position as allophones of /b d g/ in English. The opposition between word-initial /p t k/ and /b d g/ in English is thus one of aspiration, rather than voice (unlike in Spanish). In terms of VOT, English word-initial /b d g/, if realized as voiceless, may be identical to Spanish /p t k/. This can give rise to confusions in both directions in second-language situations: native English speakers may produce initial /b d g/ as voiceless in Spanish, causing them to be misperceived as Spanish /p t k/ (e.g. *bollo* misperceived as *pollo*), and, on the other hand, native Spanish speakers

Table 8.5 Voice Onset Time contrasts in initial position and phonological categories in Spanish and English.

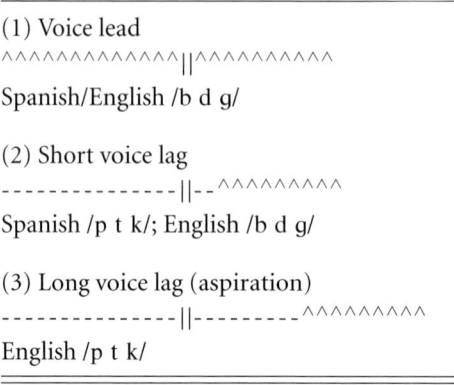

(1) Voice lead
∧∧∧∧∧∧∧∧∧∧∧∧||∧∧∧∧∧∧∧∧∧
Spanish/English /b d g/

(2) Short voice lag
---------------||--∧∧∧∧∧∧∧∧
Spanish /p t k/; English /b d g/

(3) Long voice lag (aspiration)
---------------||---------∧∧∧∧∧∧∧∧
English /p t k/

learning English often produce English /p t k/ without aspiration, leading to confusion with /b d g/ (e.g. *pier* misinterpreted as *beer*).

To repeat, in utterance-initial position the two series of Spanish plosives contrast in voicing: voiceless /p t k/ [p t k] contrast with voiced /b d g/ [b d g]. In English on the other hand, these two phonological series contrast in aspiration in this position: /p t k/ are voiceless aspirated [pʰ tʰ kʰ] whereas /b d g/ are unaspirated and may be realized as either voiced [b d g] or as voiceless [b̥ d̥ g̥] (= [p t k] in VOT, although with differences in release properties).

Word internally, the position of the stress is crucial to determine the allophony of /p t k/ in English. As mentioned, after the stressed vowel these consonants are realized as unaspirated. The contrast between *rapid* and *rabid* is one of voicing, not aspiration. In addition, in this position the consonantal contrast is cued by the length of the preceding vowels: vowels are considerably longer before voiced than before voiceless segments. This is especially apparent in word-final position, where the consonant may undergo partial or total devoicing, but the contrast is still robust thanks to the durational effects on the preceding vowel, as in *mat* [mæt] vs *mad* [mæːd̥]. This effect is not found in Spanish.

In American English, and in some other English varieties, /t/ and /d/ after a stressed vowel and before an unstressed one (as in *petal, pedal, writer, rider, butting, budding*) are neutralized and realized as a segment known as 'flap', an oral stop with a very short closure (although the contrast may be recoverable from the length and quality of the preceding vowel, at least in some varieties). This 'flap' is very much like Spanish /ɾ/, although not identical to it (see 11.3.1). Spanish, of course, does not display flapping of /t/ or /d/. The transfer of this process from English to Spanish is to be carefully avoided, since the realization of, e.g., *todo* 'all' with a 'flap' will tend to be interpreted as *toro* [tóɾo] 'bull'.

An additional difference between the two languages has to do with place of articulation. In Spanish, /t/ and /d/ are (apico-)dental. In English these consonants have a more retracted, alveolar, articulation.

EXERCISES

1 For the following examples indicate whether the underlined segment represents (a) the voiceless velar fricative [x], (b) the voiced velar plosive [g] or (c) the voiced velar approximant [ɣ].

   le*j*os, si*gu*e, á*g*il, *gu*erra, ten*g*o, al*g*o, *g*ime, la*g*o

2 The contrast between the two phonological series /p t k/ and /b d g/ in Spanish is generally considered to depend on the feature 'voice' (voiceless vs voiced). Martínez Celdrán (1991b), on the other hand, argues that this is essentially a contrast of 'tension' (tense vs lax) primarily manifested in differences in duration. Evaluate this proposal.

3 Williams (1977) performed a perception experiment in which Spanish speakers were asked to identify plosive-initial words before and after modification. His results showed that the presence of prevoicing is very important for the correct perception of initial voiced plosives, since when the initial voice bar is removed in an example like *baño* correct identification declines considerably and listeners tend to hear *paño* instead. However, the change in perception is not categorical: it is not the case that such modified tokens are perceived as unambiguously starting with a voiceless plosive. How can you explain these results?

9 Fricatives and affricates

9.1 Affricates

Affricates differ from plosives in the presence of strong friction at the release of the occlusion. Affricates thus have two phases: occlusion and friction, at the same place of articulation.

Spanish has a single affricate phoneme /t͡ʃ/ which we may define as a prepalatal voiceless affricate, as in *mucho* /mút͡ʃo/ 'much'. The exact place of articulation of this segment, however, varies a great deal. A very advanced, alveolar articulation [t͡s] is found in areas of Chile and, as a more recent and socially variable phenomenon, in the speech of young female speakers in the Bilbao area (Basque Country). On the other hand, in the Canaries and Cuba this consonant can have a fully palatal articulation, properly becoming a palatal plosive (known as *ch adherente* in Spanish dialectology). Furthermore, in keeping with the tendency to voice intervocalic plosives in these dialects, it can be realized as either a voiceless palatal plosive [c] or as its voiced counterpart [ɟ]: Can./Cu. *muchacho* [mucáco] ~ [muɟáɟo] 'boy' (see Trujillo 1980 for spectrographic evidence).

Another important dialectal phenomenon is the deaffrication of /t͡ʃ/; that is, the loss of the occlusive element of the affricate, resulting in the fricative [ʃ] (as in English *sheep*): *muchacho* [muʃáʃo]. This lenitive development has been attested in a number of separate areas including parts of Andalusia, Northern Mexico (Sonora and Chihuahua), Panama and parts of Chile.

The phoneme /t͡ʃ/ is limited in its distribution to the prevocalic position. Final [t͡ʃ] is, however, found in spelling pronunciations of Catalan names with orthographic *-ch*, such as *Llorach*, *Blanch*, *Domenech*, etc.[1]

Old Spanish had, in addition to preplatal /t͡ʃ/, a pair of dental affricate phonemes, voiceless /t͡s/ and voiced /t͡z/. These sounds eventually become

---

[1] Even though this traditional Catalan spelling represents /-k/ in this language.

/θ/ in Castilian Spanish and merged with /s/ in Andalusian and all of Latin American Spanish (more details below).

In Mexican Spanish, dental /t͡s/, written *tz*, is found in toponyms of indigenous origin such as *Netzahualcóyotl*.

In Peninsular Spanish dental and alveolar affricates from other languages are usually adapted as either fricatives or as the affricate /t͡ʃ/, although an attempt to preserve the affricate suggested by the spelling is made in the case of technical terms such as *mosca tsetsé* 'tsetse fly'. In surnames, place names and other words of Basque origin the apico-alveolar fricative *ts* /t͡s̺/ of Basque is sometimes replaced by /s/ as in Bq. *Altsasua* > Sp. *Alsasua* (name of a town), and other times replaced by /t͡ʃ/, as in Bq. *otsoa* 'the wolf' > *Ochoa* (surname). The predorso-dental fricative *tz* /t͡s̻/ of Basque, on the other hand, is traditionally rendered as Castilian /θ/, as in *elortza* 'hawthorn' > *Elorza* (surname), but in recent borrowings this pronunciation sometimes competes with /t͡ʃ/; e.g. Bq. *abertzale* 'patriot, nationalist' may be heard in Peninsular Spanish as either [aβerθále] or [aβert͡ʃále] and both pronunciations are also heard for the name *Itziar*.

9.2 Fricatives

Spanish dialects vary both in terms of inventory of fricative phonemes and in the phonetic realization of these phonemes. Standard Peninsular Spanish has four voiceless fricative phonemes: /f θ s x/. The phoneme /s/ is realized as apico-alveolar [s̺] and /x/ has a strident postvelar or even UVULAR realization, [χ]. In contrast, what we may term Standard Latin American Spanish has three voiceless fricatives: /f s x/, where /s/ is predorso-alveolar [s̻] and /x/ medio-velar [x] or LARYNGEAL [h].

9.2.1 /s/ and /θ/

Although the contrast between /s/ and /θ/ (*distinción* /s/-/θ/), as in *sien* /sién/ 'temple, side of head' vs *cien* /θién/ 'a hundred', is part of Standard Peninsular Spanish, it is not found in all of Spain, as it is not made in the Canary Islands, in large areas of Andalusia or in parts of Extremadura. In Andalusia we find a great degree of social and geographical variation. In some Andalusian areas there is a contrast between /s/ and /θ/, with /s/ generally realized as predorsal, not as apical, unlike in Castilian. In most of Andalusia, however, there is a single phoneme, which is realized as predorso-alveolar [s̻] in some areas (*seseo*), but as a less sibilant dentalized sound [θ̞], which resembles Castilian [θ], in other areas (*ceceo*). Due to recent mobility, nowadays in

Andalusian cities such as Seville and Granada it is possible to find speakers who practise *distinción*, speakers who employ *seseo* and speakers who use *ceceo*. In terms of social distribution in Andalusia, *distinción*, as part of the Peninsular standard, has greater prestige, followed by *seseo*, which can be considered the local standard, whereas *ceceo* is considered 'rural' and is evaluated negatively by Andalusian city-dwellers.

Within northern and central Spain, the phonological contrast /s/-/θ/ is completely general (except for perhaps a few native speakers of Basque and Catalan). The realization of /s/ is generally apico-alveolar in this area, with the apex against the upper alveolar region. In the northernmost area of the Peninsula, that is, in the Basque Country and surrounding area, the articulation is slightly more retracted, which gives it a more sibilant sound. In many Latin American countries there is much awareness of Castilian apical [ṣ] as a foreign pronunciation, which is very much part of the humoristic stereotype of people of northern Peninsular origin.

In Latin America *distinción* /s/-/θ/ is not found anywhere.[2] The most widespread articulation of the phoneme /s/ is as predorso-alveolar [s̻] (which is also the most common realization of /s/ in English). The Castilian apical [ṣ] has been reported for Antioquia, Colombia (Canfield 1981:36). As for *ceceo* with predorso-dental [θ̻], this phenomenon appears to be common, but subject to individual variation, in the Central American countries of El Salvador, Honduras and Guatemala.

9.2.2 Variation in the articulation of /x/

Besides the pronunciation of /s/ and /θ/, another characteristic feature of northern and central Peninsular Spanish is a retracted pronunciation of /x/ as a strident postvelar fricative [χ]: *jota* 'letter *j*; a dance', *ajo* 'garlic', Cast. [χóta], [áχo]. In Andalusian and Canary Island varieties, on the other hand, this phoneme is realized as an aspiration (laryngeal fricative) [h], which may be voiced [ɦ] between vowels: And. [hóta], [áɦo].[3]

In Latin American Spanish, two main pronunciations of this sound are found. One is a velar [x], not as retracted as the Castilian sound and less strident: Mex./Arg. [xóta], [áxo]. The other main pronunciation is as [h], very much like the corresponding English sound: Col. [hóta], [áho]. The laryngeal

---

[2] As already noted in 2.3, there have been reports of its marginal existence in the Cuzco area of Peru, where perhaps a few words are contrastively pronounced with /θ/ by some speakers (Caravedo 1992).

[3] This pronunciation is also found in some rural dialects of Cantabria, in northern Spain (Penny 1978; Nuño Alvarez 1996).

pronunciation [h] predominates in Caribbean, Central American and Colombian varieties, whereas velar [x] is found in Mexico, Peru, Chile and Argentina.

When /x/ is produced with dorsal constriction, this constriction is more advanced in the mouth before a front vowel /i e/ (*gente, ágil*) than before a central or back vowel /a o u/ (*baja, rojo, justo*). This assimilation in place is also found with the other velar consonants /k/, /g/, and also occurs in English (cf. *car key*). In Chilean Spanish, however, the assimilation has been taken further resulting in a distinctive voiceless palatal fricative [ç] before a front vowel: Chil. *gente* /xénte/ [çéṇte] 'people', vs *ajo* /áxo/ [áxo] 'garlic'. One may speak of two quite distinct allophones in complementary distribution in this dialect. To speakers of other Spanish dialects, this palatal fricative of Chilean Spanish often produces the impression of a palatal glide inserted after the consonant. They may insist, for instance, that Chileans say '*giente*' for *gente*.

9.2.3 Summary of dialectal variation in the place of articulation of the fricatives

Table 9.1 summarizes the details of dialectal variation in the place of articulation of fricatives.

9.2.4 /s/ and /θ/ and Spanish 'jota' in historical perspective

Although this is not a book on historical phonology, it seems appropriate to devote a few paragraphs to considering the historical developments that gave rise to the *seseo* and *distinción* /s/-/θ/ systems, since this is the most important phonological difference between the Spanish of all of Latin America and Standard Peninsular Spanish. It is also worth considering briefly the historical reason for the unusual value that orthographic *j, g(e,i)* is given in Spanish, when compared with the other Romance languages and English, and the rather striking sound correspondences we find: e.g. Eng. *general*, It. *generale*, both with /d͡ʒ/, Fr. *général* with /ʒ/, but Sp. *general* with /x/. Both phenomena are, in fact, related.

Medieval Castilian had four sibilant (or 's-like') phonemes instead of the two of modern northern-central Peninsular Spanish and the one of Latin American Spanish. From diverse sources of information, it has been established that Old Castilian distinguished between voiceless /s/ and voiced /z/, although the contrast was limited to the intervocalic position. In the orthography, the voiceless intervocalic fricative /s/ was generally represented as -*ss*-, whereas intervocalic -*s*- indicated the voiced fricative phoneme /z/ – e.g. *passa* /pása/ 's/he passes' vs *casa* /káza/ 'house' (very much as in modern Portuguese and Catalan). In at least the original Castilian area, these fricatives were apico-alveolar [s̺], [z̺];

Fricatives and affricates

Table 9.1 Spanish fricative phonemes: dialectal variation in place of articulation.

/f/	[f] voiceless labiodental fricative	Standard variant.
	[ɸ] voiceless bilabial fricative	Reported as common variant in both Spain and Latin America, especially in rural areas.
/θ/	[θ] voiceless interdental fricative	A phoneme only in northern and central Spain (Standard Peninsular Spanish).
/s/	[s̺] voiceless apico-alveolar fricative	Northern and central Spain (most retracted in the Basque Country and adjacent areas), also in parts of Colombia (Antioquia).
	[s̻] voiceless predorso-alveolar fricative	Standard Latin American variant, also parts of southern Spain.
	[θ̱] voiceless predorso-dental fricative	'Ceceo'. Common in parts of Andalusia and in some Central American areas (El Salvador, Honduras, Nicaragua).
/x/	[χ] voiceless postvelar or uvular fricative	Castilian Spanish. More advanced before /i e/.
	[x] voiceless velar fricative	Mexico, Peru, Argentina, etc. Mid-velar before /a o u/, prevelar before /i e/.
	[ç] voiceless palatal fricative	Found in Chile before /i e/.
	[h] voiceless laryngeal fricative	Caribbean, Central America, Colombia, Andalusia, Canary Islands.

that is, the type of articulation still found in the northern part of the Peninsula. In addition to these two fricatives, Old Castilian had a pair of dental affricates also contrasting in voice: voiceless dental affricate /t͡s/, spelled with ç (*c cedilla*)[4] (before a front vowel, also *c*), as in *braço* /brát͡so/ 'arm', *plaça* /plát͡sa/ 'square'; and voiced dental affricate /d͡z/, written *z*, as in *dezir* /ded͡zír/ 'to say', *fazer* /had͡zér/ 'to do'.

There was also a third pair of fricatives, which we may include among the 'sibilants', employing this term in a loose sense: voiceless prepalatal /ʃ/, written *x*, as in *dixo* /díʃo/ 's/he said', *caxa* /káʃa/ 'box', and its voiced counterpart /ʒ/, written *j*, *i* or *g* (before a front vowel) as in *ojo*, *oio* /óʒo/ 'eye', *mugér* /muʒér/ 'woman', *coger* /koʒér/ 'to take, grab'. See Table 9.2.

---

[4] Although this letter is no longer used in Spanish its name betrays Castilian origin: *c cedilla* 'c with a small zed'. From Castilian this letter spread to other languages that still have it in their orthography, such as Portuguese, Catalan and French.

9.2 Fricatives

Table 9.2 The Old Spanish sibilants.

Phoneme		Spelling	Example
/s/	voiceless apico-alveolar fricative	s-, -ss-	*saco* /sáko/ 'sack', *passa* /pása/ 's/he passes'
/z/	voiced apico-alveolar fricative	-s-	*cosa* /kóza/ 'thing'
/t͡s/	voiceless dental affricate	ç, c	*caça* /kát͡sa/ 'hunt'
/d͡z/	voiced dental affricate	z	*dizia* /did͡zía/ 's/he said, *imp.*'
/ʃ/	voiceless prepalatal fricative	x	*dixo* /díʃo/ 's/he said, *pret.*'
/ʒ/	voiced prepalatal fricative	j, i, g(e,i)	*ojo* /óʒo/ 'eye'

Over several centuries, starting in the late Middle Ages and continuing up to the seventeenth century, these sounds underwent a series of changes that profoundly altered the phonological system. This transformation started with two quite distinct changes. First of all, the affricates lost their occlusion, becoming fricatives. Secondly, the voiced/voiceless contrast was lost through the devoicing of the voiced phonemes. These processes started in some areas before others, although eventually they spread to all dialects of Spanish. In particular, the devoicing of the voiced sibilants started very early in the northernmost Castilian-speaking areas of the Peninsula, in the Burgos area, and only centuries later became established also in Toledo and Seville. In fact, modern Judeo-Spanish, still spoken by some of the descendants of the Jews expelled from Spain in the fifteenth and sixteenth centuries, preserves the voiced/voiceless distinction (see 2.5).[5]

After these two changes, the Spanish spoken in northern and central regions of the Peninsula ended up with a system containing three voiceless fricatives produced in a relatively small articulatory region: predorso-alveolar or predorso-dental /s̻/ (from the older dental affricates /t͡s/ and /d͡z/), apico-alveolar /s̺/ (from both older /s/ and /z/) and prepalatal /ʃ/ (from both older /ʃ/ and /ʒ/). Notice that, after the older dental affricates lost their occlusive

---

[5] Menéndez Pidal (1973[1904]) identifies some small areas of the Peninsula, mostly in Extremadura, where the Old Spanish distinction between voiced and voiceless sibilants was still found at the beginning of the twentieth century. Since then, it appears to have been lost everywhere except in the dialect of Serradilla (Ariza 1994). Among the other local dialects mentioned by Menéndez Pidal, a particularly interesting geographical point is Malpartida de Plasencia, an island of *ceceo* in the province of Cáceres where, in the local dialect, known as *chinato*, the Old Spanish voiceless fricatives /s/ and /t͡s/ had become /θ/ and the voiced ones, /z/ and /d͡z/, had evolved to /d/ (intervocalically [ð]) (see Menéndez Pidal 1906; Catalán 1958; Hualde 1991a).

Table 9.3 Evolution of the Old Spanish 'sibilants' in northern and central Spain.

a. Evolution of the OSp. dental affricates			
Deaffr. & devoicing	Interdentaliz.	Mod. Cast.	
/t͡s/ ⟶ /s̪/ > /d͡z/ ⟶		/θ/	Examples: /brát͡so/ > /brás̪o/ > /bráθo/ *brazo* /ded͡zír/ > /des̪ír/ > /deθír/ *decir*

b. Evolution of the OSp. alveolar fricatives			
Devoicing		Mod. Cast.	
/s/ ⟶ /s̺/ = /z/ ⟶		/s/ [s̺]	Examples: /pása/ (no change) *pasa* /káza/ > /kása/ *casa*

c. Evolution of the OSp. prepalatal fricatives			
Devoicing	Velarizat.	Mod. Cast.	
/ʃ/ ⟶ /ʃ/ > /ʒ/ ⟶		/x/	Examples: /óʒo/ > /óʃo/ > /óxo/ *ojo* /éʒe/ > /éxe/ *eje*

element, their difference in place of articulation from the older (apico-alveolar) fricatives, which before was redundant, became distinctive.

After this, these three fricatives increased their articulatory distance. Both /s̪/ and /ʃ/ moved away from apico-alveolar /s̺/. The most fronted phoneme, /s̪/, advanced its place of articulation even further becoming the interdental /θ/. Modern Castilian Spanish thus has the phoneme /θ/ in those words where Old Castilian had dental affricates. In turn, prepalatal /ʃ/ retracted its place of articulation to velar /x/, perhaps with a palatal fricative /ç/ as an intermediate stage. The new velar pronunciation /x/ became the norm only towards the end of the sixteenth century.[6] See Table 9.3.

It is likely that in Andalusia the old fricatives were predorso-alveolar or predorso-dental and not apico-alveolar, unlike in more northerly regions of the Peninsula. The fact is that when the affricates deaffricated, they simply merged with the fricatives. The end result of the deaffrication and devoicing process is that the four phonemes of Medieval Spanish /s/, /z/, /t͡s/ and /d͡z/

---

[6] We may note that other Romance varieties in the area of influence of Castilian, such as Galician, Asturian, Aragonese and some varieties of Valencian Catalan, also devoiced the old fricatives, but did not undergo velarization of /ʃ/ (cf., for instance, Gal. *xunta* /ʃúnta/ for Sp. *junta* /xúnta/). On the other hand, Gipuzkoan Basque did share the change /ʃ/ > /x/.

9.2 Fricatives

Table 9.4 Evolution of the Old Spanish sibilants in Andalusia and Latin America

Deaffr. & devoicing	Andal. & Lat Am.	Examples:
/s/ /z/ /t͡s/ /d͡z/	/s/ [s̺] (predorso-alveolar or dental)	/pása/ > /pása/ /káza/ > /kása/ /brát͡so/ > /bráso/ /ded͡zír/ > /desír/

became a single phoneme /s/ in southern Spain and in all of Latin American Spanish. See Table 9.4.

As in the north and centre, the old prepalatal fricatives retracted their point of articulation after merging in a single voiceless sound. However, in parts of Andalusia the retraction process went further, resulting in [h]: *ojo* [óho].[7]

9.2.5 Syllable-final and word-final fricatives

Fricatives in the coda are subject to two phonological processes: assimilation in voice to a following consonant and weakening (aspiration and deletion).

9.2.5.1 Voice assimilation of coda fricatives

In dialects where /s/ is normally preserved in the coda, this segment often assimilates in voice to a voiced consonant, both word internally, *mismo* [mízmo] 'same', and across word boundaries, *dos más* [dóz más] 'two more'. Although we use the symbol [z], this segment may present only partial or incomplete voicing.

Voice assimilation takes place before a word-initial glide (including cases of prefixation with *des-*), since glides are consonantized in this position (see 9.3): *los hielos* /los iélos/ [lozɟélos] 'the ices', *los huesos* /los uésos/ [lozɣuésos] 'the bones'.

On the other hand, most Spanish dialects do not voice word-final /s/ before a vowel: *las alas* [lasálas] 'the wings', *los amigos* [losamíɣos] 'the friends' (voicing of word-final /s/ before a vowel has nevertheless been reported for Highland Ecuadorian Spanish: Ec. *los amigos* [lozamíɣos] 'the friends' – Lipski 1994:248 and references therein – and is also sometimes found as a bilingual transfer phenomenon in the speech of Catalan–Spanish bilinguals).

---

[7] A direct change from /ʒ/ and /ʃ/ to [h] is attested, for instance, in dialects of Quebec French (Morgan 1975). Furthermore, the posteriorization of /ʃ/ is attested in Andalusia at an earlier date than in Castile (Eddington 1990 and references therein). It is thus not necessary to assume that in all areas there was a gradual process of retraction.

Table 9.5 Voice assimilation of syllable-final /s/.

Contexts of possible voicing (complete or partial)		Contexts where voicing is not possible	
/sb/	*esbelto* [ezβélto] 'svelte'	/sp/	*espía* [espía] 'spy'
/sd/	*desde* [dézðe] 'from'	/st/	*este* [éste] 'this'
/sg/	*rasgo* [r̄ázɣo] 'trait'	/sk/	*rasco* [r̄ásko] 'I scratch'
/sm/	*mismo* [mízmo] 'same'	/sf/	*esfera* [esféra] 'sphere'
/sn/	*asno* [ázno] 'donkey'	/ss/	*los sacos* [los:ákos] 'the bags'
/sl/	*isla* [ízla] 'island'	/sx/	*los jardines* [losxarðínes] 'the gardens'
/sr̄/	*Israel* [izɹaél]	/stʃ/	*los chicos* [lostʃíkos] 'the boys'
/siV/	*deshielo* [dezjélo] 'thawing'	/sV/*	*los hijos* [losíxos] 'the children'

*Voicing in Ecuadorian.

The interdental fricative /θ/ of Castilian Spanish also undergoes voicing in the same contexts as /s/. The resulting allophone is a voiced interdental fricative, which differs from the continuant allophone of /d/, since it is more interdental and is a fricative. It is in fact rather more similar to the English voiced interdental fricative sound in *this*. We may symbolize this voiced allophone of /θ/ as [ð̪], since we are using [ð] without a diacritic for the continuant allophone of /d/: *juzgado* Cast. /xuθgádo/ [xuð̪ɣáðo] 'court'. Alternatively, we could transcribe this sound as [θ̬] adding a diacritic for voicing to the symbol for the voiceless interdental fricative. The important thing to note is that this voiced fricative is different from the voiced approximant of, say, *cada* [káða] 'each'. Nevertheless, in Castilian Spanish syllable-final /-d/ may also be realized as voiceless and with friction so that, in this dialect, we may indeed find the same sound in *ju<u>z</u>gar* 'to judge' and *a<u>d</u>junto* 'adjunct', *pe<u>z</u>* 'fish' and *re<u>d</u>* 'net'.

The labiodental fricative is very infrequent in syllable-final position. In the few words where it appears before a voiced consonant it undergoes voicing: *afgano* [avɣáno]. Notice that this is the only context where the voiced labiodental fricative [v] is found in standard dialects of Spanish.

On the other hand, /x/, which is also very rare in the coda, appears to resist voicing assimilation: *boj verde* [bóxβérðe] 'green box bush'. In fact, we noted in 8.2.4 that the tendency is for coda /g/ to devoice to [x] in Castilian and Mexican Spanish, even before voiced consonants, as in *signo* [síxno] 'sign'.

It is important to note that in standard Spanish, unlike in English, the voiced fricatives [z] and [v] are only allophones of the corresponding voiceless consonants /s/, /f/. These allophones, furthermore, have a very limited distribution: they are only found before a voiced consonant. English speakers sometimes display a tendency to pronounce orthographic -s- as voiced in cognates such as *presidente* 'president', *visitar* 'to visit'. This does not correspond to native Spanish pronunciation. Word-internal intervocalic /s/ is never voiced in Spanish: [presiðénte], [bisitár]. As mentioned in the section above, Old Spanish did have intervocalic /z/ (like most other Romance languages), but this sound was devoiced centuries ago. Remember also that orthographic *z* represents /θ/ in northern-central Peninsular Spanish and /s/ in other dialects: *zona* is [θóna] in Castilian and [sóna] in Latin American Spanish; it is never *[zóna] (cf. Eng. *zone* /zon/). As for orthographic *v*, it has exactly the same value as orthographic *b*; that is /b/, with allophones [b] ∼ [β] (except for some bilingual varieties in contact with English or with other languages with phonemic /v/).

9.2.5.2 Aspiration and deletion of /s/

The weakening of /s/ is one of the most intensively researched phenomena of phonological variation in Spanish. In Spain, the phenomenon is widespread in roughly the southern part of the Peninsula (Andalusia, Murcia, Extremadura, and, with less intensity, Castilla-La Mancha and even Madrid), as well as in the Canary Islands; but small islands of /s/ aspiration are also found as far north as Cantabria (Penny 1978; Nuño Alvarez 1996). Nowadays the weakening of syllable-final (especially preconsonantal) /s/ has gained a foothold in Madrid speech (Quilis 1965) and appears to be spreading throughout the Peninsula in colloquial registers. In Latin America, lack of /s/-weakening is characteristic of the highlands of central Mexico and Guatemala, central Costa Rica and the Andes. Elsewhere in Spanish-speaking Latin America, we find some greater or lesser degree of /s/-weakening, the process being especially prevalent in the Caribbean and in parts of the Pacific coast of South America.

Everywhere where the phenomenon is found in the Spanish-speaking world, it appears to be subject to variation. This variation is in part social, with more weakening in more casual styles and among less educated speakers, and in part phonologically conditioned, being more frequent in certain phonological environments than in others. In the weakening process we may distinguish two main variants: the realization of /s/ as a laryngeal aspiration [h] and its complete deletion.

In general, the phonological context which most favours the weakening of /s/ is the preconsonantal one, whether the following consonant is in the same word, as in *pastel* [pahtél] 'cake', or across word boundaries, as in *más tarde* [máh tárðe] 'later'; the next context, in terms of frequency of weakening, is before pause, *vamos* [bámoh] 'let us go'; and finally, with less frequency, we find weakening of word-final /s/ before a vowel, as in *otros amigos*

Fricatives and affricates

Table 9.6 Weakening of /s/ by context in Buenos Aires and Cuba.

	Buenos Aires			Cuba		
	[s]	[h]	0	[s]	[h]	0
__C	12%	80%	8%	3%	97%	0%
__##C	11%	69%	20%	2%	75%	23%
__##V	88%	7%	5%	18%	48%	34%
__//	78%	11%	11%	61%	13%	26%

Adapted from Bybee (2000).

[ótɾoh amíɣoh] 'other friends' – although there are dialects where the effacement of /s/ displays somewhat different frequency patterns (Lipski 1984, 1986).[8] In the consciousness of many speakers, preconsonantal aspiration goes almost undetected, whereas there is greater awareness, and sometimes some degree of stigmatization, of prevocalic and prepausal aspiration.

Bybee (2000), comparing Buenos Aires area Spanish and Cuban Spanish (with data from Terrell 1977, 1978, 1979), finds that, although the overall rate of /s/ weakening is much greater in Cuban than in Buenos Aires, in both dialects the relative scale of contexts is essentially the one we have mentioned in the paragraph above (with one exception for Cuba; see Table 9.6). She concludes, in agreement with other researchers, that the weakening must have started in the preconsonantal position, spreading from there to other word-final environments.

As we can see from Table 9.6, in Buenos Aires word-final /s/ is mostly maintained before a vowel and also before pause, whereas it tends to be aspirated or deleted before a consonant at about the same high rate as word-internal preconsonantal /s/. That is, Buenos Aires speakers tend to aspirate in, e.g., *fiesta* [fi̯éhta] (__C) 'holiday', *es tarde* [éh táɾðe] (__##C) 'it is late', and, on the other hand, to maintain final [s] in, e.g., *jamás* [xamás] (__//) 'never' and *es algo* [és álɣo] (__##V) 'it is something'.

In Cuba, [s] is almost never pronounced in either of the two preconsonantal contexts (word internal or across word boundaries). Systematically, we find [h] in the preconsonantal context. There are also lower rates of retention than in Buenos Aires in the two other contexts. The only somewhat unexpected fact,

---

[8] In the *chinato* dialect, mentioned in n. 5, word-final [ð] (from OSp. /-z/, /-d͡z/) is (or was) found only in *liaison* contexts, before a vowel. Both prepausally and preconsonantally there is aspiration instead: e.g. la[ð] ala[h] 'the wings' (standard *las alas*) but la[h] coda[h] 'the things' (standard *las cosas*); va[ð] a mi cada 'you are going to my house' (standard *vas a mi casa*), but ande va[h] 'where are you going?' (standard *a dónde vas*).

in these Cuban data, is that there is more weakening of final /s/ before a vowel than before pause.[9]

If we now compare the distribution of the two weakened variants of /s/ in Table 9.6, [h] and zero, we see that preconsonantally [h] is overwhelmingly favoured, whereas, in the case of word-final /s/ before a vowel or pause, both [h] and zero are found, with more similar frequencies. That is, something like *este* is much more commonly pronounced [éhte] in dialects with /s/-weakening than [éte], whereas complete deletion, when it occurs, tends to affect word-final /s/ either before pause, as in *vamos* [bámoh] ∼ [bámo] or before a vowel, as in *otros amigos* [ótɾoh amíɣoh] ∼ [ótɾo.amíɣoh].

Buenos Aires represents a relatively conservative stage among dialects with /s/-weakening,[10] although, of course, it is less conservative than the Spanish of Highland Mexico or Bilbao, which do not have any significant weakening of /s/, and that of Madrid, where the overall rates of weakening are much lower in the speech of educated speakers, being mostly limited to certain preconsonantal contexts.[11]

Caribbean Spanish, as a whole, has higher rates of aspiration and deletion. The Cuban data in Table 9.6 are representative in this respect. Furthermore, we should note that the Cuban data in the table represent the semiformal speech of educated middle-class speakers (Terrell 1979). Undoubtedly, comparable data from speakers of lower educational and socioeconomic levels and from more casual styles would show an even greater degree of weakening (including higher percentages of zero allophones).

In particular, the most advanced stage of weakening of syllable- and word-final /s/ in Latin America appears to be found in lower sociolects of the Dominican Republic, where the complete deletion of the segment is extremely frequent (Terrell 1986). In this variety, final [s] is only regularly preserved in sequences of plural determiner followed by a stressed vowel (as in *los otro(s)*) (see also Alba 1982). In all other contexts, deletion is the norm (96 per cent of all occurrences of final /s/ for semiliterate speakers) and [h] is very rare. This has given rise to a hypercorrection phenomenon locally known as *hablar fisno*, where

---

[9] Terrell (1979:607), however, points out that the word-final prevocalic context includes a number of more specific subcontexts with very different allophonic distribution. In particular, [s] appears to be retained almost categorically in groups where a determiner is followed by a stressed vowel, as in *los otros* 'the others', *mis hijos* 'my children', etc. He also notes that the prepausal position is where the greatest individual variation was found among the Cuban speakers in his study (p. 609).

[10] Even within Argentina, other varieties have a much higher rate of weakening of word-final /s/ in the prevocalic and prepausal contexts than that of Buenos Aires (see Lipski 1994:169–70 and references therein).

[11] In Madrid aspiration of /s/ appears to be especially common before /p/, *espera* [ehpéɾa] 'wait!', and before /k/, where /s/ is often realized as a velar, *es que* [éxke] 'it is that'.

in formal or semiformal styles speakers may introduce [s] where it does not belong etymologically (as in *fisno* for *fino* 'refined'). Terrell (1986) proposes that rather than speaking of deletion of /s/ in Dominican Spanish, one should speak of a process of /s/ insertion, since /s/-less forms are clearly the norm.

As mentioned above, weakening of /s/ is also extremely common in all of southern Spain. In Spain, the complete loss of the segment is most frequent in Eastern Andalusian, where it is accompanied by the vowel phenomena described in section 7.4.1. In Andalusian speech the aspiration of preconsonantal /s/ sometimes has striking effects on the following consonant. Sequences of /s/ + voiceless plosives result in preaspirated geminates:[12] *caspa* [ká^{h}p:a] 'dandruff', *costa* [kó^{h}t:a] 'coast', *asco* [á^{h}k:o] 'disgust' (Rodríguez Castellano and Palacio 1948; Alarcos Llorach 1958, etc.). In these sequences the plosive is preceded by a brief aspiration and has a longer occlusion than when in intervocalic position (Gerfen 2002). Aspirated /s/ may also assimilate to a following sonorant, resulting in a partially voiceless geminate: *isla* [iḷla] 'island', *mismo* [mim̥mo] 'same'. But the most striking effects are found before [β ð ɣ], which may become voiceless geminates in the context of a preceding aspirated /s/: *las botas* [læɸːɔ́tæ] 'the boots', *los dedos* [lɔθːɛ́ɔ] 'the fingers', *los gatos* [lɔxːátɔ] 'the cats' (see Alarcos Llorach 1958; Salvador 1957–8; Penny 2000:122–5; cf. also Montes 1996 and Becerra 1985 for similar facts in coastal Colombian).

In Canary Island Spanish, on the other hand, the sequences /sb/, /sd/, /sg/ may be realized as tense voiced plosives [bː dː ɡː], in opposition to intervocalic /b d g/, which are realized as [β ð ɣ]: *las velas* [labːéla] 'the sails; candles' vs *la vela* [laβéla] 'the sail; candle'; *las damas* [ladːáma] 'the ladies' vs *la dama* [laðáma] 'the lady'; *sesgar* [seɡːár] 'to slant' vs *segar* [seɣár] 'to reap' (Trujillo 1981; Dorta and Herrera Santana 1993).

The type of /s/-weakening we have discussed so far affects syllable-final /s/, even if, before a word-initial vowel, this segment may be resyllabified in the onset, as in *las alas* [lahála] 'the wings'. In Andalusia, central Colombia and some other areas, medial /-s-/ is often aspirated in *nosotros* (Eastern Andal. [nɔhɔ́trɔ]), but this can also be interpreted as an extension of word-final aspiration, given the compound structure of this word (*nos* + *otros*) and the analogical model provided by the phrase *los otros* 'the others' (Penny 2000:123). The same explanation can be applied to aspiration of the /s/ in the prefix *des-*, as in *desarmado* [deharmáo] 'unarmed', which is not uncommon in Andalusian. More extensive aspiration of word-internal intervocalic and even word-initial /s/ has, however, been noticed for some areas, including parts of Andalusia, Honduras (Lipski 1985a), Central Colombia (Flórez 1951) and northern

---

[12] The colon indicates lengthening of the closure duration of the consonant.

New Mexico (Espinosa 1930): *la semana* [lahemána] 'the week', *sí señor* [híheɲó] 'yes, sir', *basura* [bahúɾa] 'garbage'. Since in these areas /x/ is also usually rendered as [h], this process can potentially lead to restructuring of lexical entries. A common view is that syllable-initial aspiration of /s/ is a further development, an extension, of the same process to yet another environment in some of the dialects with most pervasive weakening of syllable- and word-final /s/ (Méndez Dosuna 1996). However, some of the dialects with weakening of syllable-initial /s/ have relatively low rates of syllable-final /s/-weakening, which suggests that the development path may not be the same in all dialects (Lipski 1984; Brown and Torres Cacoullos 2003).[13]

The aspiration and deletion of syllable- and word-final /s/ is a process that ran its full course in French some centuries ago (e.g. Lat. TESTA > [tehtə] > Fr. *tête* 'head') and is also found in many other languages, related and unrelated to Spanish. It seems uncontroversial that in this process aspiration precedes complete deletion. The phonetic origin of aspiration is generally seen in a relaxation in the articulation of /s/. If the lingual gesture is reduced, the constriction will not be narrow enough in the alveolar region to produce friction at this place, resulting in pure glottal friction or [h] (Quilis 1993:275–80; Terrell 1979; among others). Widdison (1993) shows that a period of glottal friction is always present in the transition between a vowel and [s] and claims that the reduction of [s] in the preconsonantal context (taken to be the original environment of the change) will naturally lead to the perception of [h], causing reanalysis on the part of the listener.[14]

In aspirating Peninsular dialects with a /s/-/θ/ contrast (some Andalusian, Murcian and Extremaduran varieties, among others), both phonemes undergo aspiration and deletion, e.g. *una vez* [úna βé] 'one time', *cuatro veces* [ku̯átɾo βéθɛ] 'four times'.

9.3 On the phonemic status of /ʝ/

We have been using the symbol /ʝ/ to refer to a voiced palatal consonant of very variable constriction which in most dialects corresponds to orthographic syllable-initial *y* and *ll*, as in *mayo* and *calle*. In Castilian Spanish and many other dialects this consonant is realized with a broad range of constriction degrees from glide [i̯], to fricative [ʝ], to stop [ɟ] or affricate [ɟ͡ʝ] (see Aguilar 1997:69–73). The most common realization in Standard Castilian is a voiced palatal weak fricative or approximant consonant [ʝ] (*mayo* [máʝo] 'May'), except that

---

[13] The use of [hí] as a casual form of *sí* 'yes' is found in many areas.
[14] Following John Ohala's view of language change (see, for instance, Ohala 1974).

the (affricated) stop [ɟ] occurs after a nasal or lateral (as in *inyección* 'injection', *un yunque* 'an anvil', *el yeso* 'the plaster') and also frequently but variably utterance-initially: *yo lo sé* [ɟó losé] 'I know it' vs *lo sé yo* [losé ʝó] (Navarro Tomás 1977:127–31). However, in other dialects or sociolects, both in Spain and Latin America, there are different allophonic distributions. For instance, in the colloquial speech of Madrid (and also in the colloquial speech of, for instance, Lima) the stop/affricate is often found after all consonants and even in intervocalic position: *oye* [óɟe] 'listen!'.

As has already been mentioned, other dialects have yet more different pronunciations. Notably, Standard Argentinian Spanish has a voiced prepalatal fricative [ʒ], similar to the sound in French *jamais* or in English *pleasure*: Arg. *mayo* [máʒo], *oye* [óʒe], *yéso* [ʒéso]. This fricative is affricated to [d͡ʒ] (as in English *John*) after a nasal or lateral. This pronunciation is associated with Argentinian Spanish, because of its prestigious social consideration and widespread diffusion in that country (although it does not affect the entire country), nevertheless it is also found in parts of Andalusia and Extremadura in Spain, as well as in some regions of Mexico, at least as a variable phenomenon. Among the younger generations in Buenos Aires and surrounding area this sound is becoming more and more frequently devoiced to [ʃ].

Rather than being optional, as in Castilian, in Argentinian obstruent realizations are obligatory. For instance, whereas, in Castilian, *yo* 'I' may be realized as [i̯ó] ~ [ʝó] ~ [ɟó] depending, perhaps, on degree of emphasis, in Argentinian only obstruent allophones are found: [ʒó] ~ [ʃó].

At the other phonetic extreme, in northern Mexico and the Spanish of the US Southwest, as well as in parts of Central America, the corresponding segment is realized with very little constriction, as a pure glide, which, furthermore, may be deleted in intervocalic position after a front vowel: northern Mex. *pollo* [pói̯o] 'chicken', *mayo* [mái̯o] 'May', *silla* [sí̯ia] ~ [sía] 'chair' (see 2.3.1).

Some phonologists have proposed eliminating the phoneme /ʝ/ from the phonemic inventory of Spanish. In this proposal this sound or family of sounds would simply be the realization of the high front vowel phoneme /i/ when unstressed, prevocalic and in syllable-initial position. The fricative and (affricated) plosive voiced palatal segments are thus analysed as resulting from the variable reinforcement of the glide [i̯] in word-initial and syllable-initial position, and, therefore as allophonic variants of /i/. That is, in this analysis, the phoneme /i/, besides its vocalic realization as in *piso* /píso/ [píso] 'floor', has a glide allophone – as in *tieso* /tieso/ [ti̯éso] 'straight', in the context of the Gliding rule (5.4) – and a consonant allophone (or allophones), also in the context of the Gliding rule, when the segment is furthermore word initial or syllable initial, as in *mayo* /máio/ [má.ʝo] 'May', *yeso* /iéso/ [ʝéso] 'plaster'.

9.3 On the phonemic status of /ʝ/

Table 9.7 Distribution of allophones of /i/ in Standard Castilian in an analysis without phonemic /ʝ/.

Allophone	Example	Context
[i]	*piso* /píso/ [píso] *bahía* /baía/ [baía]	
[i̯]	*tieso* /tiéso/ [ti̯éso]	– non-stress bearing and – adjacent to different V
[j]	*de yeso* /de-iéso/ [dej̯éso] *mayo* /máio/ [máj̯o]	– non-stress bearing and – adjacent to different V and – word or syllable initial
[ʝ]	*con yeso* /kon-iéso/ [konʲʝéso] # *yéso* /iéso/ [ʝéso]	– non-stress bearing and – adjacent to different V and – word or syllable initial and – after nasal/lateral or (optionally) after pause

For instance, under this proposal, the segmental difference between the following examples derives from an independent contrast in syllabification resulting from the presence of word boundaries:

italiano /italiáno/ [italiáno] 'Italian, *masc.*' vs
y tal llano /i-tál-iáno/ [itál ʝáno] 'and such a plain'

In this analysis, thus, the distribution of allophones of /i/ in Standard Castilian Spanish (the variety described by Navarro Tomás) would be as indicated in Table 9.7, where the appropriate allophone for the most restrictive context is selected in all cases.

This analysis is particularly attractive for dialects where the sound that we are concerned with has very little constriction. Nevertheless, there are also some difficulties with it. To begin with, notice that in an example like *con yeso* /kon-iéso/ the phonological representation suggests that there should be resyllabification, since we have a CV sequence across word boundaries (see 5.5.1). This would put /i/ in non-syllable-initial position, wrongly producing *[ko.ni̯é.so]. To prevent this incorrect result, the correct consonantal allophone must be chosen taking into account its syllabic position *at the word level*. That is, there is no resyllabification in *con yeso* because in the word /iéso/ the segment /i/ is syllable initial and adjacent to a vowel, in a context where it would be consonantized, thus blocking resyllabification. In an analysis with ordered rules, the consonantization of the word-initial glide (phonemic /i/) 'bleeds' resyllabification (i.e., consonantization applies before the rule of resyllabification, preventing its

Table 9.8 Contrasting [i̯] vs [ʝ] ~ [ɟ] deriving from a contrast in syllabification.

	One syllabification domain			word-internal syllable boundary	
orthography	phonological representation	pronunciation	orthography	phonological representation	pronunciation
desierto	/desiérto/	[desi̯érto]	*deshielo*	/des-iélo/	[dezʝélo]
abierto	/abiérto/	[aβi̯érto]	*abyecto*	/ab-iékto/	[aβɟékto]
boniato	/boniáto/	[boni̯áto]	*cónyuge*	/kón-iuxe/	[kónʲɟuxe]

application). In an analysis with ranked constraints, consonantization would be ranked higher than resyllabification.

We, furthermore, find a handful of near-minimal pairs where there is a contrast between the glide [i̯] and the consonant [ʝ] ~ [ɟ] in the same phonological context, as in *abierto* 'open' vs *abyecto* 'abject', *desierto* 'desert' vs *deshielo* 'thawing', and *boniato* 'sweet potato' vs *cónyuge* 'spouse' (phonetic transcriptions are given in Table 9.8). These problematic cases can, however, be reduced to a contrast in syllabification, for the most part morphologically driven. The example *desierto* vs *deshielo* was discussed in 5.6. As we saw, productive prefixes are independent domains for syllabification. In *deshielo*, the pronunciation is in accordance with the distribution in Table 9.7, under the explanation just developed for the example *con yeso*, given the fact that the prefix boundary is also a boundary of two syllabification domains: /des-iélo/. That is, for syllabification purposes *deshielo* is no different from a phrase like *con yeso* or *es hielo* /és-iélo/ [ez ʝélo] 'it is ice' (see also the pair *italiano* vs *y tal llano* discussed above). The correct allophone will be chosen if in /des-iélo/ the phoneme /i/ is taken to be word initial (again, consonantization blocks resyllabification). The same explanation can be extended to the other few cases of seemingly anomalous allophony. Regarding *abyecto*, the syllable *ab-*, unlike *des-*, is not a transparent prefix in Spanish; nevertheless, the existence of *proyecto* 'project', *inyectar* 'inject', etc., makes this morphological segmentation at least possible. The syllabification of glides as syllable initial after prefixes in fact goes back to Latin (Pensado 1989), which explains this example as well as *cónyuge*, which etymologically has the same prefix as words like *conlleva* 'it implies', *compañero* 'companion', and many others. Nevertheless, given its stress pattern and the opacity of the stem, from a synchronic point of view it is perhaps most sensible to treat *cónyuge* as a case of anomalous syllabification.

An additional problem for the reduction of /ʝ/ to /i/ is presented by the fact that many speakers tend to pronounce orthographic *hiV*, in words such as

9.3 On the phonemic status of /j/

Table 9.9 Contrast between /ʒ/ and /i/ in Argentinian Spanish.

/ʒ/ [ʒ ~ ʃ]	/i/ [i̯ ~ j]
yeso 'plaster'	*hielo* 'ice'
llena 'full, *fem*.'	*hiena* 'hyena'
tramoya 'artifice', *cebolla* 'onion'	*paranoia* 'paranoia'
yerba '*mate* leaves'	*hierba* 'grass'

hielo 'ice', *hierro* 'iron', etc., with less constriction than orthographic *y* or *ll*, as in *yeso*, *lleno*, etc.[15] This orthographically induced contrast is especially clear in dialects such as Buenos Aires Spanish where the pronunciation of *y*, *ll* is always as an obstruent consonant, acoustically very different from a glide [i̯]. In Standard Argentinian Spanish, thus, there is a clear contrast between the prepalatal fricative in *yeso* [ʒéso], *lléno* [ʒéno], and the glide of *hielo*, *hierro*, which may be pronounced with some palatal constriction, but always with little stridency [i̯élo] ~ [jélo]. Pronunciations such as [ʒélo] for *hielo* are frowned upon in Standard Argentinian as a sign of low cultural level (or lack of familiarity with the standard orthography). There is even a minimal pair. Whereas the RAE provides the alternative spellings *hierba* ~ *yerba* for the same word, meaning 'grass, weed',[16] in Argentinian Spanish these are two words with different meanings. The popular development [ʒérβa] has been specialized with the meaning '*mate* leaves' (*mate* is the national tea of Argentina) and is written *yerba*, whereas for 'grass' the spelling *hierba* and the pronunciation [i̯érβa] are used. It is thus clear that Argentinian Spanish has a phoneme /ʒ/ which contrasts with the nonsyllabic allophone of the phoneme /i/. In word-internal position the contrast is between words like *cebolla* 'onion', *tramoya* 'artifice', on the one hand, and the technical word *paranoia*, on the other. In Argentinian Spanish, thus, the phonemic link between /ʒ/ [ʒ] ~ [ʃ] and /i/ [i̯] ~ [j] has been broken.[17]

Even more problematically, other dialects without obligatory fortition of initial glides also have an orthographically based (but nonetheless real) 'quasi-contrast'. Just like in Argentina, both in other areas of Latin America and in Spain, many educated speakers avoid pronouncing words spelt with *hie-* with a strong fricative or noncontinuant consonant, at least in formal styles (as

---

[15] Words like *hielo* 'ice', even if they may be pronounced with a glide, [i̯élo], cannot, on the other hand, be syllabified with a sequence in hiatus, and are thus different from an example such as the word *hiato* [i.áto] 'hiatus', which is a case of exceptional hiatus (see 5.4).

[16] Other words with alternative spellings are *hiedra* ~ *yedra* 'ivy' and *hiero* ~ *yero* 'vetch'.

[17] For a different view see Harris and Kaisse (1999).

Table 9.10 Range of pronunciations for different words in Castilian Spanish.

*hi*ato 'hiatus'	i-á ~	i̯á
*hi*ena 'hyena'	i̯é ~	ʝé
*y*ema 'yolk'	i̯é ~	**ʝé** ~ ɟé

noted by Navarro Tomás 1977:50; Dalbor 1997:217; and other authors). The greater the phonetic distance between the most common pronunciation of the consonant spelt *y* or *ll* and a pure glide in the dialect, the greater is the likelihood of speakers establishing separate categories for words with the spelling *hie-* and those with *y-* or *ll-*.

This applies mostly to the phrase-initial context. As noted above, in this context the full range from glide [i̯] to palatal stop [ɟ] is found in Castilian Spanish and other dialects. Given the association of the spelling *(h)i* with a vowel in the mind of Spanish speakers, speakers often restrict the range of pronunciations of (some) words with this spelling to the least constricted end of the range. That is, in the phrase-initial environment, different words allow a different range of realizations along the constriction parameter, in careful style, this being in part orthographically driven and in part dependent on word frequency. In my own speech I am aware of the existence of three classes of words in this respect, if we include words with initial exceptional hiatus. Examples are given in Table 9.10.

The regular case is that presented by *yema* 'yolk', whose regular pronunciation is as [ʝéma], but which also allows pronunciations with either less or greater constriction. (The pronunciation taken as 'basic' for each item is in boldface in Table 9.10.) As mentioned, the word *hiato* belongs to the class with exceptional hiatus /i.áto/ (just like, e.g., /di.áblo/ 'devil'). The hiatus may be contracted to a diphthong by syllable reduction (see 5.5), but this initial diphthong is not reinforced. That is, *hiato* /i.áto/ has the same range of pronunciations as a phrase like *y atas* /i átas/ [i.átas] ~ [i̯átas] (but usually not *[ʝátas]) 'and you tie'. Finally, *hiena* should in principle have the same range of pronunciations as *yema* or *llena* 'full, *fem.*', but in fact it tends to be realized with much less constriction. This is no doubt due to the orthography and to the learned character of this word. There is thus a quasi-categorical contrast in this dialect, reflected in the existence of minimal pairs such as *hiena* vs *llena*, which differ in their possible range of pronunciations, as in Table 9.10. In citation form the words *hiena* and *llena* are not likely to be confused (although they may indeed become homophonous in natural

9.3 On the phonemic status of /ʝ/

Table 9.11 Initial u.V, u̯V, gu̯V.

*hui*da	**u.i**	u̯i	
*hue*so		**u̯e**	gu̯e
*gua*sa		u̯a	**gu̯a**

conversation). Given all of this, we may consider /ʝ/ a 'quasi-phoneme' in Spanish.[18]

The same situation of 'quasi-contrast' arises with respect to [u̯]V (spelt *hu*V or, in borrowings, *w*V: *hueso* 'bone', *hueco* 'hole', *Hawaii*, *washingtoniano* 'Washingtonian') and [gu̯]V (*guasa* 'humour', *cigüena* 'stork', *güito* 'fruit stone'). After pause, some speakers tend to maintain a contrast, corresponding to the difference in spelling, pronouncing, e.g., *hueso* [u̯éso] with less constriction than *guasa* [gu̯ása], pronounced with a stop in this context (see Aguilar 1997:190–1).[19] From these two classes we must distinguish again a third class of words that have an exceptional hiatus, such as *huida* [u.íða] 'flight', which do not allow consonantal reinforcement.[20] In each case, the most representative pronunciation in initial position in careful speech is in boldface in Table 9.11.

The contrasts that we are concerned with, to the extent that they are made, are basically limited to the phrase-initial position (after pause). In the same dialects (e.g. Standard Castilian), there is no contrast word internally between, say, the sounds represented by the bolded segments in *paranoia* and in *tramoya* (unlike in Argentinian), both with [-ója] ∼ [-ói̯a], or, for the velar place, in *cigüeña* 'stork' and *vihuela* 'type of guitar', both with [-iɣu̯é-] ∼ [-iu̯é-]. Regardless of the spelling, we tend to find an approximant consonant (of variable constriction). This also applies to contexts across word boundaries. After a

---

[18] In written Spanish (and to a lesser extent in the oral language) there is a rule whereby the conjunction *y* 'and' is replaced by *e* before the vowel [i] as in *geografía e historia* 'geography and history'. This rule does not apply before words with orthographic *y-* or *ll-*: *cal y yeso* 'lime and plaster', *nieve y lluvia* 'snow and rain'. Before orthographic *(h)iV-* there is a certain amount of variation (Whitley 1995). The application of the *y → e* rule is common (but not totally consistent) with words like *hiato*, which allow a pronunciation in hiatus: *diptongo e hiato* 'diphthong and hiatus'. For some speakers, the context of the rule is the nuclear vowel [i], not the glide [j], and thus they would not apply it in *leones y hienas* 'lions and hyenas' even if the word-initial segment is pronounced as a pure glide. Whitley (1995) nevertheless reports that some of his respondents used *e* in this case. One explanation could be that some Spanish-speakers tend to apply this *y → e* substitution before both the vowel [i] and the glide [j].

[19] Nevertheless, for several words there are alternative spellings: *huarache* ∼ *guarache* 'type of sandal'; *huero* ∼ *güero* 'empty', Mex. 'blond'; *huiro* ∼ *güiro* 'type of gourd'. When the Spanish Academy decided to nativize the word *whisky* as *güisqui*, some people complained that with this spelling the Academy was promoting a colloquial or substandard pronunciation.

[20] To this hiatus class belong surnames such as *Huidobro* and *Huarte*.

Table 9.12 'Quasi-phonological' contrasts.

Possible contrast: after pause	No contrast	
yeso [ɟéso] ~ [ʝéso] ~ [i̯éso]	*de yeso* [deɟéso] ~ [dei̯éso]	*con yeso* [konʲɟéso]
hielo [i̯élo]	*de hielo* [deɟélo] ~ [dei̯élo]	*con hielo* [konʲɟélo]
guasa [gu̯ása]	*de guasa* [deɣu̯ása] ~ [deu̯ása]	*con guasa* [koŋgu̯ása]
hueso [u̯éso]	*de hueso* [deu̯éso] ~ [deɣu̯éso]	*con hueso* [koŋgu̯éso]

nasal or lateral consonant, on the other hand, a plosive is normally pronounced, both for the palatal and for the velar, also regardless of spelling. Examples are given in Table 9.12.

For practical reasons, in this book we distinguish a phoneme /ɟ/ in our phonological representations. From the preceding discussion, it should be clear, though, that the phonemic status of this segment is not as secure as that of other phonemes.

EXERCISES

1. In what ways are affricates like and unlike plosives? Would it be possible to analyse affricates as sequences of two segments?

2. In some Latin American countries the English borrowing *watchman* has been adapted as *guachimán*. Can you explain this adaptation?

3. What is the historical origin of the difference between Peninsular and Latin American Spanish in the pronunciation of orthographic *z*, *c(e,i)*?

4. Terrell (1986) reports examples such as *gasto* for 'gato', *astrás* 'atrás', *esquipo* 'equipo', *las ochos* 'las ocho', *yo vivos* 'yo vivo', *tengos* 'tengo', in the speech of some of his Dominican informants. How do you explain these forms?

5. In some areas of Castilla-La Mancha *oler* 'to smell' has a colloquial, substandard, form *goler*. How can you explain this development?

6. What are the arguments in favour of, and against, considering /ɟ/ an independent phoneme in Spanish?

10 Nasals

10.1 Nasal phonemes

Spanish has three nasal phonemes in its consonantal inventory, as summarized and exemplified in Table 10.1.

These three nasal phonemes are in contrast in onset position but undergo neutralization in the syllable coda, as explained in the following section.

English, of course, lacks a palatal nasal in its inventory. The closest approximation is found in words like *canyon* (itself a borrowing from Spanish), but the palatal nasal actually contrasts in Spanish with a sequence of alveolar nasal + palatal glide (for most speakers). Minimal pairs illustrating this contrast are *huraño* /uráɲo/ 'shy' vs *uranio* /uránio/ [uránio̯] 'uranium', *uñón* /uɲón/ 'big finger nail' vs *unión* /unión/ [unió̯n] 'union', and *Miño* /míɲo/ 'a river in Galicia' vs *minio* /mínio/ [mínio̯] 'minium'.

The palatal nasal is rare in word-initial position. The dictionary of the Spanish Academy lists only forty-nine words starting with *ñ*, including many regionally restricted words. There is an obvious historical reason for the rarity of word-initial /ɲ/. Latin did not have a phoneme /ɲ/. In Spanish this phoneme has one of three main origins: (1) a geminate sequence *-nn-*, as in ANNU(M) > *año* 'year'; (2) a sequence *n* + front vowel before another vowel, as in VĪNEA > *viña* 'vineyard', HISPANIA > *España*; and (3) the sequence *-gn-*, as in PUGNU(M) > *puño* 'fist' (see Penny 2002:61–72, among others). Of these three sources, only the second one could in principle have given rise to word-initial /ɲ/, but, in fact, the change did not affect word-initial sequences. It follows that word-initial /ɲ/ has origins other than regular evolution from Latin. Spanish words with initial /ɲ/ can be borrowings from other languages such as *ñame* 'yam', *ñandú* 'South American ostrich' and *ñu* 'gnu', expressive formations such as *ñiquiñaque* 'worthless thing', and dialectal variants (since in Leonese varieties

Table 10.1 Nasal phonemes.

/m/ voiced bilabial nasal	*cama* /káma/ 'bed', *mata* /máta/ 'bush'
/n/ voiced alveolar nasal	*cana* /kána/ 'grey hair', *nata* /náta/ 'cream'
/ɲ/ voiced palatal nasal	*caña* /káɲa/ 'reed, cane', *ñandú* /ɲandú/ 'South American ostrich'

initial /n/ underwent palatalization) such as *ñublado* (= *nublado*) 'cloudy' and *ñudo* (= *nudo*) 'knot'.

The Spanish (and English) nasal consonants are produced with complete blockage of the airflow through the oral cavity. They are thus properly defined as nasal stops.

10.2 Nasals in coda position

10.2.1 Word-internal coda nasals

In word-internal preconsonantal position (in a syllable coda) nasals are always homorganic with following consonants; that is, they share the point of articulation of the following consonant. The contrast among three nasal phonemes differing in point of articulation that we find in syllable-onset position is thus neutralized in the coda. This phenomenon was discussed and exemplified in 6.2.

We may note that conventional Spanish orthography, which is generally phonemic, is somewhat inconsistent in this respect. The orthographic rule is to write *m* before *p* and *b* and *n* elsewhere. In, for instance, *campo* [kámpo] 'field', *cambio* [kámbi̯o] 'change', the orthography reflects the phonetic reality. However, before all other consonants, *n* is uniformly written, regardless of the actual place of articulation of the nasal: *énfasis* [éɱfasis] 'emphasis', *ancho* [ánʲt͡ʃo] 'wide', *ángel* [áŋxel] 'angel'. Notice, furthermore, that *n* is also written before *v*, which represents the same bilabial phoneme as orthographic *b*, as in *envía* [embía] 's/he sends', *invita* [imbíta] 's/he invites', and also before *m*, as in *inmortal* [immortál] 'immortal'. Conventional Spanish orthography thus falls short of providing an adequate phonological representation in this case.

As we explained in 6.2, we may adopt a phonologization with a nasal /N/ whose place of articulation is determined by the following consonant, equivalent to the nasal archiphoneme proposed in Praguean analyses.

The only exception is the sequence /mn/, which is found in examples such as *himno* 'hymn', *alumno* 'student' and *columna* 'column'.

10.2 Nasals in coda position

Table 10.2 Word-internal coda nasals: homorganic with following consonant.

campo	/káNpo/	[kámpo]	'field'
cambio	/káNbio/	[kámbi̯o]	'change'
envía	/eNbía/	[embía]	's/he sends'
inmortal	/iNmortál/	[immortál]	'immortal'
énfasis	/éNfasis/	[éɱfasis]	'emphasis'
canto	/káNto/	[kán̪to]	'I sing'
ando	/áNdo/	[án̪do]	'I walk'
manso	/máNso/	[mánso]	'tame'
ancho	/áNt͡ʃo/	[ánʲt͡ʃo]	'wide'
enyesar	/eNɟesár/	[enʲɟesár]	'to plaster'
ángel	/áNxel/	[áŋxel]	'angel'
mango	/máNgo/	[máŋgo]	'handle'
hinco	/íNko/	[íŋko]	'I drive in'
Exception: /mn/			
columna	/kolúmna/	[kolúmna]	'column'

Table 10.3 Preconsonantal nasal allophones.

[m]	bilabial nasal	campo, cambio, envía
[ɱ]	labiodental nasal	énfasis
[n̪]	dental nasal	canto, ando (interdental in Cast. encía)
[n]	alveolar nasal	ansia, enredo, enlatar
[nʲ]	palatalized nasal	ancho, enyesar
[ŋ]	velar nasal	mango, hinco, ángel

It is interesting to note that, although Spanish generally lacks geminate consonants, we do find the morpheme-internal sequence [nn] (analysable as /Nn/) in two or three words: *perenne* 'perennial', *pinnípedo* 'seals and related mammals'. Other than these, there are almost no examples of morpheme-internal geminates in Spanish.[1] With the prefix *in*-, there are examples like *innoble* 'ignoble', *innatural* 'unnatural', etc.

Notice that before palatal consonants nasals are palatalized, but without becoming identical to the palatal nasal [ɲ] (Quilis 1993:229–30). The symbol [nʲ], which includes the IPA superscript for palatalization, is intended to represent a palatalized nasal. In terms of allophones we can thus distinguish the segments as in Table 10.3.

---

[1] With geminate /b/, we have *obvio* [óβːi̯o] 'obvious'.

10.2.2 Word-final nasals

In word-final position we find only one nasal consonant in Spanish: /n/. Final -*m* is found in a few borrowings such as *álbum, ítem, referéndum*, and Catalan toponyms like *Benidorm*. The pronunciation of these exceptional words is very variable: some speakers pronounce [m] in words spelt with final -*m*, but this seems to be a minority pronunciation. Integrated words with final -*m* in the original language have changed this consonant to -*n* as we can see in the biblical names *Adán* 'Adam', *Jerusalén* 'Jerusalem' and *Belén* 'Bethlehem'.

The palatal nasal is totally excluded from word-final position. The French word *champagne* has been adapted as both *champán* and *champaña*, to avoid final [ɲ]. Catalan surnames ending in /ɲ/, which is spelled -*ny* in this language, as in *Company*, are usually given a Spanish spelling pronunciation: [kompáni]. Compare also the verb *desdeñar* 'to disdain' and the noun *desdén* 'disdain'.

Before a pause or a vowel, word-final /n/ is pronounced [n] in most Spanish dialects, but a velar articulation [ŋ] is common in many areas including western and southern Spain, the Caribbean and the Pacific coast of South America. The phenomenon is known as nasal VELARIZATION and can be considered a weakening of the articulation of the consonant. In both Andalusia and the Caribbean there is further reduction, so that instead of a final nasal consonant one often hears only a nasalization of the preceding vowel: *comen* [kómẽŋ] ~ [kómẽ] 'they eat'. It is not clear to what extent the presence of word-final [ŋ] may be contrastive in velarizing dialects when occurring before a vowel as in *en aguas* [eŋáɣu̯as] 'in water' vs *enaguas* [enáɣu̯as] 'petticoats', since even in these dialects final nasals may be articulated as [n] when resyllabified with a following vowel (5.5.1).

Much less common is the pronunciation of final nasals as bilabial [m]: *pan* [pám] 'bread', *melón* [melóm] 'melon'. This (variable) phenomenon has been attested in several isolated areas, including the Yucatán peninsula of Mexico, the Valle del Cauca of Colombia (Montes 1979) and Tucumán, Argentina.

In plurals of words ending in a nasal and derived words, we have [-n-] regardless of the pronunciation that word-final nasals receive in the dialect of the speaker. In velarizing dialects, we have for instance, *pan* [páŋ] but *panes* [pánes] (not *[páŋes]), *camión* [kami̯óŋ] / *camiones* [kami̯ónes] 'truck/-s', etc.

Before a consonant, word-final nasals assimilate in place of articulation: *camión pequeño* [kami̯ómpekéɲo] 'small truck', *un camión feo* [úŋkami̯ómɱféo] 'un ugly truck', *son grandes* [sóŋgráṉdes] 'they are big', *son felices* Cast. [sómɱfelíθes] ~ LatAm. [somɱfelíses] 'they are happy'. Depending on speech rate, doubly articulated nasals can also be found in this context. As was explained in 6.9, an alveolar (or, in velarizing dialects, velar) occlusion may be produced partially overlapping with a second occlusion, corresponding to the place of articulation of the following consonant, while the velum is still lowered: [kami̯ónm̑pekéɲo], or, in velarizing dialects, [kami̯óŋm̑pekéɲo].

EXERCISES

1. Consider the following Catalan data:

   a. *son* [són] 'they are'
      son pocs [sómpɔ́ks] 'they are few' (= 'we are few')
      son dos [sóṉdós] 'they are two'
      son seks [sónsɛ́ks] 'they are dry'
      son grans [sóŋgɾáns] 'they are big'

   b. *som* [sóm] 'we are'
      som pocs [sómpɔ́ks] 'we are few'
      somdos [sómdós] 'we are two'
      som secs [sómsɛ́ks] 'we are dry'
      som grans [sómgɾáns] 'we are big'

   c. *any* [áɲ] 'year'
      any passat [áɲpəsát] 'last year'
      any dos [áɲdós] 'year two'
      any sec [áɲsɛ́k] 'dry year'
      any gran [áɲgɾán] 'big year'

   How would you say Catalan differs from Spanish in terms of the phonological phenomena of nasal neutralization and nasal assimilation?

2. Compare the articulation of /ɲ/ in Spanish *cañón* with that of the sequence in English *canyon*.

11 Liquids (laterals and rhotics)

11.1 Liquid consonants: laterals and rhotics

The term 'liquid consonant' is used to include both laterals (or *l*-like sounds) and rhotics (or *r*-like sounds). These segments often share distributional and other properties. For instance, in Spanish only lateral /l/ and rhotic /ɾ/ can occur after another consonant in an onset cluster (e.g. *blusa* 'blouse', *bruto* 'brute').

11.2 Laterals

11.2.1 Phonemes and allophonic distribution

Lateral consonants are produced with central obstruction in the mouth, allowing free passage of the air flow through one or both sides of the tongue. Most Spanish dialects nowadays have a single lateral phoneme /l/, whose basic allophone is a voiced apico-alveolar lateral. To produce this segment, the tip of the tongue moves to create an occlusion in the alveolar region but allows airflow either on one or on both sides of the tongue, depending on speaker preferences. Notice that, although the kind of contact that is produced is similar to that for [t] (full contact between the tongue tip and the passive articulator, albeit slightly further back), the sound of [lllll] can be maintained, unlike that of [t], which does not produce any sound until it is released. That is because, when [l] is produced, the air escapes through the space between the tongue and one or both sides of the mouth in spite of the central obstruction.

In English, /l/ has both a 'clear' or 'light' allophone, [l], as in *light*, and a 'dark' or velarized allophone, [ɫ], as in *tall*, with a secondary velar constriction, produced by bunching the tongue body towards the velum. In most English varieties 'clear' [l] is used in syllable onset and 'dark' [ɫ] in the coda, but there

Table 11.1 Assimilation of [l].

Assimilation of /l/ before consonants articulated with front part of the tongue		No assimilation of /l/ before labial and velar consonants	
dental [l̪]	*alto* [áḻto] 'tall'		*golpe* [gólpe] 'blow'
	caldo [káḻdo] 'broth'		*alba* [álβa] 'dawn'
alveolar [l]	*balneario* [balneár̯io] 'spa'		*el faro* [elfáro] 'the lighthouse'
	balsa [bálsa] 'raft'		
palatalized [lʲ]	*colcha* [kólʲt͡ʃa] 'bedspread'		*belga* [bélɣa] 'Belgian'
	el yeso [elʲʝéso] 'the plaster'		*alcoba* [alkóβa] 'bedroom'
			el jarro [elxár̄o] 'the pot'

are English-speakers who have a dark [ɫ] in all positions.[1] In Spanish, instead, /l/ is always light. It is always produced without bunching the tongue body, whether in the onset or in the coda: *lata* [láta] 'can', *tal* [tál] 'such'. This is except in Catalonia, where Catalan-dominant bilingual speakers sometimes transfer the dark [ɫ] of this language to Spanish.

When followed by a consonant articulated with the front part of the tongue, /l/ assimilates in place of articulation (see Table 11.1). There is, however, no assimilation either to labial consonants, since it is not possible to produce a labial lateral, or to velars. Notice, in particular, that [l] is still 'clear', not velarized, when preceding a velar consonant, as in *algo* 'something'. The assimilation in place of preconsonantal /l/ is thus more limited than that of nasals in the same position.

11.2.2 The fate of the lateral palatal /ʎ/: *yeísmo* and related phenomena

Some Spanish dialects have a second lateral phoneme: a voiced palatal lateral /ʎ/. In dialects with this phoneme, it occurs in words where the spelling has *ll*, such as *llorar* /ʎorár/ 'to cry', *calle* /káʎe/ 'street', etc. (For the spelling *ll* to represent this sound, see Appendix B.) This sound also occurs in Italian, where it is spelled *gli*, as in *paglia* 'straw'. Impressionistically, as a first approximation, it is somewhat like [l] plus a palatal glide [i̯] pronounced simultaneously. It is, nevertheless, crucially different from the sequence [li̯]. For Spanish speakers who have this phoneme, *pollo* [póʎo] 'chicken' is not confused with *polio*

---

[1] In fact, English /l/ typically has a secondary velar constriction. What provides the 'clear' [l] percept in the onset and the 'dark' [ɫ] percept in the coda is a difference in the relative timing and magnitude of the dorsal and apical constrictions in these two positions (Sproat and Fujimura 1993).

[pólio] 'polio'. In [ʎ] there is contact between the tongue dorsum and the central part of the palate, with free air flow through one of the sides of the tongue.

Even though, at some historical point, all Spanish dialects must have had the palatal lateral phoneme, nowadays it is part of the phonological system of only a minority of Spanish speakers. Phonological descriptions of Standard Peninsular Spanish produced in the first part of the twentieth century, and even more recent ones, include the palatal lateral /ʎ/ as part of the inventory in this variety (e.g. Navarro Tomás 1977; Quilis 1993; Martínez Celdrán et al. 2003). The fact is, however, that the great majority of speakers in Spain under the age of fifty or so have merged this phoneme with /ʝ/ and do not distinguish between, for instance, *pollo* 'chicken' and *poyo* 'stone bench', both pronounced [pójo]. As mentioned in 3.5, the lack of contrast between the sounds corresponding to orthographic *ll* and orthographic prevocalic *y* is known as *yeísmo*. The phenomenon of *yeísmo* probably originated from a relaxation of the central occlusion of /ʎ/, which led to merger with /ʝ/. The existence of *yeísmo* has been attested since the end of the Middle Ages, but until very recently, within Spain, it was confined mostly to Andalusia, and not even to the whole of this region. In the last century or so, however, *yeísmo* has become the dominant pronunciation and the lateral palatal phoneme /ʎ/ is consistently preserved only in some rural areas, primarily of northeastern Spain. We may note that the same process took place in French some time earlier.

In Latin America the lateral palatal is still found as an independent phoneme in Paraguay and the Andean region: parts of Colombia, Ecuador, Peru, Bolivia, and also relatively small areas of Chile (Canfield 1981:31) and Argentina (Canfield 1981:24). As in Spain, in most of these South American nations the phoneme is quickly disappearing in the speech of the younger urban generations. An exception is Paraguay, where /ʎ/ is still found in firm contrast with /ʝ/, which in this country is generally realized as the affricate [d͡ʒ]; e.g.: Par. *calle* [káʎe] 'street' vs *mayo* [mád͡ʒo] 'May' (see Canfield 1981:70; Alvar 1996c:203–4). It is interesting to note that, although the preservation of /ʎ/ in parts of the Andean area may be plausibly attributed to the influence of Quechua and Aymara, two languages that also have this phoneme (as in *llama*, which in a borrowing from Quechua), Guaraní, the dominant language of Paraguay, does not have this sound, so that a different explanation is needed for its maintenance in Paraguayan Spanish.

In parts of Ecuador (central highlands; see Canfield 1981:48) and in a small area of Argentina (Canfield 1981:23), the lateral palatal has become a strident prepalatal fricative [ʒ], without merging with the palatal phoneme /ʝ/, which is not strident in this area.

Finally, we may note that Spanish words never have final *-ll* indicating /ʎ/ in the conservative *lleísta* pronunciation. Where we would expect this word-final consonant for historical and morphological reasons, we find /-l/ instead, cf. *él/ella* 'he/she', *aquel/aquella* 'that over there, *masc./fem.*', *doncel/doncella* 'lad/maiden', etc.

11.3 The rhotics

11.3.1 Phonemes and allophonic distribution

Spanish has two contrastive rhotics or r-sounds: a tap /ɾ/ (*vibrante simple*), as in *caro* /káɾo/ 'expensive' and a trill /r̄/ (*vibrante múltiple*), as in *carro* /kár̄o/ 'cart', *roca* /r̄óka/ 'rock'. Both rhotic phonemes are usually realized as voiced and as alveolar, although other realizations are also attested in several areas, as we will see below. The fundamental difference between tap and trill is the following: the tap is produced with a single rapid contact of the tip of the tongue against the alveolar ridge. The trill is produced with several such rapid contacts, generally two or three. It is not completely accurate, however, to define a trill as a sequence of taps, since the articulation is somewhat different. The trill requires a more precise articulatory gesture, which restricts its coarticulation with neighbouring segments (see Recasens 1991; Recasens and Pallarès 1999).

The Spanish intervocalic tap is very similar to the flap allophone of /t/ and /d/ produced in American English, and some other English dialects, after a stressed vowel and preceding an unstressed one, as in *better, ladder* and the second *t* in *potato*. In both consonants, there is a brief alveolar occlusion, and the acoustic effect is similar. Articulatorily, however, the two sounds are not identical. In the production of the American English flap the tongue tip is first retracted and then rapidly brought forward to make contact with the alveolar ridge. In the Spanish tap, on the other hand, there is a rapid vertical upward–downward movement of the tongue tip, without anticipatory retraction (Ladefoged and Maddieson 1996:232).

English /r/ is generally an approximant alveolar or postalveolar [ɹ] (without occlusion), often with retroflection and a constriction in the pharynx. It has a very different acoustic effect from the Spanish rhotics. Transfer of the English [ɹ] to Spanish is one of the most noticeable marks of a foreign accent in the perception of Spanish speakers.

The distribution of the rhotics in Spanish presents unique characteristics. Tap and trill are found in phonemic contrast only in word-internal intervocalic position. In this environment numerous minimal pairs can be found, as illustrated in Table 11.2.

Table 11.2 Examples of minimal pairs contrasting tap and trill.

tap /ɾ/	trill /r̄/
pe*r*o 'but'	pe*rr*o 'dog'
pe*r*a 'pear'	pe*rr*a 'dog, *fem.*'
pa*r*a 'for'	pa*rr*a 'grapevine'
co*r*o 'choir'	co*rr*o 'circle'
que*r*ía 'I wanted'	que*rr*ía 'I would want'
ca*r*o 'expensive'	ca*rr*o 'cart; car'
mo*r*o 'Moor'	mo*rr*o 'snout'
ce*r*o 'zero'	ce*rr*o 'hill'
mi*r*a 'look'	mi*rr*a 'myrrh'
va*r*a 'stick'	ba*rr*a 'bar'

Outside of the intervocalic context, however, there is no contrast. Word initially and after a consonant in a different syllable, only the trill is found: *rata* /r̄áta/ 'rat', *honra* /ónr̄a/ 'honour'. In an onset cluster, only the tap is found: *broma* /bɾóma/ 'joke', *abre* /ábɾe/ [áβɾe] 's/he opens' (but see 11.3.3; see also 6.7 on *svarabakhti* vowels). The tap also occurs to the exclusion of the trill word finally before another vowel: *mar ancho* [máɾán ͡ʲt ͡ʃo] 'wide sea'. In coda position, where there is no possible resyllabification – that is, before a consonant (within a word or across word boundaries) and before pause – we find a nondistinct rhotic, which we could represent simply as [r]. In most regions this neutralized coda [r] usually resembles the tap more closely, but it can also be realized as a trill in somewhat emphatic speech: *arte* [áɾte] = [áɾte] ~ [ár̄te] 'art', *amor* [amóɾ] = [amóɾ] ~ [amór̄] 'love'. In the Basque Country and other areas of northwestern Spain a trill-like realization is also the norm in nonemphatic speech in coda contexts (Alonso 1945:95–6).

The distribution of rhotics is summarized in Table 11.3.

Importantly, the tap /ɾ/ is the only consonant in Spanish that is clearly contrastive word-medially and yet is systematically excluded from the word-initial position.

In phonological representations, we will represent word-final and syllable-final rhotics as /ɾ/, e.g., /máɾ/, /páɾte/, as shown in the table. A tap [ɾ] is what we invariably have in Spanish when a word-final consonant resyllabifies with a following vowel. This phonemization must be complemented with the statement that preconsonantal and phrase-final /ɾ/ (as in pa<u>r</u>te, ma<u>r</u>, ma<u>r</u> seco) can be variably strengthened. If, on the other hand, we followed classical European structuralist practice in postulating an archiphoneme both in

11.3 The rhotics

Table 11.3 Distribution of rhotics in Spanish.

a) Contrast tap /ɾ/ vs trill /r̄/	V__V	Intervocalic
		/káɾo/ 'expensive' vs /kár̄o/ 'cart; car'
b) Only trill /r̄/	#__	Word-initial
		/r̄óka/ 'rock'
	C.__	After a heterosyllabic consonant
		/alr̄ededóɾ/ 'around', /enr̄edo/ 'mess', /isr̄aelita/ 'Israeli'
c) Only tap /ɾ/	C__	After a tautosyllabic consonant (onset cluster)
		/bɾóma/ 'joke', /gɾámo/ 'gram'
	V__#V	Word-final before a vowel
		/séɾ amígos/ 'to be friends'
d) Variable rhotic (most commonly [ɾ])	V__C	Before a consonant
		/páɾte/ [páɾte] ~ [pár̄te]
	V__#C	Word-final before a consonant
		/séɾ poéta/ 'to be a poet'
	V__##	Word-final before pause
		/séɾ o nó séɾ/ 'to be or not to be'

word-internal preconsonantal position and in word-final position, we would still need a statement to account for the fact that the archiphoneme is necessarily realized as a tap when resyllabified (as in *mar ancho*) but varies between tap and trill otherwise. Other phonologizations are also possible (see Exercise 1).

In the group /sr̄/ (e.g., *israelita* 'Israeli', *dos rocas* 'two rocks') it is common for the sibilant to be deleted, so that, for instance, *te lo regalo* 'I give it to you' and *te los regalo* 'I give them to you' may become homophonous [telor̄eɣálo]. Another common possibility is for the trill to be realized as an approximant rhotic in this sequence: [doɹr̄ókas].

Notice that both word-initial and word-final rhotics may occur in the intervocalic environment in connected speech, in which case they may contrast with word-internal sequences. Since word-initial rhotics are always trills, they may contrast with word-internal taps. For instance, the phrase *a Roma* [ar̄óma] 'to Rome' forms a minimal pair with the word *aroma* [aɾóma] 'aroma', and, on the other hand, *de rota* [der̄óta] 'of a broken one' and *derrota* [der̄óta] 'defeat' are homophonous. As for word-final rhotics, if intervocalic, they contrast with word-internal trills, as in *amar a ese* [amáɾaése] 'to love that one' vs *amarra ese* [amár̄aése] 'tie that one up'.

Table 11.4 Sequences of rhotics across word- and prefix-boundaries.

Across word-boundaries:			
a.	ɾ	*dar ocas*	'to give geese'
b.	r̄	*da rocas*	's/he gives rocks'
c.	ɾr̄	*dar rocas*	'to give rocks'
Across prefix-boundaries:			
a.	ɾ	*super-ávido* 'super avid'	
b.	r̄	*extra-rápido* 'extra rapid'	
c.	ɾr̄	*super-rápido* (vs *supe rápido* 'I found out quickly')[2]	

Across word- and prefix-boundaries we could in principle have a three-way contrast, as in the examples in Table 11.4.

It is sometimes stated that the contrast between trill and sequence of final rhotic followed by word-initial trill is necessarily neutralized (J. Harris 1983:63; Quilis and Fernández 1985:148; Lipski 1990), the logic being that the only possible contrast in Spanish is between one occlusion (tap) and two or more occlusions (trill) and thus the number of occlusions beyond two cannot make any phonological difference. However, as mentioned in 5.8, in an experiment reported in Hualde (2004) a difference in duration was found between the sequences in examples such as *salí rápido* 'I left quickly' vs *salir rápido* 'to leave quickly', comparable to that between single and double /s/, as in *sabe siempre* 's/he always knows' vs *sabes siempre* 'you always know'. It appears that, as in sequences of identical continuant consonants across word boundaries, the contrast between (b) and (c) in Table 11.4 may be neutralized, but may also be preserved by durational means (see 5.8).

An additional morphophonological restriction is that a word-final rhotic always corresponds to /ɾ/, never to /r̄/, before a vowel in morphologically related words. Thus, there are sets of related words such as *olor* 'smell', *olores* 'smells', *oloroso* 'smelly'; *señor* 'gentleman', *señores* 'gentlemen', *señora* 'lady'; but not *olor*, *olorres, *olorroso; *señor*, *señorres, *señorra (with very few exceptions, see next section).

---

[2] These two examples also differ in their basic stress pattern, but this difference can be eliminated either by placing stress on the initial of the compound (*súper-rápido*) or by deaccenting the verb in *supe rápido*.

11.3.2 Historical origin of the tap/trill contrast

The limited contrast between tap and trill has an obvious historical explanation: it derives from an earlier contrast between single and geminate consonants. In Latin, a single vs geminate contrast existed for almost all consonants. The contrast was found only in word-internal intervocalic position. In the evolution from Latin to Spanish, geminates became single consonants, -CC- > -C- – e.g., BUCCA > *boca*, GUTTA > *gota* – except that /-ll-/ > /ʎ/, /-nn-/ > /ɲ/ and /-rr-/ > /r̄/ (Menéndez Pidal 1973[1904]:134–5; Lloyd 1987:242–4; Penny 2002: 81–2).

Notice that, in spite of its historical origin, the Spanish intervocalic trill is not a geminate since it syllabifies as onset with the next vowel. The syllabification of *carro* is *ca-rro*.[3]

In other contexts, the distribution between tap and trill in Spanish is not exactly the same as that between single and geminate /r/ in Latin because of independent evolutions. In particular, from the distribution of geminate and single consonants in Latin, we would expect to find taps and not trills in word-initial position in Spanish. What has happened here is that in Spanish and some other Romance languages there has been historical fortition of word-initial /r-/; e.g. Lat. /romá:na/ > Sp. /r̄omána/ 'Roman, *fem*.'.[4]

The limited context for the contrast between tap and trill in Spanish is thus explained by its origin in a single vs geminate opposition.

The lack of contrast in the case of word-final rhotics (e.g. *olor/olores* but not **olor/olorres*) also has an obvious historical origin: if /r/ was already word-final in Latin, it couldn't be a geminate. Word-final consonants also arose from the deletion of /e/ after a single coronal consonant, as in *pane/panes* > *pan/panes* 'bread, *sg./pl.*', *amore/amores* > *amor/amores* 'love, *sg./pl.*'. Since, on the other hand, the few words ending in *-rre*, such as *torre* (< Lat. TURRE) did not lose their final vowel, there is no **tor/torres* (cf. *torre/torres*, see 12.7.1).

Given this evolution, there cannot be any native words of the **olor/olorres* type. Such words could only be incorporated into the Spanish lexicon by borrowing from a language with the relevant pattern. This has happened in the Spanish of Navarra in adjectives/nouns referring to towns in the Roncal Valley, which are borrowed from Basque. For instance a person from *Garde* is a *gardar*. This word has a plural *gardarres* 'people from Garde' and a feminine

---

[3] On the other hand, in Italian, where the single/geminate contrast of Latin has been preserved for all nonpalatal consonants, *carro* is syllabified as *car-ro*, just like, for instance *fat-to* 'fact' (see, e.g., Muljačić 1972).

[4] In other Ibero-Romance languages /l-/ and /n-/ also underwent fortition, cf. Cat. and Ast. *lluna* 'moon', Ast. *ñome* 'name'.

gardarra 'woman from Garde'. Similarly we have *burguiar/burguiarres* (from Burgui), *izabar/izabarres* (from Isaba), etc. These seem to be the only words in the Spanish language with this pattern.[5]

11.3.3 Dialectal phenomena involving the rhotics

At the beginning of section 11.3 we described what can be considered the normative articulation of the Spanish tap and trill. These are not, however, the only ways in which these phonemes may be realized. To begin with, any Spanish speaker may produce both tap and trill without full occlusion, as approximants or fricatives (see Blecua 2001; Hammond 1999). The frequency with which these allophonic realizations are produced depends on both speaker and dialectal preferences. In addition, we find a number of dialectal pronunciations that differ from the norm.

a) Assibilation of rhotics

In some areas, fricative or assibilated (s-like) allophones are part of the local dialect, either consistently or in variation with more 'standard' variants. These assibilated allophones of the rhotics can be either voiced or voiceless and may be found in different contexts depending on the dialect. There is no special IPA symbol for this sound (or collection of sounds) but in the Spanish dialectological tradition the symbol [ř] is generally employed for this purpose.

In central Mexico an assibilated, generally voiceless, allophone of /r/ is found with some frequency before pause: *comer* [koméř̥] (Moreno de Alba 1994:126–34).

Assibilated variants of onset /r̄/, generally voiced (*carro* [kářo], *roca* [řóka], are found in parts of Central America (Guatemala, Costa Rica) and in the Andean region (highlands of Colombia, Ecuador, Peru, Bolivia and northern Chile), as well as in Paraguay and northern Argentina. In some countries where these variants are found they are somewhat stigmatized (i.e. they are not part of the national standard). In Costa Rica a frequent (but somewhat stigmatized)

---

[5] In Basque, unlike in Spanish, word-final rhotics surface as trills before vowel-initial suffixes in most words – *lur* 'land', *lurra* 'the land', *lurrak* '(the) lands' – although there are a few exceptions: *ur* 'water', *ura* 'the water', *urak* '(the) waters'. The town adjectives under discussion belong to the general class in Basque, e.g. *gardar, gardarra, gardarrak*. In other areas of contact with Basque, the pattern has not arisen because the corresponding adjectives have been borrowed with the Basque singular article *-a* incorporated, as in *un donostiarra* 'a person from Donostia – San Sebastián'. In most Basque dialects words are cited with the article, but this was not the case in the extinct Roncalese Basque dialect. This is what has allowed for the borrowing of the Basque pattern of rhotics in Roncalese Spanish.

variant of the trill is an approximant very similar to American English /r̄/; that is, [ɹ].

In Highland Ecuador Spanish, an assibilated rhotic is found before a dental consonant, but not in other preconsonantal contexts (Argüello 1978, cited in Bradley 2004).

The group /tr/ (and sometimes /dr/ as well) is assibilated, with a pronunciation that resembles English *tr* (as in *tree*) in Ecuador, Costa Rica, Chile and, in Spain, in an area of La Rioja and the south of Navarra.

b) Dorsalization of the trill

A widespread, relatively recent, historical change in parts of western Europe has been the replacement of apical /r/ with a dorsal articulation, either a trill [ʀ] or a fricative, produced with the dorsum against the velar or uvular region. Dorsal rhotics are nowadays found in Standard French, in Standard German, in some varieties of Dutch, in southern Swedish and in Lisbon Portuguese,[6] among other European varieties. In many Spanish-speaking areas one occasionally, or frequently, depending on the region, encounters speakers who produce a dorsal instead of an apical trill, but this is generally at the level of individual idiosyncrasy. In the Spanish-speaking world, a dorsal articulation of /r̄/ has become an established dialectal variant only in Puerto Rico, although, even here, it is by no means the case that all Puerto Ricans use this variant. In Puerto Rican Spanish, dorsal [ʀ] may be either voiced or voiceless and is found both word initially and word medially: *roca* [ʀóka], *carro* [káʀo] (word finally other processes take place instead, see next section). The social consideration of dorsal [ʀ] in Puerto Rico is quite interesting: whereas some speakers consider it a low-prestige variant, a deviation from standard pronunciation, for some other Puerto Ricans it is a sign of Puerto-Ricanness (López Morales 1979, 1983:137–46).

c) 'Preaspiration' of trills

In Puerto Rico, Cuba and the Dominican Republic, a common variant of the intervocalic trill is a partly devoiced consonant that starts with pharyngeal friction and ends with one or more apical occlusions. Sometimes this is transcribed with a preceding [h]: *carro* [káhro].

d) Strengthening of rhotics in codas and onset clusters

As mentioned above, in an area of northern and western Spain, comprising the Basque Country and parts of Leon and Old Castile, preconsonantal rhotics are typically realized as trills in normal speech. In addition, in the Spanish spoken in the Basque Country, it is frequent to find trills in onset clusters, e.g.

---

[6] In many Brazilian Portuguese varieties, velar [x] or aspirated [h] are found.

primo [pr̃ímo] 'cousin', *droga* [dr̃óɣa] 'drug'. It is likely that this phenomenon is due to influence from Basque, although this pronunciation is also common among monolingual Spanish speakers in this area. On the other hand, the realization of trills also in word-final position before a vowel, as in, e.g., *por eso* [por̃éso] 'because of that', is stigmatized as a sign of a heavy Basque accent.

11.4 Neutralization and deletion of liquids in the coda of the syllable in Spanish dialects

In parts of Andalusia and Extremadura and in the Caribbean, the contrast between /l/ and /ɾ/ before a consonant or at the end of the word tends to be neutralized, so that words like *harto* 'full' and *alto* 'tall', *mar* 'sea' and *mal* 'evil', etc., are not distinguished in pronunciation. The result of this neutralization is very variable, so that, for instance, *carne* 'meat' may be realized as [káɾne] ~ [kálne] ~ [káhne] ~ [kánne], among other possibilities, in dialects with weakening of coda liquids, often with variation in the speech of the same speaker. In parts of Andalusia the most common pronunciation of liquids in preconsonantal position is as rhotics, *muy alto* [múáɾto] 'very tall', *e[ɾ] niño* 'the boy', whereas at the end of a word (other than an article) deletion of the segment is most common: Andal. *vamos a cantar* [bámo.akaṇtá] 'let's sing', *el hospital* [elohpitá] 'the hospital', *mujer* [muhé] 'woman'. In Puerto Rico the usual solution is [l] or an intermediate sound between lateral and rhotic: PR *puerta* [pu̯éʳlta] 'door', *por favor* [poʳlfaβól] 'please'. In Cuba it is common for preconsonantal liquids to assimilate to the place of articulation and other features of the following consonant: Cu. *el golpe* [eggóbpe] 'the blow', *el verde* [ebbédde] 'the green one', *pulga* 'flea' = *purga* 'purgative' [púgga] (see Guitart 1976; notice that /b d g/ are realized as plosives in this environment). Typical of the El Cibao region of the Dominican Republic (especially in the lower socioeconomic strata) is the vocalization of liquids as palatal glides before a consonant and word finally in words with final stress: Dom. *algo* [ái̯ɣo], *mujer* [muhéi̯] (if stress is not final, final liquids are deleted instead: *el árbol* [elái̯βo]; Alba 1979). Another solution in many dialects is the aspiration of the liquid, *carne* [káhne] 'meat'. Usually in dialects with neutralization and deletion of word-final liquids, the etymological consonants are preserved in plurals and derived words; e.g. Andal. *mujer/mujeres* [muhé]/[muhéɾe] 'woman/women' and *papel/papeles* [papé]/[papéle] 'paper/papers'. Nevertheless, nonetymological plurals do occur.

EXERCISES

1. Some authors who adopt a Praguean structuralist framework, such as Quilis (1993:41–2, 329–43), postulate an archiphoneme /R/ to represent the neutralization of the two rhotic phonemes in syllable- and word-final position. What are the empirical problems for adopting an archiphoneme /R/ in word-final position? Consider the following examples (where [r] is a nondistinct surface rhotic (that is, [ɾ] ~ [r]) and /R/ is the archiphoneme). What rule/statement do you need in order to make the mapping between phonological and phonetic representations explicit?

    | *dar más* | /dáR más/ | [dármás] | 'to give more' |
    | *dar uno* | /dáR úno/ | [dáɾúno] | 'to give one' |

2. D'Introno *et al.* (1995:295–303) propose a generative analysis of the Spanish rhotics with two phonemes, tap and trill, but without making use of archiphonemes (they discuss two slightly different hypotheses). Other generativist phonologists, such as J. Harris (1983:62–71), have proposed an analysis with a single rhotic phoneme, where the trill is derived from an underlying geminate sequence. Compare these analyses. What are the advantages of each of them in terms of economy and clarity? (To complete this exercise you need to read the sources.)

3. In some dialects of Brazilian Portuguese, including Standard Brazilian Portuguese, the trill has become [h] by historical evolution; e.g. *carro* [káhu] 'car'. In these Brazilian varieties we find [h] in the coda, *amor* [amóh] 'love', *Artur* [ahtúh], but a tap [ɾ] in word-final position before a vowel, *amor eterno* [amóɾɛtéhnu] 'eternal love' (Perini 2004:42–3). How does Brazilian Portuguese differ from Spanish in this respect?

4. This author recently noticed the sign *delantares/aprons* in a shop in Puerto Rico, for standard *delantales*. How do you explain this nonstandard orthographic form?

5. Obtain spectrograms of the words *polio*, *pollo* and *poyo* pronounced by a *lleísta* speaker. How would you characterize the difference among these spectrograms?

12 Main morphophonological alternations

12.1 Morphophonological rules

Sometimes the same MORPHEME (unit of meaning) has different shapes in words related by INFLECTION or DERIVATION. Thus, for instance, the root of the verb *soñar* 'to dream' has a diphthong in forms of its paradigm such as *sueño* 'I sleep'. We say that the root of *soñar* has two ALLOMORPHS or variants, one with the vowel /o/ and another one containing the diphthong /ue/. In this particular case, it turns out that the same /o/-/ue/ alternation is found in many other verbal paradigms (and in many words related by derivation: e.g. *puerta* 'door' / *portero* 'doorman'). It also happens to be the case that the distribution of /o/ and /ue/ has a phonological condition: in verbal roots with an /o/-/ue/ alternation, the diphthong /ue/ appears when the syllable is stressed. In cases like this we speak of MORPHOPHONOLOGICAL RULES. Unlike phonological rules, like those discussed in previous chapters, which determine the distribution of allophones of the same phoneme, morphophonological rules involve alternations between phonemes in words of the same 'family'.

Whereas with phonological rules we often find phonetic gradualness, morphophonological rules are categorical, since they are relations between phonemes. In our example, there are no intermediate forms between /o/ and /ue/ (e.g. a slightly diphthongized vowel). In a given word we either have one or the other. A morphophonological rule may be optional in certain instances (for example, the so-called superlative of *nuevo* 'new' is either *novísimo* or *nuevísimo* 'very new'), but it cannot be phonetically gradual, because phonemes are, in principle, distinct categories.

Let us consider another example to illustrate this difference between phonology and morphophonology. As we know, in many Spanish dialects syllable-final /s/ can be weakened to different degrees. This is the phonological rule we know as aspiration of /s/, which may involve the complete deletion of the segment as

12.1 Morphophonological rules

the most advanced stage of weakening. On the other hand, all Spanish dialects also have a morphophonological rule resulting in the deletion of the final /s/ of the verb in first person plural imperatives followed by the clitic pronoun *nos*: *vamos* but *vámonos* 'let's go' (not *vámosnos). In this instance there is neither optionality nor gradualness: /s/ is obligatorily removed in this context. Whereas in dialects with phonological aspiration the final /s/ of *vamos* may be weakened to different degrees in other contexts ([bámos] ~ [bámoh] ~ [bámo], and intermediate forms), the loss of the /s/ in *vámonos* is categorical in both aspirating and nonaspirating dialects.[1]

Morphophonological alternations are, by definition, restricted in their application to specific morphological contexts or lexical items and, consequently, are never completely predictable from the phonological environment alone, in the sense that a given phonological context predictably triggers a change (they may even be restricted to a single combination of morphemes, as is the case with V-*mos* + *nos* → V-*monos*).[2] In fact, for some alternations there is no obvious phonological context. Whereas, for instance, in the /o/-/ue/ alternation we can find a phonological condition (word-stress), some other alternations in the phonological shape of morphemes are not phonologically conditioned in any obvious way. The alternating phonemes may indeed appear in essentially the same phonological context, as, for instance, do /n/ and /ɲ/ in *vino* 'wine' vs *viña* 'vineyard', and /ue/ and /u/ in *puedo* 'I can' vs *pudo* 's/he could'.

Both roots and suffixes may show allomorphy. For instance, the plural suffix in Spanish has two allomorphs, as it appears as /-s/ in some cases and as /-es/ in other cases.

Differences between related words may involve a single phoneme that changes or they may involve more extensive alternations (e.g. *decir* 'to say' vs *dije* 'I said'; *padre* 'father' vs *paternal* 'fatherly'; *ojo* 'eye' vs *oculista* 'eye doctor'; *leche* 'milk' vs *lácteo* 'lacteous'). In the most extreme case, forms of a single paradigm, related by meaning, are completely different, as is the case, for instance, with *voy* 'I go' and *fui* 'I went'. In this case we speak of SUPPLETION. Of course, outside of INFLECTIONAL PARADIGMS we don't always have clear criteria for determining when two words should be considered to be related.

The relative productivity of alternations can be very variable. For instance, the alternation between /o/ and /ue/, as in *soñar/sueño*, affects a large number of roots, as mentioned above. On the other hand, the alternation in *fruto* 'fruit' vs *fructificar* 'to fructify' is very weakly represented in the Spanish lexicon. Some

---

[1] Except as some sort of hypercorrection in dialects with aspiration.
[2] This is not to say that the reverse always holds. 'Purely' phonological rules may also be restricted to certain classes of words or apply more frequently in certain contexts than in others.

alternations appear to apply quite consistently in a given environment, but affect a small number of morphemes.

In this chapter we cannot consider all alternations observable between derivationally related words (for a summary, see Pensado 1999). Instead, we will examine only the most important morphophonemic alternations that affect inflectional paradigms and 'affective' derivation, addressing also the historical explanation for their existence when this is useful for understanding the facts.

12.2 Historical origin of morphophonological alternations

We may distinguish three main situations.

a) In many cases where we have a morphophonological alternation this is the consequence of a sound change that applied in a specific context, not affecting all words containing the same morpheme when the relevant phonological context was not present in all of them. Thus, as will be explained in more detail later, a sound change produced the diphthongization of the Latin short vowel /o/ when it was in stressed position, but not when it was in an unstressed syllable. This is the origin of the /o/-/ue/ alternation in Modern Spanish. Latin /f/ became /h/ (ultimately lost) before a vowel, but not before the diphthong /u̯e/. The result is that we have *fuego* 'fire' but *hogar* 'fireplace'.

b) Many morphophonological alternations in Spanish have resulted from the way the Spanish lexicon has grown. Throughout its history, Spanish has borrowed words from Classical Latin. These learned words, adopted from written Latin, do not show many of the changes undergone by the native lexicon, orally transmitted from generation to generation. For instance, the Latin intervocalic stops /p t k/ became voiced in their evolution in Spanish: Lat. CAPILLU > Sp. *cabello* 'hair', Lat. VĪTA > Sp. *vida* 'life', Lat. LACU > Sp. *lago* 'lake'.[3] At a later point, however, Spanish borrowed related adjectives from the same Latin source and now we have morphophonological alternations between intervocalic voiced and voiceless stops, as in *cabello/capilar, vida/vital, lago/lacustre*. It is interesting to note in this respect that English has also borrowed a large part of its technical vocabulary from Classical Latin, but since in English the native lexicon has a different source (Germanic) what we find is many pairs

---

[3] Following an established convention, forms given as Latin etyma of Spanish nouns (in small capitals and italics) generally correspond to the Latin accusative, without the final -M of the accusative singular, which we know was lost in pronunciation fairly early. An exception is constituted by some neuter nouns such as Lat. LAC 'milk' whose accusative form was also LAC. In this case it is assumed that Spanish *leche* derives from a non-Classical form *LACTE created by analogy with genitive LACTIS and other forms of the declensional paradigm. Another example of this would be *NŌMINE > *nombre* 'name', where the Classical Latin forms are nominative and accusative NŌMEN, genitive NŌMINIS, etc.

12.3 Diphthongs and mid vowels: *e/ie, o/ue*

of semantically related words with different roots, as in *life/vital, moon/lunar, sea/marine, tree/arboreal*, etc.

c) In a few cases, an alternation that we find in Spanish was already present in Latin. To give an example, in Latin the nasal of the negative prefix *in-*, besides assimilating in place to a following consonant, assimilated in all features when the following consonant was a liquid. This Latin assimilation rule accounts for the fact that in Modern Spanish, together with *tolerante/intolerante* 'tolerant/intolerant', *posible/imposible* 'possible/impossible', etc., we have *legal/ilegal* 'legal/illegal', *racional/irracional* 'rational/irrational', etc., where now, in Spanish, the final /n/ of the prefix deletes before a liquid. As can be seen by the glosses, English has also borrowed this alternation from Latin.

Also of Latin origin is the alternation between /a/ in a word-initial syllable and /e/ after a prefix shown in examples such as *apto/inepto* 'apt/inept', *arma/inerme* 'arm/unarmed', *barba/imberbe* 'beard/beardless', *año/bienio* 'year/biennium', etc.[4] This alternation has its origin in a sound change in pre-Classical Latin.

12.3 Alternations between diphthongs and mid vowels: *e/ie, o/ue*

One of the most conspicuous alternations in Spanish affects the diphthongs *ie, ue*. For the most part, these diphthongs are found only in stressed position. In morphologically related words, *ie* is reduced to *e* and *ue* to *o* when the stress is shifted to a different syllable.

12.3.1 Verbs with *e/ie, o/ue* alternations

This alternation has systematic aspects in verb forms. From the infinitive, one cannot predict which verbs alternate and which do not, since in the infinitive the stress is on the ending, not on the root. Thus, in this direction, it is an unpredictable fact that from, say, *coser* 'to sew' we have *coso, coses* 'I sew, you sew' but from *cocer* 'cook, boil' the forms are *cuezo, cueces* 'I cook, you cook'. To give another example, there appears to be no predictability in the fact that from *defender* 'to defend' we have *defiendo* 'I defend' but from *ofender* 'to offend' the corresponding form is *ofendo* 'I offend'. If we know only the infinitive and the root has a mid vowel, we will not be able to guess whether in present tense forms with stress on the root there is a diphthong or not.[5]

---

[4] In *arte/inercia* 'art/inertia' the semantic connection has been lost.
[5] A clear demonstration of this is provided by the fact that the verb *apostar* 'to bet' diphthongizes – *apuesto* 'I bet' – but the homonymous infinitive *apostar* 'to post, station' does not: *aposto* 'I station'.

Looking at the phenomenon from the opposite direction, on the other hand, there is much greater predictability. Almost all verbs that have *ie* or *ue* in the root have these diphthongs in all and only those forms of the paradigm where the root receives the stress, and have *e* or *o*, respectively, in forms of the paradigm where the stress is on a syllable containing a suffix. That is, if we know that some forms of the present tense of a given verb have a diphthong *ie*, we can be almost certain that this diphthong is reduced to *e* in unstressed position throughout the verbal paradigm, and similarly for *ue* and *o*. The diphthongs *ie* and *ue* appear only in the present indicative and subjunctive (all singular and third plural forms), as well as the singular imperative, since these are the forms and tenses where the stress falls on the root. To give an example, the verb *pensar*, which shows an *e/ie* alternation, has *ie* forms (stressed nucleus in bold): *pi**e**nso, pi**e**nsas, pi**e**nsa, pi**e**nsan* (present indicative); *pi**e**nse, pi**e**nses, pi**e**nse, pi**e**nsen* (present subjunctive); and imperative *pi**e**nsa*. This is the complete set of forms of this verb with stress on the root. All other forms show *e*, since the stress does not fall on the alternating vowel of the root. This includes the first and second person plural of the present indicative and subjunctive, *pens**á**mos, pens**á**is* (present indicative), *pens**é**mos, pens**é**is* (present subjunctive), as well as all other tenses: *pensé, pensaste*, etc. (preterite); *pensaba, pensabas*, etc. (imperfect); *pensaré, pensarás*, etc. (future); *pensaría, pensarías*, etc. (conditional); *pensara, pensaras*, etc. (imperfect subjunctive); *pensando* (present participle); *pensado* (past participle); *pensar* (infinitive).

There are only a few exceptional verbs with a different distribution of the diphthongs *ie, ue*, or a different alternating pattern involving these diphthongs. First of all, in a couple of cases the diphthongs alternate with high vowels. In *jugar* 'to play', *juego* 'I play', the alternation is between *u* and *ue*, and in *adquirir* 'to acquire', *adquiero* 'I acquire' (as well as in *inquirir* 'to inquire', *inquiero* 'I inquire'), it is between *i* and *ie*.

A second exceptional case is presented by a handful of verbs with nonalternating diphthongs; that is, where the diphthong appears in all forms of the paradigm. These are verbs related to nouns or adjectives, such as *arriesgar* 'to risk' (from *riesgo* 'risk'), *secuestrar* 'to kidnap' (from *secuestro* 'kidnapping'), *frecuentar* 'to frequent' (from *frecuente* 'frequent') and *amueblar* 'to furnish' (from *mueble* 'piece of furniture'). These examples, like those mentioned in the paragraph above, are very few. Not all verbs derived from nouns or adjectives with a diphthong fail to monophthongize in unstressed position. For instance, *desterrar/destierro* 'to banish' / 'I banish' from *tierra* 'land, country', *cegar/ciego* 'to blind' / 'I blind' from *ciego* 'blind', and *despoblar/despueblo* 'to depopulate' / 'I depopulate' from *pueblo* 'town, people', etc., show the expected

12.3 Diphthongs and mid vowels: *e/ie, o/ue*

Table 12.1 Distribution of *ie*, *ue* diphthongs in verb roots.

I. GENERAL PATTERN OF ALTERNATION
Diphthong in all and only those forms where the stress is on the root
e.g. *pensar* 'to think', *negar* 'to deny', *volar* 'to fly', *morder* 'to bite'

Stressed syllables: *ie*, *ue*	Unstressed syllables: *e*, *o*
(1sg., 2sg., 3sg. & 3pl. pres. ind.; subj.)	(all other forms of the verb)
ie: pienso, piensas; piense, pienses; niego, niegas; niegue, niegues	*e*: pensamos; pensé; pensaré; negamos; negué; negaré
ue: vuelo, vuelas; vuele, vueles; muerdo, muerdes; muerda, muerdas	*o*: volamos; volé; volaré; mordemos; mordí; morderé

II. EXCEPTIONAL PATTERNS

IIa. Verbs with diphthong / high vowel alternation
e.g. *jugar* 'to play', *adquirir* 'to acquire'

Stressed syllables: *ue*, *ie*	Unstressed syllables: *u*, *i*
ue: juego, juegas; juegue, juegues	*u*: jugamos; jugué; jugaré
ie: adquiero, adquieres; adquiera, adquieras	*i*: adquirimos; adquirí; adquiriré

IIb. Nonalternating diphthongs
e.g. *arriesgar* 'to risk', *frecuentar* 'to frequent'

Stressed	Unstressed
ie: arriesgo, arriesgas; arriesgue, arriesgues	*ie*: arriesgamos; arriesgué; arriesgaré
ue: frecuento, frecuentas; frecuente, frecuentes	*ue*: frecuentamos; frecuenté; frecuentaré

IIc. Alternating verbs with mid vowels in some stressed syllables
1. *tener* 'to have' and *venir* 'to come'

Stressed syllables	Unstressed syllables
ie: tienes, tiene	*e*: tenemos, tendré
But *e* in forms with -g- and imperative	
e: tengo; tengas, tenga, ten.	

2. Alternating verbs with rhyzotonic preterites:
tener: *tiene* 's/he has' / *tuvo* 's/he had'
venir: *viene* 's/he comes' / *vino* 's/he came'
querer: *quiere* 's/he wants' / *quiso* 's/he wanted'
poder: *puede* 's/he can' / *pudo* 's/he could'

pattern of alternations. (With some derived verbs there may be more than one alternative. Thus, the dictionary of the Real Academia Española (1992) lists both *despezar* and *despiezar* 'to disassemble' from *pieza* 'part'.)

The alternating verbs *tener* 'to have' and *venir* 'to come' (*venir* actually has a more complex alternation *e/ie/i*, see next section), which irregularly insert a -g- in the first person singular of the present indicative and in all forms of the present subjunctive (see section 12.5), are also irregular in the fact that they do not have a diphthong in stressed syllables in forms with this velar increment: *tienes, tiene, tienen* 'you have, s/he has, they have' but *tengo* 'I have', and present subjunctive *tenga, tengas*, etc., in spite of the stress on the root. The *tú*-imperative forms of these verbs, which are also irregular in not having a final vowel, also fail to diphthongize: *ten* 'have!', *ven* 'come!' (This also applies to all other verbs related to these two by prefixation: *contener* 'to contain', *retener* 'to retain', *mantener* 'to support', *detener* 'to detain', *convenir* 'to agree', *prevenir* 'to warn', etc.)

Another exception to the stress condition for diphthongizing verb roots is represented by irregular or 'strong' preterites. RHYZOTONIC (root-stressed) preterite forms of diphthongizing verbs do not have diphthongs, but high vowels: *quiero* 'I want', *quise* 'I wanted'.

12.3.2 The mid vowel / diphthong alternation in derivational morphology

Outside of verbal paradigms, we find the same stress-conditioned alternations between *e* and *ie*, and *o* and *ue*, in derivational morphology, although with much less systematicity in the reduction of the diphthongs when unstressed (stressed nuclei are bolded and alternating nuclei are underlined): *ti̲erra* 'land', *te̲rreno* 'terrain'; *pu̲erta* 'door', *po̲rtal* 'doorway'. In derived words with certain suffixes the reduction is systematic; with other suffixes the diphthong is generally maintained in unstressed position and with yet other suffixes we find both possibilities with similar lexical frequency (Eddington 1996, 1998).

In adjectives and nouns with suffixes such as *-al, -(i)dad, -oso* and *-ero*, derived from bases with a diphthong *ie, ue*, the diphthong is most commonly reduced to a mid vowel (although there are some exceptions): *diente* 'tooth', *dental* 'dental'; *bueno* 'good', *bondad* 'goodness'; *fuego* 'fire', *fogoso* 'fiery'; *hierro* 'iron', *herrero* 'blacksmith'.

On the other hand, with diminutive, augmentative and pejorative suffixes, as well as in words bearing the 'superlative' suffix *-ísimo/a*, the diphthong is usually maintained in an unstressed syllable: *puerta* 'door', *puertita, puertecita* 'little door'; *viejo* 'old', *viejito, viejecito* 'old, dim.'; *fuerte* 'strong', *fuertote* 'strong, augm.'; *bueno* 'good', *buenísimo* 'very good'. There are nevertheless a few exceptions. Thus, the diminutive of *caliente* 'hot' is *calentito*, with reduction of the diphthong. It should be noticed that in the diminutive of many words ending in *-o, -a* with a diphthong in the root, both allomorphs of the diminutive suffix, *-ito/a* and *-ecito/-a* are used, whereas similar words without a diphthong only admit the allomorph *-ito/a*. For instance, whereas the diminutive of *cesta* 'basket' is *cestita*, not **cestecita*, for *siesta* we can have either *siestita* or *siestecita*.

Table 12.2 Reduction and maintenance of diphthongs *ie, ue* in unstressed syllables in derived nouns and adjectives.

I. Suffixes that regularly trigger reduction of diphthongs

-al ~ -ar
diente 'tooth'	*dental* 'dental'
escuela 'school'	*escolar* 'school-'
muerte 'death'	*mortal* 'mortal'
infierno 'hell'	*infernal* 'infernal'
huevo 'egg'	*oval* 'oval'
sentimiento 'feeling'	*sentimental* 'sentimental'

-(i)dad
bueno 'good'	*bondad* 'goodness'
nuevo 'new'	*novedad* 'novelty'
ciego 'blind'	*ceguedad* 'blindness'

-ero/a
puerta 'door'	*portero* 'doorman'
tienda 'shop'	*tendero* 'shopkeeper'
BUT *huevo* 'egg'	*huevera* 'eggcup'

-oso
ciénaga 'marsh'	*cenagoso* 'marshy'
vergüenza 'shame'	*vergonzoso* 'shameful'
BUT *miedo* 'fear'	*miedoso* 'fearful'

Other less productive suffixes
cielo 'sky'	*celeste* 'sky' (adj.)

II. Suffixes that normally do not trigger reduction of diphthongs

-ito/a (and other affective suffixes)
puente 'bridge'	*puentecito*
fiesta 'party'	*fiestecita ~ fiestita*
BUT *caliente* 'hot'	*calentito (~ calientito)*

-ísimo/a
bueno 'good'	*buenísimo*
cierto 'certain'	*ciertísimo ~ certísimo*
caliente 'hot'	*calientísimo ~ calentísimo*[6]
fuerte 'strong'	*fuertísimo ~ fortísimo*
nuevo 'new'	*nuevísimo ~ novísimo*

III. Suffixes presenting both patterns with similar frequency

-ista
cuento 'tale'	*cuentista* 'storyteller'
fuero 'law'	*fuerista* 'defender of local laws'
juerga 'party'	*juerguista* 'partygoer'
concierto 'concert'	*concertista* 'soloist'
diente 'tooth'	*dentista* 'dentist'

[6] Superlatives in *-ísimo* with a reduced diphthong (*novísimo, fortísimo*) are felt to belong to a more formal register than their unreduced variants, although *calentísimo* is also colloquial.

As mentioned, there are also suffixes for which a general pattern (maintenance or reduction of the diphthong) is hard to establish, since similar numbers of examples can be found for each of the two patterns. Thus, with the suffix *-ista*, both possibilities, the reduction pattern illustrated by *diente* 'tooth' / *dentista* 'dentist' and the maintenance of the diphthong as in *cuento* 'tale' / *cuentista* 'storyteller', are abundantly attested and it is hard to give a general rule.

12.3.3 Historical origin of the alternation between diphthongs and mid vowels

As we saw in section 7.1, Classical Latin had a ten-vowel system, of which five were short, /i e a o u/, and five long, /i: e: a: o: u:/. When discussing Latin it is customary to represent the phonologically short vowels with a micron or half-moon superscript, /ĭ ĕ ă ŏ ŭ/, and the long vowels with a macron, /ī ē ā ō ū/, since this is more convenient for the description of the evolution of the different vowels.

As in other languages with a contrast between short and long vowels, the two sets of vowels also came to be pronounced with different qualities, the longer vowels being higher and more tense than the corresponding short vowels. Over time, the original ten phonemes were reduced to a seven-vowel system in stressed position in the spoken Latin of the Iberian Peninsula, as well as in Gaul (France) and most of Italy (perhaps via an intermediate stage with nine vowels differing in quality). As shown in Table 12.3, the original short high and long mid vowels merged, so that both /ĭ/ and /ē/ gave /e/, contrasting now with /ɛ/ from the short mid vowel /ĕ/, while /ŭ/ and /ō/ gave /o/, contrasting with /ɔ/ from short /ŏ/. The distinction between the low vowels /ă/ and /ā/ was also lost.

In unstressed position there was further merger. All of original /ĭ/, /ē/ and /ĕ/ gave /e/ and, correspondingly, /ŭ/, /ō/ and /ŏ/ gave /o/ when unstressed, as shown in Table 12.4.

The Western Romance result after these changes is that, whereas in stressed position there is a contrast between /e/ and /ɛ/ and between /o/ and /ɔ/, this contrast is not found in unstressed position, where only /e/ and /o/ can appear. This is basically the system still found in Portuguese where, for instance, *p*[ɛ]*dra* 'stone' (< PĔTRA), *p*[ɔ]*rta* 'door' (< PŎRTA) have low-mid vowels and *v*[e]*rde* 'green' (< VĬRĪDE) and *b*[o]*ca* 'mouth' (< BŬCCA) have high-mid vowels. The contrast is not found in unstressed position and there are alternations such as *v*[ɔ]*lves* 'you return' and *v*[o]*lvemos* 'we return'.

In the Castilian area, there was a further change, as shown in Table 12.3. The stressed mid-low vowels /ɛ/ and /ɔ/ became, respectively, the rising diphthongs /ie/ and /ue/.

12.3 Diphthongs and mid vowels: *e/ie, o/ue*

Table 12.3 Evolution of the vowel system in <u>stressed</u> position from Classical Latin (CL) to Western Romance (WR) to Spanish.

CL	ī	ĭ	ē	ĕ	ā	ă	ŏ	ō	ŭ	ū
	i	ɪ	e	ɛ	a		ɔ	o	ʊ	u
WR	i		e	ɛ	a		ɔ	o	u
Sp.	i		e	ie	a		ue	o	u

Examples
VĪTA > vida 'life'   PĀLU > palo 'stake'   LŪNA > luna 'moon'
PĬRA > pera 'pear'   MĂLU > malo 'bad'   LŬPU > lobo 'wolf'
TĒLA > tela 'cloth'   FLŌRE > flor 'flower'
TĔRRA > tierra 'land'   BŎNU > bueno 'good'

Table 12.4 Evolution of the vowel system in <u>unstressed</u> position from Classical Latin to Western Romance.

CL	ī	ĭ	ē	ĕ	ā	ă	ŏ	ō	ŭ	ū
WR	i		e		a		o		u

Table 12.5 Evolution of Latin /ĕ/, /ŏ/, and origin of the alternation between diphthongs and mid vowels in Spanish.

a. Stressed
PĔTRA > pɛdra > piedra
PŎRTA > pɔrta > puerta
VŎLVĬS > vɔlves > vuelves

b. Unstressed
VŎLVĒMŬS > volvemos

Although there were analogical changes in both directions and other complications in the evolution, the majority of instances of the diphthongs /ie/, /ue/ of Modern Spanish go back to the mid-low vowels /ɛ/, /ɔ/ of Late spoken Latin or Western Romance, and ultimately to the short mid vowels /ĕ/, /ŏ/ of Classical Latin in stressed position. Since in unstressed position Late spoken Latin had only five vowels /i e a o u/, instead of the seven vowels /i e ɛ a ɔ o u/ then found in stressed syllables, the diphthongs /ie/

and /ue/ of Spanish are essentially restricted in their occurrence to stressed syllables.

In a few cases, /ie/ and /ue/ have origins other than the breaking of stressed mid-low vowels. These sequences were already present in Latin in words such as CLIENTE > *cliente*, CRUENTU > *cruento*, and were separated by a consonant in other words such as CRUDĒLE > *cruel*, FIDĒLE > *fiel*. In these cases there is no alternation (e.g. *clientela* 'clientele', *crueldad* 'cruelty') and, for some of these examples, the sequences can in fact be pronounced as hiatus by some speakers (*cru-el*, *cli-ente*).

12.4 Alternation between high and mid vowels in verbs: *i/e, u/o*

In third conjugation verbs, there is an alternation between high and mid vowels, as illustrated by *servir* 'to serve' but *sirvo* 'I serve'. Unlike the alternation discussed above in 12.3, this alternation is restricted to verbs and, even more specifically, to third conjugation verbs (infinitive in -*ir*). For verbs presenting this alternation, the rule that accounts for the distribution of the two vowels is the following: /e/ is found in forms where the following syllable contains the nuclear vowel /i/ (*servir, servido, servimos, serví*) and /i/ is found where the following syllable contains any other vowel or a diphthong (*sirvo, sirva, sirviendo, sirvió*).

Some common third conjugation verbs with a mid vowel in the root in their infinitive have a more complex alternation. These verbs present both the mid/high vowel alternation and diphthongization. These verbs thus have three allomorphs of the root, with a mid vowel (*hervir* 'to boil', *dormir* 'to sleep'), with a high vowel (*hirvamos* 'we boil, subjunct.', *durmamos* 'we sleep, subjunct.') and with a diphthong (*hiervo* 'I boil', *duermo* 'I sleep'). The distribution of the three allomorphs follows the two rules given for verbs with only one of these two alternations. Diphthongization in stressed position has priority. The diphthong is found in forms where the root vowel in question (the last vowel of the root) is stressed (*duermo, duermes, duerma*); the mid vowel is found when the stress is on the ending and the next syllable contains the high vowel /i/ (*dormí, dormir, dormido*); and the high vowel is found otherwise (i.e. when the stress is on the ending and the next syllable contains a vowel /a/ or a diphthong /ie/, /io/: *durmamos, durmiendo, durmió*).

There are relatively large numbers of verbs with either an *e/i* or an *e/ie/i* alternation. On the other hand, the only examples with an alternation *o/ue/u* are *dormir* 'to sleep' and *morir* 'to die', and the simpler alternation *o/u* is only found in *podrir* ~ *pudrir* 'to rot', for which forms with -*o*- actually compete with variants in -*u*-, except in the participle *podrido* 'rotten'. (The verb *poder*

12.4 High and mid vowels in verbs: *i/e, u/o*

Table 12.6 Alternations between mid and high vowels in verb roots.

Ia. Verbs with *e/i* alternation
a) Mid vowel *e* if the following syllable has the vowel /i/; e.g.: *servir, serví, servimos*.
b) High vowel *i* otherwise (if the following syllable has a different vowel or a diphthong); e.g.: *sirvo, sirvió*.

Other examples: *medir (mido), pedir (pido), repetir (repito), seguir (sigo), vestir (visto)*.

Ib. Verbs with *o/u* alternation: only *podrir ~ pudrir (pudro)*. Past Part. *podrido*.

IIa. Verbs with *e/ie/i* alternation
a) Mid vowel *e* if unstressed and followed by a vowel /i/; e.g.: *hervir, herví, hervimos*.
b) Diphthong *ie* if stressed; e.g.: *hiervo, hierves, hierva*.
c) High vowel *i* otherwise (unstressed and followed by vowel /a/ or diphthong); e.g.: *hirvamos, hirvió, hirviera*.

Other examples: *sentir (siento, sintió), mentir (miento, mintió), herir (hiero, hirió), preferir (prefiero, prefirió), arrepentir (arrepiento, arrepintió), convertir (convierto, convirtió)*.

IIb. Verbs with *o/ue/u* alternation: only *dormir* and *morir*.
a) Mid vowel *o* if unstressed and followed by vowel /i/; e.g.: *dormir, dormí, dormimos*.
b) Diphthong *ue* if stressed; e.g.: *duermo, duermes, duerma*.
c) High vowel *u* otherwise (unstressed and followed by vowel /a/ or diphthong); e.g.: *durmamos, durmió, durmiera*.

'to be able' also has an *o/ue/u* alternation in the root, but with a different distribution.) This is summarized in Table 12.6.

The historical origin of the *i/e, u/o* alternation in verb roots is much less straightforward than that of the *e/ie, o/ue* alternation. It is the result of complex sound changes triggered by a glide in the suffix of Latin verbs in *-īre*. These involved glide-triggered metaphony (e.g. MĒTIO(R) > mido 'I measure', MĒTIĀMUS > midamos 'we measure, subjunct.') and subsequent analogical processes within and across verb paradigms (Penny 2002:185–90). This development also involved exchanges between the second and third conjugations (e.g. OSp. *sofrer* > *sufrir* 'to suffer'). Related consequences are the fact that virtually all third conjugation verbs with a mid vowel in the last syllable of the infinitive root have either a mid vowel / high vowel or a mid vowel / diphthong / high vowel alternation, and that, on the other hand, there are no second conjugation verbs with a high vowel /-i-/ or /-u-/ in the root in Modern Spanish (Elvira 1998; Penny 2002: 173).

12.5 Verbs with velar increment

A small number of second and third conjugation verbs show insertion of /-g-/ between root and ending in the first person singular of the present indicative and in all persons of the present subjunctive. The context for this alternation can also be defined in phonological terms: in verbs of this group, /-g-/ is inserted immediately after the root and before either /-o/ or /-a/ (a nonfront vowel). The root of all verbs with this alternation ends in either /-n/ or /-l/ (but not all verbs with roots ending in one of these two consonants undergo the alternation). Forms with this velar increment have the same root vowel as the infinitive even in verbs which otherwise show one of the two alternations mentioned in the sections above: *tener* 'to have', *tengo* 'I have', *tienes* 'you have'; *venir* 'to come', *vengo* 'I come', *vienes* 'you come', *viniendo* 'coming'.

A related alternation is found in another group of second and third conjugation verbs like *caer* 'to fall', whose root ends in a vowel. These verbs have insertion of /-ig-/ in the same context.

Most second conjugation verbs in *-ecer* (e.g. *parecer* 'to seem'), as well as *conocer* 'to know, be acquainted', etc., and third conjugation verbs in *-ucir* (*conducir* 'to drive'), have an alternation *-c-/-zc-*, phonologically /-θ-/–/-θk-/ in Northern-Central Peninsular Spanish and /-s-/–/-sk-/ in other dialects, also with the same distribution as in the two other cases above. That is, in these verbs /-k-/ is inserted between /-θ-/ ~ /-s-/ and a nonfront vowel.

12.5.1 Historical origin of the velar increment

The velar increment alternation has different origins in different classes of verbs. In verbs like *conocer* 'to know' and *crecer* 'to grow' (from Latin inceptive or inchoative verbs), the present-day alternation has resulted from the distinct evolutions of /-sk-/ before front and nonfront vowels: Lat. CRESCES > *creces* 'you grow' (OSp. *cresçes*) vs Lat. CRESCŌ > *crezco* 'I grow' (OSp. *cresco*, with irregular change from *-sc-* to *-zc-* /-θk-/ in Modern Spanish by analogy with the other forms of the verb). In verbs ending in *-ducir* (and *lucir*), on the other hand, the alternation must have been analogically introduced, as we find no source for it in Latin (DŪCŌ 'I lead').

12.5 Verbs with velar increment

Table 12.7 Verbs with velar increment.

inf.	pres. indic. (1sg, 2sg)	pres. subjunct. (1sg, 2sg)
a. Insertion of /-g-/ after lateral or nasal:		
Ø → g / {l, n} ___ {o, a} (some 2nd and 3rd conjugation verbs)		
salir 'to leave'	*salgo, sales*	*salga, salgas*
valer 'to be worth'	*valgo, vales*	*valga, valgas*
poner 'to put'	*pongo, pones*	*ponga, pongas*
tener 'to have'	*tengo, tienes*	*tenga, tengas*
venir 'to come'	*vengo, vienes*	*venga, vengas*
b. Insertion of /-ig-/ after a vowel:		
Ø → -ig- / V ___ {o, a} (some 2nd and 3rd conj. verbs)		
caer 'to fall'	*caigo, caes*	*caiga, caigas*
traer 'to bring'	*traigo, traes*	*traiga, traigas*
oir 'to hear'	*oigo, oyes*	*oiga, oigas*
c. Insertion of /-k-/ after /θ/ ∼ /s/		
Ø → -k- / θ ___ {o, a} (2nd conj. verbs in *-ecer, conocer*, and 3rd conj. verbs in *-ucir*)		
conocer 'to know'	*conozco, conoces*	*conozca, conozcas*
merecer 'to deserve'	*merezco, mereces*	*merezca, merezcas*
crecer 'to grow'	*crezco, creces*	*crezca, crezcas*
conducir 'to drive'	*conduzco, conduces*	*conduzca, conduzcas*
lucir 'to shine'	*luzco, luces*	*luzca, luzcas*

In verbs with insertion of /-ig-/ after a vowel, the epenthesis would seem to have the function of avoiding a hiatus – Lat. TRAHŌ > *traigo* 'I bring' – and also appeared after deletion of *-d-* : Lat. CADŌ > **cao* > *caigo* 'I fall'. Nevertheless, historically we find first forms of the type *trayo, cayo, oyo*, without a velar increment. Notice also that the hiatus is tolerated in other forms of the paradigm, *traes, caes*.

The origin of the epenthesis of /-g-/ in verbs like *tener, venir, salir*, etc., is also somewhat unclear. Lat. TENEŌ, VENIŌ by regular evolution should have given *teño, veño*, as they did in Galician-Portuguese. A possibility is that the *-g-* spread from verbs like *tañir* 'to play an instrument' (from Lat. TANGERE 'to touch') whose first person singular was *tango* by regular evolution, first to *tener* and then to other verbs with a similar shape (Penny 2002:178–80). The phenomenon of *-g-* epenthesis is found in Italian as well.

12.6 Other alternations in verbs

As is well known to all who have learned Spanish in a school setting, Spanish verbs have quite a few other alternations and irregularities. Here we will briefly mention the most important ones not covered in previous sections of this chapter. For more extensive exemplification of verb paradigms the reader is referred to Butt and Benjamin (2000) as well as the online list of verb paradigms on the website of the Real Academia Española, among other sources of information.

The first person singular of the present indicative has a final -*y* in the four verbs *soy* 'I am', *estoy* 'I am, stay', *voy* 'I go' and *doy* 'I give'. In spite of the fact that there are only four verbs with this ending, this is an almost completely regular irregularity, since this is the complete set of monosyllabic first person singular forms – including *estoy* where the initial /e/ is historically epenthetical (Lat. STŌ 'I stand') – if we leave aside the even more irregular *sé* 'I know' and *he* 'I have'. A morphophonological rule could thus be formulated stating that -*y* is added after -*o* in monosyllabic first person singular forms. The final -*y* may derive from the medieval clitic *y*, from Lat. IBI 'there'.

The fact that *estar* is the only verb with final stress also in other forms of the present indicative (*estás* 'you are', *está* 's/he is') is also related to the fact that historically these forms were monosyllabic.

An important irregularity is shown by verbs with a strong or rhyzotonic preterite (with stress on the root in the first and third person singular). In addition to different endings in the preterite from those of regular verbs, these verbs have a different root in the preterite (and the imperfect subjunctive) from that in other tenses: *ten-er/tuv-e* 'have' (inf / 1st sg. pret.), *est-ar/estuv-e* 'be, stay', *hab-er/hub-e* 'have', *pod-er/pud-e* 'be able', *and-ar/anduv-e* 'walk', *sab-er/sup-e* 'know', *cab-er/cup-e* 'fit', *tra-er/traj-e* 'bring', *dec-ir/dij-e* 'say', *conduc-ir/conduj-e* 'drive', *pon-er/pus-e* 'put', *quer-er/quis-e* 'want', *hac-er/hic-e* 'do, make', *ven-ir/vin-e* 'come', *s-er/fui* 'be', *ir/fui* 'go'. In some of these cases the alternation represents a direct evolution from Latin, which had a complex set of modifications in the *perfectum*. In other cases, we have analogical developments. The preterite *fui* 'I was / I went' was originally the preterite of 'to be' only.

The future and conditional historically derive from constructions with the infinitive followed by, respectively, the present and the imperfect indicative of the verb HABĒRE 'to have': CANTĀRE HABEŌ 'I have to sing' > */kantar ajo/ > cantar (h)e > cantaré* 'I will sing'; CANTĀRE HABĒBAM 'I had to sing' > *cantaría* 'I would sing'. Consequently with this evolution, in regular verbs the whole infinitive is contained in future and conditional forms, although, from a synchronic point of view it might be preferable to analyse these forms as containing a future/conditional marker /-ɾ-/. In a few irregular forms the vowel following the root (the theme vowel) has been deleted before the future/conditional suffix: *saber* 'to know'/ *sabré* 'I will know' (expected *saberé*), *haber/habré* 'have', *poder/podré* 'be able', *caber/cabré* 'fit', *querer/querré* 'want' (with a /ɾ/ - /r̄/ contrast). In verbs with root-final *n* or *l*, deletion of the theme vowel was historically followed by epenthesis of *-d-* between root and suffix: *poner/pondré* 'put' (expected *poneré*), *tener/tendré* 'have', *venir/vendré* 'come', *salir/saldré* 'leave', *valer/valdré* 'be worth'. Whereas the deletion of the theme vowel is an irregular process (it is not possible to predict which verbs show this alternation), the epenthesis of *-d-* is regular in this context: all verbs that irregularly drop their theme vowel in the future and conditional insert *-d-* in its place if the root ends in *n* or *l*. That is, the sequences *-nr-*, *-lr-* are systematically avoided in this context and repaired as *-ndr-*, *-ldr-*. Finally, for two verbs the root has a contracted form in the future and conditional: *hacer/haré* 'do, make', *decir/diré* 'say'.

The *tú*-imperative ends in a vowel (the theme vowel) and is identical to the third person singular form of the present indicative: *hablar* 'to speak', *habla* 's/he speaks' = *habla* 'speak!'; *comer* 'to eat', *come* 's/he eats' = *come* 'eat!'. In five verbs, however, the final vowel is missing in the imperative form: *tener/ten* 'have', *venir/ven* 'come', *poner/pon* 'put', *salir/sal* 'leave', *hacer/haz* 'do, make'. From a historical point of view, these imperatives are in fact regular in their ending, since word-final /e/ was regularly lost in this context (see next section): *pone* > *pon* 'put!' like *pane* > *pan* 'bread'. It is actually the third person forms *pone*, *sale*, etc., that underwent analogical restoration of the final vowel to conform with other present tense forms. Three other imperatives are more irregular: *decir/di* 'say', *ser/sé* 'be', *ir/ve* 'go'.

Finally, another important verbal irregularity is that found in the past participle of a handful of verbs; e.g. *escribir/escrito* 'write', *abrir/abierto* 'open', *romper/roto* 'break', *decir/dicho* 'say', etc. These irregular participles have many idiosyncrasies and there is no general rule of allomorphy that would cover all of them.

12.7 Plural formation

In Spanish, plural formation involves allomorphy of the plural marker. In principle, all nouns and adjectives can have a plural form. This is the general rule: words ending in a vowel form their plural by adding *-s*, as in *casa/casas* 'house/houses', and words ending in a consonant add *-es* in the plural, as in *papel/papeles* 'paper/papers'.

As we know, the consonants that are possible at the end of a native Spanish word are *-d, -z, -s, -l, -n, -r* and, marginally, *-j*; that is, the phonemes /d (θ) s l n ɾ x/: *pared/paredes* 'wall/walls', *arroz/arroces* 'rice/rices', *mes/meses* 'month/months', *sol/soles* 'sun/suns', *canción/canciones* 'song/songs', *mujer/mujeres* 'woman/women', *reloj/relojes* 'watch/watches'. These are all the coronal consonants, except for /t/, and including also velar /x/, which appears as a final segment only in a handful of nouns. At the phonological level, it is to be noted that word-final *-r* is always /ɾ/ before a suffix (11.3). Regarding orthography, it should be noted that *-z* is replaced by *c* before *e*. Notice also that OXYTONIC singular forms ending in *-n* and *-s* lose their orthographic accent mark in the plural, since they become regular PAROXYTONES in *-s*. Native words ending in *-y* also behave as consonant-final for plural formation: *rey/reyes* 'king/kings'.

The general rule of plural formation has a systematic exception (or subrule): words with an unstressed final syllable ending in *-s* are invariable in the plural. We may say that the plural suffix has a 'zero' or empty allomorph in this case. Thus, the plural of *el lunes* 'Monday' is *los lunes* 'Mondays', *la tesis* 'the thesis' has plural *las tesis* 'the theses', and for *un virus* 'a virus' the plural is also *virus* 'viruses'. Notice that in stating this subregularity we wrote *-s* and not /s/. This is because words ending in *-z* follow the general rule: *lápiz/lápices* 'pencil/pencils'. For dialects with a /s/ vs /θ/ contrast, the zero plural rule is phonologically conditioned: it affects paroxytonic and proparoxytonic words ending in /s/, but not those ending in /θ/, e.g. /tésis/ 'sg. = pl.' but /lápiθ/ – /lápiθes/. For speakers of dialects without this phonemic contrast, on the other hand, the only certain guide for determining the plural of these words is the orthography. Notice also the contrast between *el autobús / los autobuses* 'bus/buses' but *el ómnibus/los ómnibus* 'bus/buses' (used in some South American countries), where the position of the stress determines which rule applies.

Another special rule of plural formation applies to nouns and adjectives ending in a stressed high vowel, *-í, -ú*. These words may either add *-s* or *-es*: *rubí/rubís* ∼ *rubíes* 'ruby/rubies', *menú/menús* ∼ *menúes* 'menu/menus'. Words ending in nonhigh stressed vowels follow the general rule for vowel-final words and can only add *-s* in the plural: *café/cafés* 'coffee/coffees', *sofá/sofás* 'sofa/sofas', *dominó/dominós* 'domino/dominoes' (there are nevertheless a few nouns ending in *-á* that may also form a plural in *-aes*: *bajá/bajáes* 'pasha/pashas').

Recent borrowings ending in a consonant do not always follow the regular rule of plural formation. In particular, nouns ending in a consonant or consonant cluster not found in word-final position in the native lexicon usually add only *-s* in the plural: *coñac/coñacs* 'cognac/-s', *mamut/mamuts* 'mammoth/-s', *robot/robots* 'robot/-s', *chef/chefs* 'chef/-s', *pub/pubs* 'pub/-s', *ítem/ítems* 'item/-s', *récord/récords* 'record/-s', although some are adapted to the regular pattern, *club/clubs* ~ *clubes* 'club/-s'. However, even borrowings with a common consonant ending may irregularly pluralize in *-s*, as in *póster/pósters* 'poster/posters' (vs regularized *váter/váteres* 'toilet/toilets', used in Spain). This also applies to borrowed nouns in *-y*, such as *jersey/jerseys* 'sweater/sweaters' (Spain), although some are adapted to the native pattern: *convoy/convoys* ~ *convoyes* (never if the final glide is orthographically represented as *-i*: *bonsái/bonsáis*).

A special problem is presented by PROPAROXYTONIC nouns ending in a consonant other than *-s*, such as *régimen* 'regime; diet', *hipérbaton* 'hyperbaton', *déficit* 'deficit'. If the regular rule of plural formation applied to these nouns, the result would be a word with the stress four syllables from the end, beyond the 'THREE-SYLLABLE WINDOW' for stress placement (see 13.2). Here we thus have a conflict involving the plural formation rule and stress requirements:

(a) Words ending in a consonant regularly form the plural adding *-es*.
(b) The stress is placed on the same vowel in the plural as in the singular.
(c) The stress always falls on one of the last three syllables of the word.

There is no uniform solution for this conflict. The 'stress-window' generalization in (c) is always satisfied, but this is done by violating (a) in some cases and (b) in other cases. Two words in this group pluralize in *-es*, but also shift the accent one syllable towards the end, so it stays within the window: *régimen/regímenes* 'regime-s, diet/-s', *espécimen/especímenes* 'specimen/-s'. Greek proparoxytonic words ending in *-on* fluctuate between two solutions, shift of the stress <u>two</u> syllables towards the end or irregular plural in *-os*: *hipérbaton/hiperbatones* ~ *hipérbatos* 'hyperbaton/-s', *asíndeton/ asindetones* ~ *asíndetos* 'asyndeton/-s'. Other words in this group either add only *-s* or are invariable in the plural: *el déficit / los déficits* ~ *los déficit, el currículum / los currículums* ~ *los currículum* (~ *los currícula* ~ *los currículos*).

Finally, *carácter/caracteres* 'character/-s' is the only example in the language showing an unmotivated violation of generalization (b) above. In this word, the stress is shifted one syllable towards the end in the plural, even though the stress would stay within the 'window' even if it were not shifted.

The different rules, subrules and exceptional patterns of plural formation just reviewed are summarized in Table 12.8.

12.7.1 Historical origin of the *-s*/*-es* allomorphy of the plural suffix

Most native Spanish nouns and adjectives can be reconstructed as deriving from the Latin accusative. Except for neuter forms, in Latin the accusative singular ended in *-M* and the accusative plural in *-s*. In the accusative case we thus find singular/plural pairs in *-AM/-ĀS* (*PORTAM/PORTĀS* 'door/-s'), in

Table 12.8 Plural formation.

General rules in A apply unless the word falls under one of the specific rules in B

A. General rules

A1. Words ending in a vowel

pl: -s
casa/casas 'house/-s'
gato/gatos 'cat/-s'
noche/noches 'night/-s'
bici/bicis 'bike/-s'
espíritu/espíritus 'spirit/-s'

A2. Native words ending in a consonant or *-y*

pl: -es
pared/paredes 'wall/-s'
marqués/marqueses 'marquis/-es'
nariz/narices 'nose/-s'
peral/perales 'pear tree/-s'
amor/amores 'love/-s'
boj/bojes 'box bush/-es'
buey/bueyes 'ox/oxen'

B. Specific rules

B1. Words ending in unstressed syllable with final *-s* (not *-z*)

pl: Ø (sg. = pl.)
el lunes / los lunes 'Monday/-s'
el análisis / los análisis 'analysis/analyses'
la tesis / las tesis 'thesis/theses'
el ómnibus / los ómnibus 'bus/buses'
el virus / los virus 'virus/viruses'
el atlas / los atlas 'atlas/atlases'
el biceps / los biceps 'biceps'
BUT, with *-z*: *el lápiz / los lápices* 'pencil/-s', *el alférez / los alféreces* 'standard bearer/-s'

B2. Words ending in stressed high vowel *-í, -ú*

pl: *-s* ~ *-es*
israelí/israelís ~ *israelíes* 'Israeli/-s'
jabalí/jabalís ~ *jabalíes* 'wild boar/-s'
tabú/tabús ~ *tabúes* 'taboo/-s'

B3. Borrowings with a final consonant or cluster not found in the native lexicon

pl: -s
esnob/esnobs 'snob/-s'
chef/chefs 'chef/-s'
robot/robots 'robot/-s'
tic/tics 'tic/-s'
anorak/anoraks 'anorak/-s'
bulldog/bulldogs 'bulldog/-s'
récord/récords 'record/-s'
test/tests 'test/-s'

12.7 Plural formation

Table 12.8 (*cont.*)

*A few take *-es* (optionally):
club/clubes ~ *clubs* 'club/-s', *álbum/álbumes* ~ *álbums* ~ *álbunes* 'album/-s'

* Plural *-s* is also found with all borrowings in *-y* and some with common final consonants:
jersey/jerseys 'sweater/-s' (Spain), *póster/pósters* 'poster/-s'

B4. Proparoxytones ending in a consonant other than *-s*

Regular plural formation is in conflict with 'three-syllable window' restriction for stress. This is solved in one of three different ways, depending on the word:

a. pl: *-es* + shift of stress one syllable towards the end (words in *-en*)
   régimen/regímenes 'regime/-s, diet/-s'
   espécimen/especímenes 'specimen/-s'
b. pl: *-es* + shift of stress two syllables towards the end or irregular plural in *-os* (Greek words in *-on*)
   hipérbaton/hiperbatones (also *hipérbatos*) 'hyperbaton/-s'
   asíndeton/asindetones (also *asíndetos*) 'asyndeton/-s'
   ómicron/omicrones 'omicron/-s'
c. pl: *-s* or invariable (other words)
   déficit/los déficits ~ *los déficit* 'deficit/-s'
   superávit/los superávits ~ *los superávit* 'superavit/-s'

* The paroxytone *carácter/caracteres* 'character/-s' also has stress shift as in B4a. Only case of unmotivated shift.

-UM/-ŌS (AMĪCUM/AMĪCŌS 'friend/-s') and in -EM/-ĒS (NĀVEM/NĀVĒS 'ship/-s', PĀNEM/PĀNĒS 'bread loaf/loaves'), for the three main declensions. In Late or Vulgar Latin, final -M was lost, and -U(M) became -o. In Early Medieval Spanish, nouns in all three groups mentioned would have had the same singular/plural alternation: an *-s* was added in the plural[7] – *amore/amores* 'love/-s' was no different from *amiga/amigas* 'friend/-s, *fem.* or *amigo/amigos* 'friend/-s, *masc.*' Later on, in Medieval Spanish, unstressed final *-e* was also lost, but only when preceded by a single coronal consonant (dental, alveolar and sometimes prepalatal): *pane* > *pan*; not otherwise (*monte, nave*). The *-e* was not lost in plural forms, where it was followed by *-s* (*panes*). The nouns and adjectives that make their plural in *-es* in Modern Spanish are then essentially

---

[7] Neuter words, which had different correspondences, were eventually transferred to the other genders.

Table 12.9 Historical origin of the main morphophonological rule of plural formation.

Classical Latin Accusative	Early Medieval Spanish	Modern Spanish
PORTAM/PORTĀS[8]	puerta/puertas 'door/-s'	
AMĪCAM/AMĪCĀS	amiga/amigas 'friend/-s, fem.'	
MŪRUM/MŪRŌS	muro/muros 'wall/-s'	
AMĪCUM/AMĪCŌS	amigo/amigos 'friend/-s, masc.'	
PĀNEM/PĀNĒS	pane/panes >	pan/panes 'loaf/loaves'
AMŌREM/AMŌRĒS	amore/amores >	amor/amores 'love/-s'
SŌLEM/SŌLĒS	sole/soles >	sol/soles 'sun/-s'
MŌNTEM/MŌNTĒS	monte/montes 'mountain/-s'	
FORTEM/FORTĒS	fuerte/fuertes 'strong'	
PAUPEREM/PAUPERĒS	pobre/pobres 'poor'	
NŪBEM/NŪBĒS	nube/nubes 'cloud'	

those that lost final *-e* in the singular in Medieval Spanish.[9] That is, whereas now it looks as if /e/ is added before /s/ in the plural of modern sg./pl. pairs such as *canción/canciones* 'song/-s', *sal/sales* 'salt/-s', *mujer/mujeres* 'woman/women', *ciudad/ciudades* 'town/-s', etc., historically a final /e/ was lost in the singular instead. See Table 12.9.

12.8 Feminine *el*

Some feminine nouns such as *agua* 'water' take the article *el* instead of *la*. The fact that these nouns are feminine is apparent from agreement with other modifiers (*el agua clara* 'the clear water') and from the plural form (*las aguas* 'the waters'). This allomorphy of the feminine article is subject to both phonological and morphological contextual conditions. Feminine *el* is used before nouns starting with stressed /á/: *el alma* 'the soul', *el hacha* 'the axe', *el águila* 'the eagle', *el ave* 'the bird', *el ansia* 'the anxiety'. Nouns starting with unstressed /a/, on the other hand, take the regular feminine article *la*: *la almendra* 'the almond', *la araña* 'the spider'. Furthermore, the allomorphy does not take place

---

[8] Vowels not marked with a macron are short.
[9] In some varieties of Medieval Spanish final *-e* was also lost after two consonants (*monte* > *mont* 'mountain', *corte* > *cort* 'court') and after nonalveolar/dental consonants (*nube* > *nuf* 'cloud'), but these variants did not prosper.

before adjectives, even if they meet the phonological conditions of starting with stressed /á/: *la árida estepa* 'the arid steppe', *la alta torre* 'the high tower'. Names of letters are also exceptions to this morphophonological rule: *las aes* 'the *a*'s', *las haches* 'the *h*'s'.

la → *el* / ___ [$_{Noun}$ á (exception: names of letters)

In affective derivation and compound forms, the (main) stress shifts from the initial vowel, but the allomorphy of the article conditioned by the basic form is maintained: *el agüita* 'the water, *dim.*'. In the case of compounds ending in /-e/ or a consonant this creates opacity (since the stress condition is not present and the ending of the word does not provide a clue for gender), which has been resolved by transfer of the etymologically compound noun to the masculine gender in words such as *aguardiente* 'brandy' (from *(el) agua ardiente* 'burning water') and *avestruz* 'ostrich' (based on feminine *(el) ave* 'bird'). The noun *aguafuerte* 'etching' is also usually masculine, but it is listed in the dictionary of the Spanish Academy as either masculine or feminine. On the other hand, in the case of a word such as *aguamala* 'jellyfish', literally interpretable as 'bad water', the ending of the adjective *mala*, agreeing with *agua*, clearly shows this to be a feminine word. The uncertainty in this case has to do with the shape of the article: is it *el aguamala*, like *el agua*, or *la aguamala*, since the initial vowel does not bear main stress?

The existence of this rule of article allomorphy is also the cause of uncertainty regarding the gender of some other /á-/ initial nouns with endings other than /-a/. Thus, *(el) arte* 'art' is usually masculine (*el arte español* 'Spanish art'), but takes feminine agreement in some set phrases such as *el arte poética* 'ars poetica' and *el arte amatoria* where the original Latin gender agreement is preserved. Moreover, in the plural it is always feminine: *las bellas artes* 'fine arts', *las artes españolas* 'Spanish arts'. This uncertainty extends to the word *(el) azúcar* 'sugar'. Given the fact that this noun does not meet the stress condition for feminine *el* (stress is not initial), the presence of this article should unambiguously indicate masculine gender; but, in fact, there is some fluctuation in usage. In Spain, standard terms are *azúcar moreno* 'brown sugar', with a masculine adjective, but *azúcar blanquilla* 'white sugar', with feminine agreement.

12.8.1 Historical origin of feminine *el*

Although, in Modern Spanish, expressions such as *el agua* would appear to involve the use of what normally is a masculine article with a feminine noun, historically we do not find any gender shift in this use of the article. It is simply the case that the Latin feminine demonstrative ILLA(M) 'that' had a different

Table 12.10 Affective forms.

Plain	Diminutive -ito/a, -illo/a, -ico/a	Augmentative -azo/a, -ón/ona, -ote/ota	Pejorative -ucho/-a, -ejo/a, -uelo/a
perro 'dog'	perrito perrillo perrico	perrazo	perrucho
libro 'book'	librito librillo librico	librazo librote	librucho librejo
casa 'house'	casita casilla casica	casaza casona casota	casucha
hombre 'man'	hombrecito hombrecillo hombrecico	hombrazo hombrón hombretón	hombrezuelo

evolution in the context represented by ILLA(M) AQUA(M) > *el(a) agua* > *el agua*, than it did in, for instance ILLA(M) CASA(M) > *(e)la casa* > *la casa* 'the house'.

Originally feminine *el* had a more extensive usage in Spanish, being used regardless of stress and also before feminine words starting with other vowels, as in *el espada* for modern *la espada* 'the sword'. Progressively, this use of feminine *el* became more restricted until it was limited to its present-day context of application.

12.9 Diminutives

'Affective' morphology (diminutive, augmentative and pejorative forms) has a certain degree of productivity in Spanish. Examples are given in Table 12.10.

Dictionaries, in general, only list these forms when they have acquired an unpredictable meaning (e.g. *bolsillo* 'pocket', from *bolso* 'purse'; *mesilla* 'night table'), have some formal irregularity (e.g. *hombretón*) or both (e.g. *manecilla* 'hand of a clock'), since it is assumed that, to a certain extent, speakers can create and interpret affective forms productively.

The common diminutive suffix *-ito/a* presents allomorphy. We can distinguish minimally a 'short form' of the suffix, as in *librito* 'book, *dim.*', and a

12.9 Diminutives

'long form', containing the consonant -c-, as in *hombrecito* 'little man'. The same allomorphy also applies to the variants -*ico/a*, -*illo/a*, -*ete/a* and to the diminutive/pejorative -*uelo/a*. Here we will concentrate on the diminutive with /-it-/, since it is the most common one (although regionally one of the other forms may be preferred) and the alternation applies to all variants. The question that arises is whether the allomorph of the suffix that is selected can be predicted from the phonological shape of the plain form. In general we do in fact find some clear patterns, although there are also exceptions and irregularities.

A first relevant fact is the number of syllables in the plain form. A second factor is the vowel or consonant with which it ends. The presence of a diphthong in the plain form is also relevant for this allomorphy.

It is convenient to consider two-syllable forms before shorter and longer words.

a) Two-syllable words with inflectional endings -*a*, -*o*, as a general rule, take the 'short' diminutive.

General rule: 'short' diminutive; e.g.

oso	→ *osito*	'bear'
foca	→ *foquita*	'seal'
rojo	→ *rojito*	'red, *masc.*'
roja	→ *rojita*	'red, *fem.*'

There are, however, two exceptional patterns.

Exceptional pattern 1: if the base contains a diphthong /ie/, /ue/, both 'short' and 'long' diminutive can be used. The short form is the normal one in South America, whereas the long form is more common in most areas of Spain:

hueso	→ *huesito* ~ *huesecito*	'bone'
fiesta	→ *fiestita* ~ *fiestecita*	'party'
viejo	→ *viejito* ~ *viejecito*	'old, *masc.*'
vieja	→ *viejita* ~ *viejecita*	'old, *fem.*'
piedra	→ *piedrita* ~ *piedrecita*	'stone'

Exceptional pattern 2: if the plain form ends with a diphthong /-ia/, /-io/, addition of -*ito/a* with removal of the inflectional vowel of the base would create a sequence [ií]. This is often avoided by using the 'long' diminutive; e.g.:

rabia	→ *rabiecita*	'rage'
vidrio	→ *vidriecito*	'glass'

Alternatively, the stem-final glide is deleted, as in

limpio	→ *limpito*	'clean, *masc.*'
rubia	→ *rubiecita* ~ *rubita*	'blond, *fem.*'

b) Two-syllable words with inflectional ending *-e* usually take *-ecito/a*.

noche	→ *nochecita*	'night'
parte	→ *partecita*	'part'
coche	→ *cochecito*	'car'
verde	→ *verdecito/a*	'green'
leche	→ *lechecita* ~ *lechita*	'milk'
torre	→ *torrecita*	'tower'
monte	→ *montecito*	'mountain'
pobre	→ *pobrecito/a*	'poor'

This allomorphy allows for unambiguous recovery of the base. Thus e.g. *cortecita* from *(la) corte* 'court' contrasts with *cortita*, from *corta* 'short, *fem.*'. There are nevertheless some exceptions and a certain amount of variation with specific lexical items. Thus the diminutive of *nene* 'baby' is *nenito* and, for instance, that of *tigre* 'tiger' may be *tigrecito* or *tigrito*.

c) Two-syllable words without an inflectional suffix (consonant-final) take *-ito/a* or *-cito/a* depending on the final phoneme. As we will recall, the final consonants that are common in native Spanish words are *-l, -r, -n, -s, -z, -d*; that is, /l ɾ n s (θ) d/. Words ending in *-l* generally take *-ito/a* (but *-cito/a* in Bolivian Spanish; see Prieto 1992). Words ending in *-n* or *-r*, on the other hand, usually take *-cito/a*. The contrast between the two allomorphs disappears after /s/ in non-Peninsular dialects and after /θ/ in Peninsular dialects with this phoneme. In Castilian, words ending in *-s* take *-ito/a*. With words ending in *-d* the diminutive is not commonly used. Those words with final *-d* that are used in the diminutive take *-ito/a* in Spain, but in some Latin American dialects *-cito/a* is preferred instead.

-l

papel	→ *papelito* ~ Bol. *papelcito*	'paper'
hotel	→ *hotelito*	'hotel'

-r

pintor	→ *pintorcito*	'painter'
mejor	→ *mejorcito/a*	'better'
mujer	→ *mujercita*	'woman'

But:

señor	→ *señorito*	'gentleman'

12.9 Diminutives

-n
camión	→	*camioncito*	'truck'
lección	→	*leccioncita*	'lesson'
virgen	→	*virgencita*	'virgin'

-s
anís	→	*anisito*	'anise'

-z
nariz	→	*naricita*	'nose'
matiz	→	*maticito*	'nuance'

-d
ciudad	→	*ciudadita* ~ Lat Am. *ciudadcita*	'town'
pared	→	*paredita* ~ Lat Am. *paredcita*	'wall'

d) One-syllable words take *-ecito/a* in Spain, but *-cito/a*, without the *-e-*, in some parts of South America. In other parts of Latin America both forms of the long diminutive may be used in variation or with different lexical items.

sol	→	*solecito* (SA *solcito*)	'sun'
mal	→	*malecito*	'illness'
flor	→	*florecita* (SA *florcita*)	'flower'
tren	→	*trenecito* (SA *trencito*)	'train'
té	→	*tecito*	'tea'

Again, the use of the long diminutive in this case avoids ambiguity as to the base. For instance, *solecito* from *sol* 'sun' contrasts with *solito* from *solo* 'alone', and *salecita* from *sal* 'salt' contrasts with *salita* from *sala* 'living room'.

The word *pie* 'foot' has the irregular diminutive *piececito*.

e) Words of three or more syllables show a greater preference for the short suffix than shorter words. Regarding words ending in *-o*, *-a*, no exception is made for items containing a diphthong *ue/ie*. These take the short diminutive if they contain three or more syllables. Thus, from trisyllabic *abuelo* 'grandfather' we obtain *abuelito*, not **abuelecito* – cf. bisyllabic *vuelo* 'flight' whose diminutive may be *vuelito* or *vuelecito*. For words of three or more syllables ending in *-e* or a consonant such as *-n* or *-r*, the short diminutive suffix is also available as an option, in spite of the fact that bisyllabic words with the same endings normally take the long suffix. Compare the following examples with those given above for bisyllabic words with the same relevant structure:

pañuelo	→	*pañuelito*, not **pañuelecito*	'handkerchief'
invierno	→	*inviernito*, not **inviernecito*	'winter'

chocolate →	*chocolatito* ~ *chocolatecito*	'chocolate'
elefante →	*elefantito*	'elephant'
alcalde →	*alcaldito* ~ *alcaldecito*	'mayor'
profesor →	*profesorito* ~ *profesorcito*	'teacher'
alemán →	*alemanito* ~ *alemancito*	'German'

Words with certain derivational suffixes such as *-ción*, however, form the diminutive in *-cito*, like bisyllabic words with the same ending: *contaminación/contaminacioncita* 'pollution', like *canción/cancioncita* 'song', *nación/nacioncita* 'nation', etc.

Regarding the inflectional ending of the diminutive form, bases ending in *-e* or a consonant take *-o* or *-a* in their diminutive depending on their morphological gender: *coche/cochecito* 'car (*masc.*)', *noche/nochecita* 'night (*fem.*)', *verde/verdecito* 'green, *masc.*', *verde/verdecita* 'green, *fem.*', *canción/cancioncita* 'song (*fem.*)', *motor/motorcito* 'motor (*masc.*)'.

Bases ending in *-a*, on the other hand, maintain this suffix in the diminutive regardless of gender: *mesa/mesita* 'table (*fem.*)', *artista/artistita* 'artist, *masc.* or *fem.*', *programa/programita* 'programme (*masc.*)'.

Nouns ending in *-o* are almost exclusively masculine. For exceptionally feminine *(la) mano* 'hand' the diminutive is *manita* in some areas (e.g. Spain) but *manito* in others (e.g. Peru). For the few other feminine nouns in *-o* resulting from truncation of longer words such as (la) *foto* 'photograph', *(la) moto* 'motorcycle' and, in some dialects, *(la) radio* 'radio', there is a certain amount of insecurity and the diminutive is usually avoided: *foto/?fotito, ?fotita*.

For producing the diminutive of a feminine form of an adjective or a noun with two gender forms, there are two strategies: the diminutive feminine can be created either from the plain feminine form or from the diminutive masculine. In the case of adjectives and nouns whose masculine form ends in a consonant, this may result in two different patterns.

12.9.1 Historical origin of the alternation

The origin of the allomorphic variation of the diminutive suffixes can be traced back to Latin. The Latin diminutive -ULUS/A/UM (as in CELLULA, diminutive of CELLA 'room') had a variant -CULUS/A/UM (as in PARTICULA, diminutive of PARS, PARTIS 'part' and FRĀTERCULUS 'little brother', diminutive of FRĀTER 'brother'), which resulted from an earlier agglutination of two diminutive suffixes. The distribution of these two allomorphs was morphologically conditioned in Latin. The -ULUS variant was used to form the diminutive of nouns and adjectives of the first and second declensions and the consonant-initial variant -*CULUS* was used with the other declensions. A suffix-initial -*c*- could also be found with the diminutive -*ELLUS/A/UM*, which is the ancestor of Sp -*illo/a*. The Spanish alternation between the short diminutive ending -*illo/a* and the long diminutive ending -*(e)cillo/a* thus has direct origins in Latin, although the distribution of the long and short forms has changed. The present-day distributional rules for the two allomorphs developed in Old Spanish (see Penny 2002:294–9, and Pharies 2002 under -*illo*, -*ulo*). From -*illo* ~ -*ecillo* the alternation spread to -*ito*, -*ico*, -*ete* and -*uelo*, which have or had a similar value, and to the augmentative -*ón*.

12.10 Morphophonology and phonological schools

Most studies of Spanish phonology that you will encounter are likely to be theoretically aligned with one of two main schools: Praguean structuralism or generative phonology. The place that morphophonological alternations occupy is very different in these two traditions of phonological analysis.

In textbooks offering an analysis of Spanish phonology from a Praguean structuralist perspective, such as Quilis (1993) and Quilis and Fernández (1985), there is no discussion of the phenomena considered in this chapter, since they are taken to fall outside of the purview of phonology.

In generative studies, such as J. Harris (1969), on the other hand, such alternations play a central role. This is because, within this phonological school, the assumption is made that, in principle, a morpheme must be given the same 'underlying representation' in all contexts where it occurs. For instance, instead of the phonological representations /puédo/ 'I can', /podémos/ 'we can', that we employ in this book, Harris (1969:118) proposes the 'systematic phonemic representations' /pOdo/, /pOdemos/, where /O/ is a vowel bearing an abstract feature [+D] (= diphthongizing). Upon these representations, which respect the principle of morphophonological invariance, a number of 'phonological rules' apply. Relevantly, /O/ becames [we] (= [u̯e]) when stressed, and [o], when unstressed, finally deriving the 'phonetic' forms [pwéðo] and [poðémos]. This 'one morpheme one underlying representation' principle often leads followers of this school to propose rather abstract 'systematic phonemic representations'. Thus, for instance, in Harris (1969) we find that *protejo* is analysed as /proteg+e+o/ (p. 72), because of *protección*, *protector*; *agresor* is represented as /agred+t+or/ (p. 146), because of *agredir*; *edición* as /edi+t+ionE/ (p. 150), because of *editar*; *opacidad* as /opakidad/ (p. 168) because of *opaco*; *cuece* as /kOke/ (p. 168) because of *cocción*; *leche* as /lakte/ (p. 170), because of *láctico*, etc.

EXERCISES

1. Consider the following alternation between /e/ and /i/:

   examen 'exam'   *examinar* 'to examine'
   margen 'margin'   *marginal* 'marginal'
   virgen 'virgin'   *virginal* 'virginal'
   volumen 'volume'   *voluminoso* 'voluminous'
   origen 'origin'   *original* 'original'
   crimen 'crime'   *criminal* 'criminal'

   How would you define the context for this alternation?

2. Define the phonological contexts for the allomorphs of the root of the verbs *pedir, servir, preferir, vestir, perder*. State the context for the allomorph with the least restricted distribution as 'elsewhere'. Which of these verbs present the same pattern of allomorphy?

3. Define the phonological and morphological contexts for the allomorphs of the roots of *hacer* and *decir*. Do you see any important difference between these verbs and those in Exercise 2 regarding the distribution of allomorphs?

4. Define the phonological context for the occurrence of the allomorph /i-/ of the negative prefix /in-/.

5. Consider the plural of the nouns *régimen*, *análisis* and *carácter*. Are all three of them equally anomalous? Explain.

6. Examples such as *don/doña (courtesy title)*, *desdén/desdeñar* 'disdain N/V' show the existence of a morphophonological alternation involving the phonemes /n/ and /ɲ/.

   (a) Is this a phonologically conditioned alternation? If so, what is the rule or generalization of the phonology of Spanish that explains the alternation?
   (b) What could the historical origin of this alternation be? (See Appendix B.)
   (c) A few other sets of morphologically related words have an alternation between /l/ and /ʝ/: *aquel* /akél/ – *aquella* /akéʝa/ 'that, *masc./fem.*', *doncel/doncella* 'lad/maiden'. In what ways is this alternation like the one involving /n and /ɲ/? What differences do you see?
   (d) A generative analysis of the alternations mentioned in the paragraphs above is presented in J. Harris (1983:50–5). This analysis follows the principle or practice of generative phonology of favouring analyses where there is an invariant 'underlying representation' per morpheme. Harris

(following in part an earlier analysis by H. Contreras) thus postulates phonological representations such as /desdeɲ/ for *desdén*, and /akeL/ for *aquel*, where *L* is a 'phonetically uninterpreted symbol' (p. 143, note 7). In your opinion, what are the advantages and disadvantages of such an analysis? (To answer this question, read Harris 1983:50–5, first.)

13 Stress

13.1 What is stress?

Stress is the degree of relative prominence that a syllable receives in comparison with the other syllables in a given domain. Both Spanish and English are stress languages, but not all languages of the world have stress. In Spanish, as in English, the basic domain of stress assignment is the word (in other languages it may be the phrase). In a word-domain, in principle, only one syllable can receive primary stress. In a word like /papa/, we may have primary stress on the first or on the second syllable, but it cannot be on both syllables at the same time. Furthermore, if this is a lexical word (e.g. a noun or a verb), one of the two syllables must carry primary stress. In this *culminative* character, stress fundamentally differs from segmental features, as Trubetzkoy (1939) pointed out. It also differs from lexical tone: in a tone language a word like /papa/ may have lexical high tone on one syllable, on both syllables or on neither one.

In languages like Spanish and English, stress has a *distinctive* function in Trubetzkoy's terminology, since segmentally identical words may differ in the position of the stress. That is, stress is phonologically contrastive. There are other languages where the position of the stress is always predictable. In Hungarian, Finnish and Czech, for instance, stress is always on the first syllable of the word; in French, it is always on the last syllable with a full vowel. In Classical Latin as well, the position of the stress was always predictable, as we will see, although the rule was slightly more complicated.

In languages where the stress has a fixed position with respect to the beginning or the end of the word, we say that the feature of stress has a *delimitative* function, also in Trubetzkoy's terms, since it serves to locate word boundaries in the stream of speech. In Spanish this function is not as obvious as in, say, Hungarian. Nevertheless it is the case that the stress is never too far from the end of the word.

Table 13.1 Examples illustrating the lexically contrastive nature of stress in Spanish.

n**ú**mero 'number'	num**e**ro 'I number'	numer**ó** 's/he numbered'
t**é**rmino 'term'	term**i**no 'I finish'	termin**ó** 's/he finished'
c**é**lebre 'famous'	cel**e**bre 's/he celebrate, subjunct.'	celebr**é** 'I celebrated'
ánimo 'courage'	an**i**mo 'I encourage'	anim**ó** 's/he encouraged'
s**á**bana 'sheet'	sab**a**na 'savanna'	
	pl**a**to 'dish, plate'	plat**ó** 'stage'

In the next sections we will consider the generalizations that can be made regarding the position of the stress in Spanish words. The phonetic realization of stress in Spanish will be considered in 13.8.

13.2 Generalizations regarding stress in Spanish

Stress in Spanish is phonologically contrastive. By this we mean that it is possible to obtain words with different meaning solely by altering the position of the stress, as we can see in *número* 'number', *numero* 'I number' and *numeró* 's/he numbered', and in the other examples in Table 13.1 (the nuclear vowel of the stressed syllable is in bold face – redundantly so when the word carries an orthographic accent mark, since these orthographic marks are always placed on stressed vowels).

Spanish is thus a language with 'free' stress: stress does not automatically fall on the same syllable in all words with the same structure. Nevertheless, this freedom is relative, since the position of the stress is also subject to some constraints.[1] It is not the case that any syllable whatsoever can bear the stress.

The strongest of the constraints limiting the placement of stress is one dictating that the stress must fall on one of the last three syllables of the word. We can have words with stress on the final syllable, such as *revolución* 'revolution' (= OXYTONES: in Spanish *palabras agudas*); with stress on the penultimate, like *elefante* 'elephant' (= PAROXYTONES: *palabras llanas* or *graves*); and with stress on the antepenultimate, like *murciélago* 'bat' (= PROPAROXYTONES:

---

[1] These constraints on stress assignment have been discussed in great detail in the literature on this topic. See J. Harris (1995; and other work by this author), Roca (1990, 1999; and other work by this author), Aske (1990), Bárkányi (2002), among others.

palabras esdrújulas); but there are no other possibilities. There are no words like **élefante* with stress four syllables or more from the end. It is as if we had a 'THREE-SYLLABLE WINDOW' aligned with the end of the word, outside of which the stress could not be seen.

The only apparent exceptions to this generalization are verb forms with attached enclitics such as *cantándomelo* 'singing it to me'. These examples, however, are explained by the fact that the domain for stress assignment is the bare verb, without pronouns. Enclitic pronouns simply have no effect on the position of the stress (although they are taken into account for the orthographic accent rules): *cantando* 'singing', *cantándome* 'singing to me', *cantándomelo* 'singing it to me'; *los conejos se me están comiendo los tomates* 'rabbits are eating up my tomatoes' → *están comiéndosemelos* 'they are eating them up on me'. This neutral behaviour of enclitics can be compared with the stress effects of derivational suffixes, which always determine the stress pattern of the word; e.g. *urbe* 'town', *urbano* 'urban', *urbanístico* 'urban', *urbanizar* 'urbanize', *urbanidad* 'urbanity', *urbanización* 'urbanization'.

Adverbs in *-mente* '-ly' such as *rápidamente* are not exceptions either, since they have two stressed syllables, as we shall explain below. They contain two stress domains.

Beyond this three-syllable-window restriction, which affects all Spanish words, for the description of stress patterns and generalizations it is convenient to distinguish four classes of words, according to grammatical category. Some generalizations apply to nouns and adjectives together. Adverbs have similar stress properties to nouns and adjectives, but also some peculiarities. Verbs, on the other hand, are best studied separately from these other classes of words. Finally, closed classes (pronouns, prepositions, conjunctions, etc.) also have some specific properties regarding stress. In the next sections, we will study stress in these different classes of words separately.

13.3 Stress properties of nouns and adjectives

13.3.1 Unmarked, marked and exceptional stress patterns

A first observation regarding nouns and adjectives is that the stress pattern of plural forms is predictable from the singular: the stress falls on the same vowel in the plural as in the singular, *elefante/elefantes* 'elephant/-s', *apóstol/apóstoles* 'apostle/-s' (with only one purely arbitrary exception, *carácter/caracteres* 'character/-s', and a handful of systematic exceptions in proparoxytones ending in a consonant other than /-s/: *régimen/regímenes* 'diet/-s, regime/-s', *hipérbaton/hiperbatones* 'hyperbaton/-s'; see 12.7).

13.3 Stress properties: nouns and adjectives

Table 13.2 Stress patterns of nouns and adjectives (singular forms).

	Cons./glide-final	Vowel-final
(a) Unmarked pattern (95%)	OXYTONIC e.g.: can*ción* 'song' especta*dor* 'spectator' fe*liz* 'happy' fran*cés* 'French' pa*red* 'wall' pai*pay* 'type of fan'	PAROXYTONIC e.g.: ar*tis*ta 'artist' cala*ba*za 'pumpkin' a*mar*go 'bitter' igno*ran*te 'ignorant' *tri*bu 'tribe' ta*re*a 'task'
(b) Marked pattern	PAROXYTONIC e.g.: *ár*bol 'tree' *lá*piz 'pencil' e*xa*men 'exam' *ú*til 'useful' *cés*ped 'lawn'	PROPAROXYTONIC e.g.: ve*hí*culo 'vehicle' sim*pá*tico 'nice' *sá*bana 'sheet' heli*cóp*tero 'helicopter' *á*rea 'area'
(c) Exceptional pattern	PROPAROXYTONIC e.g.: *sín*tesis 'synthesis' *ré*gimen 'regime; diet' *Jú*piter 'Jupiter' *Ál*varez (surname) *ó*micron 'omicron'	OXYTONIC e.g.: pa*pá* 'dad' jaba*lí* 'wild boar' domi*nó* 'domino' ca*fé* 'coffee' cane*sú* 'camisole'

When we consider singular forms, the following generalizations emerge.

(a) In the general or unmarked case, stress falls on the final syllable if the word ends with a consonant (responsabili*dad* 'responsibility') or glide (ca*rey* 'tortoise shell') and on the penultimate syllable if the word ends in a vowel (pano*ra*ma 'panorama'). About 95 per cent of Spanish nouns and adjectives follow this rule.

(b) In most singular words of these grammatical classes which do not follow rule (a), stress falls one syllable earlier: on the penult in words ending in a consonant (a*pós*tol 'apostle') and on the antepenult in words ending in a vowel (*brú*jula 'compass'). This is the marked pattern.

(c) Exceptional words not following either of the two rules above fall into two groups: in a small group of consonant-final words there is antepenultimate stress (a*ná*lisis 'analysis') and in another small set of vowel-final words there is final stress (Pana*má*).

These patterns are summarized and further exemplified in Table 13.2.

It is possible to draw some further generalizations regarding the lexical distribution of the marked and exceptional stress patterns. Proparoxytonic stress is never found in words with certain syllabic structures and paroxytonic stress in consonant-final nouns and adjectives has a very skewed distribution. These two patterns will be examined in the next two subsections.

13.3.2 Proparoxytones

Regarding the distribution of proparoxytonic stress, there are two generalizations or constraints.

(a) Words that contain a rising diphthong in the final syllable are never proparoxytonic. There is, e.g., *caricia* 'caress', *Maciá*, but not *cáricia.

(b) Words whose penultimate syllable contains either a diphthong or a syllable-final consonant do not have proparoxytonic stress either. That is, a condition for proparoxytonic stress is that the penultimate syllable must be LIGHT (= not closed by a consonant). Exceptions to this generalization are borrowings such as *rémington* 'type of rifle', *básquetbol* 'basketball', the obsolete *límiste* 'a type of cloth'[2] and the Spanish toponym of Gothic origin *Frómista*. Foreign surnames and toponyms which violate this generalization also maintain antepenultimate stress even when they are phonetically adapted: *Anderson, Washington, Manchester*, etc. On the other hand, it is interesting to note that the native pattern is preserved in a neologism such as *alomorfo* 'allomorph' (with a HEAVY penultimate syllable and penultimate stress, not *alómorfo) as opposed to *alófono* 'allophone' (with a light penultimate syllable).

These two lexical restrictions in the native Spanish vocabulary regarding antepenultimate stress find an explanation within the stress system of Latin (see 13.7).

Some specific endings are particularly common in proparoxytones. These include 'superlative' -*ísimo/a* (*riquísimo/a* 'very rich'), adjectival -*ico/a* (*automático/a* 'automatic', not the diminutive) and the ending -*ulo/a* (*tabernáculo* 'tabernacle', *ridículo/a* 'ridiculous', *fábula* 'fable').

13.3.3 Consonant-final paroxytones

As mentioned above, whereas penultimate stress is the unmarked pattern for words ending in a vowel, final stress is unmarked for singular nouns and adjectives ending in a consonant. As for paroxytones ending in a consonant in the singular (marked pattern), we find a biased distribution. Not all consonant-final endings are equally common in paroxytones. For instance, about 50 per cent

---

[2] From the name of an English town, Lemster or Leominster. This word is listed in the dictionary of the Real Academia Española (1992) as *limiste* without an accent mark, but there is solid evidence that it was proparoxytonic, see Corominas and Pascual (1980) under 'límiste' and also Larramendi (1729:341–9).

of commonly used nouns and adjectives ending in *-en* have paroxytonic stress (*examen* 'exam', *resumen* 'summary', *virgen* 'virgin', *volumen* 'volume', etc.), but very few ending in *-n* preceded by a different vowel have this stress pattern (Aske 1990). Paroxytonic stress is also not uncommon in words ending in *-il* (*útil* 'useful', *ágil* 'nimble', *hábil* 'skilful', *difícil* 'difficult', etc. vs the unmarked pattern represented by *sutil* 'subtle', *fusil* 'rifle', *juvenil* 'youthful', etc.).

Interestingly, by a sort of hypercharacterization of foreign words, recent loanwords ending in a consonant are sometimes adapted with penultimate stress, even when in the source language they have final stress. This is the case with *cártel*, from English *cartel* (in spite of the existence of *cartel* 'poster'), and *chófer*, from French *chauffeur* (both normally with penultimate stress in Spain, although in other areas they have final stress).

All native words ending in a glide – but this is a small group of words – are oxytones (*Paraguay*). Borrowings ending in a glide also receive final stress, as in *samuray*, *bonsái*, *jersey*, *cowboy*, although there are exceptions among recent borrowings from English, such as *hockey* [xókei̯], *yóquey* 'jockey' (accepted with this orthography in the dictionary of the RAE) and proper English names used in a Spanish context, e.g. *Walt Disney* vs non-English *Tolstoy*, *Trubetzkoy*.

13.3.4 Unifying the statement of stress patterns for consonant- and vowel-final nouns and adjectives

We can achieve greater generalization in the statements of stress patterns of nouns and adjectives by disregarding all inflectional suffixes, not only plural suffixes. The final unstressed vowels of nouns and adjectives are inflectional suffixes. They are deleted in derivation – *cas-a* 'house', *cas-ero* 'domestic'; *libr-o* 'book', *libr-ería* 'bookstore'; *urb-e* 'town', *urb-ano* 'urban' – and participate in gender alternations: *gat-o/gat-a* 'tomcat/she-cat', *jef-e/jef-a* 'boss, *masc./fem.*'. The relevant observation is that gender vowels are, in fact, as neutral for stress purposes as plural suffixes are, as we can see in examples where the feminine adds a vowel to the masculine: *francés/franceses/francesa* 'French, *masc. sg. / masc. pl. / fem. sg.*'; *profesor/profesores/profesora* 'teacher, *masc. sg. / masc. pl. / fem. sg.*'; *huésped/huéspedes/huéspeda* 'guest, *masc. sg. / masc. pl. / fem. sg.*'. We may thus unify the stress patterns of consonant- and vowel-final nouns and adjectives by stating that in the unmarked case the last vowel of the *stem* bears the stress and in the marked case the stress is placed on the penultimate vowel (or diphthong) of the stem (Hooper and Terrell 1976).

Even vowel-final oxytones like *sofá* 'sofa' (right column under (c) in Table 13.2) can be understood as falling within the purview of the general pattern under the assumption that in these words the final vowel is not an inflectional suffix, but part of the stem. Usually the final vowel of these words is not deleted in

Table 13.3 Unmarked and marked patterns of stress in nouns and adjectives.

Unmarked pattern (~ 95%) stress on last vowel of stem	Marked pattern (~ 4%) stress on penultimate vowel of stem
calab*a*z-a, calab*a*z-as	simp*á*tic-o, simp*á*tic-os
profes*o*r, profes*o*r-a, profes*o*r-es	hu*é*sped, hu*é*sped-a, hu*é*sped-es
par*e*d, par*e*d-es	ap*ó*stol, ap*ó*stol-es

derivation, as in *maní* 'peanut', *manisero* 'peanut seller', not *manero (although the adjective derived from *Panamá* is *panameño*).

The only group of words that remains unaccounted for under the generalizations in Table 13.3 is the handful of proparoxytonic words ending with a consonant (left column under (c) in Table 13.2). These words constitute a rather exceptional group. It should be noticed that except for those ending in -*s* (*análisis*, *ómnibus*), which are regularly invariable in the plural (like, e.g., *lunes* 'Monday'), there is no straightforward way to form the plural of these nouns (*régimen*, *ómicron*, *hipérbaton*, *Júpiter*) since regular pluralization in /-es/ would place the stress beyond the window (see 12.7).

13.3.5 Stress in compounds

In N+N compounds each member of the compound may receive its own stress as in *camión-cisterna* 'tank truck', *cartón-piedra* 'cardboard', *hombre-rana* 'frogman'.

In other compound nouns, however, including the following types, only the stress of the second member is preserved.[3]

(a) Opaque N+N compounds: *bocacalle* 'entrance to a street'.
(b) N+A compound nouns: *yerbabuena* 'mint', *camposanto* 'cemetery' (contrasting with the phrases *yerba buena* 'good grass', *campo santo* 'holy field'). This also applies to A+N compound nouns: *medianoche* 'midnight'.
(c) Exocentric N+N compounds: *cara-huevo* 'egghead'.
(d) Compound names: *José Antonio*, *María Rosa* [mar̯i̯ar̄ósa], *Luis Enrique*.
(e) V+N compounds: *tocadiscos* 'record player', *lavavajillas* 'dishwasher', *paraguas* 'umbrella', *recogepelotas* 'ball catcher'. These compounds thus contrast in stress with segmentically identical phrases, which have two stresses: *toca discos* 's/he plays records', *recoge pelotas* 's/he gathers balls', etc.

---

[3] For an overview of Spanish compounds see Val Alvaro (1999).

13.3 Stress properties: nouns and adjectives

Compound colour adjectives with a structure A+N or A+A preserve the two stresses: *amarillo limón* 'lemon yellow', *azul marino* 'navy blue'. On the other hand, N+A adjectives have a single stress: *carirredondo* 'round-faced', *manirroto* 'prodigal', *barbilampiño* 'beardless'.

Among words used as titles, a contrast is made between, (a) those that can only be titles, such as *don* 'Mr', *doña* 'Ms' and *Fray* 'Friar, Brother', and (b) those such as *señor* 'Mr; gentleman', *señora* 'Mrs; lady', *señorita* 'Ms, young lady', *padre* 'Father, father', etc., which are also common nouns. Those title words in group (a) are always unstressed: *aquí está don Antonio* 'Don Antonio is here'; *aquí está, don Antonio* 'here it is, Don Antonio'. On the other hand, those title words in group (b), which are also common nouns, are only unstressed when used to accompany a proper name in vocatives, but receive stress (and must be used with the definite article) in nonvocative function: *señor Fernández, señorita Emilia, padre Antonio, pasen por favor* 'Mr Fernández, Miss Emilia, Father Antonio, please come in' vs *llegaron el señor Fernández, la señorita Emilia y el padre Antonio* 'Mr F., Miss E. and Father A. arrived' (see Quilis 1993:395).

Compound numerals from 16 to 99 are usually pronounced with a single stress, on the last member: *dieciocho, cuarenta y dos*. Compounds with *mil* 'thousand' and *cientos* 'hundreds' also have a single stress. For instance, there are three stresses in *cinco mil cuatrocientos veintitrés* '5423'. On the other hand, with *millones*, preceding numbers preserve their stress: *cinco millones* '5 million'. This is related to the fact that *millones* is a noun, as is evident from the fact that its complement must begin with *de*: *cinco millones de euros*. When *miles* is used as a noun, preposed numbers also preserve their stress: *cinco miles de euros* vs *cinco mil euros*.

13.3.6 Stress in truncated forms

A morphological process employed mostly in informal registers is the truncation or shortening of nouns. The resulting truncated form is a bisyllabic word ending in a vowel and with penultimate stress, regardless of the stress pattern of the base, as in the following examples:

profesor → *profe* 'teacher'   *universidad* → *uni* 'university'
bolígrafo → *boli* 'ball pen'   *fotografía* → *foto* 'photograph'
bicicleta → *bici* 'bicycle'   *televisión* → *tele* 'television'
policía → *poli* 'police(man)' *película* → *peli* 'film'

If the second syllable ends in a consonant, this consonant may be retained, but stress is still on the first syllable:

facultad → *facul* 'faculty, university department'

This process is also used to form hypocoristic forms of names (sometimes with further modifications): *Teresa* → *Tere*, *María* → *Mari*. Glides are syllabified as vowels in this process: *Daniel* → *Dani*, *Santiago* → *Santi*, *Manuel* → *Manu*. Another interesting example is *José* → *Jose*, where only the stress pattern is altered in the hypocoristic form, since the base is already bisyllabic.

13.4 Adverbs

In general, adverbs follow the same stress rules as nouns and adjectives. They usually have penultimate stress, if ending in a vowel, and final stress, if ending in a consonant: *mañana* 'tomorrow', *ayer* 'yesterday'; *delante* 'ahead', *detrás* 'behind'; *nunca* 'never', *jamás* 'never'. Some basic place adverbs ending in a vowel have final stress: *aquí* ~ *acá* 'here', *ahí* [a.í] ~ [ái̯] 'there', *allí* ~ *allá* 'over there'. The adverb *lejos* 'far' mimics the stress and morphological behaviour of a plural noun (cf. diminutive *lejitos*, derived adjective *lejano*, and *alejar* 'to remove', with deletion of -*os*). The stress of *apenas* 'almost', on the other hand, is etymologically justified in a transparent manner (< *a penas* 'with pains').

Adverbs ending in -*mente* historically derive from expressions involving the noun *mente* 'mind' (in the ablative case); e.g. *claramente* 'clearly' < CLARĀ MENTE 'with a clear mind'. This historical origin is still evident from several properties of these adverbs, such as the fact that they are formed from the feminine form of the adjective (the noun *mente* is feminine) whereas, otherwise in derived forms, word-internal inflectional endings are deleted; and the fact that in coordination it is possible to add -*mente* only to the last of the coordinated adjectives with an adverbial function: *habló clara, rotunda y concisamente* 's/he spoke clearly, emphatically and concisely'. Regarding stress, this phrasal origin is also evident in the fact that these adverbs have two stressed syllables: *rápidamente* 'rapidly', *sencillamente* 'simply', *naturalmente* 'naturally'. In natural discourse either the first or the second of the two stresses may be eliminated, but it is also perfectly normal for both stresses to be preserved.

13.5 Verbs

Unlike the situation with other classes of words, with verbs we find no contrast between marked and unmarked stress patterns. All morphologically regular verbs show exactly the same stress patterns. Even morphologically irregular verbs generally abide by the general rules of stress assignment, the only partial exceptions being the so-called 'strong preterites' and the present tense of *estar* 'to be, stay'. See Table 13.4.

On the other hand, we find quite different rules depending on the tense.

13.5 Verbs

Table 13.4 Present tense stress pattern.

General rule e.g. *alabar* 'to praise'		Only exception *estar* 'to be, stay'	
Pres. indi.	Pres. subjunct.	Pres. indic.	Pres. subjunct.
alabo	*alabe*	*estoy*	*esté*
alabas	*alabes*	*estás*	*estés*
alaba	*alabe*	*está*	*esté*
alabamos	*alabemos*	*estamos*	*estemos*
alabáis	*alabéis*	*estáis*	*estéis*
alaban	*alaben*	*están*	*estén*

13.5.1 Present tense (indicative and subjunctive) and imperative

In the present tense, the stress falls on the penultimate syllable, except in the second person plural (*vosotros*) form, where it is final. There is a single verb that does not follow this stress rule: *estar*, which has final stress in all singular and third person plural forms, as well as in second person plural.

The exceptionality of the verb *estar* is due to the fact that in its Latin ancestor the forms that now irregularly show final stress were monosyllabic and therefore stressed on their only syllable: STŌ, STĀS, STAT, STĀMUS, STĀTIS, STANT. These forms acquired one more syllable as a result of initial prothesis of /e-/ (like all other words with initial *sC* clusters), but that did not cause a shift in the inherited stress.

The second person plural forms (only used in Spain) can also be analysed as following the penultimate stress rule if we consider that they contain a falling diphthong and that there is no contrast in Spanish between bisyllabic [a.is] and monosyllabic [ai̯s]. This analysis, however, would require a greater amount of abstraction in order to account for third conjugation forms, where we find a monophthong in the final syllable in the surface: *(vosotros) vivís* 'you-*pl.* live', *preferís* 'you-*pl.* prefer'.

In Argentina and some other Latin American areas of VOSEO, second person singular familiar forms derive by contraction from forms like the *vosotros* forms of Peninsular Spanish. These also have final stress: *(vos) alabás* 'you praise', *merecés* 'you deserve', *vivís* 'you live'.

Verbs with infinitives ending in *-iar*, *-uar* may have either a diphthong (e.g. *cambiar: cambio* 'to change'; *copiar: copio* 'to copy'; *envidiar: envidio* 'to envy'; *averiguar: averiguo* 'to find out'; *apaciguar: apaciguo* 'to pacify'; *menguar: menguo* 'to diminish') or a hiatus (e.g. *enviar: envío* 'to send'; *variar: varío*

Table 13.5 Present indicative verbs in *-iar, -uar, -ear, -oar, -uir*.

-iar		-uar		-ear, -oar	-uir
diphthong	hiatus	diphthong	hiatus		
cambiar	*enviar*	*averiguar*	*continuar*	*pelear*	*huir*
cambio	envío	averiguo	continúo	peleo	huyo
cambias	envías	averiguas	continúas	peleas	huyes
cambia	envía	averigua	continúa	pelea	huye
cambiamos	enviamos	averiguamos	continuamos	peleamos	huimos
cambiáis	enviáis	averiguáis	continuáis	peleáis	huis
cambian	envían	averiguan	continúan	pelean	huyen

'to vary'; *espiar: espío* 'to spy'; *continuar: continúo* 'to continue'; *evaluar: evalúo* 'to evaluate'; *actuar: actúo* 'to act') in a lexically specific manner. With a few of these verbs both patterns are accepted in the standard language; e.g. *licuar: licúo ~ licuo* 'to liquify'. Notice that in either case, they conform to the paroxytonic stress rule in the present: these two classes of verbs differ in syllable structure but not in accentual structure. On the other hand, verbs in *-ear, -oar* always have a hiatus in the present tense, since sequences of nonhigh vowels are heterosyllabic in careful speech (*pelear: peleo* 'to fight'; *menear: meneo* 'to move'; *loar: loo* 'to praise'; *incoar: incoo* 'to initiate'). The only exception is found in the verbs derived from *línea* 'line', *alinear* 'to align' and *delinear* 'to delineate', which for some speakers have *alineo, delineo* (in which case they are pronounced with a diphthong [ẹo]),[4] as already noticed by Menéndez Pidal (1973[1904]:276); standard forms are *alineo, delineo*. Verbs ending in *-uir* do not have a diphthong in the present either, since with these verbs *-y-* is systematically inserted after the root in all forms except those containing the theme vowel *-i- – huir: huyo, huimos;* subjunct. *huya, huyamos* 'to flee'; *construir: construyo* 'to build'. See Table 13.5.

Aside from the complication introduced by verbs with infinitives in *-iar, -uar*, there are no irregularities in the stress patterns of present tense forms. In particular, we do not find the contrast between proparoxytonic and paroxytonic forms found in nouns and adjectives. In verbs morphologically derived from proparoxytonic nouns and adjectives, the stress is shifted to conform to the paroxytonic pattern of all verbs, as can be seen by comparing the pairs of nouns/adjectives and segmentally identical verb forms derived from them (see Table 13.6; J. Harris 1969:120; RAE 1973:258).

[4] The Spanish Academy rejects this stress pattern as incorrect, while admitting that it is becoming more and more common (RAE 1973:258–9).

13.5 Verbs

Table 13.6 Shift of the stress in verbs derived from proparoxytonic nouns and adjectives.

N/A		V	
fórmula	'formula'	*formula*	's/he formulates'
número	'number'	*numero*	'I number'
fábrica	'factory'	*fabrica*	's/he fabricates'
plática	'conversation'	*platica*	's/he converses'

Table 13.7 Past tenses: columnar or morphological stress on theme vowel.

Preterite	impf. indic.	impf. subjunct. A	impf. subjunct. B
alabé	*alababa*	*alabara*	*alabase*
alabaste	*alababas*	*alabaras*	*alabases*
alabó	*alababa*	*alabara*	*alabase*
alabamos	*alabábamos*	*alabáramos*	*alabásemos*
alabasteis	*alabábais*	*alabarais*	*alabaseis*
alabaron	*alababan*	*alabaran*	*alabasen*

Imperative *tú* 'you, informal', *usted* 'you, formal' and *ustedes* 'you-*pl.* (formal)' forms are always identical to other forms of the present indicative or subjunctive paradigm (except for exceptional monosyllabic *tú* affirmative imperatives, e.g. ¡*sal!* 'leave!') and therefore do not require any additional comment. Affirmative *vosotros* 'you-*pl.*, informal' commands, on the other hand, have special forms in -*d*, which receive final stress: ¡*alabad!* 'praise! you-*pl.*', ¡*comed!* 'eat! you-*pl.*'. The /d/ is deleted before the enclitic reflexive pronoun *os*: ¡*sentaos!* 'sit! you-*pl.*' (in colloquial usage, forms identical to the infinitive are used instead: ¡*comer!*, ¡*sentaros!*). In Argentinian *voseo*, forms historically related to the Peninsular *vosotros* forms, but without the -*d*, are used: ¡*comé!* 'eat! you-*sg.*', ¡*sentate!* 'sit! you-*sg.*'.

13.5.2 Past tenses

All simple past tense forms (preterite, imperfect indicative and imperfect subjunctive) are stressed on the vowel immediately after the root. This is illustrated in Table 13.7 with all three simple past tenses of the verb *alabar* 'to praise'. In these tenses we thus have columnar stress, where the position of the stress is not regulated with respect to the end of the word, but rather falls on the same

Table 13.8 Strong preterites: *poder, estar*.

pude	*estuve*
pudiste	*estuviste*
pudo	*estuvo*
pudimos	*estuvimos*
pudisteis	*estuvisteis*
pudieron	*estuvieron*

Table 13.9 Future and conditional: columnar or morphological stress on -rV-.

Future	Conditional
alabaré	*alabaría*
alabarás	*alabarías*
alabará	*alabaría*
alabaremos	*alabaríamos*
alabaréis	*alabaríais*
alabarán	*alabarían*

syllable with respect to the root in all forms of the paradigm. One may also speak of morphological stress, since the stressed syllable always contains the same morpheme: the theme vowel (i.e., the first vowel after the stem).

The so-called strong preterites are the exception to this rule, since they receive stress on the root vowel in the first and third person singular forms (= RHYZOTONIC forms). This is illustrated with the preterites of *poder* 'to be able' and *estar* 'to be, stay' in Table 13.8. All irregular or strong preterites have the same set of endings, regardless of conjugation, and show the same stress pattern.

13.5.3 Future and conditional

In the future and conditional tenses we also find columnar/morphological stress, but on a different morpheme from the one in the past tenses. These forms are stressed on the syllable containing the future/conditional tense marker -*r*-. Counting from the end of the word this may be the final, penultimate or antepenultimate syllable.

As was explained in 12.6, historically future and conditional derive from Latin periphrases.

13.5.4 Compound tenses

In compound tenses both auxiliary and main verb receive stress: *he comido* 'I have eaten', *hemos hablado* 'we have spoken'. Thus, for instance, *ha lavado* 's/he has washed', with two stresses, minimally contrasts with *alabado* 'praised', with a single stress.

13.6 Grammatical words

Grammatical words (pronouns, determiners, prepositions, conjunctions) can be either stressed or unstressed (Quilis 1993:390–5). Unstressed words do not normally receive intonational or other prominence when used in the context of a sentence. For instance, in the phrase *para la capital* 'for the capital city' there is a single stressed syllable; both preposition and article are unstressed in this example. The intonational contour of this phrase will normally show a single PITCH ACCENT, on the last syllable. Lexically unstressed words may receive stress only when cited or contrastively emphasized (capitalization is used here to indicate emphasis): *la preposición 'para'* 'the preposition "para"'; *he dicho 'LA capital', no 'el capital'* 'I said "*la capital*" [city] not "*el capital*" [funds]' (but even in corrections of this type it is also normal to leave lexically unstressed words unstressed: *he dicho la capiTAL, no el capital*, see 14.4.1).

13.6.1 Pronouns

Clitic pronouns (*me, te, se, lo, la, le, nos, os, los, las, les*) are unstressed. Subject pronouns and pronouns used with prepositions (*yo, tú, él, ella, usted, nosotros/as, vosotros/as, ustedes, ellos/as, mí, ti, sí*) are stressed:

yo te lo doy a ti 'I give it to you'
ellos nos las trajeron a nosotros 'they brought them to us'
véndemelos 'sell them to me!'
no me los vendas 'don't sell them to me!'
se los vendieron a ellas 'they sold them to them'

In normal nonemphatic pronunciation the syllables marked as stressed by bolding will receive intonational prominence, whereas no such prominence will appear on unstressed items.

As noted before, clitic pronouns are syntactically attached to verbs, either preceding or following them, but do not affect the stress pattern of the verbs to which they attach.

Table 13.10 Examples of unstressed and stressed determiners.

Unstressed determiners: definite articles and possessives	Stressed determiners: indefinite articles and demonstratives
el amigo 'the friend'	*un amigo* 'a friend'
la montaña 'the mountain'	*una montaña* 'a mountain'
mis amigos 'my friends'	*estos amigos* 'these friends'
nuestros amigos 'our friends'	*aquellas montañas* 'those mountains'

13.6.2 Determiners

Determiners can also be either stressed or unstressed. In general, the stressed or unstressed nature of specific determiners is not predictable from other considerations. Definite articles (*el, la, los, las, lo*) and possessives (*mi, tu, su, nuestro/a, vuestro/a*) are unstressed. On the other hand, both indefinite articles (*un, una, unos/as*) and demonstratives used as determiners (*este*, etc.) are stressed. See Table 13.10.

When not used as determiners, possessives receive stress; e.g. *esas cosas son vuestras* 'those things are yours' (cf. *vuestras cosas son ésas* 'your things are those'), *un amigo mío* 'a friend of mine'. Notice the contrast between demonstratives, always stressed, and possessives, which are unstressed when functioning as determiners in prenominal position: *estos libros / los libros éstos* 'these books'; *nuestros libros / los libros nuestros* 'our books'.

Dialectally, possessives functioning as determiners may be stressed in an area of northwestern Spain (León).

13.6.3 Prepositions

Prepositions are unstressed: *iba desde la montaña hasta la costa* 'it went from the mountain up to the coast'; *por nuestros hermanos* 'because of our brothers'; *eran para los de mis amigos* 'they were for those of my friends'.[5]

Notice the following contrasts between prepositions (unstressed) and homophonous verbs:

para las máquinas	's/he stops the machines'
para las máquinas	'for the machines'
bajo las sábanas	'I lower the sheets'
bajó las sábanas	's/he lowered the sheets'
bajo las sábanas	'under the sheets'

---

[5] As Quilis (1993:392) remarks, *según* 'according to' is stressed.

13.6.4 Question words (interrogative pronouns)

Interrogative words such as *qué* 'what', *quién* 'who', *cuándo* 'when', *cuánto* 'how much', *cómo* 'how' are stressed in interrogative and exclamative sentences, including indirect questions: *¿Qué quieres?* 'What do you want?', *¡Cuánto sabe el maestro!* 'The teacher knows so much!', *No sé cómo lo hizo* 'I don't know how s/he did it.' In other contexts, when they function as relative pronouns or conjunctions, however, these words are unstressed. This difference is orthographically indicated. When unstressed, these words do not carry an orthographic accent mark: *hazlo como quieras* 'do it whichever way you want', *como no llegabas, me fui* 'since you did not seem to be arriving, I left', *cuando llegó Juan, nos fuimos* 'when Juan arrived, we left', *quien lo sepa, que levante la mano* 'whoever knows it should raise his or her hand'.

13.6.5 Conjunctions

Most conjunctions are unstressed. These include the most common conjunctions: *y* 'and', *o* 'or', *pero* 'but', *sino* 'but', *que* 'that', *aunque* 'although', *mientras* 'while', *si* 'if'. Among subordinating expressions some are usually unstressed and others are stressed. Compare the following pairs of near-synonymous expressions differing in stress:

en cuanto llegue Juan 'as soon as Juan arrives'
apenas llegue Juan 'as soon as Juan arrives'
puesto que lo sabes 'since you know it'
dado que lo sabes 'since you know it'
aun cuando se lo pedí 'even though I asked him/her for it'
a pesar de que se lo pedí 'even though I asked him/her for it'

The transparent lexical origin of some of these expressions seems to explain in part their stress behaviour: *apenas* is also an adverb meaning 'barely' and *dado* is also a verbal participle 'given' (but *puesto* 'put' is also a participle and is unstressed in *puesto que* 'since'). On the other hand, *luego* 'then; therefore' and *mientras* 'in the meantime; while' are stressed as adverbs but unstressed as conjunctions. The expression *mientras que* 'as long as' is also unstressed:[6]

luego lo traigo 'I will bring it later'
luego lo traigo 'therefore I bring it'
mientras, hablábamos 'in the meantime we were speaking'
mientras hablábamos 'while we were speaking'
mientras que lo traigas 'as long as you bring it'
mientras, que lo traigas 'in the meantime, (I'm telling you to) bring it'

[6] For a more extensive listing of stressed and unstressed words see Quilis (1993:390–5).

13.7 The Latin stress system and its continuation in Spanish

As the great Spanish linguist Ramón Menéndez Pidal (1973[1904]:36) put it : 'El acento se mantiene inalterable desde el tiempo de Plauto, de Horacio, de Prudencio, hasta el de Cervantes y hasta el nuestro, informando como un alma a la palabra' ('the stress-accent remains inalterable from the time of Plautus, Horace and Prudentius to that of Cervantes and to our own, and it is like the soul shaping the word'). Given this conservatism in the position of the Spanish stress, it is useful for our understanding of Spanish stress to consider the Latin stress assignment rules here.

In Latin, vowels could be contrastively short or long and intervocalic consonants could also be either single or geminate. The position of the stress was completely predictable from segmental facts. Stress always fell on the penultimate syllable in bisyllabic words and either on the penultimate or on the antepenultimate syllable in words of three or more syllables, according to the following exceptionless rule.

(1) Latin stress rule
Stress the penultimate syllable if heavy, otherwise the antepenultimate (where HEAVY is defined as a syllable containing either (a) a long vowel or (b) a syllable-final consonant – including the first part of a geminate).

In accordance with this rule, the examples in (2) were stressed as in (3), where the stressed vowel is bolded. Long vowels are indicated with a macron. Notice that the only syllable whose weight is relevant for the assignment of stress is the penult.

(2) Some Latin words
ANIMA 'wind, soul', AMĪCA 'friend, *fem.*', ANGUSTUS 'narrow', FURIŌSUS 'furious', FŪNEBRIS 'deadly', LĪTIGIUM 'contention', SPECULUM 'mirror', GARRULITĀS 'chattering', GARRULITĀTIS 'of the chattering'

(3) Stress
  a. Heavy penult → paroxytones:
     A.MĪ.CA, AN.GUS.TUS, FU.RI.Ō.SUS, GAR.RU.LI.TĀ.TIS
  b. Light penult → proparoxytones:
     A.NI.MA, FŪ.NE.BRIS, LĪ.TI.GI.UM, SPE.CU.LUM, GAR.RU.LI.TĀS

As noted by Menéndez Pidal, in almost all cases the stress has been kept on the same vowel in all Spanish words of Latin origin; e.g.:

(4) From Latin to Spanish
AMĪCA > *amiga* 'friend, *fem.*',
ANIMA > **alma**, **ánima** 'soul'

13.7 The Latin system and its continuation in Spanish

Whereas the position of the stress was always predictable in Latin, it became unpredictable once the phonological distinction between long and short vowels, which conditioned it, was lost, as the examples just given show. In Latin the word AMĪCA was predictably stressed on the penultimate syllable, since its vowel was long, and ANIMA was predictably stressed on the antepenultimate syllable, since the vowel of the penultimate syllable was phonologically short. In Spanish, on the other hand, there is nothing in the segmental composition of *amiga* and *ánima* that accounts for their different stress patterns. The position of the stress has not varied, but it has become unpredictable.

On the other hand, the Latin stress rule also placed the stress on the penultimate syllable when this syllable was closed by a consonant. No sound change has affected the predictability of the stress in this context and the effects of this restriction are still observable in Spanish. In words with a closed penultimate syllable the stress is almost as predictable in Spanish as it was in Latin (aside for the possibility of final stress). There are no possible Latin sources for the pattern CV(C).CVC.CV(C) (antepenultimate stress in words with a penultimate syllable ending in a consonant). The only words with this pattern in Spanish are borrowings from other languages; in particular Germanic borrowings. As mentioned above, these words include the old toponym *Frómista* (from Gothic *frumisti* 'beginning'; see Corominas and Pascual 1980, under 'límiste') and a number of foreign surnames, place names and other words more recently borrowed from English.

In this connection we may also note that there are no proparoxytonic words in Spanish with a trill in the onset of the final syllable. The only exceptions are surnames of non-Latin origin such as *Chávarri* (< Bq. *etxa-barri* 'new house') and *Achúcarro*, the onomatopoetic *cháncharras-máncharras* 'excuses', and the noun *tábarro* (a type of wasp), of unknown etymology (variant of *tábano*). The intervocalic trill derives from a geminate /rr/ in Latin, which necessarily produced a heavy syllable.

The three-syllable-window restriction itself has its obvious origin in Latin. In this case, however, language contact has not introduced any exceptions in Spanish. Names from Russian and other languages with contrastive stress that do not use the Latin alphabet are sometimes transcribed in Spanish texts with the stress indicated with an accent mark. In such foreign names we may find the stress outside of the window: 'El gobernador de Kémerovo, Amán Tuléyev' (*El País*, 3 Aug. 2003, p. 2). Presumably Spanish readers do not have much trouble pronouncing such (obviously foreign) names as transcribed.

Let us consider now the origin of the restriction in Spanish against proparoxytonic stress in words with a rising diphthong in their last syllable (i.e. the absence of words with the pattern illustrated by hypothetical *palacio – cf. *palacio* 'palace'). This also follows from the Latin stress rule. Latin did not have rising diphthongs. Sequences of the type /Cia/ were syllabified as hiatus. This being the case, words like PA.LA.TI.UM, I.TA.LI.A had antepenultimate stress. Stress could thus not be any further towards the beginning of the word. In Late Latin such sequences became diphthongs, but since the stress was not shifted, such words systematically became paroxytones: I.TA.LI.A > I.ta.l̯ia.[7] In Spanish words of Latin origin with a rising diphthong in the last syllable it is thus impossible to have proparoxytonic stress.

Although, with very few exceptions, the same syllable nuclei are stressed in Spanish as were in Latin, the actual stress pattern of specific words has changed. First of all, a pervasive process of syncope has eliminated (necessarily short) nonlow vowels in the penultimate syllable of proparoxytones; e.g. TABULA > *tabla* 'board', PŌPULU > *pueblo* 'people; village', FĒMINA > *hembra* 'female', ANIMA > *alma*. Although sometimes words were reintroduced as learned terms with the shape they had in Classical Latin, as is the case with *fémina* and *ánima*, the general effect of the syncope process was to reduce the percentage of proparoxytones in the lexicon.

Another important difference is that, together with paroxytones and proparoxytones, Spanish also has oxytones, a pattern not found in Latin. These have been produced by deletion of final vowels, e.g. SENIŌRE 'older' > *señor* 'lord', CIVITĀTE > *ciudad* 'town', and also by contraction, e.g. AMĀVI > *amé* 'I loved'.

Finally, let us consider the few contexts where stress was actually shifted from Latin to Spanish. We find two cases, both systematic but including very small groups of words (Menéndez Pidal 1973[1904]:38–41). One involves the shift from a high vowel to an immediately following vowel in hiatus, in sequences that became diphthongs in Vulgar Latin (VL), e.g. MULIERE(M) > VL mul̯iere > *mujer* 'woman', FILIOLU(M) > VL fil̯iɔlu > *hijuelo* 'son, dim.'. The other case is presented by words where the vowel of the penultimate syllable is followed by a stop + liquid sequence. These sequences of consonants were syllabified as onset clusters in Classical Latin, thus leaving an open penultimate syllable: CA.THE.DRA 'chair', IN.TE.GRUM 'whole', TE.NE.BRAE 'darkness'. When borrowed as learned vocabulary, those words do indeed have proparoxytonic stress also in Spanish, *cátedra, íntegro*. In natively transmitted words with this structure, on the other hand, we observe that the stress has been shifted to the penultimate: CATHEDRA > *cadera* 'hip', INTEGRU(M) > *entero* 'whole', TENEBRAE > *tiniebla* 'darkness' (with contamination from *niebla* 'fog'). It is

---

[7] In regularly evolving native words most of such rising diphthongs on final syllables later disappeared by palatalization (FĪLIA > *hija*) or by metathesis (PRIMĀRIU(M) > *primairo > primeiro > primero*).

likely that this stress pattern corresponds to a nonstandard pronunciation in Latin for words with this segmental structure.

In historically more recent times we also find changes in the position of stress motivated by the reduction of hiatus sequences to diphthongs as in Lat. REGĪNA > re.ina > reina 'queen'. This 'anti-hiatus tendency' is also apparent in nonstandard reductions with stress shift such as ma.iz → maiz 'corn', ma.estro → maistro 'master bricklayer [in Mexico]', etc. (A. Alonso 1930; Quilis 1993:297–398; see 5.5.3). Aside from this context, there are also a few other cases of fluctuation or shift explainable by analogies with words of a similar ending, e.g. Lat. MEDULLA > medula ~ médula (most common words in -ula are proparoxytonic), sutil ~ nonstandard sútil (cf. útil 'useful'), mendigo ~ nonstandard méndigo 'pauper', intervalo ~ nonstandard intérvalo 'interval', etc. (see A. Alonso 1930).

Regarding the accentuation of verbal forms, the mobile stress pattern of the present continues the Latin situation – e.g. AMŌ 'I love', AMĀMUS 'we love' > amo, amamos. In native verbs with proparoxytonic stress, the pattern became paroxytonic by general deletion of the posttonic vowel, as in COLLOCŌ > cuelgo 'I hang'. Learned verbs borrowed from Latin with antepenultimate stress eventually shifted the stress to conform with the general pattern of the language, as in COLLOCŌ > coloco 'I place' (Menéndez Pidal 1973[1904]:274–5).[8]

In tenses other than the present with variable stress in the Latin paradigm, the stress was shifted so that it falls on the same syllable in all forms of the Spanish tense paradigm with respect to the root, as in the imperfective forms CANTĀBAM, CANTĀBĀMUS > cantaba, cantábamos 'I sang, we sang' (the stress pattern cantabamos is still found in Galician, as well as in Italian cantavamo). This tendency in Spanish to regularize the stress of tense paradigms in a columnar fashion has also spread to the present subjunctive of second and third conjugation verbs in nonstandard usage of parts of Andalusia and Latin America, e.g. vaya 'I go, subjunct.', vayamos 'we go' (Standard vaya, vayamos).

13.8 Phonetic correlates of stress

Stressed syllables receive greater prominence by means of pitch, duration and intensity. There are languages, such as English and Portuguese, where vowels in unstressed syllables are also reduced and/or centralized, which contributes

---

[8] It is interesting to note that in Italian, where medial posttonic vowels have for the most part been preserved (TABULA > It. tavola 'table' vs Sp. tabla 'board'), we still find a contrast between verbs with paroxytonic and with proparoxytonic stress in the present; e.g. imparo 'I learn' vs abito 'I live', cf. Sp. habito 'I live'. Incidentally, the addition of a final -o to the third person plural form has created exceptions in Italian to the three-syllable-window restriction: HABITANT > It. abitano 'they live'.

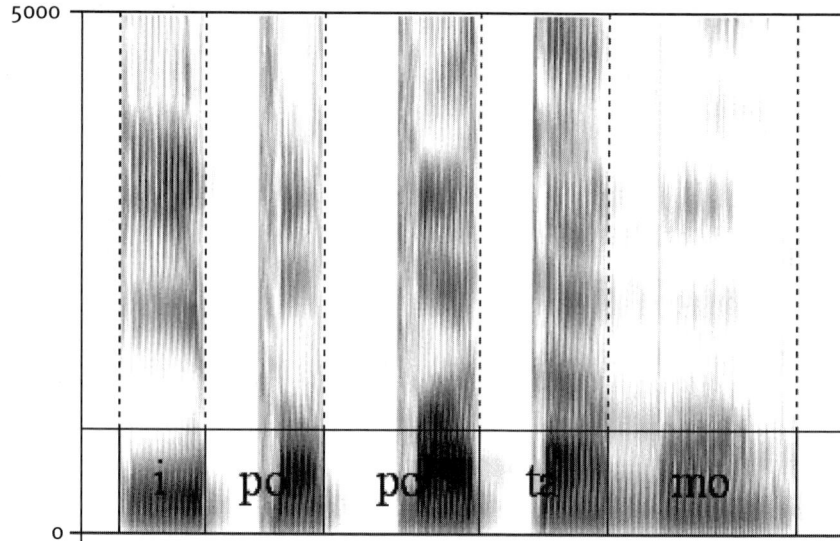

Figure 13.1a. Spectrogram of *hipopótamo*. The stressed syllable is longer than the preceding phonologically identical /po/ syllable, but the difference is relatively small. There are no significant differences in vowel quality.

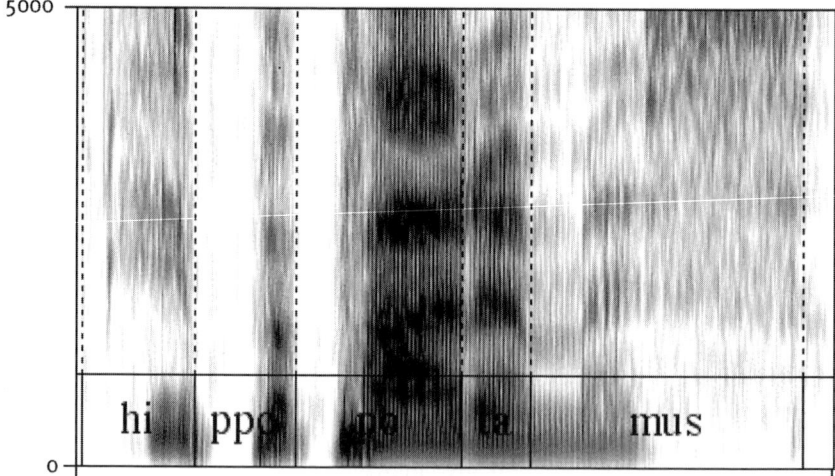

Figure 13.1b. Spectrogram of *hippopotamus* [hɪpəˈpʰɑɾəməs]. Comparing the two *po* syllables, notice the greater amount of aspiration at the release of the /p/ and the much greater duration of the vowel in the stressed syllable. Notice also that the /t/ after the stress is realized as a flap in this example.

13.8 Phonetic correlates of stress

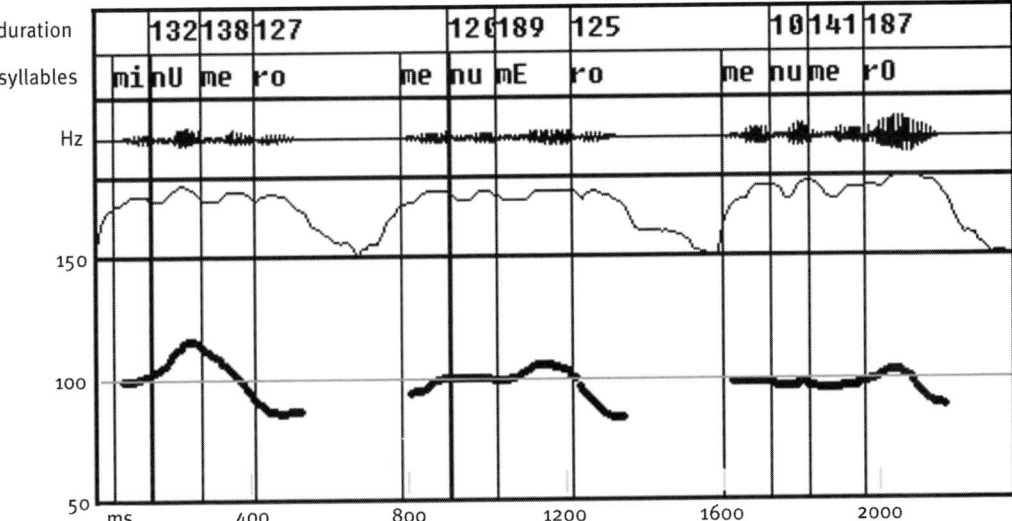

Figure 13.2. *Mi número, me numero, me numeró*. Tiers: duration of each syllable in ms, syllables, waveform, intensity curve and F0 curve. Durations: *nú-me-ro* (132–138–127), *nu-me-ro* (120–189–125), *nu-me-ró* (109–141–187).

to the greater relative distinctiveness and prominence of stressed syllables. In Spanish, on the other hand, the difference in quality between stressed and unstressed vowels is very small (Quilis and Esgueva 1983). In English, vowels in unstressed syllables are reduced to a neutral vowel [ə], known as schwa. In Spanish there is no such reduction. Compare, for instance, American English *banana* [bə'nænə],[9] where only the stressed syllable has a clear vowel, with Spanish *banana* [banána], where all three vowels are an unreduced [a] (see 7.2). The effect of stress on consonants is also smaller in Spanish than in English. Consider, for instance, how different the pronunciation of the two instances of /t/ in an English word like *potato* is, as a function of their position with respect to the stress (especially in American English, where the second /t/ undergoes flapping, [pə'tʰeɪɾo] ~ [pə'tʰeɪɾə]). In Spanish *patata*, on the other hand, the difference between the two /t/'s is much smaller: [patáta]. Similarly, to give another example, the difference between the two /-po-/ syllables in *hipopótamo*, unstressed and stressed, is very small compared to the corresponding sequence in English *hippopotamus* [ˌhɪpə'pʰɑɾəməs], where stress has a great effect both on vowel quality and on the aspiration of the /p/. See Fig. 13.1a/b.

An important function of stressed syllables in Spanish is to serve as anchoring points for intonational events. In Fig. 13.2, we have the intonational contours

---

[9] In the transcription of English words we employ IPA symbols for primary and secondary stress.

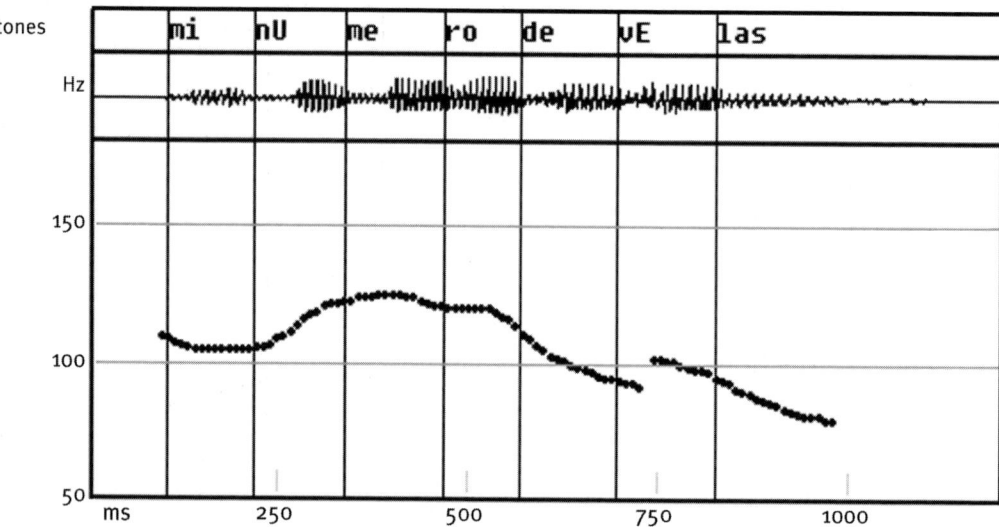

Figure 13.3a.   *Mi número de velas* 'my number of candles'.

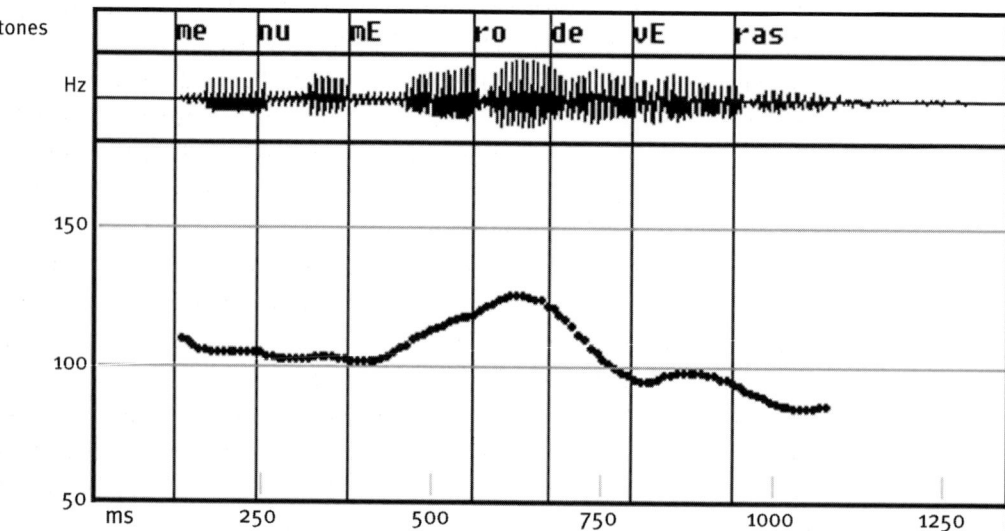

Figure 13.3b.   *Me numero de veras* 'I truly number myself'.

of the examples *mi número* 'my number', *me numero* 'I number myself' and *me numeró* 's/he numbered me', which have been uttered with declarative intonation. We can see that in all three examples there is a pitch rise whose peak is aligned with the lexically stressed syllable.[10]

---

[10] Pitch contours in this and the next chapter were produced with the commercial program PitchWorks by Sciconrd.

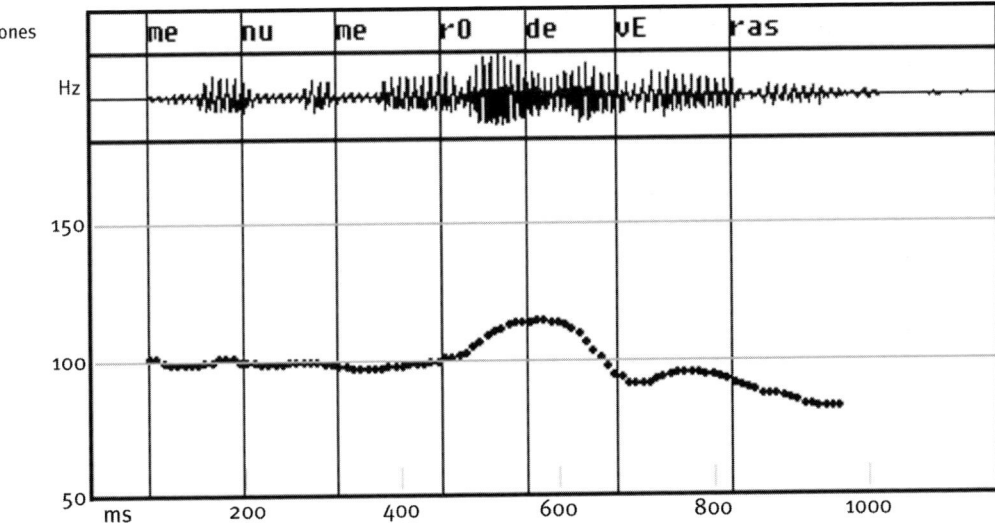

Figure 13.3c.   *Me numeró de veras* 's/he truly numbered me.'

From observation of words in isolation we might conclude that stressed syllables are associated with the highest pitch in the word. This would be, however, an erroneous conclusion. In other contexts, where the word is not in nuclear position in a declarative sentence, the pitch contour over the sentence will be different, and we will not necessarily find that the stressed syllable has the highest pitch in the word. What remains constant across contexts is that the location of the stressed syllable is the crucial point of reference for the alignment of pitch events. We can see this by applying the same intonational structure to texts differing in the position of the lexical stress. In Fig. 13.3, the words *número, numero, numeró* are also embedded in a declarative utterance, but, unlike in Fig. 13.2, they are not in final position. Here the nuclear accent of the utterance falls on *de velas* 'of candles' / *de veras* 'truly' and the contrasting words are in prenuclear position. We can see in the pitch contours that in our target word the highest pitch in the word is not found in the stressed syllable but, rather, is reached in the posttonic. This is typical of words in prenuclear position in declarative sentences (see next chapter). The anchoring function of stress can nevertheless still be seen in the fact that there is a pitch rise that coincides with the stressed syllable. In all three examples the pitch starts rising at the onset of the stressed syllable and rises throughout this syllable, the peak being reached late, on the posttonic.

Finally, in Fig. 13.4 we have the contrasting triplet *número/numero/numeró* at the end of a phrase with a question contour. Notice that here again one could not say that the stressed syllable is the one with the highest pitch. Rather, in these examples, there is a low point in the stressed syllable, after

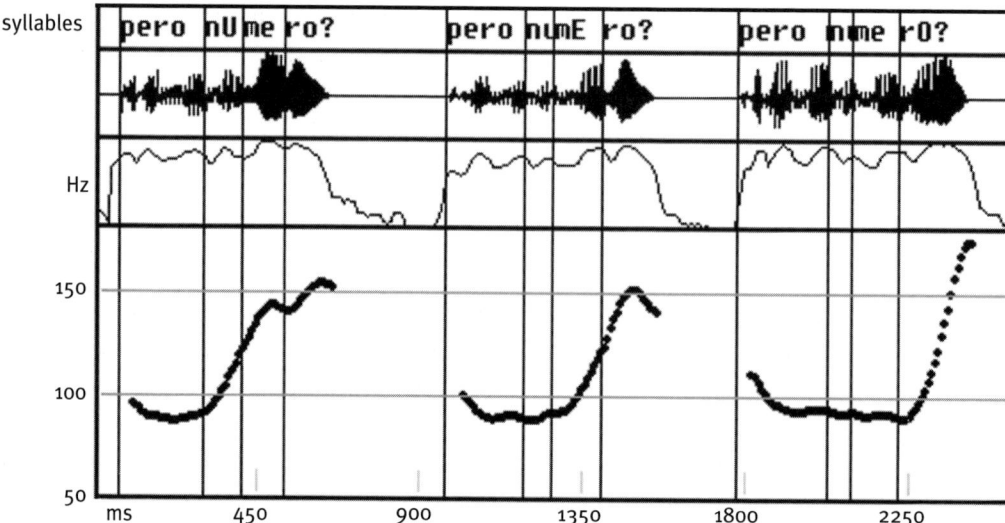

Figure 13.4. ¿*Pero número?* 'But number?', ¿*Pero numero?* 'But I number?', ¿*Pero numeró?* 'But s/he numbered?'. The final rise in these interrogative contours starts after a low point in the stressed syllable.

which there is a final rise to the end of the utterance. These examples again show that stressed syllables have the property of serving as anchoring points for pitch movements, but they are not necessarily associated with higher pitch than other syllables in the word.

In Fig. 13.2 we have noted the duration of each syllable in the target word on the highest tier above the sound wave (in milliseconds). By comparing the three examples we can see that each of the three syllables /nu/, /me/ and /ro/ is longest in the word where it is stressed. Duration is indeed another correlate of stress. Notice that this is not the same thing as saying that the stressed syllable will always be the longest syllable of the word, since some segments are intrinsically longer than others (and, in addition, duration also has other linguistic functions). See Simoẽs (1996), Manrique and Signorini (1983).

The durational effects of stress appear to go beyond the lengthening of the stressed syllable and may also affect adjacent syllables to the stressed one. For instance, the vowel /u/ is normally longer in *número* 'number', where it is stressed, than in *numero* 'I number' and in *numeró* 's/he numbered', where it is unstressed. However, Hualde and Chitoran (2003) found that vowels also tend to be longer in immediately pretonic position than further away from the stressed syllable, so that in our examples, there tends to be the following durational cline regarding the vowel /u/, from longest to shortest: *n<u>ú</u>mero* >> *n<u>u</u>mero* >> *n<u>u</u>meró*.

Finally, intensity also plays some role in enhancing the prominence of stressed syllables, although its role only becomes significant when combined with the other factors above. (In Fig. 13.2 and Fig. 13.4 the intensity contour appears between the sound wave and the pitch contour.)

To conclude, it appears that the most important correlate of stress in Spanish is pitch (fundamental frequency). The relationship between lexical stress and pitch is, nevertheless, somewhat abstract. It is by no means the case that the stressed syllable always has a higher fundamental frequency value than other syllables in the word or that it shows a consistent tonal contour. Instead, what we find is that stressed syllables function as anchoring points for intonational events (pitch accents). When bearing an intonational pitch accent, stressed syllables will normally also be enhanced by greater duration and intensity. Experimental work on the perception of stress in Spanish has shown that fundamental frequency, in combination with either duration or intensity, functions as a strong predictor of stress, whereas intensity and duration by themselves or in combination are not enough for determining the location of the stressed syllable (see Llisterri *et al.* 2003). Experimental work is still needed to determine whether, in natural discourse, stressed syllables bear significant durational or intensity prominence in contexts where pitch excursions are greatly reduced or eliminated, such as the position after another word with narrow focus.

Spanish stress is thus different in important ways from English stress. Although in both languages stressed syllables are used for the positioning of intonational excursions or pitch accents, in English lexically stressed syllables are also normally identifiable in the absence of pitch prominence because of intrinsic segmental features (including vowel quality and duration and certain consonantal phenomena). In Spanish, instead, pitch is a much more crucial correlate of stress. Stressed syllables that anchor pitch movements are also given greater duration and intensity (as in English), but there are only small differences in quality between segments in stressed and unstressed syllables (but see 8.2.2) and it is still unclear to what extent duration and intensity may serve to identify stressed syllables in the absence of tonal cues (i.e. in utterances where the word does not bear a pitch accent).

Something that makes the nature of word-stress particularly complex in a language like Spanish is that the parameters that are used to lend prominence to stressed syllables also have other linguistic functions. Thus, as we will see in the next chapter, some tonal movements (pitch accents) are prominence-lending and are associated with lexically stressed syllables, but tonal contours are also used to mark the end of intonational phrases. In a similar fashion, increased duration is used to indicate phrasal boundaries (final lengthening), in addition to serving as a cue for lexical stress.

13.9 Secondary stress

Besides their lexical or primary stress, words may receive a secondary stress two or more syllables before the lexically stressed syllable for special emphasis. This emphatic stress is usually placed on the first syllable of the word or on a lexically unstressed word preceding it in the phrase: *seguridad* 'certainty', *perspectiva* 'perspective', *del senado* 'of the senate'. The secondary emphatic stress may also fall on a noninitial syllable two or more syllables to the left of the lexically stressed syllable of the word: *con normalidad* 'with normality', *un lugar privilegiado* 'an extraordinary place', *clases particulares* 'private lessons'. Emphatic stress is a feature of public speech in Spanish. In certain contexts such as news broadcasting, other types of public reading, and the public speech of politicians, this phenomenon can reach very high frequency. In conversational speech, on the other hand, it is very seldom used. The syllable with secondary stress receives an intonational pitch accent.

13.10 Lexical stress and orthography

The goal of the orthographic accent rules in Spanish is to indicate the position of the lexical stress in every word without ambiguities and in an efficient and economic manner. If an accent mark were placed on the stressed vowel of every word (as we do in our phonetic transcriptions) we would have an unambiguous system, but this would not be the most efficient system. In the Spanish orthographic system the stress of most words, those that conform to the general patterns of the language, is left unmarked and accent marks are used to indicate deviation from the general patterns.

It should be pointed out that the unmarked general patterns for the orthographic rules are not exactly identical to those we have described above, since for orthographic purposes no distinction is made among different classes of words.

13.10.1 Basic orthographic accent rules

There are three basic orthographic rules for the use of accent marks.

1) All proparoxytonic words carry an accent mark on the stressed vowel; e.g.: *armónico* 'harmonious', *espectáculo* 'spectacle', *régimen* 'regime; diet', *cantábamos* 'we sang'.

Verbs with orthographically attached clitics count as single words for these purposes and bear an accent mark if the stress is three or more syllables away from the end of the word: ¡*cántalo!* 'sing it!', *cántamelo* 'sing it to me'.

13.10 Lexical stress and orthography

2) Paroxytonic words carry an accent mark when they end in a consonant other than -*n* or -*s*; e.g. *árbol* 'tree', *césped* 'lawn', *lápiz* 'pen', *ámbar* 'amber', but *examen* 'exam', *cantaban* 'they sang', *lunes* 'Monday', *casas* 'houses'. Consonant-final words are mostly oxytonic. The accent mark is thus employed in the marked case. The exception made in the orthographic rule for words ending in the consonants -*n* and -*s* is because of the high textual frequency of these final consonants in inflectional suffixes. Even though singular nouns and adjectives ending in -*n* and -*s*, like those ending in any other consonant, are mostly oxytonic (e.g. *nación* 'nation', *compás* 'compass', etc.), the exception made for -*n* and -*s* allows us to leave paroxytonic plurals (e.g. *casas* 'houses', *calabazas* 'pumpkins') and verb forms in -*n* and -*s* orthographically unmarked (e.g. *cantas, cantamos, cantabas, cantan, cantaban, cantaron*), which is more economical.

It is important to note that the exception for -*s* does not extend to -*z*, even though in Latin American Spanish these two letters represent the same phoneme. Thus *lápiz* 'pencil', *cáliz* 'chalice', *Fernández*, etc., are written with an accent mark, since they are paroxytonic words ending in a consonant (letter) different from -*n* or -*s*. An accent is also used in paroxytones in -*x* (e.g. *tórax* 'thorax') as well as those ending in a consonant cluster (e.g. *bíceps* 'biceps').

3) Oxytonic words have an accent mark if they end in a vowel, -*n* or -*s*. As we already know, the overwhelming majority of words ending in a vowel are paroxytonic. These are left orthographically unmarked, e.g. *calabaza* 'pumpkin', and so are their plurals. According to this rule, an accent mark is needed in, e.g., *café* 'coffee', *israelí* 'Israeli', *aquí* 'here', *anís* 'anise', *jamás* 'never', *inglés* 'English', *camión* 'truck', *alemán* 'German' and in several verbal forms, e.g. *canté, cantó, cantaré, cantarás, cantarán, cantáis*. Notice that the plural forms of oxytones in -*n* and -*s* do not have the accent mark of the singular, since they are paroxytones in -*s*; e.g.: *camión/camiones* 'truck/-s', *alemán/alemanes* 'German/-s', *inglés/ingleses* 'English, sg./pl.'. On the other hand, in words such as *examen/exámenes* 'exam/-s', the plural has an accent mark because it is a proparoxytone.

Oxytones ending in consonant cluster with -*s* do not bear an accent mark: *robots* (vs *bíceps*).

For accentual purposes, final -*y* (which represents a glide) is considered a consonant. Therefore oxytonic words ending in -*y* do not have an accent mark. This is also economical since, with the exception of only a few recent borrowings, all words ending in a glide are oxytonic; e.g. *Paraguay, convoy* (vs *yóquey* 'jockey'). On the other hand, when a final glide is represented as -*i*, as in a couple of borrowings from Japanese, the word is treated as vowel-final: *samurái, bonsái*.[11]

13.10.2 Diacritic use of accent marks to indicate hiatus

In addition to the rules above, an accent mark is placed on the vowels *í, ú*, when immediately preceded or followed by a vowel of the set *a, o, e* to indicate that the sequence is to be pronounced as a hiatus with stress on the high vowel; e.g. *vacío* 'void', *María* (vs *Mario*), *continúa* 's/he continues' (vs *continua* 'continuous, fem.'), *caída* 'fall' (vs *vaina* 'sheath'), *caí* 'I fell', *país* 'country', *maíz* 'corn', *países* 'countries', *maíces* 'corns', *reímos* 'we laugh', *reúno* 'I gather', *baúl* 'luggage trunk'.

Anti-economically, the accent mark is also used when the two vowels are separated by an *h*: *prohíbe* 's/he prohibits', *búho* 'owl', *vahído* 'faintness', although the *h* by itself would seem to provide enough of a cue for syllabification.

Somewhat inconsistently, the rule does not apply to the sequences *ui, iu*. Thus, the hiatus of *huida* 'flight', *huimos* 'we flee', is not orthographically distinguished from the diphthong in *cuida* 's/he cares for', *fuimos* 'we went/were'. For orthographic purposes, this phonological contrast is not supposed to exist, although it appears to be found in the pronunciation of most Spanish speakers.[12]

13.10.3 Monosyllables and pseudo-monosyllables

The rules above do not apply to one-syllable words. Monosyllables only bear an accent mark in the case of the diacritically distinguished minimal pairs mentioned below in 13.10.4. The problem is that it is not always clear when we have a monosyllable and when we have a bisyllabic word instead. As explained in 5.4, there is dialectal and idiolectal variation in the pronunciation of sequences where an unstressed high vowel is immediately followed by another vowel. This has potential orthographic consequences when the difference in syllabification would determine whether a given word is monosyllabic or bisyllabic. For some speakers, including perhaps most Peninsular speakers, words such as *pie* [pi.é] 'I chirped', *guion* [gi.ón] 'hyphen', *rio* [ɾi.ó] 's/he laughed', *hui* [u.í] 'I fled' are bisyllabic, with a sequence in hiatus, and contrast in syllable count with monosyllabic *pie* [pi̯é] 'foot', *dios* [di̯ós] 'god', *dio* [di̯ó] 's/he gave', *fui* [fu̯i] 'I

---

[11] The dictionary of the Real Academia Española (1992) lists *samuray* with plural *samuráis*.
[12] In examples such as *jesuítico* 'jesuitic' (proparoxytone), *intuís* 'you-*pl.* know by intuition' (oxytone in *-s*), the accent mark is according to the general rules.

13.10 Lexical stress and orthography

went/was', for instance, which contain a diphthong. If bisyllabic, the examples in the former group are oxytones and should carry an accent mark according to the general rule for oxytones. Until recently such words were indeed written with an accent mark. In the most recent edition of the academic orthographic rules, however, the accent mark has become only optional in these words and the preferred spelling is without the accent: 'En este caso es admisible el acento gráfico, impuesto por las reglas de ortografía anteriores a estas, si quien escribe percibe nítidamente el hiato y, en consecuencia, considera bisílabas palabras como las mencionadas: *fié, huí, riáis, guión, Sión*, etc.' (RAE 1999: 46) ('The graphic accent, demanded by earlier orthographic rules, is admissible in this case if the writer clearly perceives a hiatus and, consequently, considers that words like those mentioned above are bisyllabic: *fié, huí, riáis, guión, Sión*, etc.'). As a default case, then, all words in this group are considered monosyllabic, in which case the accent mark is superfluous. It is likely that this recent change in the orthography of these words is due to a recognition that the pronunciation as diphthong of all these sequences is widespread in many areas of Latin American Spanish.

13.10.4 Diacritically distinguished pairs

Orthographic accent marks are also used in contexts where they would not be required according to the rules above, in order to differentiate some pairs of segmentally identical words. In some instances, but not all, the graphic distinction is related to the phonological distinction between unstressed and stressed words (i.e. if one member of the pair is unstressed and the other stressed, the lexically stressed word bears a graphic accent). Several subcases must be distinguished.

13.10.4.1 Monosyllabic segmental homophones

Orthographic accent marks are used to distinguish several pairs of segmentally homophonous one-syllable words. In all these pairs, the word with an accent mark is lexically stressed and the other member of the pair is lexically unstressed. The accent mark is thus a clear indication of stress status. The following list is exhaustive:

a) *el* 'the' vs *él* 'he'
   el programa 'the programme'
   él programa 'he programmes'

b) *se* 'reflexive/reciprocal/impersonal/dative pronoun' vs *sé* 'I know; be!'
   se la cantaba 's/he sang it to him/her'
   sé la palabra 'I know the word'
   ¡sé la primera! 'be the first one!'
c) *tu* 'your' (possessive) vs *tú* 'you' (subject pronoun)
   tu pregunta 'your question'
   ¡tú pregunta! 'you ask!'
d) *mi* 'my' (possessive) vs *mí* 'me' (prepositional pronoun)
   para mi tío 'for my uncle'
   para mí, tío 'for me, uncle'
e) *si* 'if' vs *sí* 'yes'; third person prepositional reflexive pronoun
   si lo sabes 'if you know it'
   sí, lo sabes 'yes, you know it'
   por si viene 'in case it comes'
   por sí viene 'it comes by itself'
f) *de* 'of' vs *dé* 'I/he/she give, *subjunct.*; give!'
   de su dinero 'of his/her/your/their money'
   ¡dé su dinero! 'give your money!'
g) *que* 'that' vs *qué* 'what'
   no me dijo que quería 's/he didn't tell me that s/he wanted some'
   no me dijo qué quería 's/he didn't tell me what s/he wanted'
h) *mas* 'but' vs *más* 'more'
   no tristes, mas alegres 'not sad, but happy'
   no tristes, más alegres 'not sad, happier'
i) *aun* 'even though' (and *aun cuando*) vs *aún* 'still'. The unstressed conjunction *aun* 'even though' is monosyllabic. The adverb *aún* 'still' is bisyllabic.
   aun cansados, llegamos a la meta 'even though tired, we reached the goal'
   aún cansados, llegamos a la meta 'still tired, we reached the goal'
   aun cuando ganaste 'even though you won'
   aún cuando ganaste 'even when you won'
j) *te* 'you' (clitic pronoun) vs *té* 'tea'
   quererte 'to love you'
   querer té 'to want tea'

13.10.4.2 Question words

As explained above, question words (*quién* 'who', *cuándo* 'when', *cómo* 'how', etc.) are unstressed in noninterrogative nonexclamative usage. When unstressed, they are written without a written accent. The accent mark is thus an indication of lexical stress, which implies interrogative/exclamative function: *lo escribí como me dijiste* 'I wrote it the way you told me', *como poeta no es muy bueno* 'he is not very good as a poet' vs *no me acuerdo de cómo lo dijiste* 'I don't remember how you said it' (implicit question), *¡Cómo lo sabes!* 'You know it so well!' (exclamative). See 13.6.4 for more examples.

13.10.4.3 Demonstratives

Demonstratives may function as determiners (*este libro* 'this book') or as pronouns (*no me gusta este* 'I don't like this one'). In both cases they are stressed. According to the most recent orthographic rules of the Spanish Academy, demonstratives with a pronominal function must be written with an accent mark in cases of possible ambiguity, as in the following example taken from the Academy's official book of orthographic rules (RAE 1999:49):

Dijo que ésta mañana vendrá 's/he said that this one will come tomorrow'
Dijo que esta mañana vendrá 's/he said that s/he will come this morning'

(In speech there would normally be a difference in phrasing.)

If there is no possible ambiguity, the use of accent marks with demonstrative pronouns is only optional. Nevertheless, many writers consistently employ accent marks on demonstratives used as pronominals: *No quiero éstas ni ésas, sino aquéllas* 'I don't want these or those, but those over there' vs *No quiero estas rosas, ni esas margaritas, sino aquellas gardenias* 'I don't want these roses or those daisies, but those gardenias.' This only applies to demonstratives that can be both determiners and pronouns. The so-called neuter forms, *esto* 'this', *eso* 'that' and *aquello* 'that over there', are never written with an accent mark since they can only be pronouns.

13.10.4.4 Other cases of diacritic accent

Many writers consistently write the adverb *sólo* 'only' (= *solamente*) with an accent mark and the homophonous adjective *solo* 'alone' without it. Both words are lexically stressed on the first syllable. The most recent orthographic rule is that the accent is to be used on the adverb only when there is a risk of ambiguity; e.g. *Juan ha vivido solo en Lima* 'Juan has lived in Lima alone' vs *Juan ha vivido sólo en Lima* 'Juan has lived only in Lima.'

No other pairs of segmental homophones are distinguished graphically by the use of accent marks. For instance the noun *sino* 'fate' and the unstressed conjunction *sino* 'but' are written identically (but differently from *si no* 'if not'): *triste sino el del carretero* 'sad fate, that of the cartwright'; *no triste, sino contento* 'not sad, but happy'; *estoy triste si no estás contento* 'I am sad if you are not happy.'

Finally, a somewhat different case of diacritic accent is the use of an accent mark on the conjunction *o* 'or' when it is between numbers to distinguish it graphically from the number zero: *3 ó 4* '3 or 4'.

EXERCISES

1. Indicate whether the following examples belong to the unmarked, the marked or the exceptional stress pattern: *caníbal, animal, pánico, manifestación, examen, régimen, sintaxis, rabia*.

2. Divide the following words into syllables, underline the stressed syllable and write an accent mark in the examples that need it according to the orthographic rules of Spanish: *area, tarea, monopolio, petroleo, neuralgia, analogia, versatil, serafin, ingenuo*.

3. What is the main difference between the stress pattern of the present and that of the past and future tenses?

4. What are the main generalizations regarding the stress of nouns in Spanish? To what extent is Spanish stress predictable?

5. Are there any important differences between Spanish and English regarding the physical expression of stress?

14 Intonation

14.1 Tone and intonation

The pitch with which we pronounce a syllable or sequence of syllables is determined by the rate of vibration of the vocal folds. A faster rate of vibration results in a higher pitch. The acoustic correlate of pitch is the fundamental frequency or F0 of the sound wave (see 4.2).

In all languages pitch variation is used for linguistic purposes. In many languages of the world differences in pitch are employed to establish lexical contrasts. For instance, in Mandarin Chinese, to give a well-known example, the syllable /ma/ can have four different lexical meanings depending on the tone with which it is pronounced: /ma/ pronounced with a high level tone is the word 'mother'; with a rising contour starting from a mid point, it is 'hemp'; with a low falling–rising contour, it is 'horse'; and with a high falling contour, it is 'to scold'. Languages that make contrastive use of pitch at the lexical level are known as TONE LANGUAGES. Besides Chinese, Thai and other languages of South East Asia, many languages of Sub-Saharan Africa and a number of indigenous languages of Mexico and Central America are tone languages.

In languages like English and Spanish, on the other hand, differences in pitch are not used to distinguish words, but, rather, to express pragmatic meanings. For instance, in Spanish, whether we pronounce /más/ with a high tone, a low tone, a rising tone or a falling tone, among other possibilities, we always have the same word *más* meaning 'more'. What changes is the pragmatic meaning of the utterance. With different pitch contours, the one-word utterance /más/ may be, for instance, a command ¡Más!, a question ¿Más?, a declarative Más (for instance, as a reply to ¿Juan obtuvo el mismo número de puntos que Pedro? 'Did Juan obtain the same number of points as Pedro?'), an incomplete declarative *Más . . .*, etc. It is clear, then, that, unlike in Chinese, words in Spanish do not have any lexical tonal specification. Pitch in Spanish, as in English, is used exclusively to convey discourse-related meanings. Different pitch contours specify different types of utterances, not different words. In the example that we have just used, the utterance happens to be a one-syllable-word utterance, but the same contours, expressing the same pragmatic meanings, are found spread over several syllables and words in longer utterances. The use of pitch for pragmatic or discourse purposes is known as INTONATION and languages, like Spanish and English, which use pitch only at this level are referred to as INTONATIONAL LANGUAGES (as opposed to TONE LANGUAGES). There are also languages, such as Swedish, that combine lexical and intonational uses of pitch.

The fact that in a language like Spanish, pitch is not used to distinguish one word from another does not mean that pitch (intonation) is unimportant in Spanish. We may note, for example, that very often the only difference between a declarative and an interrogative sentence in Spanish is provided by intonation, as in *Llegaron mis amigos* 'my friends arrived' vs *¿Llegaron mis amigos?* 'Did my friends arrive?' Intonational differences also allow us to mark information as relatively more or less important and to express many other meanings at the level of discourse.

14.2 The atoms of intonation

As just mentioned, in languages like Spanish and English, the same 'text' can be pronounced with very different intonational contours, depending on the contribution that it is intended to make to the discourse. These utterance-level intonational contours or melodies can be analysed as consisting of specific tonal events associated with certain syllables in the text. In Spanish (and English) there are two main landmarks for the realization of tonal events: lexically stressed syllables and ends of phrases. Tonal contours associated with stressed syllables are known as PITCH ACCENTS and tones aligned with phrasal boundaries receive the name of BOUNDARY TONES in the Autosegmental-Metrical theory of intonation analysis, which is the theoretical framework that we will employ in this chapter (see Pierrehumbert 1980; Beckman and Pierrehumbert 1986; Ladd 1996).[1]

As we already know from Chapter 13, pitch accents may be of various types. We may have a high tone or tonal peak aligned with the stressed syllable (H*), a low tone or tonal valley (L*) or a more complex configuration such as a rise from a valley at the onset of the stressed syllable with a peak reached perhaps

---

[1] Applications of this model to Spanish include Sosa (1999, 2003), Face (2001, 2002a, 2002b), Beckman *et al.* (2002) and Hualde (2002, 2003a).

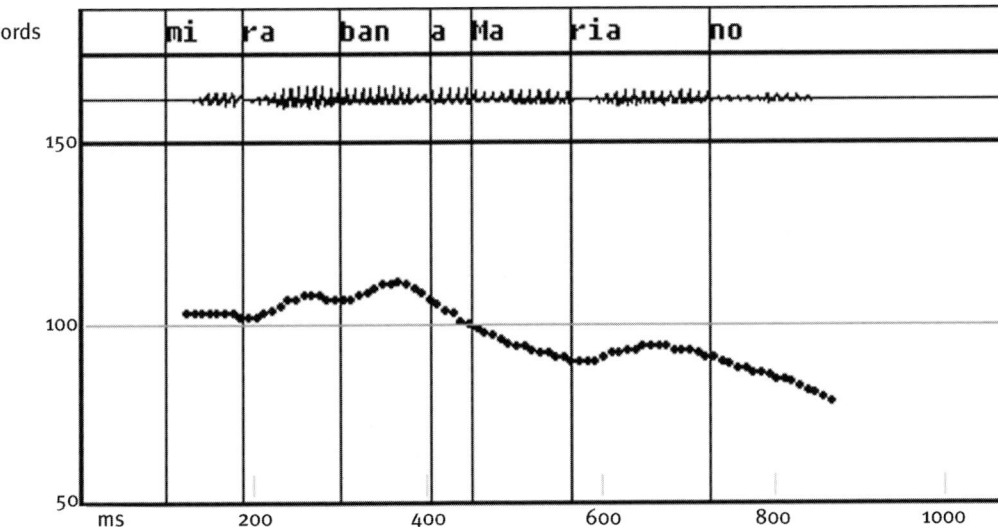

Figure 14.1. *Miraban a Mariano* 'They were watching Mariano.' Example of final declarative with two rising accents, prenuclear and nuclear. Notice the displacement of the prenuclear peak to the posttonic and the overall declining trend.

on the next syllable (L*H) or a fall from a high point in the pretonic to a valley in the stressed syllable (HL*), among other possibilities. Notice that, in the formalism that we are using, an asterisk indicates that the tone is associated with a stressed syllable. In the case of bitonal pitch-accents (rising and falling contours), the asterisk is placed after whichever of the two tones appears to be more closely aligned with the stressed syllable.

Boundary tones (indicated with the symbol %) can also be of different types: we may have a final high tone (H%), a final low tone (L%) or more complex endings. We will also make use of the symbols H- and L- to indicate tonal targets at the end of intermediate phrases (intermediate boundary tones). The complete intonational contour of an utterance is the result of interpolation between tonally specified landmarks.

14.3 Simple declarative sentences: nuclear and prenuclear accents

Here we will consider some typical examples of basic Spanish intonational contours. In the examples used in the figures in this chapter voiceless consonants are avoided as much as possible since they cause interrupted stretches in the F0 curve, as they are produced without vibration of the vocal folds. On the other hand, voiced obstruents and other voiced consonants produce small localized dips in F0. In Fig. 14.1 the /b/ of *miraban* can be seen to have that effect. These relatively small (microprosodic) segmental effects should be ignored in the analysis of the curve.

In Fig. 14.1, we have an F0 tracing of the sentence *Miraban a Mariano* 'They were watching Mariano', produced with declarative intonation.[2] As we can see in this figure, in neutral declarative sentences the overall contour shows a progressive lowering of the pitch, from a rise associated with the first stressed syllable to the end of the sentence (see Prieto *et al.* 1996). Examining the F0 contour in more detail, the contour in Fig. 14.1 can be analysed as consisting of two rising pitch accents associated with the lexically stressed syllables of the two words *mi<u>ra</u>ban* and *Ma<u>ria</u>no*, plus a final low boundary tone L%.

If we now consider the shape of the two pitch accents in our example, we notice that in *Ma<u>ria</u>no* the pitch rises from a low point or valley at the beginning of the stressed syllable to a peak approximately in the middle of this syllable. In *mi<u>ra</u>ban*, on the other hand, there is also a rise from a valley through the stressed syllable but the pitch continues rising after the end of this syllable and reaches its peak in the middle of the next syllable (the posttonic).

Generally, the last pitch accent is perceived as having greater prominence than preceding accents, although, as in this example, it normally has a smaller rise in F0, given the overall declining pattern of neutral declarative sentences. We will say that it is the NUCLEAR ACCENT of the phrase, whereas other pitch accents before it in the phrase are called PRENUCLEAR ACCENTS. In our example there is, thus, a nuclear accent associated with the stressed syllable of *Ma<u>ria</u>no* and a prenuclear accent associated with the stressed syllable of *mi<u>ra</u>ban*. The displacement of the peak to the posttonic that we have noticed is extremely frequent in prenuclear accents in Spanish.[3] We will represent a rising accent with a delayed peak as L*H. This notation is intended to indicate that of the two tones, L and H, in a rising configuration, in this case the L tone is the one that is realized within the accented syllable (at the beginning). This allows us to reserve the notation LH* (with the asterisk on the second tone) for rising accents whose peak is realized within the accented syllable. As mentioned, the overall contour in this example is falling after the first peak, so that the nuclear peak has a lower F0 value than the prenuclear one, even if it is perceived as more prominent. For greater clarity we will indicate the nuclear accent in boldface in our transcriptions. The syllable with which the nuclear accent is associated

---

[2] All contours were produced by the author, except when otherwise indicated.
[3] See Prieto *et al.* (1995) for a controlled study of factors affecting peak displacement in Spanish.

14.4 Differences from English in placement

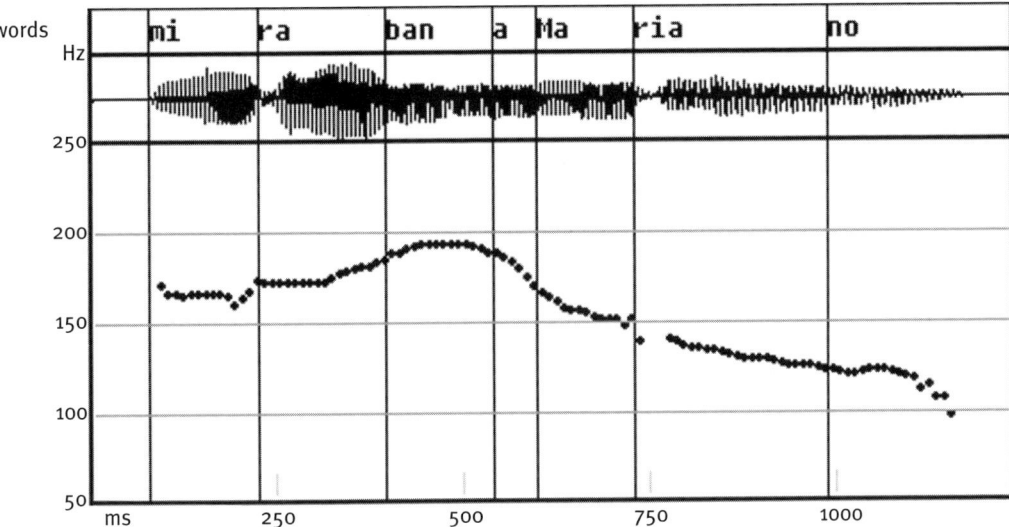

Figure 14.2. *Miraban a Mariano* 'They were watching Mariano.' Example of declarative with falling nuclear accent. As in Fig. 14.1, notice the displacement of the prenuclear peak to the posttonic. This contour was produced by a female speaker, which accounts for the higher F0 values than in the rest of the contours in this chapter.

is in small capitals:

(1) mi<u>ra</u>ban a Ma<u>RIA</u>no]   (= Fig. 14.1)
      | | |
    L*H   LH* L%

Nuclear accents in declaratives in Spanish may have one of two common shapes. One of the them is the rise followed by a fall illustrated in Fig. 14.1. The other possibility is a fall throughout the stressed syllable (represented as HL*), as in Fig. 14.2. Different Spanish varieties appear to make use of these two nuclear configurations to different degrees. The rising nuclear contour LH* is more emphatic than the falling one HL* in varieties where both are used.

14.4 Differences from English in the placement of nuclear accents

In Spanish the position of the nuclear accent is to a very large extent fixed on the last word of the intonational phrase, except for special cases of narrow contrastive focus. In this, Spanish differs from English, which has both more complex rules and a greater flexibility in the assignment of nuclear accents to nonfinal words. This seems to be in fact a general difference between Romance and West Germanic languages. Spanish agrees with Italian, Catalan, Portuguese and other Romance languages in displaying a very strong tendency for always placing the nuclear accent on the last content word, whereas English, like Dutch and German, places the nuclear accent on nonfinal words in a number of contexts. Here we will consider some of the main cases where we seem to have systematic differences in nuclear accent placement between English and Spanish (or West Germanic and Romance). The description is to a large extent based on Ladd (1996).

14.4.1 Repeated information

To begin with, whereas in English repeated information at the end of the sentence is deaccented, so that the nuclear accent falls on an earlier word, in Spanish the tendency is to keep the nuclear accent at the end of the sentence even in the case of repeated noninformative words. We can see this in the following examples. The syllable with nuclear accent is in small capitals. Prenuclear accents are not indicated in this section:

(2) a. Por favor pon en su SITIO todo lo que está fuera de su SITIO.
Please put in its PLACE everything that is OUT of place.
b. ¿El café lo quieres con AZÚCAR o sin AZÚCAR?
You want your coffee with SUGAR or withOUT sugar?

Similarly, in an example like (3) where the prefix is the object of correction and everything else is repeated, the nuclear accent would be placed on that syllable in English. In Spanish instead it would be common to keep the accent on the lexically stressed syllable:

(3) No es un negocio de importaCIÓN, es un negocio de exportaCIÓN.
It is not an IMport business, it is an EXport business.

14.4.2 Object pronouns and indefinites

In English object pronouns are generally unaccented. Thus whereas in the English sentence in (4a) the nuclear accent falls on the object, in (4b) it falls on the verb, the object pronoun being deaccented. The same pattern would seem to occur in the corresponding Spanish sentences. An important difference, however, is that Spanish clitic pronouns cannot be accented, even if contrastive focus is intended. These pronouns are lexically unstressed and form a single phonological word with their host verb. Thus, under contrastive focus, we may

14.4 Differences from English in placement

have nuclear accent on *him* in (4c), but in Spanish a nonclitic object would have to be added to obtain the same pragmatic effect:

(4) a. Tengo que llamar a JUAN.
   I have to call JOHN.
 b. Tengo que llaMARle.
   I have to CALL him.
 c. Tengo que llamarle a ÉL. (not *tengo que llamarLE)
   I have to call HIM. (contrastive focus)

Spanish does not make the accentual contrast between indefinite and other arguments that has been described for English (Ladd 1996:179–80).[4] In the Spanish examples in (5) the nuclear accent is uniformly placed on the last word. In English, on the other hand, the nuclear accent is usually on the verb when the object is an indefinite, as in (5c–d). That is, in English these indefinite pronouns have the same accentual behaviour as object pronouns, but in Spanish they are fully accentable words:

(5) a. Conozco a JUAN.   b. He visto una VAca.
   I know JOHN.   I saw a COW.
 c. Conozco a ALguien. d. He visto ALgo.
   I KNOW someone.   I SAW something.

14.4.3 Final predicates and adverbials

In English (and the other West Germanic languages) there is a tendency to place the nuclear accent on the subject in simple intransitive sentences where the whole sentence is intended as new information. The nonfinal nuclear accent does not necessarily indicate narrow focus on the word bearing it. In comparable sentences in Spanish, we usually have a postverbal subject, which will bear the nuclear accent by virtue of its position at the end of the sentence:

(6) a. Ha salido el SOL.   b. Se ha roto la MÁquina.
   The SUN came out.   The maCHINE broke.

More generally, it has been said that in English the preference is for placing the nuclear accent on arguments (subject, object, etc.) rather than on verbs, especially when the latter are semantically predictable or not very informative. As Ladd (1996) shows, this rule does not operate in languages like Spanish and its close relatives, where, instead, the nuclear accent is uniformly

---

[4] In this too Spanish is like other Romance languages, whereas English agrees with Dutch (Ladd 1996:179–81).

placed on the last content word of the sentence. This is particularly clear in cases where Spanish and English use the same word order, as in the following examples:

(7) a. Tengo mucho trabajo que haCER.   b. Le dieron un paquete para enviAR.
    I have a lot of WORK to do.   They gave him a PACKage to send.

Sentence-final time and place adverbials and prepositional phrases are also commonly deaccented in English, as in the example in (8) (adapted from Ladd 1996:182), but will regularly receive nuclear accent in Spanish, which we give above the English:

(8) Hay una mosca en la sopa.
    There is a FLY in the soup.

14.4.4 Narrow focus

One may say that Spanish, like other Romance languages, prefers to make use of different word orders instead of shifting the nuclear accent to a nonfinal word as in English (Vallduví 1992; Ortiz-Lira 1994). This also applies to cases where narrow contrastive focus on a constituent is intended. Thus, whereas in English narrow focus on the subject would be expressed by placing the nuclear accent on this constituent without altering the order of constituents in the sentence, in Spanish it would be more natural to shift this element to sentence-final position, where it too will receive nuclear accent, as in (9):

(9) Lo ha traído mi herMAno.
    My BROther brought it.

Placing the nuclear accent on a nonfinal word to express contrastive narrow focus is not impossible in Spanish (*mi herMAno lo ha traído, no María*), but this is a more marked option than that in (9). (See section 14.5.2 for the tonal contours associated with contrastive narrow focus.)

14.5 Non-neutral declarative sentences

14.5.1 Old and new information

In a declarative sentence the whole sentence may be intended as new information. In such cases we will typically find a descending staircase contour, where pitch accents are progressively lower, as mentioned above. An example of such a contour is given in Fig. 14.3, *Mariana miraba la luna* 'Mariana was watching the moon.'

14.5 Non-neutral declarative sentences

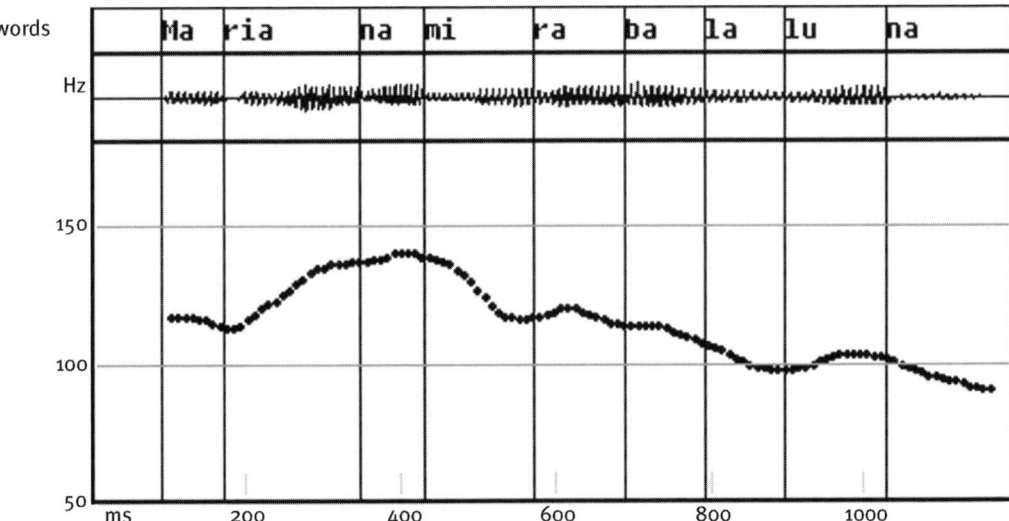

Figure 14.3. *Mariana miraba la LUNA* 'Mariana was watching the moon.' The whole sentence is new information. Descending staircase pattern.

On the other hand, if part of the sentence is 'given' or repeated information, the pitch will typically rise to reach a high point at the end of the 'given' portion of the utterance. Figure 14.4 is an example of the same sentence as Fig. 14.3, *Mariana miraba la luna*, as may be produced as an answer to the question *¿Qué miraba Mariana?* 'What was Mariana watching?', or perhaps to *¿Mariana miraba las estrellas?* 'Was Mariana watching the stars?', where the portion *Mariana miraba* is repeated information. Notice that the highest point is reached at the end of *miraba*. We may transcribe this pattern as containing a high boundary tone H- at the end of an intermediate phrase, which signals an overall rising pattern up to this point. After this high boundary tone, there is fall to a valley at the beginning of the syllable with nuclear accent, *lu-*, which bears a LH* pitch accent, as in other examples:

(10) Mariana miraba] la LUna]   (= Fig. 14.4)
         | | | |
        L*H   L*H H- **LH*** L%

context: *¿Qué miraba Mariana?*

To give another example, in the contour in Fig. 14.5, *Emilio viene mañana* 'Emilio is coming tomorrow', a H- tone appears at the end of *viene*, separating out the portion *Emilio viene* as given information. This pattern

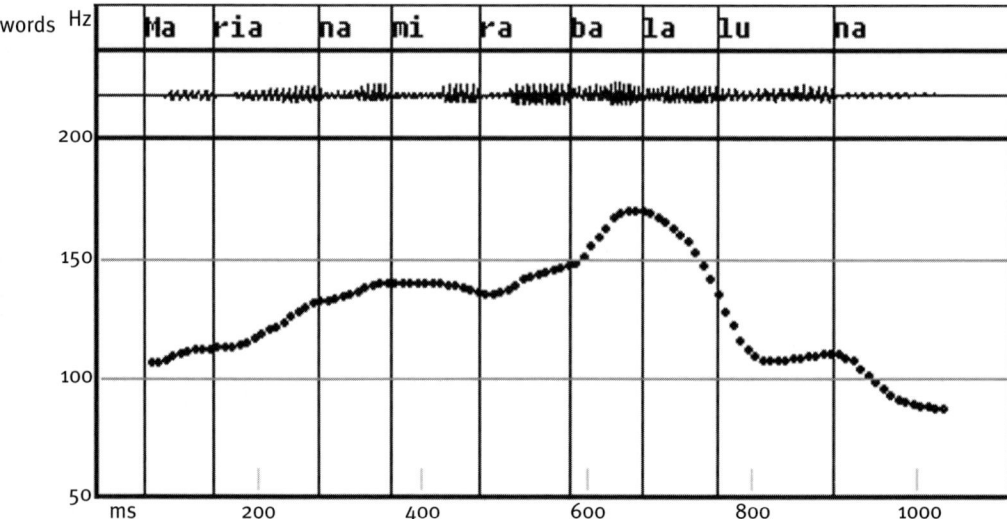

Figure 14.4. *Mariana miraba*_{H-} *la LUna* 'Mariana was watching the moon.' *Mariana miraba* is 'given' information.

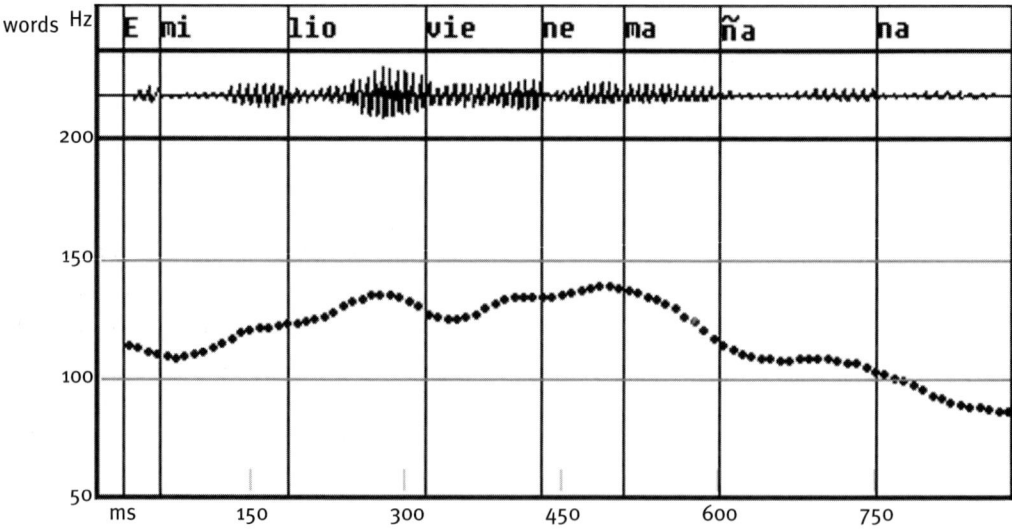

Figure 14.5. *Emilio viene*_{H-} *mañana* 'Emilio is coming tomorrow', where *Emilio viene* is 'given' information; e.g. as an answer to the question *¿Cuándo viene Emilio?* 'When is Emilio coming?'

14.5 Non-neutral declarative sentences

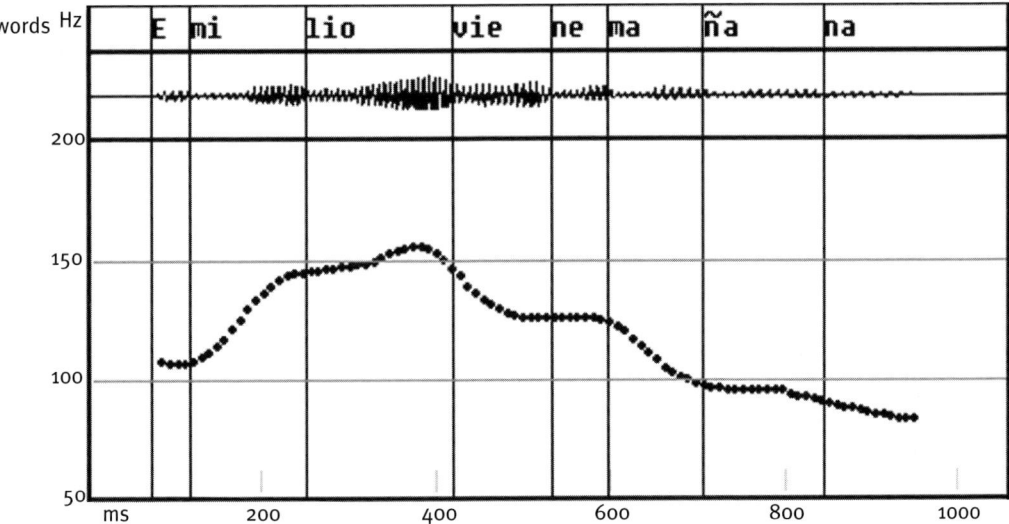

Figure 14.6. Emilio_H. viene mañana '(As for) Emilio, he is coming tomorrow.'

would be appropriate as an answer to the question ¿*Cuándo viene Emilio?* 'When is Emilio coming?':

(11) E<u>mi</u>lio <u>vie</u>ne] ma<u>ÑA</u>na]   (= Fig. 14.5)
         | | | | |
        L*H   L*H   H-   **LH***   L%

context: ¿*Cuándo viene Emilio?*

In Fig. 14.6 we have another rendition of *Emilio viene mañana* with a different contour, corresponding to a different division of given and new information. In this case, *Emilio* is given information and *viene mañana* is new information. We may gloss it with a topicalized structure: '(as for) Emilio, he is coming tomorrow'. This could be an answer to ¿*Qué sabes de Emilio?* 'What do you know about Emilio?' Now the intermediate H- boundary tone is placed at the end of *Emilio*.

(12) E<u>mi</u>lio] <u>vie</u>ne ma<u>ÑA</u>na]   (= Fig. 14.6)
         | | | | |
        L*H H-L*H   **LH***   L%

context: ¿*Qué sabes de Emilio?*

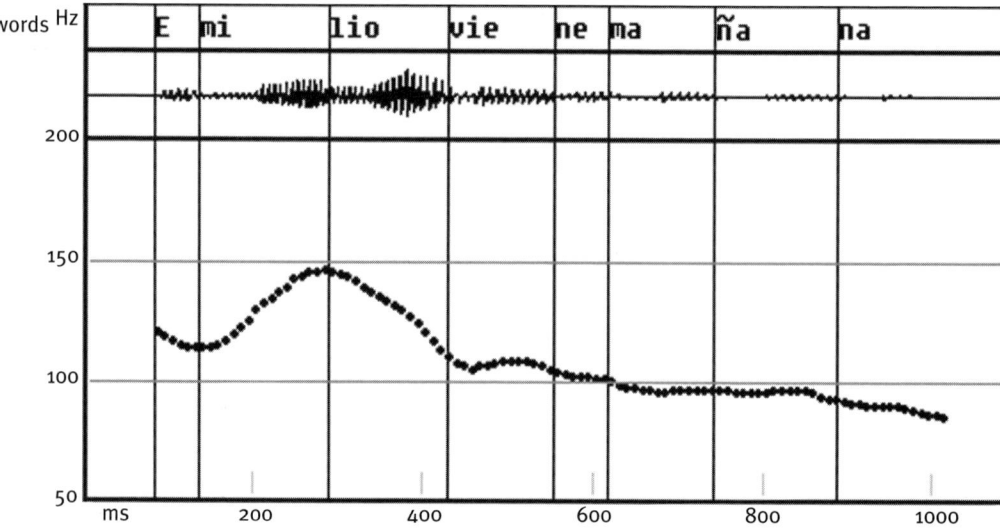

Figure 14.7. *Emilio viene mañana* 'Emilio is coming tomorrow.' Narrow contrastive focus on *Emilio*.

14.5.2 Contrastive narrow focus on nonfinal words

As explained above, to a great extent Spanish uses different word orders to produce the effects obtained in English by shifting the position of the nuclear accent. In particular, constituents may be highlighted by positioning them at the end of the sentence, where they will receive nuclear accent. It is, however, also possible to have contrastive narrow focus on a nonfinal word by shifting the nuclear accent, as in English. This is a more marked option in Spanish. For instance as a reply to *Mañana viene María ¿verdad?* 'María is coming tomorrow, right?' we may have *No, mañana viene Emilio*, but also *No, Emilio viene mañana* 'No, Emilio is coming tomorrow' with contrastive focus on a nonfinal word. The corresponding contour is illustrated in Fig. 14.7. Notice that in this example, where the word *Emilio* receives nuclear accent, the accentual peak is reached within the limits of the stressed syllable and there is a rapid fall on the posttonic. Another thing to notice in this contour is that other, postnuclear, accentual peaks are greatly reduced or downstepped.

A transcription of the contour in Fig. 14.7 is given in (13). We add the symbol (!) to the postnuclear pitch accents to indicate their reduced nature (this is the traditional symbol for tonal downstep in studies of tone in African languages):

14.5 Non-neutral declarative sentences

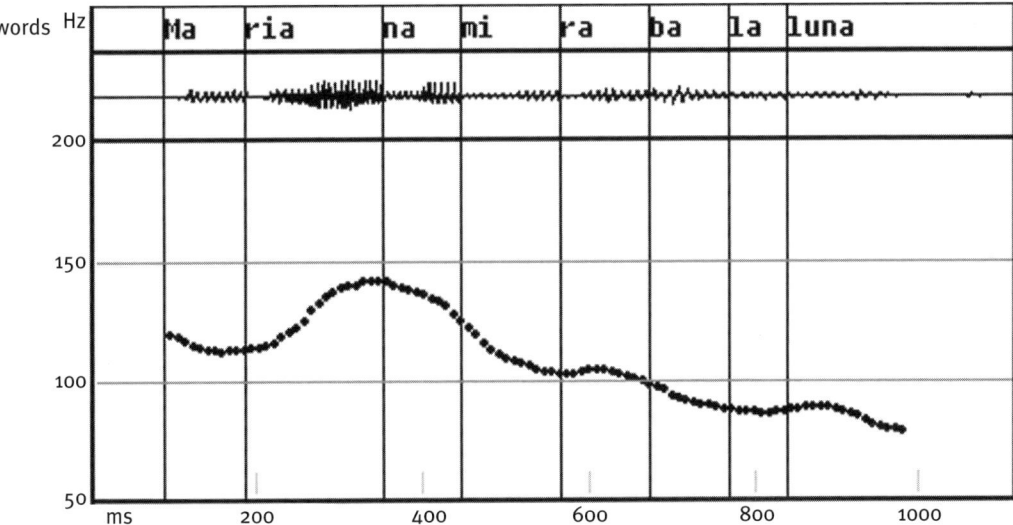

Figure 14.8. *Mariana miraba la luna* 'Mariana was watching the moon.' Narrow contrastive focus on *Mariana*.

(13) Emilio viene mañana]   (= Fig. 14.7)
 | | | |
 LH* !LH* !LH* L%

context: *Mañana viene María ¿verdad?*

Another analytical possibility would be to represent the nuclear accent in (13), a rise to a peak within the stressed syllable immediately followed by a fall in the posttonic, as tritonal LH*L, which would trigger downstep or reduction of the following postnuclear pitch accents.

Another example of the same type of contour with nuclear accent on the first word, expressing contrastive focus, is given in Fig. 14.8, *Mariana miraba la luna* 'Mariana was watching the moon.' This could be a reply to *¿Emilio miraba la luna?* 'Was Emilio watching the moon?' This figure can be compared with the broad focus contour in Fig. 14.3. Notice again that in Fig. 14.8 there is a rapid fall on the posttonic of the word under narrow focus and considerable reduction of postnuclear accents.

(14) Mariana miraba la luna]   (= Fig. 14.8)
 | | | |
 LH* !LH* !LH* L%

context: *¿Emilio miraba la luna?*

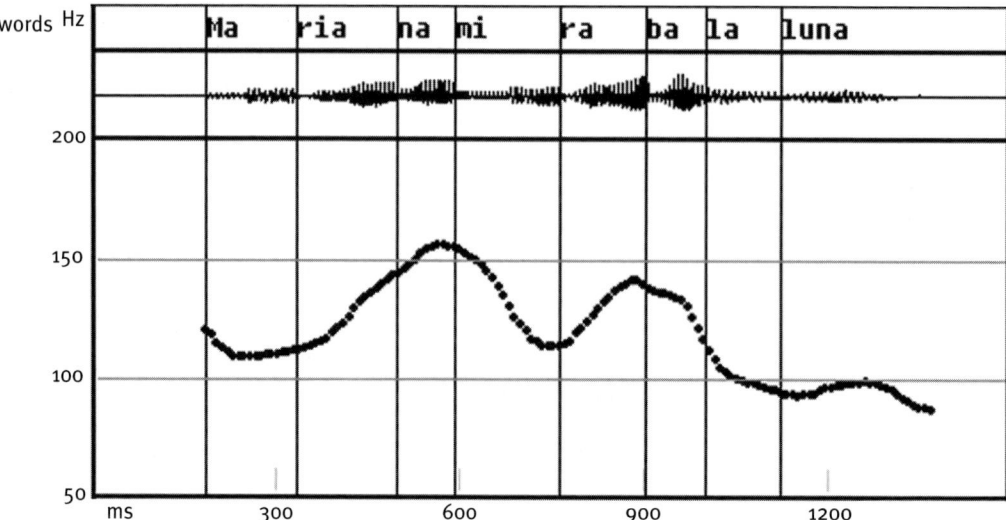

Figure 14.9. *Mariana mirAba la luna* 'Mariana was WATching the moon.' Narrow contrastive focus on *miraba*. The word *Mariana* is repeated information.

In Fig. 14.9, *Mariana mirAba la luna* 'Mariana was WATching the moon', the second word has the nuclear accent. This could be appropriate in a context where *Mariana* is given information and the speaker wants to express contrastive focus on *miraba*. The context could be, for instance, *¿Has dicho que Mariana esperaba la luna?* 'Did you say that Mariana was waiting for the moon?' Notice the contrast in the alignment of the accentual peaks. Since *Mariana* is given information, the accentual peak is displaced, and merges with the H- tone at the end of the constituent in this example. In the word *miraba*, however, as in the other examples of contrastive focus above, the accentual peak is reached within the stressed syllable and there is a fast fall on the posttonic. This difference in alignment distinguishes words expressing given information (topics) from words with narrow focus.

(15) Mariana] mirAba la luna]   (= Fig. 14.9)
     | | | | |
     L*H H- **LH*** !LH*   L%

context: *¿Mariana esperaba la luna?*

14.5.3 'Circumflex' declarative contours

The term 'circumflex' is employed in Spanish intonation to refer to a pitch contour where the pitch accent associated with the stressed syllable of the last

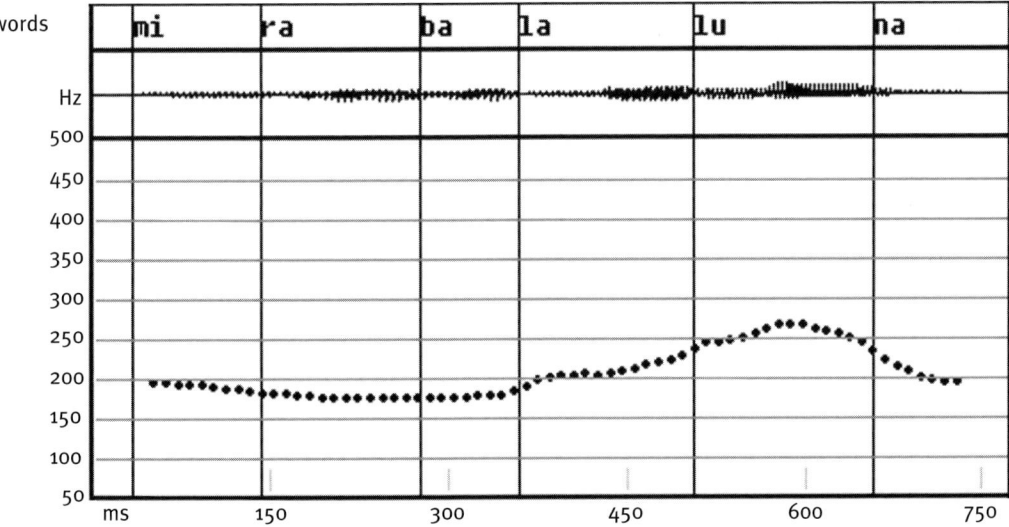

Figure 14.10. *Miraba la luna* 'S/he was watching the moon.' Circumflex declarative contour. Mexican Spanish.

content word – the nuclear accent – is higher than preceding pitch accents. In, for instance, Madrid Spanish, such contours are employed to convey special emphasis. In some other Spanish varieties, including Mexican and Puerto Rican Spanish, on the other hand, similar circumflex contours are common in pragmatically neutral contexts. A Mexican example is given in Fig. 14.10. In this example the prenuclear accent is low, L*.

(16) Mi<u>ra</u>ba la <u>LU</u>na]   (= Fig. 14.10)
       | | |
       L*   LH* L%

context: *¿Qué hacía Mariana?* (Mexico)

14.6 Questions

Structurally, there are two main types of questions: yes/no questions and pronominal or question-word questions. In pronominal questions, the presence of the question word suffices to identify the utterance as a question. In Spanish yes/no questions, on the other hand, intonation may be the only difference from a statement.

Unmarked pronominal questions have a falling contour similar to that of declaratives. The highest point corresponds to a pitch accent associated with the question word. Other pitch accents are progressively lower and there is a

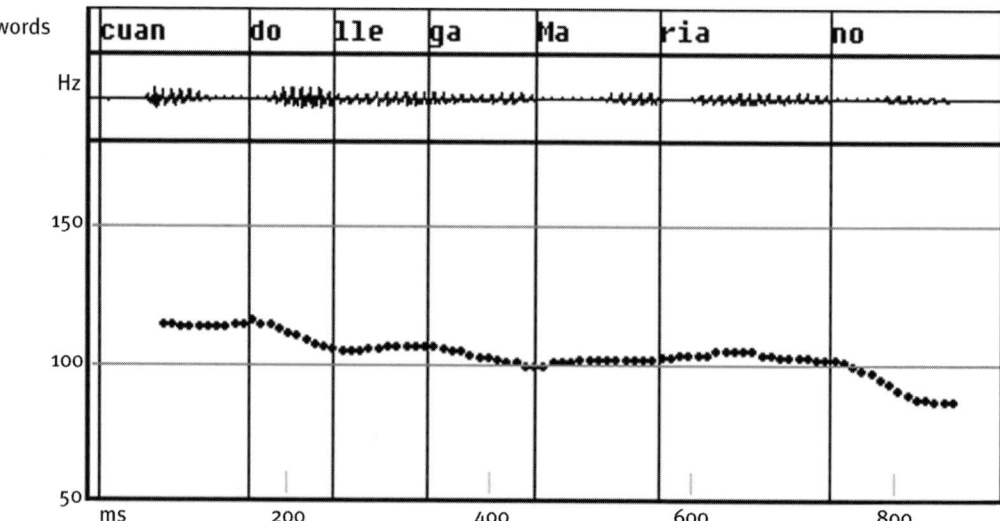

Figure 14.11.   *¿Cuándo llega Mariano?* 'When is Mariano arriving?' Neutral pronominal question.

final descent after the last stressed syllable. An example is given in Fig. 14.11: *¿Cuándo llega Mariano?* 'When is Mariano arriving?'

(17) Cuándo llega MaRIAno]   (= Fig. 14.11)
      | | | |
    L*H   L*H   **LH*** L%

It is possible, however, to find pronominal questions with a final rise (that is, a H% boundary tone), as in Fig. 14.12. These questions are less neutral. They add some pragmatic nuance, established in the context of the conversation. This added meaning may be insistence, politeness, tentativeness, etc.

As for yes/no questions, in most Spanish dialects these have a final rise (H%) from a low point on the last stressed syllable. As mentioned, this intonational feature may be the only difference from declaratives: compare Fig. 14.13 *¿Miraban a Mariano?* 'Were they watching Mariano?' with the corresponding declarative in Fig. 14.1. In the contour in Fig. 14.13 there is a target low on the last stressed syllable (a L* pitch accent) followed by a final rise (a H% boundary tone):

(18) Miraban a MaRIAno]   (= Fig. 14.13)
      | | |
    L*H   L* H%

14.6 Questions

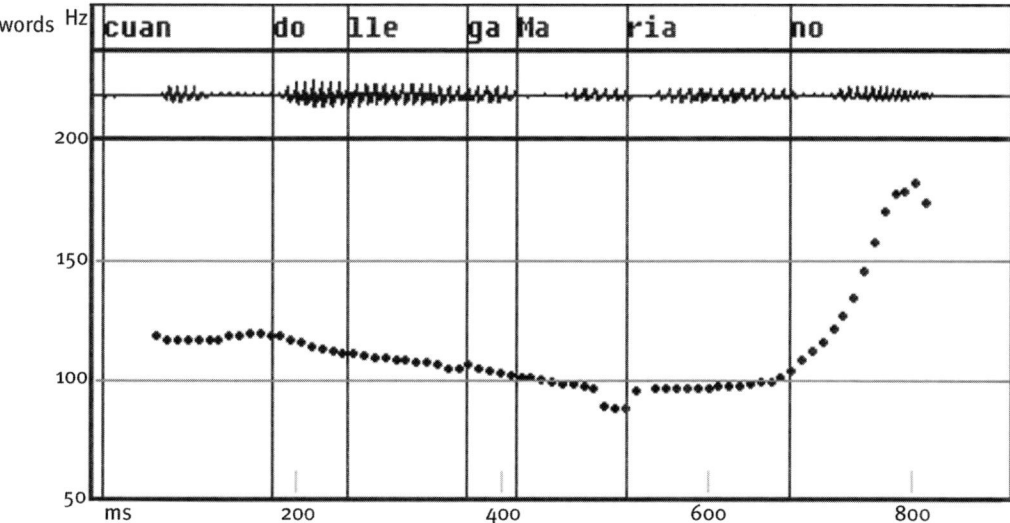

Figure 14.12.   ¿Cuándo llega Mariano? 'When is Mariano arriving?' Pragmatically marked pronominal question.

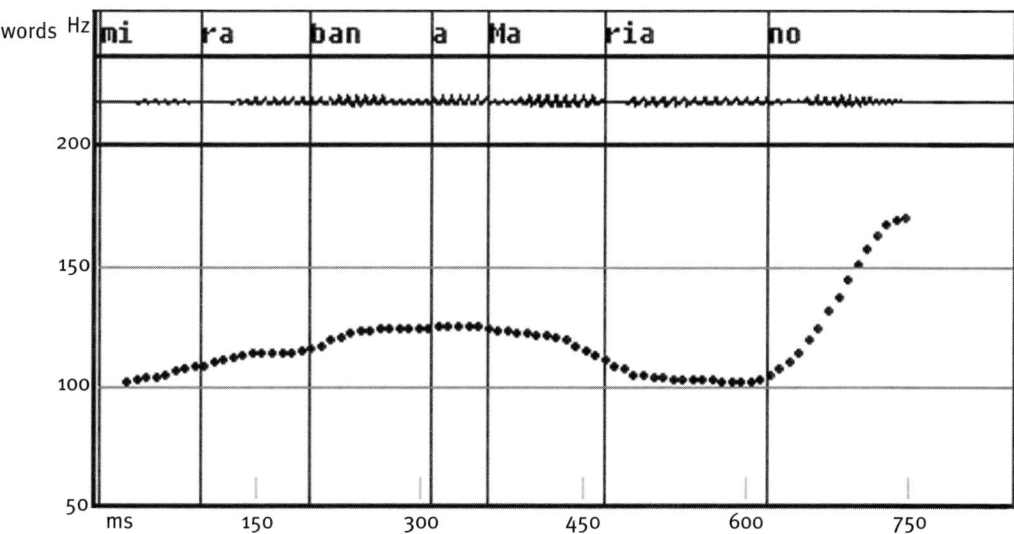

Figure 14.13.   ¿Miraban a Mariano? 'Were they watching Mariano?' Neutral yes/no question.

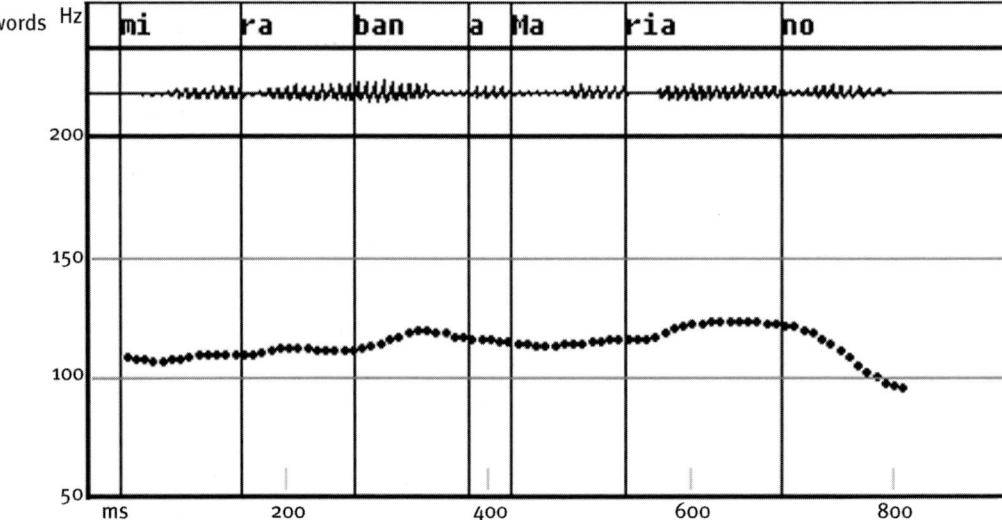

Figure 14.14.   ¿*Miraban a Mariano?* 'Were they watching Mariano?' Circumflex interrogative pattern.

Nevertheless, it is also possible to have yes/no questions with a final fall. Normally these questions have a circumflex pattern: a rise up to the syllable bearing nuclear accent and a fall from this syllable to the end of the utterance. An example is given in Fig. 14.14. We indicate the upstepping of the nuclear accent with the symbol (¡):

(19) Mir<u>a</u>ban a Mariano]   (= Fig. 14.14)

       | | |

    L*H   ¡**LH*** L%

Spanish dialects differ in the frequency with which they use circumflex patterns in yes/no questions. In Madrid Spanish, such contours are pragmatically marked and appear to be primarily used in 'checks' where the speaker wants to verify the information (see Quilis 1993:441). In Caribbean and Canary Island Spanish, on the other hand, this is the unmarked pattern in questions (Quilis 1993:469). In fact, Sosa (1999:245) finds only circumflex patterns in Caribbean questions. Circumflex questions are also unmarked in Asturias and Galicia, in northwestern Spain. As we see, one of the possible differences among dialects regarding intonation is that what is a marked pattern with a narrow set of pragmatic meanings in one dialect may be the unmarked contour in another dialect.

14.7 Intonation and phrasing

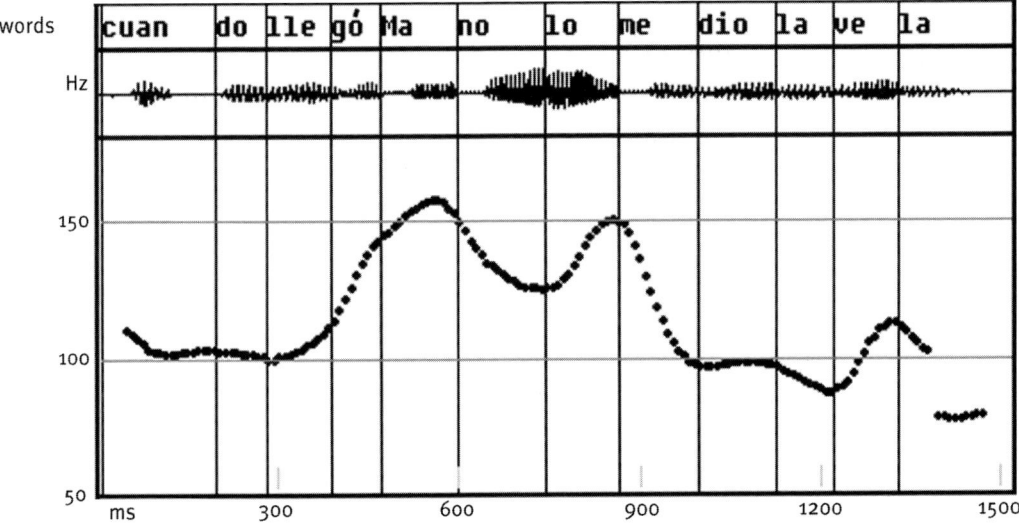

Figure 14.15. *Cuando llegó Manolo, me dio la vela* 'When Manolo arrived, he gave me the candle.'

14.7 Intonation and phrasing

Intonation is one of the main cues to phrasing, besides the introduction of pauses and the lengthening of phrase-final syllables. Consider, for instance, the following pair of examples:[5]

(20) a. Cuando llegó Manolo, me dio la vela.
    'When Manolo arrived, he gave me the candle.'
  b. Cuando llegó, Manolo me dio la vela.
    'When he arrived, Manolo gave me the candle.'

In these sentences, the comma indicates orthographically the presence of an intonational break, often realized by a high boundary tone H% and an optional pause, as in Fig. 14.15 and Fig. 14.16.

In Fig. 14.15 there is no internal pause and only the rise at the end of the first clause indicates the boundary. We may analyse this example as consisting of two intonational phrases. The first one has a L* nuclear accent on Manolo, followed by a LH% tone, indicating an incomplete sentence:

---

[5] Notice that here the word *cuando* 'when' is unstressed and does not bear a pitch accent, unlike in (17), where it is a question word (see 13.6.4).

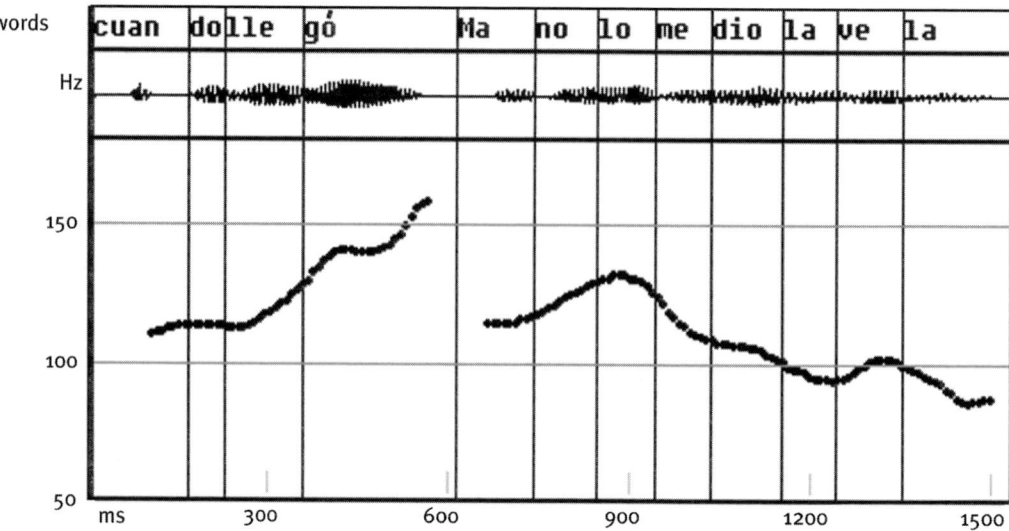

Figure 14.16.   *Cuando llegó, Manolo me dio la vela* 'When he arrived, Manolo gave me the candle.'

(21) Cuando llegó Ma<u>no</u>lo] me <u>dio</u> la <u>vE</u>la]   (= Fig. 14.15)
         | | | | | |
        L*H   L* LH% LH* **LH*** L%

In Fig. 14.16 we can see that internal phrasing is marked both by the presence of a LH% boundary and by a short pause.[6]

(22) Cuando lle<u>gó</u>] Ma<u>no</u>lo me <u>dio</u> la <u>vE</u>la]   (= Fig. 14.16)
         | | | | | |
       LH* LH%   L*H   LH* **LH***   L%

In general, a rising or level pitch at the end of an intonational group indicates continuation, lack of finality.

14.8 A note on rhythm

Besides their intonational and accentual differences, English and Spanish also differ in their rhythm. It has been said that English is a STRESS-TIMED language, whereas Spanish is SYLLABLE-TIMED. These labels refer to the auditory impression produced by the language. English 'sounds as if' the

---

[6] Notice, incidentally, that, in this example, the pitch rises through the pretonic syllable *lle-*. Crucially, however, there would be a more complex contour on this syllable (and greater duration) if the word were *llego* 'I arrive', instead of *llegó* 's/he arrived', in the same intonational context. The simple inspection of isolated pitch contours does not allow us to identify the stressed syllables in every case.

duration of intervals between stressed syllables were kept more or less constant, by reducing or expanding the duration of intervening unstressed syllables. Spanish, on the other hand, 'sounds as if' all syllables, stressed and unstressed, had the same duration. This is reflected in the respective poetic traditions. For instance, a line in an English sonnet is an iambic pentameter; that is, rhythmic well-formedness is a function of stress. In Spanish poetry, on the other hand, well-formedness is determined by the number of syllables. In a Spanish *soneto* each line must be an *endecasílabo*, or eleven-syllable line (more accurately, a line with ten syllables counting up to the last stressed syllable).

There appears to be some phonetic truth in this classification, although the facts are rather more subtle. Clearly it is not the case that all Spanish syllables have the same duration. To begin with, segments have different intrinsic durations. For instance, the tap [ɾ] is shorter than the trill [r̄] and than a voiceless stop. Also, among vowels, there are intrinsic differences in duration, with low vowels having greater duration than high vowels. In any language, the duration of syllables or sequences of syllables will thus depend in great part on their segmental composition. Besides these intrinsic differences, factors such as stress and proximity to the end of phrases also affect the duration of syllables.

If we consider the durational effects of stress on syllables with identical segmental composition (at the level of phonemes), both in English and in Spanish stressed syllables tend to have greater duration than unstressed syllables. In both languages duration is a correlate of stress. These differences in duration between stressed and unstressed syllables are, however, much greater in English than in Spanish. As we saw in section 13.2, segmental effects on the quality of both vowels and consonants in stressed and unstressed syllables are also much greater in English than in Spanish. In English the difference between stressed and unstressed syllables is thus more salient than in Spanish. (On the other hand, intonational deaccenting of less important information is more common in English than in Spanish.) This contributes to a perceptual difference between the two languages, interpretable in terms of rhythm. The fact that English has more and more complex consonant clusters than Spanish also has an effect on the perception of a rhythmic difference (see Dauer 1983; Ramus *et al.* 1999; Grabe and Low 2003; Toledo 1988).

14.9 A note on dialectal differences in prosody

For anyone who has travelled in the Spanish-speaking world or has interacted with Spanish speakers from different areas, it is evident that prosodic facts of rhythm and intonation are often enough to determine the national or regional origin of speakers. In part this is due to the fact that different dialects do not always have the same intonational contours, or that, as we have mentioned, they may employ similar contours with very different values. For instance, circumflex yes/no question patterns are pragmatically marked and thus relatively infrequent in Madrid and Mexico City, but they constitute the normal, unmarked, yes/no question pattern in many Caribbean dialects. Similarly, the circumflex declarative pattern (with a higher nuclear accent than preceding prenuclear accents) is solely emphatic in Madrid but a common nonemphatic declarative contour in Mexico City. However, besides these differences, which we may consider 'phonological', there are also differences of phonetic detail, having to do with the precise alignment of tonal targets with respect to stressed syllables and patterns of vowel lengthening and shortening. For instance, we may find a greater lengthening of certain stressed syllables, accompanied by a salient tonal contour within that syllable, or a greater lengthening of final syllables in certain contexts. To give an example, Kaisse (2001) describes a nuclear contour in Argentinian Spanish, which she calls 'the long fall', involving a pronounced fall from a peak completely contained within the stressed syllable, which is extraordinarily lengthened. The 'long fall' is typical of Argentinian Spanish, to the extent that its use may be sufficient for the speaker's dialect to be identified. (See also, on dialectal differences, Quilis, 1987; Sosa 1999:177–245; Willis 2003).

The reduction of vowels in unstressed syllables, as in Mexican and Andean Spanish (see 2.3) also contributes to producing an identifiable rhythmic effect.

EXERCISES

1 Describe and analyse the contours that we may expect for the interrogative text *¿Quiere agua o limonada?* 'Does s/he / do you want water or lemonade?' in the following three pragmatic contexts. If possible obtain actual F0 contours.

   a) Yes/no question: *¿Quiere agua o limonada?*
      Possible answer: 'Yes, I want something to drink, either water or lemonade would be fine.'
   b) Complete disjunctive question (choose one of the two): *¿Quiere agua? ¿o limonada?*
      Possible answer: 'I prefer water.'
   c) Incomplete disjunctive question (choose one, but there are more than two options): *¿Quiere agua? ¿o limonada?...*
      Possible answer: 'Tea, please, if you have any.'

2. Take a minimal pair such as *sábana* 'sheet' and *sabana* 'savannah', where the two words differ in the position of the word-stress. What acoustic differences (of F0, duration and intensity) would you expect to find between these two words pronounced in isolation or in nuclear position in a declarative sentence (e.g. *No me gusta la sábana/sabana*)? Do you expect the facts to be any different if the target words are placed in a context where they receive a prenuclear pitch accent (e.g. *La sábana/sabana estaba seca*)? Finally, what is your hypothesis regarding the realization of the word-stress contrast in a context where the target word is in a deaccented position, after another word with contrastive narrow focus (e.g. *¿Has dicho que quiere oler la sábana/sabana otra vez? No, que quiere VER la sábana/sabana otra vez*)? This is proposed here as a thought experiment. Nevertheless, it would be possible to conduct a real experiment to test your hypotheses. For that, you would need to develop adequate experimental materials, including a number of additional contrasting examples of the same type, and then follow established experimental procedures (including obtaining approval from your institutional review board as appropriate, etc.).

Appendices

APPENDIX A. SUMMARY OF MAIN ASPECTS OF SPANISH PRONUNCIATION IN CONTRAST WITH ENGLISH

- Vowels are not reduced in unstressed syllables.
- The mid vowels /e/ and /o/ are pure vowels. Avoid diphthongizing them (*le* ≠ *ley*).
- The sequences /ie/, /ue/ are generally realized as diphthongs (*sierra*, *pueblo*).
- /p t k/ are never aspirated.
- /b d g/ are always voiced. In most contexts they are realized as approximants, without full occlusion. This includes the intervocalic and some postconsonantal contexts. (In the most common pronunciation they are stops only when utterance initial, after a nasal and in the sequence /ld/.)
- Avoid a flap realization of /t d/ (*mudo* ≠ *muro*).
- There is no /z/. The voiceless fricative /s/ may only be voiced before a voiced consonant (*desde*), not before a vowel (*presidente*, *azul*).
- The palatal nasal /ɲ / (*baño*) is different from a sequence of /n/ + palatal glide.
- /l/ is always 'light'. Avoid a 'dark' or velarized pronunciation of postvocalic /l/ (*sal*).
- The tap /ɾ/ and the trill /r̄/ are both realized as apico-alveolar. The tap has a single brief contact, the trill has two or more. The two segments contrast in intervocalic position (*caro* ≠ *carro*).

A.1 Aspects of variation

- Standard Peninsular Spanish makes a phonemic contrast between /s/ and /θ/. Standard Latin American Spanish has only /s/. Adopt one pronunciation or the other consistently.

- Be aware of the sociolinguistic/stylistic value of variable phenomena such as aspiration of /s/ and deletion of /d/ in *-ado*, which is not the same in all Spanish-speaking countries!
- Nowadays most Spanish-speakers have a single palatal phoneme /ʝ/ corresponding to orthographic *y* (*mayo*) and *ll* (*calle*). In Argentinian Spanish the standard pronunciation has /ʒ/.

APPENDIX B. WHY ISN'T SPANISH ORTHOGRAPHY COMPLETELY PHONEMIC?

We saw in Chapter 1 that, although Spanish orthography follows the phonemic principle to a large extent, certainly much more than English orthography, it falls short of being totally phonemic. We may ask why this is so.

To begin with, the alphabet that we use to write both English and Spanish (as well as French, Swedish, etc.) is an adaptation of a writing system that was originally developed for Latin. For Classical Latin, this alphabet did a reasonably good job of directly reflecting the contrastive sounds or phonemes of the language in writing. Even in Classical Latin, though, the orthography was not completely phonemic; the correspondence between letters and phonemes was imperfect even then. This, however, should not be taken as an imperfection of Latin orthography, since a strict adherence to the phonemic principle does not necessarily make an orthographic system more efficient (see Coulmas 2003). Latin orthography, like all orthographies, was designed for readers who knew the language natively. Such readers do not need for every phonological contrast to be faithfully indicated in order to know how to interpret written texts correctly. For instance, Classical Latin had a contrast between short and long vowel phonemes not represented in the orthography. We know, to give an example, that the word for 'free', in the nominative singular form, was /liːber/, with a long /iː/, and that this word contrasted with /liber/ 'book, treatise', with a short /i/; but both words were written in the same way: *liber*. A Roman would figure out from the context whether the written form *liber* should be read with a long or a short vowel.[1]

The distance between orthography and pronunciation kept increasing as the pronunciation of Latin evolved through time. Thus, for instance, at some fairly early point, Latin speakers started 'dropping their aitches' when they spoke, with the result that, for example, *hora* 'hour' and *ora* 'border' came to be pronounced in the same manner, both /oːra/. At this point, Latin writers had

---

[1] Nowadays in Latin textbooks and dictionaries vowel length is often indicated with a macron (e.g. *līber* 'free'), but this diacritic was not employed in Roman times.

no other choice but to learn by heart which words ought to be spelt with an *h*. These silent *h*'s have been preserved in the orthography of a few English words of Latin origin, such as *hour, honour* and *honest*. In modern Spanish, of course, all *h*'s are silent (although not all of them were there in the Latin ancestors of the Spanish words, as we will see below).

To give another example, originally the letter *c* always represented the same phoneme in Latin, /k/; thus *casa* 'hut' and *cena* 'supper' were pronounced /kasa/ and /ke:na/, respectively. Again, with time, the initial sounds of these two words became more and more different (specifically, the sound /k/ was progressively changed to a different sound before the vowels /e/ and /i/, by palatalization). The final result of a long evolution is that in Modern Spanish the same letter *c* represents two completely different phonemes in *casa* and in *cena*, since the orthography has not been altered in this respect in spite of the change in pronunciation.

Obviously, the Latin alphabet lacked symbols for representing sounds that did not exist in Latin. As new pronunciations arose in the evolution from Latin to Spanish and the other ROMANCE languages, conventions were eventually adopted to represent the new phonemes. Thus *ch* has been adopted for a sound that did not exist in Latin. To give a couple more examples, Latin *ll*, like all other double letters in this language, represented a long or geminated consonant, as it still does in Italian *gallo* /gál:o/ 'rooster', *cavallo* /kavál:o/ 'horse'. In Spanish, Latin geminate /l:/ became the palatal sound /ʎ/ (and later /j/ in most dialects), but the spelling was preserved, with the result that what is pronounced /gáʎo/ or /gájo/ is spelt with a double *ll*, reflecting its Latin etymology. The same spelling *ll* was extended to other words where the same sound /ʎ/ emerged from other sources. The letter *ñ* was originally an abbreviated form of writing geminate *nn*, which by historical sound change became the palatal sound that we have in Spanish *año* 'year', from Lat. ANNU, etc. Again this spelling was also extended to words where the same sound resulted from other sources as in *viña* 'vineyard', from Lat. VĪNEA, and *España*, from Lat. HISPANIA.

At different historical points, the orthography has been reformed to accommodate it to major changes in the pronunciation of the language. A first standardization of the orthography was implemented by King Alfonso X of Castile-Leon (1252–84), known as The Learned (El Sabio). As centuries went by and the language kept changing, the Alfonsine orthography became antiquated.

Since its founding in 1713, the Spanish Academy has been constantly concerned with orthographic matters. Nevertheless, orthographic reform has not gone as far as needed if the goal were to produce a completely phonemic writing system. A balance was struck between phonemic radicalism and preservation of the orthographic tradition.

Let us consider three of the mismatches between orthography and phonemic reality that are a major source of insecurity in spelling for all users of the Spanish language: the lexical distribution of *b* and *v*, the distribution of *j* and *g* with the value of /x/ and the origins of orthographic *h*.

1) Medieval Castilian had a contrast between a phoneme spelt *b* and another phoneme spelt *v* (or *u*, since originally *u* and *v* were two variants of the same letter), which might have been a VOICED LABIODENTAL FRICATIVE /v/, as in Portuguese, French and Italian, or, more likely, a BILABIAL /β/ in the original Castilian area (Penny 2002). The phoneme written *v* appears in words where Latin has *v* as in *lavar* 'to wash' (Lat. LAVĀRE), *vaca* 'cow' (Lat. VACCA), but also in words where Latin had *b* between vowels, as in OSp. *dever* 'must' (Lat. DEBĒRE), OSp. *cavallo* 'horse' (Lat. CABALLU), OSp. *aver* 'to have' (Lat. HABĒRE), OSp. *cantavas* 'you sang' (Lat. CANTĀBĀS). On the other hand, in intervocalic position, OSp. *b* corresponds to Lat. *p* as in OSp. *saber* 'to know' (Lat. SAPĒRE), OSp. *lobo* 'wolf' (Lat. LUPU). This is essentially the same distribution of *v* and *b* that we still find in Portuguese. Unlike in its sister languages, Portuguese, French and Italian, however, the contrast between these two phonemes was eventually lost in Spanish. The result was that Spanish speakers no longer had any guide for knowing which words ought to be spelt with *b* and which with *v* and considerable insecurity in the spelling ensued. The Spanish Academy decided to impose some order on the resulting chaos and reformed the spelling in this point. The only solution consistent with phonemic spelling ('one sound, one letter') would have been to spell /labár/, /abér/, /debér/, /sabér/, /kantába/, etc., all in the same manner, since there is no difference in pronunciation. This is not, however, the ruling that the Academy made. The Academy decided to keep both letters, *v* and *b*, in the standard spelling system of the language. In the absence of any phonological reason for determining where to use each of the two letters, the members of the Academy concluded that the best thing would be, as a rule, to use *v* where Latin had *v*, and *b* where Latin had *b* (or *p*). The net result is that many words that in Old Spanish had been written with *v* came to be restructured according to their Latin etymology:

Lat. CABALLU > OSp. *cavallo* > ModSp. *caballo*
   (cf. Port. *cavalo*, It. *cavallo*, Fr. *cheval*)
Lat. HABĒRE > OSp. *aver* > ModSp. *haber*
   (cf. It. *avere*, Fr. *avoir*)
Lat CANTĀBĀS > OSp. *cantavas* > ModSp. *cantabas*
   (cf. Port. *cantavas*, It. *cantavi*)

In this respect it is interesting to note that some school teachers, singers and radio announcers (especially in parts of Latin America), attempt to give orthographic *v* the value of this letter in English or French in the mistaken belief that this pronunciation is somehow 'more correct'. From a historical point of view, using the spelling as a guide for pronunciation in this case is absolutely without basis, as we have seen. Spanish has never had a contrast in pronunciation with the lexical distribution that the modern orthography suggests. Medieval Spanish did have a contrast between /b/ and probably /β/, but many words that are nowadays spelt with *b* were not spelt with this letter when the contrast was present in the pronunciation of the language.

2) In Medieval Castilian the sound of the initial consonant in words such as *joven* 'young', *gente* 'people' was the VOICED PREPALATAL FRICATIVE /ʒ/ still found in Fr. *jeune, gens* and Port. *jovem, gente*.[2] In addition, as explained in 9.2.4, Medieval Castilian had the voiceless counterpart of this phoneme, a sound similar to that of English *sh* (in *sheep, shop*), IPA /ʃ/, which was spelt *x*, as *dixo* /díʃo/ 's/he said', *baxo* /báʃo/ 'short'. (In some words this sound derives from Lat. *x* /ks/, as in Lat. DĪXĪ /diːksiː/ > OSp. *dixe* /díʃe/ 'I said', Lat. AXE /akse/ > OSp. *exe* /éʃe/ 'axis', and this appears to explain the choice of spelling.) The distinction between /ʒ/ and /ʃ/ was lost in favour of only /ʃ/ in the fifteenth to sixteenth centuries and, some time later, this phoneme acquired the value that it has in modern Spanish, velar /x/. After these changes, the medieval orthography now provided three ways to write the phoneme /x/ before *e* and *i* (as in *dixe, gente, Jesús*) and two ways to write it in other contexts (as in *baxo, ojo*). Leaving nonphonological factors aside, the most rational reform of the spelling would have kept only one of these three letters with the value of /x/, as proposed by Juan Ramón Jiménez. Again, the Spanish Academy adopted a solution which was intermediate between orthographic simplicity and tradition, eliminating *x* with this value (except for established place names such as *México*, and *Oaxaca*, for which the Mexicans resisted the reformation),[3] but keeping both *j* and *g* before *e* and *i* according to generally etymological criteria.

3) For Spanish speakers, another cause of orthographic problems is the use of *h*, since this letter is never pronounced. There are several sources of orthographic *h*.

To begin with, modern Spanish orthography (unlike Italian) has preserved – or restored – orthographic *h* in those words where the Latin etymon has *h*, as

---

[2] An older Castilian variant is *yente*, with a nonstrident palatal, but this is not the form that prevailed.
[3] Until recently, the orthography *Méjico, mejicano* was common in Spain, but in its most recent orthographic norms the Academy recommends its avoidance (Real Academia Española 1999:29).

in *hora*, *haber*, *hombre* (Lat. HOMINE), etc., even though, as we already know, this sound stopped being pronounced as early as in Roman times.

Secondly, we have *h* in many words where Latin (and the other main Romance languages) have *f*, as in *hacer* 'to do, make' (Lat. FACERE), *hormiga* 'ant' (Lat. FORMĪCA), *hija* 'daughter' (Lat. FĪLIA), etc. The *h* of these words was pronounced as /h/ in Old Spanish. Before a vowel, Lat. /f/ generally became an aspiration /h/ in Medieval Castilian. This aspiration, however, was later lost (except that some of these words preserve the aspiration in regional nonstandard pronunciation in certain areas, both of Spain and of Latin America).

Thirdly, there are some orthographic aitches which have never been pronounced, either in Latin or in Old Spanish. Because of a purely orthographic rule, Spanish words cannot start with a diphthong like *ue-*; instead these words always have an orthographic *h*. Notice the alternation in examples such as *oler* 'to smell', *huelo* 'I smell'; *osario* 'ossuary', *hueso* 'bone'; *oquedad* 'hole', *hueco* 'hole', etc. The forms that otherwise would have an initial diphthong are provided with an *h*. This orthographic device was useful at the time where the letters *u* and *v* were used with the same value (*laua* ∼ *lava* 's/he washes'), so that something written *uelo* was ambiguous in pronunciation: it could be the word *velo* 'veil' or the word *huelo* 'I smell'. The *h* was there to indicate clearly that the following letter *u* was not a consonant. Incidentally, this orthographic device is also found in French, cf. *huître* 'oyster' (from Lat. OSTREA), *huile* 'oil' (Lat. OLEU). Nowadays there would be no confusion, since the letters *u* and *v* are always kept separate (except when we want to recreate the style of Latin inscriptions, as in VNIVERSITAS), but the convention has been maintained.

We thus see that the standard orthography of the Spanish language represents the compromise struck by the Spanish Academy between a rational system of phonemic spelling and the historical baggage of the language.

APPENDIX C. SPANISH AMONG THE IBERO-ROMANCE VARIETIES

C.1 A brief historical overview

The purpose of this appendix is to provide the historical background necessary to understand the linguistic situation in modern Spain, which is described in C.2.

We have only a partial picture of the linguistic situation in the Iberian Peninsula before the arrival of the Roman legions. We know that both Indo-European and non-Indo-European languages were spoken in this area. Indo-European languages were spread over the centre and western part of the Peninsula:

Celtiberian or Hispano-Celtic (a member of the Celtic family, which includes Welsh, Irish and Scottish Gaelic, and Breton, as well as the extinct language of the Gauls in France) was spoken in the central plateau. In parts of modern Portugal and neighbouring areas there are paleographic remains of the language, also Indo-European, of the Lusitanians. Non-Indo-European languages – most likely remnants of an even older linguistic stage before the Indo-European invasions – were at this time also spoken over large areas of the Peninsula. In eastern and southern regions, all along the Mediterranean coast, we find the Iberian language. A different language, Euskarian or Basque-Aquitanian, was spoken in the territory of the Vascones (modern Navarra and northern Aragon), in Aquitania, in southwestern France, and most likely also in most of the area of the modern Autonomous Community of the Basque Country. The Tartessians of the lower Guadalquivir valley, who according to classical sources were the most advanced among the peoples of the Peninsula, also appear to have spoken a distinct non-Indo-European language. In addition, both Greek and the Semitic language of Phoenicians and Carthaginians were no doubt spoken in the colonies that these sea-faring nations had founded along the Mediterranean coast of Spain (see Fig. C.1).

All of these languages, with the sole exception of Basque, were replaced by the Latin of the Roman conquerors, after a period of coexistence or bilingualism which may have lasted centuries in some parts.

As the political, military and administrative structures that kept the Roman Empire in place weakened and finally disappeared, the Latin language evolved into a number of regional varieties, which, in the absence of a common centre, grew more and more apart from each other, eventually becoming the different Romance languages. The Spanish language derives directly from the particular Romance variety that developed in the original area of the County (later Kingdom) of Castile, to the north of the city of Burgos, in close proximity to the area where Basque was spoken at the time. When Castilian appears in writing in the middle ages as distinct from its Latin ancestor, it is as a member of a dialectal continuum extending over northern Spain. To the west of its area, we find Leonese and Galician-Portuguese; to its east, Navarrese Romance, Aragonese and Catalan. This language continuum extended also outside of the Iberian Peninsula, throughout France and Italy. Undoubtedly the Romance linguistic continuum also included the centre and south of the Peninsula in early medieval times, but we know less about the medieval Romance varieties of this area. Most of the Peninsula had been conquered by the Arabs and Berbers, who first arrived in Spain in the year 711, and had Arabic as its language of culture. Romance varieties, known as a whole as Mozarabic (from the Arabic *musta'rab* 'Arabized'), continued nevertheless being spoken in Hispano-Muslim territory,

Figure C.1. Ancient languages of the Iberian Peninsula.

longer in some areas than in others (see Fig. C.2). Both the Arabic language and the Romance Mozarabic varieties that had survived under the Arabs were ultimately replaced by the languages of the Christian kingdoms of northern Spain, as they spread southwards in the centuries-long process known in Spanish history as the *reconquista* or re-conquest. The kings of Castile were particularly successful in this expansionist endeavour, and, as a consequence, the language of Castile spread, as a wedge, over a larger part of central and southern Hispania than its sister languages. Other northern languages, especially Galician-Portuguese and Catalan also spread southwards on both sides of the

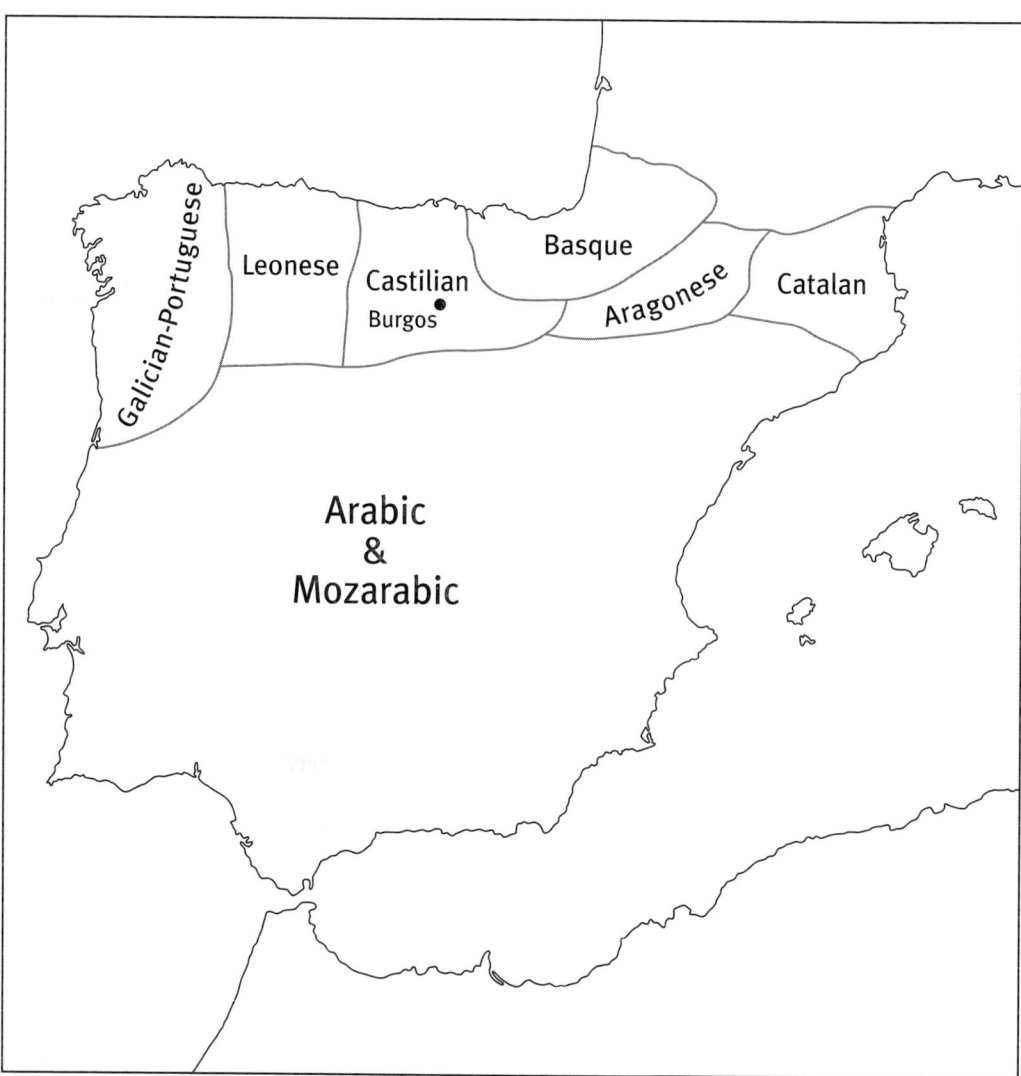

Figure C.2. Linguistic situation of the Iberian Peninsula in the tenth century. The boundaries that are drawn between Romance varieties are more or less arbitrary, since, as explained in the text, there was a single dialect continuum.

Peninsula, whereas Leonese and Aragonese had a more limited expansion on either side of the Castilian area (see Fig. C.3).

These historical events are still reflected in the present-day linguistic map of the Iberian Peninsula, in the fact that there is much more linguistic diversity in the north than in the south of the Peninsula. The linguistic continuum has been preserved to some extent in the northern area. If we travel from west to east along the northern fringe of the Peninsula, first we will hear Galician around us (in addition to Spanish with a Galician 'accent'). As we move into

Spanish in the Ibero-Romance languages

Figure C.3. The languages of the Iberian Peninsula in the fifteenth century.

Asturias, if we observe the speech of rural speakers, we will notice that Galician progressively changes into a number of Asturian varieties, which as we continue travelling eastwards become less and less like Galician and more and more like Castilian Spanish. In the region of Cantabria we will still find local forms of language that, although very similar to Standard Castilian Spanish, have some striking features, such as final /-u/ instead of /-o/ (e.g. *palu* 'stick' for Sp. *palo*) and aspirated /h/ (e.g. [hórnu] for standard Spanish *horno* [órno] 'oven'). (Portuguese and Galician have /f/ in such words.) If we keep on travelling along the coast, we will get to the Basque region, where the local language is totally different and does not form part of the continuum. If we go south to

Burgos, instead, we will be in the cradle of the Spanish language. Further to the east, in the Pyrenean valleys of northern Aragon, we can still find speakers of Aragonese varieties, which progressively deviate from Spanish and resemble Catalan more and more as we get closer to the Catalan border. Whereas, to take the two geographical extremes, a Galician fisherman and a Catalan farmer who spoke only their local variety would have a hard time understanding each other, along the way we do not find any really abrupt transition between neighbouring varieties to the extent that local varieties have been preserved (again leaving aside the Basque region). Farther south, however, the situation is quite different. Here we pass from Portuguese to Spanish or from Spanish to Catalan abruptly from one town to the next, without intermediate forms. This is because these three languages originated in more northerly regions and were brought to the central and southern part of the Peninsula by the armies and colonists of the respective medieval kingdoms.

C.2 The other languages of Spain today and their influence on the pronunciation of the regional form of Spanish in bilingual areas

We see that the different Ibero-Romance languages of the middle ages have had very unequal fortunes in later centuries, some becoming the mother tongue of millions, some others becoming extinct or nearly so.

Nowadays a number of languages coexist with Spanish in several regions of Spain. Where the local language is rather different from Spanish, as is the case with Catalan (not to mention Basque), the two varieties are generally seen as separate linguistic codes, to be used in different contexts or when speaking with different interlocutors, and most speakers avoid transferring phonological and other features from one language to the other (although, of course, they are not always successful). On the other hand, in zones where the local variety is more similar to Standard Spanish, as is the case with the Asturian-Leonese-Cantabrian varieties that still survive, many speakers see the local variety merely as a register for informal interaction with relatives and neighbours, at the end of a range of registers whose other end is Standard Castilian Spanish. In actual linguistic interaction these speakers will produce a range of speech forms which sometimes are closer to Standard Spanish and other times will have more of a local flavour. In Galicia the mixture of Spanish and Galician is known by the pejorative name *castrapo* and elicits strong condemnation on the part of those intent on preserving the purity of the Galician language.

In what follows we will consider the linguistic situation in different areas of the Iberian Peninsula where another language coexists or has coexisted with Spanish.

Spanish in the Ibero-Romance languages

Figure C.4. The languages of the Iberian Peninsula today.

As already mentioned, the Mozarabic varieties spoken in central and southern Spain before the Christian *reconquista* have not left descendants.

C.2.1 Galician and related varieties

Medieval Galician-Portuguese has given rise to two modern languages, Galician and Portuguese (including European Portuguese, Brazilian and several other Portuguese varieties around the world, in addition to various Portuguese-based Creoles), as Galicia remained attached to the Kingdom of Castile-Leon, whereas Portugal became an independent kingdom which went on to create an empire of its own. Galician is nowadays an official language (together with Spanish) in Galicia, where it is spoken by the majority of the population and is used in the school system and in the media. One major difference between both daughters of the medieval Galician-Portuguese language is that Galician, being spoken in a region within Spain, has become more similar to Spanish in its pronunciation. The phonological influence of Spanish is particularly strong in the Galician of Spanish-dominant urban speakers, which is the variety that one is most likely to hear on Galician television. Conversely, the regional form of Spanish also shows some phonological influence from Galician, including the pronunciation of final /n/ as a velar nasal [ŋ] (the final sound in English *thing*), as in *pan* [páŋ] 'bread', *son* [sóŋ] 'they are', and sometimes a very close pronunciation of final /o/, which may sound rather like [u]. Galician varieties are also spoken in border areas of Asturias and Leon. In Extremadura, along the border with Portugal, we find a couple of bilingual areas. In the town of Olivenza, Portuguese is spoken alongside Spanish, and, in Valverde del Fresno and neighbouring towns, a local dialect of a Galician-Portuguese type is spoken.

C.2.2 Modern descendants of Old Leonese

Old Leonese has had worse luck than Galician-Portuguese. It survives most strongly in the Spanish region of Asturias, as a group of local varieties mostly spoken in rural areas, which are collectively known as *asturianu* or *bable*. In recent years Asturian has become a symbol of regional pride. There is an Academia de la Llingua Asturiana, one of whose goals is to create a standard form of the language, and there is also some use of Asturian in literary creation and in the schools. In urban areas of Asturias, however, one is not likely to hear much Asturian.

Another area where a modern form of Leonese enjoys local prestige is the Portuguese region of Miranda do Douro, where the local dialect, known as *mirandês*, has been granted official recognition. Within Leon proper – nowadays merely a part of the region of Castile-Leon – the language has fared less well, with very few people still speaking Leonese dialects. As already mentioned, in Cantabria as well we find local varieties that form a transition towards Castilian Spanish, but again these are preserved mostly by elderly speakers in rural areas.

The two features noted above for the regional Spanish of Galicia, the final velar nasal [ŋ] and the very close realization of final /o/ are also found in Asturias and in other areas where Leonese varieties are or were historically spoken, including parts of Extremadura. Velar [ŋ] is a phenomenon with a wider geographical extension (being found also in Andalucia, the Caribbean and some other parts of Latin America) and is used essentially by all speakers in these areas. The raising of word-final /-o/, on the other hand, is somewhat stigmatized, especially in zones where the local dialect actually has final /-u/, and tends to be avoided in formal situations and by educated speakers in the areas where the phenomenon is found. In much of the western area of Spain, from parts of Asturias and Cantabria to Extremadura and western Andalusia, the orthographic *h* of some words such as *hondo* 'deep', *hembra* 'female', *hacer* 'to do', *hoyo* 'hole' is pronounced as [h], especially in rural areas. This is a conservative phenomenon. In Latin these words had /f/, which became /h/ in Old Castilian, as was explained above in Appendix B.

C.2.3 Aragonese varieties

Although independent from Castile until the union of both kingdoms under Ferdinand of Aragon and Isabella of Castile in the fifteenth century, most of Aragon soon became Castilian-speaking. As mentioned, the original Aragonese language has retreated to a few Pyrenean valleys, where it barely survives. Modern Aragonese dialects include *cheso*, in the Hecho Valley, *chistavino*, in Gistain, and *belsetán*, in Bielsa. As in Asturias, there have been some recent attempts to revive and standardize the language, but so far this language revival movement has not attracted much interest.

The Spanish spoken in Aragon is phonetically conservative. To other Peninsular speakers it is mostly identifiable by its distinct intonational contours.

C.2.4 The extinct Navarrese Romance

The generally accepted explanation for the disappearance of the medieval Navarrese Romance language, which developed in contact with Basque and in many respects was transitional between Castilian and Aragonese, is that, after the Kingdom of Navarre was annexed to that of Castile (in 1512), Navarrese Romance was viewed by its speakers not as a distinct language, but merely as a local form of the same language as Castilian. Progressively, Navarrese shed its distinctive traits in favour of the more prestigious Castilian variants where differences were found (see Gonzalez Ollé 1996). Probably something very similar happened with the varieties of lower Aragon (as well as much of Leon, on the other side of the originally Castilian area).

C.2.5 Catalan

Catalan, on the other hand, has been preserved in relatively good health over large areas. The Catalan language is co-official with Spanish in Catalonia, where it enjoys considerable prestige, being used in all social and public functions. Besides Catalonia proper, the Catalan language is also spoken in most of the region of Valencia, in the Balearic Islands (Majorca, Minorca and Ibiza or Eivissa – in the Catalan form of the name) and in areas of Aragon bordering Catalonia. Outside of the political boundaries of Spain, Catalan is the official language of the independent Principality of Andorra (*Principat d'Andorra*). Across the French border, Catalan is spoken in the region of Roussillon, where it lacks official recognition. It is also spoken in the town of Alghero (in Catalan, L'Alguer), on the Italian island of Sardinia, where it was brought by Catalan colonists in the middle ages.

Most Catalan-speakers in Spain also speak Spanish fluently. To a variable degree, Catalan-speakers tend to transfer certain phonological features of their native language when speaking in Spanish. Some of these features are the pronunciation of final /-d/ as [t], as in *verda*[t], *Madri*[t], the velarized pronunciation of final /-l/, in *igual*, *cual*, etc. (similar to word-final English /l/) and the VOICING of /s/ as [z] between vowels across word boundaries, as in *lo*[z] *amigos* 'the friends'. The more a speaker uses these pronunciations, the more his or her Spanish will be perceived as having a Catalan accent. Many Catalans (but not all) consistently make the contrast between /ʝ/ and /ʎ/ in Spanish.

C.2.6 Aranese Gascon

In the northwesternmost corner of Catalonia, in the Arán Valley, we find another language, which is locally known as *aranés*, or Aranese. The Arán Valley is on the northern side of the Pyrenees, but, for historical reasons, it became first part of Catalonia and then of Spain. Consistent with its geographical location, Aranese is not an Ibero-Romance variety, but, rather, a form of southern Gallo-Romance (Occitan). It is most similar to the Gascon varieties of southwestern France. Although the language enjoys official recognition, there are only a few thousand speakers of Aranese, who tend to be trilingual, speaking also Spanish and Catalan. When they speak Spanish, the people from Arán do not have much of a Catalan 'accent' at all.

C.2.7 Basque

The Basque language is now co-official with Spanish in the Autonomous Community of the Basque Country, which includes the three provinces of Vizcaya, Guipúzcoa and Álava (or, in Basque, Bizkaia, Gipuzkoa and Araba), and also enjoys a more limited official status in Navarra (in Basque, Nafarroa). Basque is also spoken across the border in the French Basque Country. The percentage of native Basque speakers in the whole region is not very high, around

20–25 percent, but much higher in parts of Vizcaya/Bizkaia and Guipúzcoa/Gipuzkoa. Although in the middle ages Basque was spoken as far south as northern parts of the provinces of Burgos and La Rioja – outside of the modern Basque provinces and adjacent to the cradle of Castilian Romance – and perhaps as far east as Huesca, in Aragon, the boundary of the Basque-speaking territory has receded considerably since then. Local varieties of Basque have been preserved in Vizcaya, east of Bilbao, in a northern corner of Alava, in all of Guipúzcoa and in northwestern Navarra, as well as in the Basque Country of France. Nowadays a standard form of Basque has been developed and the language is widely used in the educational system, with the result that knowledge of Basque is increasing among native speakers of Spanish in the younger generations, even in areas where the language had been lost a long time ago.

In the Spanish of the Basque Country the phoneme /s/ generally has a more 'sibilant' (more retracted) articulation than in other areas of the Peninsula. Before a consonant, as in pa[r̄]te 'part', /r/ tends to be trilled. Especially among native speakers of Basque, one sometimes finds a strongly trilled [r̄] also after a consonant in the same syllable, as in pob[r̄]e 'poor', and word finally, as in po[r̄] eso 'for that reason'.

One could say that the loss of /-d-/ in participles in -ado is the norm in the Basque area. Even among educated speakers and in rather formal settings, one hears very advanced forms such as [kantáu̯] for cantado 'sung'. Native speakers of Basque tend to maintain the contrast between /ʎ/ and /j/, which is also found in Basque, but the youngest generations are losing the contrast in both languages. The Basque Country is one of the few areas where the pronunciation of /ʎ/ has a very positive social consideration (at least in some circles). This is directly related to the bilingual situation. For some Basque speakers, the transfer of YEÍSMO to Basque is little less than an affront to the language and these speakers carefully maintain the contrast in both languages. Attitudes may soon start changing, though, since many young people are simply unable to produce /ʎ/ in either language.

Regarding the written language, the rule of uniform spelling in Standard Spanish finds some exceptions in the Basque area. Basque orthography is nowadays often used in Spanish-language texts not only to spell Basque names and loanwords from Basque, such as kokotxas 'cheeks of hake or cod', much more frequent than cocochas, but also sometimes in the spelling of Spanish words of other origins associated with the local culture, either because they are erroneously perceived as being Basque words or for fanciful reasons. Thus, in restaurant menus written in Spanish it is not unusual to find txuleta 'steak', for chuleta, antxoas 'anchovies' for anchoas, and txipirones 'small squids', for chipirones, for instance (in Basque orthography tx represents /t͡ʃ/ and the phoneme /k/ is

Table C.1 The Ibero-Romance varieties from the middle ages.

Middle ages	21st century
Galician-Portuguese →	Galician
	Portuguese: European, Brazilian, etc. Portuguese Creoles
Old Leonese →	Asturian
	Mirandês (Portugal), etc.
Old Aragonese →	Modern Pyrenean Aragonese dialects: Cheso, Belsetán, Chistavino, etc.
Old Catalan →	Catalan: Eastern (Barcelona, Girona), Northwestern (Lleida, Andorra), Valencian, Balearic (Majorca, Minorca, Ibiza), Rosellonés (French Catalonia), Alguerés (Sardinia)
Mozarabic	(extinct)
Old Castilian (Burgos → Toledo) →	1. Modern Spanish: Northern-Central Peninsular, Andalusian, Canarian, Mexican, Central-American, Caribbean, Andean, Chilean, River Plate
	2. Judeo-Spanish (with strong influence from other Ibero-Romance varieties)
	3. Spanish-lexicon Creoles (with strong influence from other Ibero-Romance varieties and other languages): Papiamentu (Dutch Antilles) Palenquero (Colombia) Chabacano (Philippines)

always written *k*), and in newspapers from the Basque region one reads things like *txaranga* 'music band' for *charanga* in articles written in Spanish.

In this connection, something must be said about toponyms in bilingual areas of Spain. In Franco's Spain, all names of provinces and towns, as well as other geographical names, were official only in their Spanish version, even in areas with a different language. Since then, many of them have been replaced by their Galician, Basque or Catalan forms in the respective areas. These newly official names are frequently used in Spanish discourse. Thus, in Spanish-language contexts, one now often sees and hears the official Galician *Ourense* (instead of the Spanish form *Orense*) and *A Coruña* (instead of *La Coruña*), the Catalan forms *Lleida* (for *Lérida*) and *Girona* (in Catalan, pronounced [ʒirónə], but generally mis-pronounced as [xirónə] by Spanish-speakers, instead of the traditional Spanish form *Gerona* [xeróna]), and the Basque forms *Bizkaia* and *Gipuzkoa*. When the Spanish toponym has a traditionally associated adjective, this is normally used in its traditional Spanish form, with the result that in the same text written in Spanish one may find the noun *Bizkaia*, but *vizcaíno* 'Bizkaian' as the corresponding adjective.

C.2.8 English and Spanish in Gibraltar

Although not within the political boundaries of Spain, there is a last bilingual area of the Iberian Peninsula worth mentioning: the British colony of Gibraltar. Native *gibraltareños* are for the most part bilingual in English and Spanish. Their Spanish is similar in pronunciation to that of neighbouring areas of Andalusia, perhaps freer from the prescriptive influence of Standard Peninsular Spanish and with some lexical influence from English.

C.2.9 Ceuta and Melilla

As for the Spanish enclaves of Ceuta and Melilla, on the coast of North Africa, linguistically they are essentially a continuation of Andalusia, but a high percentage of the population is bilingual in Moroccan Arabic or Berber (see Casado-Fresnillo 1995).

APPENDIX D. BILINGUALISM IN LATIN AMERICA

Indigenous or native languages are widely spoken in several Latin American areas. In Mexico there are considerable numbers of speakers of Nahuatl, Otomí, Zapotec, Maya and other languages. The Mexican areas with the greatest concentration of speakers of indigenous languages are the Yucatán Peninsula (Yucatec Maya) and the states of Chiapas and Oaxaca (both with several indigenous languages). In Guatemala one of several languages of the Maya family is spoken by a large percentage of the population. In the Andean region, there are several millions of speakers of Quechua in Ecuador, Peru and Bolivia (as well as northwestern Argentina) and Aymara is spoken by over a million people in Peru, Bolivia and northern Chile. Guaraní is an official language of Paraguay, where it is spoken by most of the inhabitants, and is also widely known in the eastern Bolivian lowlands. In the Amazon basin we find a very large number of languages.

A different case is that of northern Uruguay, where we find contact between Portuguese and Spanish. The local Spanish–Portuguese varieties (Portuguese in contact with Spanish) are known as *fronterizo*.

Spanish–English bilingualism is found not only in the USA but also in parts of Panama and Costa Rica, which are home to communities of Afro-Caribbean descent from the English West Indies, and along the Atlantic coast of Nicaragua, where the use of English (or an English-based Creole) is widespread among people of both African and indigenous Nicaraguan heritage.

In bilingual areas of Latin America, the Spanish of bilingual speakers can deviate from monolingual norms substantially more than in bilingual Spain. There are obvious sociolinguistic reasons for this, including access to education, relative proportion of monolingual speakers of both languages in the relevant area, etc. Another reason is that the native languages of the Americas are structurally much more different from Spanish than the other Ibero-Romance languages are.

A different question is the extent to which the Spanish of monolingual or Spanish-dominant speakers from the different dialectal regions of Latin America may owe some of its features to influence from the indigenous language that is or was spoken in the area. This is a difficult and highly debated issue which requires careful analysis in each particular case. Some intonational and rhythmic traits that distinguish several Latin American varieties and are unlike anything found in the Peninsula, in particular, may have their origin in the influence of native languages. Nevertheless, one should not rush to conclusions. It is tempting, for instance, to seek the origin of the deletion of certain unstressed vowels in Andean Spanish in transfer from Quechua/Aymara rhythmic patterns, but the same phenomenon is found in Mexico, where the linguistic substratum is very different. Furthermore, similar processes of reduction and deletion of unstressed vowels have arisen, for instance, in European Portuguese and, to give another example, in some Basque dialects of Navarra in the absence of any external linguistic influence in that direction. It is the case that quite radical transformations in the pronunciation of a language can be the result of purely language-internal mechanisms.

Some features of bilingual speech are clearly never transferred to the monolingual Spanish of the region. To give an often-cited example, native speakers of Quechua and Aymara who have acquired an imperfect command of Spanish as adults, may show some confusion between /i/ and /e/ and between /o/ and /u/, since in Quechua and in Aymara these pairs of sounds are allophones of the same phoneme (there are only three vowel phonemes /i a u/ in these languages). However, monolingual Spanish speakers of the Andean region show no such confusion. Nevertheless, we do seem to find examples of transfer in other cases. The insertion of a 'glottal stop' between two vowels in the regional Spanish coincides with the area where Guaraní is spoken (Paraguay and adjacent areas of Argentina and Bolivia), is a feature of this language, and appears to be more frequent in bilingual speakers who are dominant in Guaraní, but is also used by Spanish-dominant speakers (Lipski 1994:77–82).

Glossary of technical terms

Note. In the Spanish translations, terms which in Spanish are basically adjectives are provided with the most usual noun they modify (or which is understood and conditions gender agreement, if left unexpressed). For instance, *affricate* is translated as *cons(onante) africada*.

ACOUSTIC PHONETICS (*fonética acústica*)   Study of the sound waves produced in speech by the activity of the articulators.

AFFRICATE (*cons. africada*)   Consonant produced with occlusion followed by fricative release. Spanish has only one affricate phoneme /t͡ʃ/, as in <u>chico</u>, but the consonant /ʝ/ may also have affricate allophones.

ALLOMORPH (*alomorfo*)   Distinct variant of a morpheme. For example, the root morpheme of the verb 'to be able' has allomorphs /pod-/ and /pued-/. To give another example, both /-s/ and /-es/ are allomorphs of the plural suffix.

ALLOPHONE (*alófono*)   Distinct variant of a phoneme. For example, in Spanish the consonant phoneme /s/ has a voiced allophone [z] that occurs before a voiced consonant.

APPROXIMANT (*cons. aproximante*)   Consonant sound for whose production the articulators only approach each other, without enough constriction to produce friction. Examples: [β ð ɣ] in Spanish.

ARCHIPHONEME (*archifonema*)   In Prague school or European structuralism, the phonological result of the neutralization of two or more phonemes in a given position. For instance, since in Spanish /p/ and /b/ do not contrast in the coda of the syllable, an archiphoneme /P/ is postulated in the phonemic representation of words like *apto* /áPto/, *obtiene* /oPtiéne/.

ARTICULATORY PHONETICS (*fonética articulatoria*)   Study of the articulatory mechanisms involved in speech.

ASPIRATION (*aspiración*)   In Spanish dialectology this generally refers to the realization of /s/ or other phonemes as [h].

ASSIMILATION (*asimilación*)   Process by which a segment becomes more similar to a neighbouring segment. See 6.3.

BILABIAL (*bilabial*)   Sound produced with both lips as articulators. Examples are [p b β m].

BOUNDARY TONES (*tonos de frontera*)   In the Autosegmental-Metrical theory of intonational analysis, tones occurring at the beginning or, more commonly, end of phrases. For instance, yes/no questions usually have a final high boundary tone (H%).

BROAD PHONETIC TRANSCRIPTION (*transcripción fonética ancha*) Transcription of an utterance in which only major noncontrastive (allophonic) details are indicated.

CECEO In Spanish dialectology, pronunciation in which a fricative that auditorily resembles Castilian /θ/ is used for orthographic *c (e,i)*, *z* and orthographic *s*. Like in SESEO, there is a single phoneme instead of the two phonemes /s/ and /θ/ of Northern-Central Peninsular Spanish. *Ceceo* is found in parts of Andalusia and is also common as a variable phenomenon in parts of Central America.

CIRCUMFLEX (*tonema circunflejo*) Rising–falling intonational contour.

COARTICULATION (*coarticulación*) Modification in the pronunciation of a consonant or vowel under the influence of neighbouring segments. Phonological processes of assimilation generally have their origin in the phonologization of phonetic coarticulatory effects.

COMPLEMENTARY DISTRIBUTION (*distribución complementaria*) The allophones of a phoneme are said to be in complementary distribution when different allophones occur in different, nonoverlapping, phonological contexts. For instance, in Standard Spanish pronunciation, the plosive and approximant allophones of /d/ are in complementary distribution, since [d] occurs in one set of contexts (after pause, nasal and lateral) and [ð] in all other contexts.

CONTINUANT (*continuante*) Segment realized without complete closure of the passage of airflow through the oral cavity. Vowels, glides, approximant consonants and fricatives are continuant. Oral stops (plosives), nasal stops and affricates are noncontinuant. In their phonological behaviour, in Spanish, rhotics pattern with other continuant segments and laterals with noncontinuant consonants. Notice that in Spanish /l/ the apico-alveolar constriction causes blocking of the air flow through the centre of the mouth at that point.

CREOLE (*lengua criolla*) Language that has its origin in a pidgin or trade language, which at some point was acquired as a native language. When creolization happens, the language rapidly expands its linguistic structures, developing all the expressive power of a natural language.

DEFECTIVE DISTRIBUTION (*distribución defectiva*) Situation in which a phoneme is excluded from a certain position where it would be expected to occur. For instance, in Spanish the tap /ɾ/ has a defective distribution, since it is the only consonant that does not occur word initially.

DENTAL (*cons. dental*) Consonant produced with obstruction involving the upper teeth and the tip or blade of the tongue. In Spanish /t/ and /d/ are dental.

DERIVATION (*derivación*) Morphological process consisting in the creation of words from other words. For instance, the verb *gotear* 'to drip' derives from the noun *gota* 'drop'.

DEVOICING (*ensordecimiento*) Loss of voicing. Final devoicing is common in many languages. For instance, word-final /d/ may become [t] by devoicing. In Buenos Aires Spanish, [ʒ] is currently undergoing devoicing to [ʃ], so that, for instance, whereas conservative speakers in this area pronounce *mayo* as [máʒo], young speakers now tend to pronounce [máʃo]. The voiced sibilants of Old Spanish also underwent devoicing, as we see in the evolution OSp.[káza] > ModSp. [kása] 'house'.

DIALECT (*dialecto*)   Geographical variety of a language. In linguistics this is a neutral term, without any negative connotations. Standard or socially prestigious varieties are also dialects of the language. See SOCIOLECT.

DIPHTHONG (*diptongo*)   Sequence including a vowel and a glide within one syllable. If the glide occurs before the vowel, as in [i̯a], it is called a rising diphthong (because there is an increase in SONORITY or aperture). If the glide occurs after the vowel, as in [ai̯], it is a falling diphthong.

DORSAL (*dorsal*)   Segment produced with the dorsum or back of the tongue as active articulator. Both PALATALS and VELARS are dorsal segments.

EPENTHESIS (*epéntesis*)   Insertion of a segment. For example, in Spanish there is epenthesis of the vowel /e/ before word-initial *sC*- clusters in all native words, as in SPATHA > *espada* 'sword', and in borrowings.

FORMANT (*formante*)   Concentration of acoustic energy at a certain frequency range, visible in a spectrogram as a dark horizontal band. The position of the first two formants, F1 and F2, can be used to uniquely identify all five Spanish vowels. (In other languages, F3 also plays an important role. In English, for instance, F3 serves to characterize *r*-coloured vowels.)

FREE VARIATION (*variación libre*)   Two or more allophones of a phoneme are said to be in free variation in a given context if all of them may occur in that context. For instance, in some Spanish dialects [s] and [h] are in free variation word finally. Very often apparent free variation is actually stylistically conditioned.

FRICATIVE (*cons. fricativa*)   Consonant produced with a narrowing of the articulatory channel, resulting in turbulence or noise. Fricative consonants can be VOICELESS, like [f θ s ʃ x], or VOICED, like [v z ʒ]. In Spanish, [β ð ɣ], the continuant allophones of /b d g/, are sometimes regarded as voiced fricatives, but these segments are more accurately characterized as APPROXIMANTS.

GLIDE (*semivocal, deslizada*)   Vocalic segment immediately preceding or following a syllable peak and creating a single complex nucleus with it. Nonpeak element in a diphthong or triphthong. In this book glides are transcribed with a half-moon subscript, as in *pie* [pi̯é] 'foot' (prevocalic glide), *ley* [léi̯] 'law' (postvocalic glide).

GLOTTAL STOP (*cons. oclusiva glotal*)   Consonant produced with occlusion at the glottis (vocal folds). In some varieties of English it occurs as an allophone of /t/ (e.g., in *cotton*). In Arabic and other languages it is a consonantal phoneme. It is also found in many Mesoamerican languages, where it is traditionally known as *saltillo* in linguistic works written in Spanish. In Spanish, the glottal stop only occurs in varieties spoken in Paraguay and neighbouring regions of Argentina, as a segment separating sequences of two vowels. Its IPA symbol is [ʔ].

HEAVY SYLLABLE (*sílaba pesada*)   A syllable that has durational prominence. In Latin, a syllable was heavy if it contained either a long vowel or a coda consonant. If the penultimate syllable was heavy, it attracted the stress. Opposed to LIGHT SYLLABLE.

HETEROSYLLABIC (*heterosilábico*)   Belonging to different syllables; e.g., the consonants /l/ and /p/ are heterosyllabic in *culpa*. Opposed to TAUTOSYLLABIC.

HIATUS (*hiato*)   Sequence of two vowels belonging to different syllables. The Spanish word *María* [maɾí.a] has a hiatus; whereas *Mario* [máɾi̯o], has a DIPHTHONG.

HOMORGANIC (*homorgánico*)   Having the same place of articulation. In Spanish a nasal is always homorganic with a following consonant, except in the sequence /mn/.

INFLECTION (*flexión*)   Modification in the shape of a word to express grammatical notions such as number, gender and case, in nouns and adjectives, or person, tense and mood, in verbs.

INFLECTIONAL PARADIGM (*paradigma flexivo*)   Set of forms related by inflection. For instance, *como, comiéramos, comiste*, etc., form part of the inflectional paradigm of the verb *comer*.

INTERDENTAL (*cons. interdental*)   Consonant produced by protruding the tip of the tongue between the upper and lower teeth. In English both /θ/ (*think*) and /ð/ (*this*) are normally interdental. In Spanish, the approximant [ð], as in *cada*, may be defined as dento-interdental, rather than fully interdental. Northern-Central Peninsular Spanish differs from other Spanish dialects in possessing a voiceless interdental fricative phoneme /θ/ in contrast with /s/.

INTONATION (*entonación*)   Use of pitch to convey pragmatic information.

INTONATIONAL LANGUAGE (*lengua entonativa*)   Language in which all use of pitch is pragmatic. Language lacking lexical tone. Both English and Spanish are intonational languages. Opposed to TONE LANGUAGE.

LABIODENTAL (*cons. labiodental*)   Sound produced with the lower lip as active articulator and the upper front teeth as passive articulator. Examples: [f v].

LARYNGEAL (*cons. laríngea*)   Consonant produced with primary obstruction in the larynx, including the fricative [h] and the glottal stop [ʔ]. The terms laryngeal and glottal are often used as synonyms (although technically speaking glottal has a narrower sense than laryngeal).

LATERAL (*cons. lateral*)   Consonant produced with central occlusion while there is passage of air alongside one or both sides of the tongue. Examples: [l ʎ].

LIGHT SYLLABLE (*sílaba ligera*)   Syllable lacking intrinsic durational prominence. In Latin the penultimate syllable could not bear stress if it was light. A light syllable was an open syllable containing a short vowel. Opposed to HEAVY SYLLABLE.

LIQUID (*cons. líquida*)   Class of consonants including LATERALS and RHOTICS.

LLEÍSMO Conservative Spanish pronunciation that includes a palatal lateral phoneme /ʎ/, corresponding to orthographic *ll*. In most present-day Spanish dialects the phoneme /ʎ/ has disappeared, merging with /j/. Nowadays *lleísmo* is found only in parts of northern Spain, the Andean region and Paraguay. But even in most of these areas, younger speakers no longer employ *lleísmo*. Opposed to *yeísmo*.

METAPHONY (*metafonía*)   Rising of the stressed vowel, and sometimes other vowels, under the influence of a high vowel or glide in a final unstressed syllable. Pervasive metaphony phenomena are nowadays found in several Asturian and Cantabrian varieties, as well as in many Italian dialects. It is a specific type of vowel assimilation, of particular importance in Romance linguistics.

METATHESIS (*metátesis*)   Exchange in the position of segments in a word. We see the operation of metathesis, for instance, in the evolution from Lat. CRUSTA to Sp. *costra* 'crust'. See 6.8 for more examples.

MINIMAL PAIR (*par mínimo*)   Two words that differ in a single consonantal or vocalic segment and have different meaning. Minimal pairs are useful for establishing the phonemic inventory of a language. For instance the minimal pair [máta] 'bush' – [náta] 'cream' shows that /m/ and /n/ are contrasting consonants in Spanish. Minimal pairs can also be used to show the contrasting value of suprasegmental features such as stress and tone (in tone languages).

MORPHEME (*morfema*)   Minimal linguistic unit that possesses meaning. The word *pies* 'feet' contains two morphemes, the root /pie/ and the plural suffix /-s/. The word *mes* 'month' contains a single morpheme.

MORPHOPHONOLOGICAL RULE (*regla morfofonológica*)   Sound alternation that applies only in particular morphological environments. See 12.1.

NARROW PHONETIC TRANSCRIPTION (*transcripción fonética estrecha*)   Transcription of speech where many noncontrastive phonetic details are included.

NASAL (*cons. nasal*)   Sound produced with passage of air through the nasal cavity. This is accomplished by lowering the velum. The consonants [m n ɲ] have complete oral occlusion and air passage through the nasal cavity. In nasalized vowels, there is air flow through both cavities, oral and nasal.

NEUTRALIZATION (*neutralización*)   Loss of phonemic contrast in a given context. For instance, in Spanish the contrast between the two phonemes /p/ and /b/ is neutralized in the coda of the syllable. An important phenomenon in Spanish is the neutralization of nasals in the coda, see 10.2.

NUCLEAR ACCENT (*acento nuclear*)   The most prominent accent in a sentence.

OBSTRUENT (*cons. obstruyente*)   Class of consonants including PLOSIVES, AFFRICATES and FRICATIVES. Opposed to SONORANT.

OXYTONE (*palabra oxítona, aguda*)   Stressed on the last syllable; e.g. *camión, lealtad*.

PALATAL (*cons. palatal*)   Consonant (or other segment) involving a constriction between the front part of the tongue dorsum and the hard palate. Examples of palatal consonants are [ɲ ʎ j]. Besides palatal consonants, there is a palatal glide [i̯]. The term palatal may also be applied to the high front vowel [i].

PAROXYTONE (*palabra paroxítona, llana, grave*)   Stressed on the penultimate syllable; e.g. *espuma, examen*.

PHONEME (*fonema*)   Contrastive segment. Minimal contrastive unit of sound.

PHONEMIC TRANSCRIPTION (*transcripción fonémica*)   Transcription where only contrastive distinctions are indicated. Transcription in terms of phonemes.

PITCH ACCENT (*acento tonal*)   Tonal configuration phonologically associated with a stressed syllable in the utterance.

PLOSIVE (*cons. oclusiva*)   Oral stop. Consonant produced with complete closure, so that passage of air flow through both the oral and nasal cavities is impeded. The synonymous term 'oral stop' makes reference to the complete cessation of air flow during the occlusion. The term 'plosive' refers to the explosive nature of the release of the hold. Another synonym is 'occlusive'. Plosives may be voiceless, [p t k], or voiced, [b d g].

POSTVELAR (*cons. post-velar*)   Consonant whose point of articulation is in the back of the mouth and more retracted than that of a typical velar consonant. In northern Peninsular Spanish, the phoneme /x/ is usually realized as postvelar, especially before a back vowel.

PRENUCLEAR ACCENT (*acento prenuclear*)   Accent that occurs before the NUCLEAR ACCENT of the sentence.

PREPALATAL (*cons. prepalatal*)   Consonant articulated with an obstruction involving the front part of the tongue and the region between the alveolar ridge and the hard palate. Examples are [ʃ ʒ t͡ʃ].

PROPAROXYTONE (*palabra proparoxítona, esdrújula*)   Word stressed three syllables from the end; e.g. *apostólico*.

RHOTIC (*cons. vibrante*). This term means 'r-like'. In Spanish the rhotic class includes the tap /ɾ/ (*vibrante simple*), produced with a single rapid contact of the tip of the tongue against the alveolar ridge, and the trill /r̄/ (*vibrante múltiple*) which, in its standard pronunciation, involves a series of two, three or even more such rapid contacts. See 11.3.

RHYZOTONIC (*rizotónico*)   Form with stress on the root. In Spanish irregular preterites, the first and third person singular forms are rhyzotonic.

ROMANCE (*romance, lengua románica*)   Language historically derived from the evolution of Latin in a given geographical area. Some of the demographically most important Romance languages are Spanish, Italian, French, Portuguese, Catalan and Romanian.

SEMIVOWEL (*semivocal*)   Same as GLIDE. Some authors use the term semiconsonant for prevocalic glides, as in *puedo*, and the term semivowel (in a narrow sense) for postvocalic glides, as in *neura*.

SESEO   In Spanish dialectology, pronunciation where /s/ is used corresponding to the two phonemes /s/ and /θ/ of Northern-Central Peninsular Spanish (and thus for orthographic *c (e,i)*, *z* and orthographic *s*). *Seseo* is practised in all of Latin American Spanish, as well as in the Canary Islands and parts of Andalusia. If the single phoneme is more similar in its sound to Castilian /θ/ than to Castilian /s/, one speaks of CECEO. The Castilian contrast between /s/ and /θ/ is known as *distinción* /s/-/θ/.

SOCIOLECT (*sociolecto*)   Variety of a language that is defined by a social, nongeographical, feature, such as education, occupation, gender, ethnicity, social class or age. Social dialect.

SONORANT (*cons. sonorante, resonante*)   The class of sonorant consonants includes liquids and nasals; that is, all nonobstruent consonants.

SONORITY (*sonoridad*)   Degree of openness. Segments can be ordered along a scale of sonority where low vowels have the highest degree of sonority (they are the most open segments) and plosives the lowest.

STOP (*cons. oclusiva*)   Consonant produced with complete occlusion in the oral cavity. Stop consonants include the oral stops or plosives and the nasal stops. In the production of oral stops or PLOSIVES there is complete cessation of air flow during the occlusion. In NASAL stops there is air flow through the nasal cavity during the oral occlusion.

STRESS (*acento, acento de intensidad*)   Relative degree of prominence of a syllable with respect to the other syllables in the domain. When this domain is the word, the term WORD-STRESS may be used.

STRESS-TIMED   In the classification of languages according to their rhythmic properties, a language in which inter-stress intervals tend to have approximately the same duration, so that if more syllables occur between two stresses, the duration of each syllable will tend to be proportionally compressed.

STRIDENT (*cons. estridente*)   Fricative or affricate produced with a great amount of friction noise. An important dialectal phenomenon in Spanish is the use of the strident fricatives [ʒ] and [ʃ] in Argentinian Spanish, instead of the nonstrident [ʝ] of other dialects. Stridence can be used as a relative notion; e.g. /x/ has a more strident realization in Northern-Central Peninsular Spanish than in Argentina, but, in its turn, Argentinian /x/ is more strident than the corresponding Caribbean sound.

STYLISTIC VARIATION (*variación estilística*)   Variability in pronunciation or in other areas of language that is conditioned by degree of formality or other social aspects of the linguistic interaction. Regarding phonology, it generally implies that some pronunciations are more frequently used in a formal than in an informal style.

SUPPLETION (*supleción*)   Use of two or more distinct roots in a morphological paradigm. For instance, the verb *ir* 'to go' shows suppletion (*voy, fui, iré*).

SUPRASEGMENTAL (*suprasegmental*)   Features such as tone and stress which can be considered to be superimposed on vowels and consonants (segments) and analytically separable from them.

SYLLABLE-TIMED   In the classification of languages according to their rhythmic properties, a language in which all syllables tend to have approximately the same duration. Opposed to STRESS-TIMED.

TAUTOSYLLABIC (*tautosilábico*)   Belonging to the same syllable; e.g., the consonants /p/ and /l/ are tautosyllabic in *copla*. Opposed to HETEROSYLLABIC.

THREE-SYLLABLE WINDOW (*ventana de tres sílabas*)   Restriction in the placement of the WORD-STRESS to one of the three last syllables of the word, as we find in Spanish.

TONE (*tono*)   Use of pitch as a contrastive feature at the lexical level.

TONE LANGUAGE (*lengua tonal*)   Language in which differences in pitch are used contrastively at the lexical level, to distinguish different words.

UNDERSPECIFICATION (*subespecificación*)   Specific proposal within generative phonology according to which redundant features are not specified in the lexical entries.

UVULAR (*cons. uvular*)   Consonant produced with constriction at the uvula. Standard French *r* has a uvular articulation.

VELAR (*cons. velar*)   Consonant (or other segment) produced with a constriction formed by the back of the tongue against the velum (soft palate). Examples are /k g x/. The glide [u̯] is labiovelar. Sometimes the term 'velar' is also used in reference to the back vowels [o u].

VELARIZATION (*velarización*)   In Spanish dialectology this term refers to the realization of coda nasals as velar [ŋ], as in *pan* [páŋ] 'bread'. Velarization of nasals is very common in many Spanish dialects, see 10.2.2.

VOICED (*sonido sonoro*)   Segment produced with vibration of the vocal folds.

VOICELESS (*sonido sordo*)   Segment produced without vibration of the vocal folds.

VOICING (*sonorización*)   Phenomenon by which a voiceless segment becomes voiced in a given context. For instance, in many Spanish dialects /s/ may undergo voicing before a voiced consonant, as in *desde*.

VOSEO   Use of *vos* and associated verb forms as a second person singular. *Voseo* is found in many areas of Central and South America. In Argentinian Spanish, *voseo* has completely replaced the use of *tú* (*tuteo*). In some other Latin American countries both *tú* and *vos* are employed.

VOWEL HARMONY (*armonía vocálica*)   Phenomenon by which all vowels in a word or some other domain must agree in a certain feature, such as height, rounding or tenseness/laxness. See 7.4 for vowel harmony phenomena in Spanish dialects.

WORD-STRESS (*acento de palabra*)   Greater prominence of one syllable over the other syllables of the word. In Spanish (and English) the position of the word-stress is phonologically contrastive.

YEÍSMO   Majority pronunciation in Spanish in which the older palatal lateral phoneme /ʎ/ has merged with /ʝ/, so that orthographic *ll* is given the same value as orthographic *y*. The merger of these two older phonemes in a single strident fricative /ʒ/, as in River Plate Spanish, is known as *yeísmo rehilado* or *žeísmo*. See LLEÍSMO.

YOD   Term used mostly in historical linguistics to refer to a palatal glide.

References

Aguilar, Lourdes. 1997. *De la vocal a la consonante.* Santiago de Compostela: Universidade de Santiago de Compostela. (Colección Lucus-Lingua 3.)
  1999. 'Hiatus and diphthong: acoustic cues and speech situation differences'. *Speech Communication* 28: 57–74.
Alarcos Llorach, Emilio. 1958. 'Fonología y fonética: a propósito de las vocales andaluzas'. *Archivum* 8: 191–203.
  1965. *Fonología española*, 4th edn. Madrid: Gredos.
  1983. 'Más sobre las vocales andaluzas'. In *Philologica hispaniensia in honorem Manuel Alvar*, vol. I, 49–55. Madrid: Gredos.
Alba, Orlando. 1979. 'Análisis fonológico de /r/ y /l/ implosivas en un dialecto rural dominicano'. *Boletín de la Academia Puertorriqueña de la Lengua Española* 7: 1–18.
  1982. 'Función del acento en el proceso de elisión de la /s/ en la República Dominicana'. In Orlando Alba, ed., *El español del Caribe: ponencias del VI Simposio de Dialectología*, 15–26. Santiago, Dominican Republic: Universidad Católica Madre y Maestra.
Alonso, Amado. 1930. Problemas de dialectología hispanoamericana. In *Biblioteca de Dialectología Hispanoamericana*, vol. I, 314–472. Buenos Aires: Universidad de Buenos Aires.
  1945. 'Una ley fonológica del español: variabilidad de las consonantes en la tensión y distensión de la sílaba'. *Hispanic Review* 13: 91–101.
Alonso, Dámaso. 1958. 'Metafonía y neutro de materia en España (sobre un fondo italiano)'. *Zeitschrift für romanische Philologie* 74: 1–24.
  1962. 'Metafonía, neutro de materia y colonización suditaliana en la península hispánica'. In Manuel Alvar, Antoni Badia, R. de Balbín and L. F. Lindley Cintra, eds., *Enciclopedia lingüística hispánica*, vol. I, supplement: *La fragmentación fonética peninsular*, 105–54. Madrid: Consejo Superior de Investigaciones Científicas.
Alonso, Dámaso, María Josefa Canellada and Alonso Zamora Vicente. 1950. 'Vocales andaluzas'. *Nueva Revista de Filología Hispánica* 4: 209–30.
Alvar, Manuel. 1955. 'Las encuestas del Atlas Lingüístico y Etnográfico de Andalucía'. *Revista de Dialectología y Tradiciones Populares* 11: 231–74.
Alvar, Manuel. 1991. *Estudios de geografía lingüística.* Madrid: Paraninfo.

ed. 1996a. *Manual de dialectología hispánica*, vol. I: *El español de España*; vol. II: *El español de América*. Barcelona: Ariel.

1996b. 'Los Estados Unidos'. In Manuel Alvar, ed., *Manual de dialectología hispánica*, vol. II: *El español de América*, 90–100. Barcelona: Ariel.

1996c. 'Paraguay'. In Manuel Alvar, ed., *Manual de dialectología hispánica*, vol. II: *El español de América*, 196–208. Barcelona: Ariel.

Álvarez Martínez, María Ángeles. 1996. 'Extremeño'. In Manuel Alvar, ed., *Manual de dialectología hispánica*, vol. I: *El español de España*, 171–82. Barcelona: Ariel.

Ariza, Manuel. 1994. *Sobre fonética histórica del español*. Madrid: Arco/Libros.

Aske, Jon. 1990. 'Disembodied rules versus patterns in the lexicon'. *Berkeley Linguistics Society* 16: 30–45.

Bárkányi, Zsuzsanna. 2002. 'A fresh look at quantity sensitivity in Spanish'. *Linguistics* 40: 375–94.

Becerra, Servio. 1985. *Fonología de las consonantes implosivas en el español urbano de Cartagena de Indias (Colombia)*. Bogotá: Instituto Caro y Cuervo.

Beckman, Mary, and Janet Pierrehumbert. 1986. 'Intonational structure in English and Japanese'. *Phonology Yearbook* 3: 255–310.

Beckman, Mary, Manuel Díaz-Campos, Julia T. McGory and Terrell Morgan. 2002. 'Intonation across Spanish in the Tones and Break Indices framework'. *Probus* 14: 9–36.

Blaylock, Curtis. 1965. 'Hispanic metaphony'. *Romance Philology* 18: 253–71.

Blecua, Beatriz. 2001. 'Las vibrantes del español: manifestaciones acústicas y procesos fonéticos'. Doctoral dissertation, Universitat Autònoma de Barcelona.

Bradley, Travis. 2004. 'Gestural timing and rhotic variation in Spanish codas'. In Timothy L. Face, ed., *Laboratory approaches to Spanish phonology*, 197–224. Berlin: Mouton de Gruyter.

Bradlow, Ann. 1995. 'A comparative acoustic study of English and Spanish vowels'. *Journal of the Acoustic Society of America* 97: 1916–24.

Browman, Catherine, and Louis Goldstein. 1986. 'Towards an articulatory phonology'. *Phonology Yearbook* 3: 219–52.

1991. 'Gestural structures: distinctiveness, phonological processes, and historical change'. In Ignatius Mattingly and Michael Studdert-Kennedy, eds., *Modularity and the motor theory of speech perception: proceedings of a conference to honor Alvin M. Liberman*, 313–38. Hillsdale, NJ: Lawrence Erlbaum.

1992. 'Articulatory phonology: an overview'. *Phonetica* 49: 155–80.

Brown, Esther, and Rena Torres Cacoullos. 2003. 'Spanish /s/: a different story from beginning (initial) to end (final)'. In Rafael Núñez-Cedeño, Luis López and Richard Cameron, eds., *A Romance perspective on language knowledge and use*, 21–38. Amsterdam: Benjamins.

Butt, John, and Carmen Benjamin. 2000. *A new reference grammar of modern Spanish*, 3rd edn. Lincolnwood (Chicago): NTC Publishing Group.

Bybee, Joan. 2000. 'Lexicalization of sound change and alternating environments'. In Michael Broe and Janet Pierrehumbert, eds., *Papers in Laboratory Phonology 5: Acquisition and the lexicon*, 250–68. Cambridge: Cambridge University Press.

2001. *Phonology and language use*. Cambridge: Cambridge University Press.

Canellada, María Josefa, and John Kuhlmann Madsen. 1987. *Pronunciación del español: lengua hablada y literaria*. Madrid: Editorial Castalia.

Canellada, María Josefa, and Alonso Zamora Vicente. 1960. 'Vocales caducas en el español mexicano'. *Nueva Revista de Filología Hispánica* 14: 221–4.

Canfield, D. Lincoln. 1981. *Spanish pronunciation in the Americas*. Chicago: University of Chicago Press.

Caravedo, Rocío. 1992. '¿Restos de la distinción /s/ y /θ/ en el español del Perú?' *Revista de Filología Española* 72: 639–54.

Casado-Fresnillo, Celia. 1995. 'Resultados del contacto del español con el árabe y con las lenguas autóctonas de Guinea Ecuatorial'. In Carmen Silva-Corvalán, ed., *Studies in language contact and bilingualism*, 279–92. Washington, DC: Georgetown University Press.

Castañeda, María L. 1986. 'El VOT de las oclusivas sordas y sonoras españolas'. *Estudios de Fonética Experimental* 2: 91–110.

Catalán, Diego. 1958. 'Concepto lingüístico del dialecto "chinato" en una chinatohablante'. *Revista de Dialectología y Tradiciones Populares* 10: 10–28. Repr. in Diego Catalán, 1989, *El español: orígenes de su diversidad*, 105–18. Madrid: Paraninfo.

Clements, G. N. 1990. 'The role of the sonority cycle in core syllabification'. In John Kingston and Mary Beckman, eds., *Papers in Laboratory Phonology I: Between the grammar and physics of speech*, 283–333. Cambridge: Cambridge University Press.

Cole, Jennifer, José I. Hualde and Khalil Iskarous. 1998. 'Effects of prosodic context on /g/-lenition in Spanish'. In Osamu Fujimura, ed., *Proceedings of LP98*, 575–89. Prague: The Karolinium Press.

Corominas, Joan, and José Antonio Pascual. 1980. *Diccionario crítico etimológico castellano e hispánico*. Madrid: Gredos.

Coulmas, Florian. 2003. *Writing systems: an introduction to their linguistic analysis*. Cambridge: Cambridge University Press.

Dalbor, John. 1997. *Spanish pronunciation*, 3rd edn (1st edn 1969). Fort Worth: Holt, Rinehart and Winston.

Dauer, R. M. 1983. 'Stress-timing and syllable-timing re-analyzed'. *Journal of Phonetics* 11: 51–62.

D'Introno, Francesco, Enrique del Teso and Rosemary Weston. 1995. *Fonética y fonología actual del español*. Madrid: Cátedra.

Disner, Sandra F. 1984. 'Insights on vowel spacing'. In Ian Maddieson, *Patterns of sounds*, 136–55. Cambridge: Cambridge University Press.

Dorta, Josefa, and Juana Herrera Santana. 1993. 'Experimento sobre la discriminación auditiva de las oclusivas tensas grancanarias'. *Estudios de Fonética Experimental* 5: 163–88. Barcelona: Laboratorio de Fonética, Universitat de Barcelona.

Eddington, David. 1990. 'Distancing as a causal factor in the development of /θ/ and /x/ in Spanish'. *Journal of Hispanic Philology* 14: 239–45.

  1996. 'Diphthongization in Spanish derivational morphology: an empirical investigation'. *Hispanic Linguistics* 8.1: 1–13.

  1998. 'Spanish diphthongization as a non-derivational phenomenon'. *Rivista di Linguistica* 8.2: 335–54.

Elvira, Javier. 1998. *El cambio analógico*. Madrid: Gredos.

Espinosa, Aurelio. 1930. 'Estudios sobre el español de Nuevo Méjico', trans. and ed. Amado Alonso and Angel Rosenblat. In *Biblioteca de dialectología hispanoamericana*, vol. I. Buenos Aires: Universidad de Buenos Aires.

Face, Timothy. 2001. 'Focus and early peak alignment in Spanish intonation'. *Probus* 13: 223–346.

2002a. 'Local intonational marking in Spanish contrastive focus'. *Probus* 14: 71–92.

2002b. *Intonational marking of contrastive focus in Madrid Spanish*. Munich: Lincom Europa.

Fernandez, Joseph. 1982. 'The allophones of /b, d, g/ in Costa Rican Spanish'. *Orbis* 31: 121–46.

Flórez, Luis. 1951. *La pronunciación del español en Bogotá*. Bogotá: Instituto Caro y Cuervo.

García Alvarez, M. Teresa. 1960. 'La inflexión vocálica en el bable de Bimenes'. *Boletín del Instituto de Estudios Asturianos* 41: 471–87.

Gerfen, Chip. 2002. 'Andalusian codas'. *Probus* 14: 247–77.

Gómez Asencio, José J. 1977. 'Vocales andaluzas y fonología generativa'. *Studia Philologica Salmanticensia* 1: 116–30.

Gonzalez Ollé, Fernando. 1996. 'Navarro'. In Manuel Alvar ed., *Manual de dialectología hispánica*, vol. I: El español de España, 305–16. Barcelona: Ariel.

Grabe, Esther, and Ee Ling Low. 2003. 'Durational variability in speech and the rhythm class hypothesis'. In Carlos Gussenhoven and Natasha Warner, eds., *Laboratory Phonology*, vol. VII, 515–43. Berlin: Mouton de Gruyter.

Guitart, Jorge. 1976. *Markedness and a Cuban dialect of Spanish*. Washington, DC: Georgetown University Press.

Hammond, Robert. 1999. 'On the non-occurrence of the phone [r̄] in the Spanish sound system'. In Javier Gutiérrez-Rexach and Fernando Martínez-Gil, eds., *Advances in Hispanic linguistics*, 290–304. Somerville, MA: Cascadilla Press.

Harris, James. 1969. *Spanish phonology*. Cambridge, MA: MIT Press.

1983. *Syllable structure and stress in Spanish*. Cambridge, MA: MIT Press.

1984. 'Theories of phonological representation and nasal consonants in Spanish'. In Philip Baldi, ed., *Papers from the 12th Linguistic Symposium on Romance Languages*, 153–68. Amsterdam: Benjamins.

1995. 'Projection and edge marking in the computation of stress in Spanish'. In John Goldsmith, ed., *The handbook of phonological theory*, 867–87. Oxford: Blackwell.

Harris, James, and Ellen Kaisse. 1999. 'Palatal vowels, glides and obstruents in Argentinian Spanish'. *Phonology* 16: 117–90.

Harris, Tracy. 1994. *Death of a language: the history of Judeo-Spanish*. Newark: University of Delaware Press.

Hayward, Katrina. 2000. *Experimental phonetics*. Harlow: Longman.

Hillenbrand, James, Laura A. Getty, Michael J. Clark and Kimberlee Wheeler. 1995. 'Acoustic characteristics of American English vowels'. *Journal of the Acoustical Society of America* 97: 3099–111.

Hooper, Joan Bybee, and Tracy Terrell. 1976. 'Stress assignment in Spanish: a Natural Generative approach'. *Glossa* 10.1: 64–110.

Hualde, José I. 1989. 'Autosegmental and metrical spreading in the vowel-harmony systems of northwestern Spain'. *Linguistics* 27: 773–805.

1991a. 'Aspiration and resyllabification in Chinato Spanish'. *Probus* 3: 55–76.

1991b. *Basque phonology*. London: Routledge.

1997. Spanish /i/ and related sounds: an exercise in phonemic analysis'. *Studies in the Linguistic Sciences* 27: 61–79.

1998. 'Asturian and Cantabrian metaphony'. *Rivista di Linguistica* 10.1: 99–108.

2002. 'Intonation in Spanish and the other Ibero-Romance languages: overview and status quaestionis'. In Caroline Wiltshire and Joaquim Camps, eds., *Romance phonology and variation*, 101–16. Amsterdam: Benjamins.

2003a. 'El modelo métrico y autosegmental'. In Pilar Prieto, ed., *Teorías de la entonación*, 155–84. Barcelona: Ariel.

2003b. 'Segmental phonology'. In José I. Hualde and Jon Ortiz de Urbina, eds., *A grammar of Basque*, 15–65. Berlin: Mouton de Gruyter.

2004. 'Quasi-phonemic contrasts in Spanish'. *Proceedings of WCCFL 23*: 374–98.

Hualde, José I., and Ioana Chitoran. 2003. 'Explaining the distribution of hiatus in Spanish and Romanian'. *Proceedings of 15th International Congress on the Phonetic Sciences, Barcelona 3–9 August 2003*, ed. M. J. Solé, D. Recasens and J. Romero, 67–70. Universitat Autónoma de Barcelona. (CD-rom published by Causal Productions.)

Hualde José I., and Mónica Prieto. 2002. 'On the diphthong/hiatus contrast in Spanish: some experimental results'. *Linguistics* 40: 217–34.

Hualde, José I., and Benjamin Sanders. 1995. 'A new hypothesis on the origin of the Eastern Andalusian vowel system'. *Berkeley Linguistics Society 21: Parasession on historical issues in sociolinguistics / social issues in historical linguistics*, 426–37.

Johnson, Keith. 2003. *Acoustic and auditory phonetics*, 2nd edn. Oxford: Blackwell.

Kaisse, Ellen. 2001. 'The long fall: an intonational melody of Argentinian Spanish'. In Julia Herschensohn, Enrique Mallén and Karen Zagona, eds., *Features and interfaces in Romance*, 147–60. Philadelphia: John Benjamins.

Keating, Patricia. 1984. 'Phonetic and phonological representation of stop consonant voicing'. *Language* 60: 286–319.

Kenyon, John, and Thomas Knott. 1953. *A pronouncing dictionary of American English*. Springfield, MA: Merriam Webster.

Ladd, D. Robert. 1996. *Intonational phonology*. Cambridge: Cambridge University Press.

Ladefoged, Peter. 1992. *A course in phonetics*, 2nd edn. New York: Harcourt Brace Jovanovich.

1996. *Elements of acoustic phonetics*, 2nd edn. Chicago: University of Chicago Press.

2001. *Vowels and consonants: an introduction to the sounds of languages*. Oxford: Blackwell.

Ladefoged, Peter, and Ian Maddieson. 1996. *The sounds of the world's languages*. Oxford: Blackwell.

Larramendi, Manuel de. 1729. *El impossible vencido: arte de la lengua bascongada*. Salamanca: Joseph Villagordo Alcaraz. Repr. 1979, Donostia: Hordago.

Laver, John. 1994. *Principles of phonetics*. Cambridge: Cambridge University Press.

Lewis, Anthony. 2001. 'Weakening of intervocalic /p, t, k/ in two Spanish dialects: toward the quantification of lenition processes'. Doctoral dissertation, University of Illinois at Urbana-Champaign.

Lipski, John. 1984. 'On the weakening of /s/ in Latin American Spanish'. *Zeitschrift für Dialektologie und Linguistik* 51: 31–43.

1985a. '/s/ in Central American Spanish'. *Hispania* 68: 143–9.

1985b. *The Spanish of Equatorial Guinea: the dialect of Malabo and its implications for Spanish dialectology*. Beihefte der Zeitschrift für romanische Philologie, 209. Tübingen: Niemeyer.

1986. 'Reduction of Spanish word-final /s/ and /n/'. *Canadian Journal of Linguistics* 31: 139–56.

1990. 'Spanish taps and trills: phonological structure of an isolated opposition'. *Folia Linguistica* 24: 153–74.

1994. *Latin American Spanish*. London: Longman.

Lisker, Leigh, and Arthur Abramson. 1964. 'A cross-language study of voicing in initial stops: acoustic measurements'. *Word* 20: 348–422.

Llisterri, Joaquim, María Machuca, Carme de la Mota, Montserrat Riera and Antonio Ríos. 2003. 'The perception of lexical stress in Spanish'. In Maria Josep Solé, Daniel Recasens and Joaquín Romero, eds., *Proceedings of the 15th International Congress of Phonetic Sciences, Barcelona*, 2023–6. Universitat Autònoma de Barcelona. (CD-rom published by Causal Productions.)

Llorente, Antonio. 1962. 'Fonética y fonología andaluza: formas y estructuras'. *Revista de Filología Española* 45: 217–40.

Lloyd, Paul. 1987. *From Latin to Spanish*. Philadelphia: American Philosophical Society.

Lope Blanch, Juan. 1966. 'En torno a las vocales caedizas del español mexicano'. *Nueva Revista de Filología Hispánica* 17: 1–19.

    1996. In Manuel Alvar, ed., *Manual de dialectología española*, vol. II: *El español de América*. Barcelona: Ariel, 81–9.

López Morales, Humberto. 1979. 'Velarización de /rr/ en el español de Puerto Rico: índices de actitudes y creencias'. In *Homenaje a Fernando Antonio Martínez*, 193–214. Bogotá: Instituto Caro y Cuervo.

    1983. *Estratificación social del español de San Juan de Puerto Rico*. Mexico: Universidad Nacional Autónoma de México.

    1984. 'Desdoblamiento fonológico de las vocales en el andaluz oriental: reexamen de la cuestión'. *Revista de la Sociedad Española de Lingüística* 14: 85–97.

Lorenzo, Emilio. 1972. 'Vocales y consonantes geminadas'. In *Studia Hispanica in honorem R. Lapesa*, vol. I, 401–12. Madrid: Gredos.

Machuca Ayuso, María Jesús. 1997. 'Las obstruyentes no continuas del español: relación entre las categorías fonéticas y fonológicas en el habla espontánea'. Doctoral dissertation, Universitat Autònoma de Barcelona.

Mack, Molly. 1982. 'Voicing-dependent vowel duration in English and French: monolingual and bilingual production'. *Journal of the Acoustic Society of America* 71: 173–8.

Maddieson, Ian. 1984. *Patterns of sounds*. Cambridge: Cambridge University Press.

Manrique, Ana María Borzone de, and Angela Signorini. 1983. 'Segmental duration and rhythm in Spanish'. *Journal of Phonetics* 11: 117–28.

Marrero, Victoria. 1988. *Fonética estática y fonética dinámica*. Madrid: Universidad Complutense.

Martínez Celdrán, Eugenio. 1984. *Fonética (con especial referencia a la lengua castellana)*. Barcelona: Teide.

    1991a. 'Sobre la naturaleza fonética de los alófonos de /b, d, g/ en español y sus distintas denominaciones'. *Verba* 18: 235–53.

    1991b. 'Duración y tensión en las oclusivas no iniciales del español: un estudio perceptivo'. *Revista Argentina de Lingüística* 7: 51–71.

    1995. 'En torno a las vocales del español: análisis y reconocimiento'. *Estudios de Fonética Experimental* 7: 195–218.

    1998. *Análisis espectrográfico de los sonidos del habla*. Barcelona: Ariel.

Martínez-Celdrán, Eugenio, Ana M. Fernández-Planas and Josefina Carrera-Sabaté. 2003. 'Castilian Spanish'. *Journal of the International Phonetic Association* 33: 255–9.

Martínez Martín, Francisco M. 1983. *Fonética y sociolingüística en la ciudad de Burgos*. Madrid: Consejo Superior de Investigaciones Científicas.

Martínez Melgar, Antonia. 1986. 'Estudio experimental sobre un muestreo de vocalismo andaluz'. *Estudios de fonética experimental* 2: 197–248. Barcelona: Universitat de Barcelona.
    1994. 'El vocalismo del andaluz oriental'. *Estudios de Fonética Experimental* 6: 11–64.
McGurk, H., and J. MacDonald. 1976. 'Hearing lips and seeing voices'. *Nature* 264: 746–8.
McWhorter, John. 2000. *The missing Spanish Creoles: recovering the birth of plantation contact languages.* Berkeley: University of California Press.
Méndez Dosuna, Julián. 1996. 'Can weakening processes start in initial position?: the case of aspiration of /s/ and /f/'. In Bernhard Hurch and Richard Rhodes, eds., *Natural phonology: the state of the art*, 97–106. Berlin: Mouton de Gruyter.
Menéndez Pidal, Ramón. 1899. 'Notas acerca del bable de Lena'. In Octavio Bellmunt and F. Canella, eds., *Asturias*, vol. II, 332–40. Repr. in Menéndez Pidal (1962).
    1906. 'El dialecto leonés'. *Revista de Archivos, Bibliotecas y Museos.* Repr. in Menéndez Pidal (1962).
    1954. 'Pasiegos y vaqueiros: dos cuestiones de geografía lingüística'. *Archivum* 4: 7–44.
    1962. *El dialecto leonés.* Oviedo: Diputación de Oviedo.
    1973[1904]. *Manual de gramática histórica del español*, 14th edn. Madrid: Espasa-Calpe.
Monroy Casas, Rafael. 1980. *Aspectos fonéticos de las vocales españolas.* Madrid: Sociedad General Española de Librería.
Montes, José Joaquín. 1979. 'Un rasgo dialectal del occidente de Colombia: *-n > -m*'. In *Homenaje a Fernando Antonio Martínez*, 215–20. Bogotá: Instituto Caro y Cuervo.
    1996. 'Colombia'. In Manuel Alvar, ed., *Manual de dialectología hispánica*, vol. II: *El español de América*, 134–45. Barcelona: Ariel.
Moreno de Alba, José G. 1994. *La pronunciación del español en México.* Mexico: El Colegio de México.
Morgan, Raleigh. 1975. *The regional French of County Beauce, Quebec.* The Hague: Mouton.
Morillo-Velarde, Ramón. 1985. 'Sistemas y estructuras de las hablas andaluzas'. *Alfinge* 3: 29–60.
Muljačić, Žarko. 1972. *Fonologia della lingua italiana.* Bologna: il Mulino.
Navarro Tomás, Tomás. 1939. 'Desdoblamiento de fonemas vocálicos'. *Revista de Filología Hispánica* 1: 165–7.
    1977. *Manual de pronunciación española*, 19th edn. Madrid: Consejo Superior de Investigaciones Científicas (Publicaciones de la Revista de Filología Española) (1st edn, 1918).
Neira Martínez, Jesús. 1955. *El habla de Lena.* Oviedo: Diputación de Oviedo.
    1991. 'Función y origen de la alternancia -u/-o en los bables centrales de Asturias'. *Boletín de la Real Academia Española* 71: 433–54.
Núñez-Cedeño, Rafael, and Alfonso Morales-Front. 1999. *Fonología generativa contemporánea de la lengua española.* Washington, DC: Georgetown University Press.
Nuño Alvarez, María del Pilar. 1996. 'Cantabria'. In Manuel Alvar, ed., *Manual de dialectología hispánica*, vol. I: *El español de España*, 183–96. Barcelona: Ariel.
Oftedal, Magne. 1985. *Lenition in Celtic and Insular Spanish: the secondary voicing of stops in Gran Canaria.* Oslo: Universitets forpagat. (Monographs in Celtic Studies from the University of Oslo, vol. 2.)

Ohala, John. 1974. 'Experimental historical phonology'. In J. M. Anderson and C. Jones, eds., *Historical linguistics*, vol. II: 353–89. Amsterdam: North-Holland.

Olive, Joseph, Alice Greenwood and John Coleman. 1993. *Acoustics of American English speech: a dynamic approach*. New York: Springer-Verlag.

Ortega-Llebaria, Marta. 2003. 'Effects of phonetic and inventory constraints in the spirantization of intervocalic voiced stops: comparing two different measurements of energy change'. In Maria J. Solé, Daniel Recasens and Joaquín Romero, eds., *Proceedings of the 15th International Congress of Phonetic Sciences, Barcelona*, 2817–20. Universitat Autònoma de Barcelona. (CD-rom published by Causal Productions.)

Ortiz-Lira, Héctor. 1994. 'A contrastive analysis of English and Spanish sentence accentuation'. Ph.D. thesis, University of Manchester.

Penny, Ralph. 1969a. *El habla pasiega: ensayo de dialectología montañesa*. London: Tamesis.

   1969b. 'Vowel harmony in the speech of the Montes de Pas (Santander)'. *Orbis* 18: 148–66.

   1978. *Estudio estructural del habla de Tudanca*. Tübingen: Niemeyer. (Beihefte der Zeitschrift für romanische Philologie 167.)

   1994. 'Continuity and innovation in Romance: metaphony and mass noun reference in Spain and Italy'. *Modern Language Review* 89: 273–81.

   2000. *Variation and change in Spanish*. Cambridge: Cambridge University Press.

   2002. *A history of the Spanish language*, 2nd edn. Cambridge: Cambridge University Press.

Pensado, Carmen. 1999. 'Morfología y fonología: fenómenos morfofonológicos'. In Ignacio Bosque and Violeta Demonte, eds., *Gramática descriptiva del español*, vol. III, 4423–4504. Madrid: Espasa.

Perini, Mário. 2004. *Talking Brazilian: a Brazilian Portuguese pronunciation workbook*. New Haven, CT: Yale University Press.

Pharies, David. 2002. *Diccionario etimológico de los sufijos españoles*. Madrid: Gredos.

Pierrehumbert, Janet. 1980. *The phonology and phonetics of English intonation*. Ph.D. dissertation, MIT. (Published 1987, Bloomington, IN: Indiana University Linguistics Club.)

Pierrehumbert, Janet, Mary E. Beckman and D. Robert Ladd. 2001. 'Conceptual foundations of phonology as a laboratory science'. In N. Burton-Roberts, P. Carr and G. Docherty, eds., *Phonological knowledge*, 273–304. Oxford: Oxford University Press.

Prieto, Pilar. 1992. 'Morphophonology of the Spanish diminutive formation: a case for prosodic sensitivity'. *Hispanic Linguistics* 5: 169–205.

Prieto, Pilar, Jan van Santen and Julia Hirschberg. 1995. 'Tonal alignment patterns in Spanish'. *Journal of Phonetics* 23: 429–51.

Prieto, Pilar, Chilin Shi and Holly Nibert. 1996. 'Pitch downtrend in Spanish'. *Journal of Phonetics* 24: 445–73.

Quilis, Antonio. 1965. 'Description phonétique du parler madrilène actuel'. *Phonetica* 12: 19–24.

   1981. *Fonética acústica de la lengua española*. Madrid: Gredos.

   1987. 'Entonación dialectal hispánica'. In Humberto López Morales and María Vaquero, eds., *Actas del I Congreso Internacional sobre el Español de América*, 117–64. Puerto Rico: Academia Puertorriqueña de la Lengua Española.

   1993. *Tratado de fonología y fonética españolas*. Madrid: Gredos.

1995. 'El español en Filipinas'. In Carmen Silva-Corvalán, ed., *Studies in language contact and bilingualism*, 293–301. Washington, DC: Georgetown University Press.

Quilis, Antonio, and Manuel Esgueva. 1983. 'Realización de los fonemas vocálicos españoles en posición fonética normal'. In Manuel Esgueva and Margarita Cantarero, eds., *Estudios de fonética*, vol. I, 159–252. Madrid: Centro Superior de Investigaciones Científicas.

Quilis, Antonio, and Joseph A. Fernández. 1985. *Curso de fonética y fonología españolas para estudiantes angloamericanos*, 11th edn. Madrid: Consejo Superior de Investigaciones Científicas.

Ramus, Franck, Marina Nespor and Jacques Mehler. 1999. 'Correlates of linguistic rhythm in the speech signal'. *Cognition* 73: 265–92.

Real Academia Española. 1973. *Esbozo de una nueva gramática de la lengua española*. Madrid: Espasa Calpe.

1992. *Diccionario de la lengua española*, 21st edn (2 vols.). Madrid: Espasa Calpe.

1999. *Ortografía de la lengua española*. Madrid: Espasa Calpe.

Recasens, Daniel. 1991. 'On the production characteristics of apicoalveolar taps and trills'. *Journal of Phonetics* 19: 267–80.

Recasens, Daniel, and Maria Dolors Pallarès. 1999. 'A study of /ɾ/ and /r/ in the light of the "DAC" coarticulation model'. *Journal of Phonetics* 27: 143–69.

Roach, Peter. 2000. *English phonetics and phonology: a practical course*, 3rd edn. Cambridge: Cambridge University Press.

Roca, Iggy. 1990. 'Diachrony and synchrony in Spanish stress'. *Journal of Linguistics* 26: 133–64.

1999. 'Stress in the Romance languages'. In Harry van der Hulst, ed., *Word prosodic systems in the languages of Europe*, 659–811. Berlin: Mouton de Gruyter.

Rodríguez-Castellano, Lorenzo. 1952. *La variedad dialectal del Alto Aller*. Oviedo: Diputación de Oviedo.

1955. 'Más datos sobre la inflexión vocálica en la zona centro-sur de Asturias'. *Boletín del Instituto de Estudios Asturianos* 24: 123–46.

Rodríguez-Castellano, Lorenzo, and Adela Palacio. 1948. 'Contribución al estudio del dialecto andaluz: el habla de Cabra'. *Revista de Dialectología y Tradiciones Populares* 4: 378–418, 570–99.

Rosner, Burton, Luis E. López-Bascuas, José E. García-Albea and Richard P. Fahey. 2000. 'Voice-onset times for Castilian Spanish initial stops'. *Journal of Phonetics* 28: 217–24.

Salvador, Gregorio. 1957–8. 'El habla de Cúllar-Baza'. *Revista de Filología Española* 41: 161–252, and 42: 37–89.

1977. 'Unidades fonológicas vocálicas en el andaluz oriental'. *Revista Española de Lingüística* 7: 1–23.

Sanders, Benjamin. 1998. 'The Eastern Andalusian vowel system: form and structure'. *Rivista di Linguistica* 10.1: 109–35.

Simões, Antônio R. M. 1996. 'Duration as an element of lexical stress in Spanish discourse'. *Hispanic Linguistics* 8: 352–68.

Sosa, Juan M. 1999. *La entonación del español: su estructura fónica, variabilidad y dialectología*. Madrid: Cátedra.

2003. 'La notación tonal del español en el modelo Sp-ToBI'. In Pilar Prieto, ed., *Teorías de la entonación*, 185–208. Barcelona: Ariel.

Sproat, Richard, and Osamu Fujimura. 1993. 'Allophonic variation in English /l/ and its implications for phonetic implementation'. *Journal of Phonetics* 21: 291–311.

Stockwell, Robert, and J. Donald Bowen. 1965. *The sounds of English and Spanish.* Chicago: University of Chicago Press.

Terrell, Tracy. 1977. 'Constraints on the aspiration and deletion of final /s/ in Cuban and Puerto Rican Spanish'. *Bilingual Review* 4: 35–51.

    1978. 'La aspiración and elisión de /s/ en el español porteño'. *Anuario de Letras* 16: 41–66.

    1979. 'Final /s/ in Cuban Spanish'. *Hispania* 62: 599–612.

    1986. 'La desaparición de /s/ posnuclear a nivel léxico en el habla dominicana'. In Rafael Núñez-Cedeño, Iraset Páez Urdaneta and Jorge Guitart, eds., *Estudios sobre la fonología del español del Caribe*, 117–63. Caracas: Ediciones La Casa de Bello.

Toledo, Guillermo A. 1988. *El ritmo en el español: estudio fonético con base computacional.* Madrid: Gredos.

Torreblanca, Máximo. 1976. 'La sonorización de las oclusivas sordas en el habla toledana'. *Boletín de la Real Academia Española* 56: 117–45.

Tranel, Bernard. 1987. *The sounds of French: an introduction.* Cambridge: Cambridge University Press.

Trask, R. L. 1996. *A dictionary of phonetics and phonology.* London: Routledge.

Trubetzkoy, Nikolai. 1939. *Grundzüge der Phonologie.* (Travaux du Cercle de linguistique de Prague, 7.) English trans. by C. A. M Baltaxe, 1969, *Principles of phonology.* Berkeley: University of California Press.

Trujillo, Ramón. 1980. 'Sonorización de las sordas en Canarias'. *Anuario de Letras de la Universidad Autónoma de México* 18: 247–54.

    1981. '¿Fonologización de alófonos en el habla de Las Palmas?' In Manuel Alvar, ed., *Actas del I Simposio Internacional de la Lengua Española*, 161–74. Cabildo Insular de Gran Canaria: Las Palmas de Gran Canaria.

Val Alvaro, José Francisco. 1999. 'La composición'. In Ignacio Bosque and Violeta Demonte, eds., *Gramática del español*, vol. III, 4759–841. Madrid: Espasa Calpe.

Vallduví, Enric. 1992. *The information component.* New York: Garland.

Villena Ponsoda, Juan A. 1987. *Forma, sustancia y redundancia contextual: el caso del vocalismo del español andaluz.* Málaga: Universidad de Málaga.

Whitley, M. Stanley. 1995. 'Spanish glides, hiatus, and conjunction lowering'. *Hispanic Linguistics* 6/7: 355–85.

    2003. 'Rhotic representation: problems and proposals'. *Journal of the International Phonetic Association* 33: 81–6.

Widdison, Kirk. 1993. 'Hacia los orígenes de la *s* aspirada en español'. *Estudios de Fonética Experimental* 5: 33–60.

Williams, Lee. 1977. 'The voicing contrast in Spanish'. *Journal of Phonetics* 5: 169–84.

Willis, Erik. 2003. 'The intonational system of Dominican Spanish: findings and analysis'. Ph.D. dissertation, University of Illinois at Urbana-Champaign.

Zamora Munné, Juan C., and Jorge Guitart. 1982. *Dialectología hispanoamericana: teoría, descripción, historia.* Salamanca: Almar.

Zampini, Mary, and Kerry Green. 2001. 'The voicing contrast in English and Spanish: the relationship between perception and production'. In Janet Nicol, ed., *One mind, two languages: bilingual language processing*, 23–48. Oxford: Blackwell.

Index

Words in small capitals are included in the glossary.

ACOUSTIC PHONETICS 12
-*ado see* deletion of /-d-/
affective derivation 211, 212
AFFRICATE 43, 64, 76, 152
ALLOMORPH 190, 205, 212, 216, 218
ALLOPHONE 6–11, 13
Andalusian Spanish 19–20, 21, 32, 165, 176, 188
   Eastern 110, 130, 136, 164
Andean Spanish 29, 180, 186
APPROXIMANT 43, 64
Aragon 114, 289
Aranese 290
ARCHIPHONEME 104, 106, 174, 182, 189
Argentinian Spanish 31, 37, 39, 162, 166, 169, 229, 274
articulator 41
ARTICULATORY PHONETICS 12
articulatory phonology 114
ASPIRATION
   of historical /h/ from Latin /f/ 33
   of /s/ 21, 23, 25, 27, 28, 31, 50, 89, 112, 161, 190
   in voiceless plosives 52, 68, 139
ASSIMILATION 107–10
   of fricatives in voice 107, 159
   of laterals 102, 179
   of nasals 107
Asturian 109, 288

Basque 290
   affricates 43, 153
   Basque Country Spanish 187, 291
   borrowings from 237
   geographical extension 282
   palatalization 109
   rhotics 185, 186
   vowels 118, 128, 294

/x/ 158
BILABIAL 46
borrowings
   orthography 291
   plural of 206
   stress of 224, 225, 237
BOUNDARY TONES 254
breaking of lower-mid vowels 121

Canarian Spanish 22, 37, 152, 164, 165
Cantabrian 109, 134, 285, 286, 288
Caribbean Spanish 28, 29, 146, 176
Castilian *see* Northern-Central Peninsular Spanish
Catalan 289
   final devoicing 117, 127
   laterals 179
   nasals 177
   spelling 176
CECEO 56, 153, 157
Celtic 282
Central American Spanish 27, 113, 186
Chabacano *see* CREOLE
Chilean Spanish 30, 108, 152, 155
chinato 157, 162
Chinese 253
clitic pronoun 222, 233, 258
coda 71, 74
   coda clusters 76
Colombian Spanish 113, 164 *see also* Andean Spanish
columnar stress 231, 232, 239
COMPLEMENTARY DISTRIBUTION 10, 112, 155
compounds, stress in 226
consonant clusters *see* onset clusters; syllable-final clusters
continuum 282

contrast between /s/ and /θ/ *see distinción
 /s/-/θ/*
coronal 206
CREOLE 34, 287
Cuban Spanish 162, 163, 188 *see also*
 Caribbean Spanish

deaffrication 152
DEFECTIVE DISTRIBUTION 106
deletion of /-d-/ 21, 22, 23, 24, 29, 291
DENTAL 47
DIALECT 18
diminutive 212
DIPHTHONG, alternating with mid
 vowels 193 *see also* vowel sequences
dissimilation 110
distinción /s/-/θ/ 20, 23, 36, 37, 47, 56, 153,
 154, 155, 206
Dominican Spanish 163, 188 *see also*
 Caribbean Spanish
downstep 265
duration 244, 245, 273

Ecuadorian Spanish 159, 180, 187 *see also*
 Andean Spanish
emphasis 246
English
 epenthesis in 113
 flap 150, 181
 fricatives 47
 in Gibraltar 293
 in Latin America 293
 intonation 257, 258, 259, 260
 laterals 178
 lexicon 192
 nasals 51, 103, 173
 plosives 47, 52, 65, 102, 149
 rhotics 181
 rhythm 272
 syllabification 70, 79
 voicing contrast 51
 vowels 110, 122, 124–6, 239
EPENTHESIS 77, 113, 204, 205, 229
Equatorial Guinea 34
European structuralism *see* structuralism

final [m] 176
focus 260, 264, 265
FORMANT 61, 127
fortition 112, 185
French
 historical delateralization 180
 historical loss of /s/ 112, 164,
 165
 orthography 281
 Quebec 159
 stress 220
 vowels 120, 123

frequency 60
FRICATIVE 42, 63, 76, 107, 153
fronterizo 293
fundamental frequency 60 *see also* pitch
future tense 204, 232

Galician 158, 286, 287
Gascon 120
geminate 185, 237, 278 *see also* sequences of
 identical consonants
generative phonology 217, 218
GLIDE 16, 54, 71, 72
 mid 55, 90
 word-initial 89, 113
 word-final 225
Gliding rule 80, 82, 95, 166
GLOTTAL STOP 30, 50, 294
glottis 50
Guaraní 30, 123, 180, 293, 294

harmonic 61
harmony *see* vowel, harmony
HEAVY SYLLABLE 224, 236
HIATUS *see* vowel sequences
 exceptional 80, 81 *see also* Initiality
 condition; Stress condition
hypercorrection 163

Iberian 282
imperative 205, 230
Initiality condition (for exceptional
 hiatus) 84
intensity 59, 245
INTERDENTAL 46
INTONATION 254
INTONATIONAL LANGUAGE 254
Italian
 geminates 185, 278
 palatal lateral 179
 stress 239
 verbs 203

/j/ 43, 48, 165 *see also* LLEÍSMO;
 orthography
Japanese, vowels 120, 124
Judeo-Spanish 34, 157

LABIODENTAL 46
LATERAL 44, 69, 107, 178
Latin
 assimilation 108, 193
 diminutive 216
 dissimilation 110
 /f/ 281
 hiatus 86, 201
 learned words in Spanish 192
 nouns 192, 207
 orthography 277–8

stress 236
verbs 204, 229
vowels 124, 193, 198, 199
Leonese 173, 288
levels of representation 14
LIGHT SYLLABLE 224
LIQUID 45, 76, 178
LLEÍSMO 21, 24, 36, 44, 56, 290, 291
loanwords *see* borrowings

manner of articulation 41
Maya 293
METAPHONY 109, 131–5, 201
METATHESIS 114
Mexican Spanish 25–7, 186
microprosody 256
MINIMAL PAIR 6, 173, 181, 183
Mirandês 288
MORPHEME 190
MORPHOPHONOLOGICAL RULES 13, 190
Mozarabic 287
muta cum liquida 73, 114

/n/ *see* NASAL; VELARIZATION
/ɲ/ 173–4, 176
Nahuatl 25, 27, 74
NASAL 44, 69, 76, 107
    phonemes 173 *see also* NEUTRALIZATION; VELARIZATION
nasalization 110, 123, 176
Navarrese 185, 289
NEUTRALIZATION 76, 102–7
    of liquids 22, 24, 104, 188
    of nasals 103
    of plosives in voice 103, 105
New Mexican Spanish 27
Northern-Central Peninsular Spanish 20–1, 38, 39, 47, 55, 91, 146, 147, 148, 153, 154, 160, 167
NUCLEAR ACCENT 243, 256, 257, 258, 259, 260, 264, 266, 271
numerals, stress of 227

Old Spanish 152, 155, 201, 202, /h/ 279–80, 281
onset clusters 70, 73
orthographically motivated pronunciation 146
orthography 5, 174, 277
    accent marks 206, 246
    hie- 169
    letter *ch see* /t͡ʃ/
    letter *h* 6, 280, 281
    letter *-m* (final) 176
    letter *x* 3, 73
    letters *b* and *v* 5, 161, 279
    letters *c* and *z* 6, 161, 206 *see also* CECEO; *distinción* /s/-/θ/; SESEO
    letters *g* and *j* 5, 280 *see also* /x/

letters *ll* and *y* 5, 16, 19, 24, 31 *see also* LLEÍSMO *see also* phonemic orthography
OXYTONE 221, 238, 247

PALATAL 48
    nasal *see* /ɲ/
palatalization 108, 278
Palenquero *see* CREOLE
Papiamentu *see* CREOLE
Paraguayan Spanish 30, 180, 186
PAROXYTONE 221, 224, 247
participle 205
Phillipines, Spanish in 34 *see also* CREOLE
PHONEME 1, 3, 102, 190
phonemic orthography 2, 277, 279
PHONEMIC TRANSCRIPTION 3
PHONETIC TRANSCRIPTION
    NARROW 9
    BROAD 9
pitch 60, 253
PITCH ACCENT 245, 246, 254, 268
place of articulation 46
PLOSIVE 41, 59, 64, 76
    allophones 138
    intervocalic 141
    postconsonantal 144
    syllable-final 146
    utterance-initial 138, 150
    word-final 147, 148
plural 205, 222
Porteño *see* Argentinian Spanish
Portuguese 109, 198, 203, 239, 287, 293, 294
    Brazilian 108, 189
postalveolar *see* PREPALATAL
postnuclear accent 264, 265
Prague School *see* structuralism
PRENUCLEAR ACCENT 243, 256
PREPALATAL 48
preterite, irregular 204, 228, 232
PROPAROXYTONE 222, 224, 226, 230, 237, 238, 246
Puerto Rican Spanish 187, 188 *see also* Caribbean Spanish

Quechua 30, 120, 180, 293, 294
questions 235, 243, 250, 254, 267

/r/ *see* RHOTIC
resyllabification 87
RHOTIC 4, 16, 24, 29, 44, 68, 88, 103, 105, 181, 237, 291
rhyme 71
rhythm 272
River Plate *see* Argentinian Spanish

/s/ 47 *see also* ASPIRATION, of /s/; CECEO; *distinción* /s/-/θ/; SESEO

sequences of identical consonants 95, 97, 175, 184
sequences of vowels *see* vowel sequences
SESEO 33, 55, 153 *see also distinción* /s/-/θ/
shortening *see* truncation
SOCIOLECT 19
SONORITY 71, 72
spirantization 112 *see* PLOSIVE
STOP *see* PLOSIVE
STRESS *see* columnar stress; stress shift; STRESS-TIMED; WORD-STRESS
Stress condition (for exceptional hiatus) 84
stress shift 238–9
STRESS-TIMED 272
structuralism 104, 105, 106, 117, 182, 217
substratum in Latin American Spanish 294
SUPPLETION 191
syllable 70, 72, 168
syllable-final clusters 21, 25
SYLLABLE-TIMED 272
syllable weight *see* HEAVY SYLLABLE; LIGHT SYLLABLE

THREE-SYLLABLE WINDOW 222, 237, 239
TONE 2, 220
TONE LANGUAGE 253
topicalization 263, 266
toponyms in bilingual areas 292
trill *see* RHOTIC
triphthong 71
truncation 227
/t͡ʃ/ 22, 24, 27, 29, 30, 43, 75, 152

underlying representation 217, 218
UNDERSPECIFICATION 105

upstep 270
USA, Spanish in 27, 166

variation 112, 146, 161, 176, 188
    sociolinguistic 28, 33
VELAR 49
VELARIZATION 22, 24, 28, 29, 44, 88, 176
vocal cords 50
voice bar 68 *see also* VOT
VOICING 51
VOSEO 205, 231
VOT 140, 149
vowel 52, 59
    reduction 125
    triangle 120
    VOWEL HARMONY 109, 130, 134
vowel sequences 23, 25, 55, 77, 91, 203, 224, 229, 237
    accent marks in 248
    across word boundaries 89
    historical reduction 238, 239
    identical vowels 90, 91, 92, 124
    three or more vowels 93

weakening
    of intervocalic stops 111
    of /s/ *see* ASPIRATION; of /t//t͡ʃ/ *see* deaffrication; /t//t͡ʃ/
WORD-STRESS 2, 16, 220

/x/ 24, 49, 50, 154, 280

YEÍSMO 179
    rehilado 56 *see also* Argentinian Spanish